Jor...
& Syria
a travel survival kit

Damien Simonis
Hugh Finlay

Jordan & Syria – a travel survival kit

2nd edition

Published by
Lonely Planet Publications
Head Office: PO Box 617, Hawthorn, Vic 3122, Australia
Branches: PO Box 2001A, Berkeley, CA 94702, USA
12 Barley Mow Passage, Chiswick, London W4 4PH, UK

Printed by
Colorcraft Ltd, Hong Kong

Photographs by
Hugh Finlay (HF), Damien Simonis (DS), Tony Wheeler (TW)

Front cover: Wadi Rum (HF)

First Published
October 1987

This Edition
May 1993

Although the authors and publisher have tried to make the information as accurate as possible, they accept no responsibility for any loss, injury or inconvenience sustained by any person using this book.

National Library of Australia Cataloguing in Publication Data

Finlay, Hugh.
Jordan & Syria – a travel survival kit.

2nd ed.
Includes index.
ISBN 0 86442 172 9.

1. Jordan – Guidebooks. 2. Syria – Guidebooks.
I. Simonis, Damien II. Title.

915.6904

text & maps © Lonely Planet 1993
photos © photographers as indicated 1993

Damien Simonis
Damien is a London-based freelance journalist who has worked for *The Guardian*, *The Independent* and *The Daily Telegraph* magazine as sub-editor; and *The Age* and *The Australian* as sub-editor and reporter. He has also worked as an English teacher in Egypt and Sicily and travelled extensively in Australia, the Middle East and Europe.

Hugh Finlay
After deciding there must be more to life than civil engineering, Hugh took off around Australia, working in everything from spray painting to diamond prospecting, before hitting the overland trail. He spent three years travelling and working across three continents.

Since joining Lonely Planet in 1985, Hugh has co-written guides to India, North Africa and Kenya. He now lives in Central Victoria with Linda and their daughters, Ella and Vera.

From the Authors
Damien would like to thank Wafa Amr (Amman), Major Jeremy and Liz Dumas (Damascus), and Peter at the hash for their help & hospitality. Also thanks to Michael Blaha, Suzanne Smith, Vince Eichholtz, Scott Smith, Marcelo Granja, Rupert Clayton, Miriam Pinchuk, Chris Haymes and others who helped out along the way (sometimes without even knowing it). And to the many people of Jordan and Syria who did not hesitate to hold out a hand of friendship.

Hugh would also like to thank Tony Howard for continued permission to reproduce his map to Wadi Rum.

From the Publisher
This 2nd edition of *Jordan & Syria – a travel survival kit* was edited by Katie Cody, with editorial help and proofreading by Diana Saad. Ann Jeffree was responsible for design, illustrations, maps and cover design.

To all those travellers who wrote to tell us of their experiences in Jordan and Syria – thanks!

Warning & Request

Things change – prices go up, schedules change, good places go bad and bad places go bankrupt – nothing stays the same. So if you find things better or worse, recently opened or long since closed, please write and tell us and help make the next edition better.

Your letters will be used to help update future editions and, where possible, important changes will also be included in a Stop Press section in reprints.

We greatly appreciate all information that is sent to us by travellers. Back at Lonely Planet we employ a hard-working readers' letters team to sort through the many letters we receive. The best ones will be rewarded with a free copy of the next edition or another Lonely Planet guide if you prefer. We give away lots of books, but, unfortunately, not every letter/postcard receives one.

Contents

Map Legend

BOUNDARIES

▬ ▪ ▬ ▪ ▬ ▪ ▬ ....International Boundary
▬▬ ▪▪ ▬▬ ▪▪ ▬▬ ....Internal Boundary
+·+·+·+·+·+·+·+ ....National Park or Reserve
▬ ▬ ▬ ▬ ▬ ▬ ....The Equator
················· ....The Tropics

SYMBOLS

◉ NATIONAL ....National Capital
● PROVINCIAL........Provincial or State Capital
● Major ....Major Town
● Minor ....Minor Town
▪ ....Places to Stay
▼ ....Places to Eat
✉ ....Post Office
✈ ....Airport
i ....Tourist Information
⊖ ....Bus Station or Terminal
66 ....Highway Route Number
⚱ ✝ ✝ ☩ ...... Mosque, Church, Cathedral
∴ ....Temple or Ruin
✚ ....Hospital
✳ ....Lookout
⚑ ....Camping Area
⊓ ....Picnic Area
⌂ ....Hut or Chalet
▲ ....Mountain or Hill
⊦⊣▬⊦⊣ ....Railway Station
⩵ ....Road Bridge
⊦⊣⊦⊣ ....Railway Bridge
⇒ ⇐ ....Road Tunnel
→⟩ ⟨← ....Railway Tunnel
⌢⌒⌢ ....Escarpment or Cliff
‿ ....Pass
⊓⊓⊓⊓ ....Ancient or Historic Wall

ROUTES

▬▬▬▬▬ ....Major Road or Highway
▬ ▬ ▬ ▬ ▬ .... Unsealed Major Road
▬▬▬▬▬ .... Sealed Road
▬ ▬ ▬ ▬ ..... Unsealed Road or Track
⩵ .... City Street
+·+·+·+·+·+ ....Railway
▬●▬ .... Subway
··············· ....Walking Track
▬ ▬ ▬ ▬ .... Ferry Route
⊹⊦⊹⊦⊹⊦⊹⊦ .... Cable Car or Chair Lift

HYDROGRAPHIC FEATURES

.....................River or Creek
..............Intermittent Stream
........Lake, Intermittent Lake
.........................Coast Line
.................................Spring
.............................Waterfall
.................................Swamp
...Salt Lake or Oasis
.................................Glacier

OTHER FEATURES

Park, Garden or National Park
.... Built Up Area
... Market or Pedestrian Mall
.........Plaza or Town Square
.............................Cemetery

Note: not all symbols displayed above appear in this book

Introduction

If Jordan and Syria were anywhere else in the world, they would be crawling with sightseers, but Syria and Jordan are in the heart of the volatile Middle East and are low on most peoples' list of places worth visiting. Given its unflattering media profile – that of a region of barren desert and fanatics bent on revolution – it is a surprise to many that not only is it safe to travel here, but that the local Arab inhabitants are among the most hospitable in the world. The closest you'll come to being hijacked is to be dragged off to a café to drink tea and chat for a while with the locals.

Certainly, things aren't the same as at home – in many cases they are a whole lot better. Where else can you leave your belongings unattended for hours, safe in the knowledge that they will be there on your return, and where can you wander the streets any time of the day or night without fear for your safety?

With a history of permanent settlement going back some 11,000 years, the number of archaeological and historical sites is enough to satiate even the most avid ruin buff. They run the gamut from relics of Stone Age settlements through the civilisations of the Phoenicians, Greeks, Romans and Byzantines to the more contemporary Muslims, Crusaders, Ottoman Turks and even the British and the French – they have all left their mark. Add to this a few lesser known cultures such as the Nabataeans (builders of the incredible city of Petra) and the Palmyrenes, who at one stage had the audacity to threaten the might of Rome, and you start to get an idea of the diverse influences that

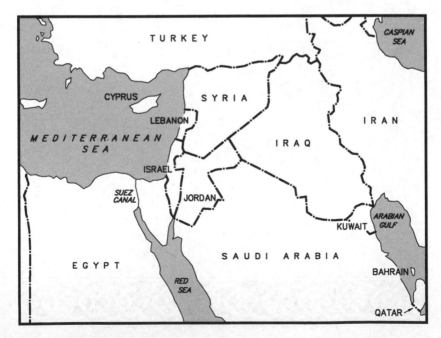

have played a part in shaping this region. Everyone from Tutankhamen to Winston Churchill has been involved at some stage.

When you've had your fill of history, you can take time out to explore some of the natural wonders on offer: take a camel ride through the incredible desert landscapes of Wadi Rum (one of Lawrence of Arabia's old stamping grounds); don a mask and snorkel and head underwater in the Gulf of Aqaba to see some of the finest coral reefs anywhere; or have a swim, or more precisely, a float, in the saline waters of the Dead Sea – the lowest point on earth.

Jordan and Syria have developed rapidly this century and both offer the visitor the facilities to make life comfortable at an affordable price. Accommodation ranges from five-star luxury for the well-heeled down to simple but perfectly adequate establishments for the impecunious. Transport is fast and efficient, and modern, air-conditioned buses or trains service all the major centres. And when it comes to food, sit yourself down to a formal banquet, or squat around a communal bowl of rice and meat with a Bedouin family in their goat-hair tent, and tuck in by hand.

Fortunately, these two countries are unlikely to ever boom as mass tourist destinations, but for those with an open mind, a bit of patience, plenty of time and a taste for something different, Jordan and Syria offer the more adventurous traveller a rare chance to really get off the beaten track.

Facts about the Region

HISTORY

The history of Syria and Jordan is one of invasion and conquest. The region was never strong enough to form an empire itself, and it was for the most part a collection of city-states, but its strategic position ensured that all the great early civilisations passed through here. The Egyptians, Assyrians, Babylonians, Hittites, Greeks, Romans, Arabs, Turks and Crusaders all helped to shape the history of the region. They traded, built cities and fought their wars here, leaving behind rich cultural influences.

Although the modern states of Jordan and Syria are creations of the 20th century, the region they encompass can lay claim to having one of the oldest civilisations in the world. Archaeological finds from Jericho, on the west bank of the Jordan River, have been positively dated at around 9000 BC. They have revealed an extensive village where the inhabitants lived in mud and stone houses and there is evidence of agriculture and animal domestication. Major finds in Syria at Ras Shamra (Ugarit, circa 6600 BC) on the Mediterranean coast and at Mari (circa 4500 BC) on the Euphrates River, show more advanced settlements that would later become sophisticated city-states.

From 3000 BC, the region was settled by the Amorites, a warlike semitic tribe, and the Canaanites, who mostly inhabited the coastal lowlands. It was around this time that the villages of Syria and Palestine came to the attention of Egypt to the south-west, and the expanding Euphrates Valley empires to the east.

Sargon of Akkad, a powerful ruler of Mesopotamia from 2334 to 2279 BC, marched to the Mediterranean in search of conquest and natural resources to supply his growing empire. From humble beginnings, he had become the greatest ruler in Mesopotamia. It is said that as a baby he was fished from the Euphrates River by a gardener who found him floating in a basket. He was raised as a gardener, but Sargon obviously had greater things in mind. After becoming cup-bearer for the ruler of the city of Kish in northern Sumer, he gathered an army and, with his great military prowess and ability to organise, set about conquering the cities of the south. He went on to become king and the world's first great empire-builder.

Sargon's ascendancy in the Mediterranean area led to the growth of many towns with strong Mesopotamian influence. Trade with Egypt flourished as it, too, needed wood, stone and metal to supply the needs of its rapidly expanding empire. Cities like Jericho and Byblos (in present-day Lebanon) became well established and prospered with this trade.

Sargon of Akkad

By about 1700 BC, Palestine was part of the Hyksos Empire of Egypt. The Hyksos were themselves Asiatic invaders and despised in Egypt. The revolt and pursuit of the Hyksos across Palestine by the Egyptians, under the leadership of Kamose of Thebes, led to a period of expansion of the Egyptian Empire. By 1520 BC, Thutmose I claims to have reached the banks of the

Euphrates River, although he was met by stubborn resistance from the local inhabitants and by no means controlled the entire area.

In 1480 BC, a revolt organised by over 300 Syrian and Palestinian rulers was easily crushed and Egypt was now firmly established in Palestine and the southern Syrian region. They would remain so for over a century. In the north, however, the various principalities coalesced to form the Mitanni Empire. They held off all Egyptian attempts at control, helped in part by their invention of the horse-drawn chariot as a weapon of war.

It was the encroachments of the Hittites from the north in about 1365 BC, under the young, ambitious leader Suppiluliumas, that led to the fall of the Mitanni Empire. Despite some half-hearted attempts by the new pharaoh, Tutankhamen, to gain control, by 1330 BC all of Syria was firmly in the hands of the Hittites.

The two powers clashed at the bloody Battle of Kadesh on the Orontes River in Syria around 1300 BC. Militarily it was an indecisive war but it dealt the Egyptians a strategic defeat and saw them retreat into Palestine. Finally, the two opposing forces signed a treaty of friendship in 1284 BC which ended a long period of clashes between empires for control of Syria. It left the Egyptians with a turbulent Palestine and the Hittites with Syria and the threat from the rising power of Assyria.

This marked the end of three prosperous centuries in this part of the Levant. The area was well placed to make the most of trade between Egypt to the south, Mesopotamia to the east and Anatolia to the north. Although suited to the production of olives, grapes, barley and wheat, as well as livestock-raising, it was the control of the natural resources of the region that really kept the foreign powers interested. The prosperity of the various cities largely depended on the extent to which they controlled the mule-caravan routes.

One of the most important contributions to world history from this period was the development of written scripts. The ancient site of Ugarit in Syria has yielded the oldest alphabet yet known. Until then only Egyptian hieroglyphics and Mesopotamian cuneiform existed. Both required hundreds of symbols that were far too difficult for anyone but the scribes to use. By 1000 BC linear, rather than pictorial scripts, were in general use. It's from these alphabets, developed further in Palestine, that today's scripts are derived.

From about the 13th century BC, Palestine was threatened by an invasion of 'Peoples from the Sea' – possibly the Philistines. The Egyptian Empire was in decline. It had over-extended itself and was under threat from Libyan tribes to the west, allowing the raiders from the Aegean to assert themselves and take control of the area. Egyptian influence rapidly dwindled and the Hittite Empire also declined, finally collapsing around 1200 BC. The Philistines settled on the coastal plain of Canaan in an area that came to be known as the Plain of Philistia and from which the name Palestine ('Filasteen' in Arabic) is derived.

The Philistines' ascendancy owed much to their use of iron for weapons and armour, which the Canaanites and Egyptians did not possess. In fact the Iron Age is traditionally given as beginning in the 12th century BC.

At about the same time the east bank of the Jordan River was settled by three other groups: the Edomites in the south, the Moabites to the east of the Dead Sea, and the Ammonites on the edge of the Arabian Desert with their capital at Rabbath Ammon, present-day Amman.

Coming of the Israelites

Much of what we know about the history of this part of the world comes from the books of the Old and, later, New Testaments, which have naturally propelled essentially Jewish history into the foreground.

It was not until the late 11th century BC that the Philistines were threatened. Led by Moses, the Israelites had left Egypt around 1270 BC – the Exodus – and, after the traditional 40 years in the wilderness, they overran the local rulers and settled in the hills of Transjordan (the name used to describe the area east of the Jordan River).

Following the victories of Moses, his successor Joshua led the 12 tribes across the Jordan River and conquered Jericho. The Israelites then suffered a severe defeat at the Battle of Ebenezer in 1050 BC, which saw the Philistines capture the Ark of the Covenant – the symbol of unity of the 12 tribes of Israel. Further disaster came after another major battle when Saul, who had been made king of Israel in 1020 BC, took his own life and left the Israelites leaderless and at the mercy of the Philistines.

The fortunes of Israel took a turn very much for the better when Saul's successor, David, was proclaimed king in 1000 BC. After defeating the Philistines near Jerusalem, he then set about regaining the territory of his neighbours east of the Jordan. By the end of his reign in 960 BC, he ruled the principalities of Edom, Moab and Ammon (the city-states of southern Syria) and was paid tribute by the Philistine princes and the tribes as far east as the Euphrates.

After the death of David and the ascent of his son Solomon to the throne, Israel entered its golden age. This period saw great advancements in trade which extended down the African and Red Sea coasts and into Asia Minor. A visit to Jerusalem by the Queen of Sheba (in present-day Yemen) is evidence that there was also overland trade to the Arabian Peninsula.

A great part of the success of Solomon's rule was derived from his administrative skills which, however, led to high tax burdens and forced labour. Resentment of these hardships led to a revolt against Solomon, and following his death in 922 BC the united kingdom was divided into the separate kingdoms of Judah in the south and Israel in the north.

The main threat to Israel was the Aramaen state of Damascus, as the two were rivals for the lucrative Syrian and Transjordanian trade. This rivalry led to an alliance between Israel and the Phoenicians when the sixth king of Israel, Omri, married off his son

Empire of David & Solomon 1000–930 BC

Ahab to the Phoenician princess Jezebel. The defeat of Ahab by Mesha, the King of Moab, is recorded in the famous Mesha Stele (Moabite Stone) found at Dhiban (north of present-day Kerak in Jordan). A short period of relative peace was shattered in 722 BC when the Assyrians under Sargon II devastated Israel and its capital Samaria, deported the citizens and replaced them with settlers from Syria and Babylonia. The northern kingdom of Israel had ceased to exist.

In the south, Judah survived for another century under Assyrian rule until the Babylonian king Nebuchadnezzar overthrew the Assyrians and took control. Rebellions under the last kings of Judah were put down and resulted in the destruction of many Judaean cities and finally the taking of Jerusalem in 597 BC. After the puppet-king installed by the Babylonians also rebelled, Jerusalem was taken for the second time in 587 BC. The Jews were deported en masse to Babylon – the Exile – ending the history of the southern kingdom of Judah.

In 539 BC Cyrus II came to power in Persia and allowed the Jews to return to Palestine, and under Nehemiah they rebuilt the walls of Jerusalem. The next two centuries were a period of calm when the Jews were able to implement various social reforms.

The Greeks & Romans

In 333 BC Alexander the Great stormed through Syria and Palestine on his way to Egypt. On his death, his newly formed empire was parcelled up among his generals. Ptolemy I gained Egypt and parts of Syria, while Seleucus established a kingdom in Babylonia.

For the next century, the Seleucids disputed the Ptolemies' claim to Palestine and tried unsuccessfully to oust the Ptolemies before finally succeeding in 198 BC under the leadership of Antiochus III. Antiochus III then tried to extend his influence westwards but met with the new power of Rome. His army was defeated by the Romans and in 188 BC he was forced to cede all his territories in Asia Minor.

After attacking Egypt the Seleucids, under Antiochus IV, sacked Jerusalem and left the Jews with no alternative but to revolt after virtually banning their religion and dedicating the Temple of Jerusalem to Zeus – the supreme god of the ancient Greeks.

Led by Judas Maccabeus of the Hasmonean family, the Jews gradually re-established themselves and by 141 BC were recognised as an independent territory, occupying a large area east of the Jordan River. During the reign of John Hyrcanus and his successors, the boundaries were further extended to cover most of Palestine and Transjordan. On Hyrcanus's death, a squabble between his sons, Aristobolus and Hyrcanus II, led to the intervention of the Romans under Pompey who took Damascus in 64 BC and Palestine the following year. The Jewish kingdom was now under Roman control and Hyrcanus II was appointed high priest.

All of western Syria and Palestine became the new Roman province of Syria. The most important cities east of the Jordan were organised into a league of 10. The Decapolis, as it was known, was formed as a commercial and military alliance for the advancement of trade, and as protection against the Jews and Nabataeans.

The Parthian kings of Persia and Mesopotamia invaded and occupied most of the province in 40 BC but Mark Antony was able to restore order, albeit with some difficulty. Antipater, minister for Hyrcanus II, was made governor of Judaea and his sons Herod and Phaesal were appointed governors of Jerusalem and Galilee, respectively. With the Parthian invasion, the Hasmonean family, now led by Aristobolus' son Antigonus, was able to seize power. Phaesal and Hyrcanus II were captured and Herod escaped to Rome where, on appeal to the senate, he was named king of Israel and returned to Palestine. With Roman help he expelled the Parthians and took Jerusalem in 37 BC in a bloody conflict. Mark Antony had Antigonus executed.

The period of Herod's rule, from 40 BC to 4 BC, was a time of relative peace and prosperity for Palestine. What followed after his death was a period of unrest that led to a Jewish revolt in 66 AD. Nero entrusted the commander Vespasian with the task of restoring order and he effectively subdued Galilee and Judaea. His son Titus captured and virtually destroyed Jerusalem.

The Herodian rulers were a perverse lot. In his later years, Herod the Great suffered from mental instability and became increasingly tyrannical. He murdered his ex-wife Mariamne, and for good measure also murdered many of her family, including her mother, brother, grandfather and her two sons. Fearing plots against him, he also disposed of three of his own sons. He tried at least once

**Kingdom of Herod
the Great
40 BC to 4 AD**

Capitolina. Captive Jews were sold into slavery and the religious practices of the survivors were strictly curtailed.

Only about 20 years before, in 106 AD, the Romans had incorporated the loose empire of the Nabataeans, centred on the rock city of Petra, into the Roman orbit. The Nabataeans were unusual in that they retained much of their nomadic character as traders rather than settling down to develop agriculture. In the previous 300 years they had established a fluid control over an area stretching from Damascus to Wejh on the coast of modern Saudi Arabia, and from modern Suez to Wadi Sirhan in the desert of eastern Jordan.

Nabataean strength lay in the control of trade routes and almost exclusive knowledge of desert strongpoints and water supplies. Their greatest economic trump was the trade monopoly they exercised over the difficult route into Arabia Felix, which the Romans attempted without success to penetrate shortly before the birth of Christ. Heavy duties imposed on goods transported on these routes and protection money to keep bandits at bay were the principal source of wealth.

The Nabataeans never really possessed an empire in the common military and administrative sense of the word, but rather a 'zone of influence'. After 106, the Nabataeans lost much of their commercial power and faded into insignificance.

In the 3rd century the Sassanians, the successors to the Parthians, invaded northern Syria but were repelled by the Syrian prince Odenathus of Palmyra. He was granted the title 'dux orientalis' (commander of the East) by his Roman overlords for his efforts, but died shortly afterwards. Suspected of complicity in his death his widow, the ambitious Zenobia, assumed the title Augusta and, with her sights set on Rome, invaded western Syria, Palestine and Egypt. In 272, Aurelian destroyed Palmyra and carted Zenobia off to Rome as a prisoner.

With the conversion of the emperor Constantine early in the 4th century, Christianity became the dominant religion. Jerusalem

to commit suicide but finally died of natural causes. His son, Herod Antipas, had John the Baptist put to death; his sister's grandson, Herod Agrippa I, had St James executed and St Peter imprisoned. The last of the line was Herod Agrippa II, son of Herod Agrippa I, who lived incestuously with his sister Berenice.

It is now widely accepted that a Jew by the name of Jesus lived in Palestine in the 1st century AD, although there is little direct evidence that he saw himself as the Messiah or intended to be the founder of a new church – this was done by those who came after him. They combined his words with elements of Judaism and paganism to form the new religion.

Apart from making the Jewish nation a province, the Romans made remarkably few changes to the Jewish way of life. This leniency led to a second revolt in 132 AD which was put down by Hadrian, who then gave Jerusalem the new name of Aelia became the site of holy pilgrimage to Christian shrines and this did wonders for the prosperity of the country. During the reign of Justinian from 527 to 565, churches were built in many towns in Palestine and Syria.

This rosy state of affairs was abruptly shattered in the 7th century when the Persians once again descended from the north, taking Damascus and Jerusalem in 614 and eventually Egypt in 616, although Byzantine fortunes were revived when the emperor Heraclius invaded Persia and forced the Persians into a peace agreement. In the south, however, the borders of the empire were being attacked by Arab invaders – no new thing – but these Arabs were ambitious Muslims, followers of Mohammed.

The Coming of Islam

With the Byzantine Empire severely weakened by the Persian invasion, and with the subordinate Aramaen population alienated by Byzantine domination, the Muslims met with little resistance and in some cases were welcomed.

In 636 the Muslim armies won a famous victory at the battle of Yarmouk which marks the modern border between Jordan and Syria. At the same time Ctesiphon, the Persian capital on the Tigris, also fell. Within 15 years the Sassanian Empire had disappeared and the Arab Muslims had reached the river Oxus on the modern northern frontier of Afghanistan.

In the west, the Byzantine forces never recovered from Yarmouk and could do little but fall back towards Anatolia. Jerusalem fell in 638 and soon after all of Syria was in Muslim hands. Egypt fell shortly after.

Because of its position on the pilgrims' route to Mecca, Syria became the hub of the new Muslim Empire which, by the early 8th century, stretched from Spain and across northern Africa and the Middle East to Persia (modern Iran) and India. Mu'awiya, the governor of Damascus, had himself declared the fifth caliph, or successor to Mohammed, in 658 and founded a line, the Omayyads, who would last for about a century. Damascus

thus replaced Medina (in present-day Saudi Arabia) as the political capital.

The Omayyad period was one of great achievement and saw the building of monuments such as the Omayyad Mosque in Damascus and the Mosque of Omar and the Dome of the Rock in Jerusalem. The Omayyads' great love of the desert led to the construction of palaces – the so-called Desert Palaces east of Amman – where the caliphs could indulge their Bedouin past. Nevertheless, it was also a time of almost unremitting internal struggle, and Damascus found itself constrained to put down numerous revolts in Iraq and Arabia itself.

Omayyad rule was overthrown in 750 when the Abbassids seized power and transferred the caliphate to Baghdad. Syria and Palestine went into a rapid decline as a result; administratively, they were no more than a coastal strip stretching as far inland as Damascus and Jerusalem.

The Abbassids, too, had their share of problems, and by the 900s had lost their grip and been replaced by other families. Imperial control slipped increasingly out of Baghdad's hands and, by 980, all of Palestine and part of Syria (including Damascus) had fallen under Fatimid Cairo's rule. Aleppo and northern Syria and Iraq were controlled by the Hamdanids, a Shi'ite group.

It was into this vacuum of central power that the Crusaders arrived, and in fact it is unlikely they would have lasted long at all if the Muslims' lands had not been so divided. They established four states, the most important being the kingdom of Jerusalem in 1099. Fortresses were built at Kerak, Shobak, Wadi Musa and the island of Far'aon just offshore from Aqaba. In Syria a string of castles, including the well-preserved Crac des Chevaliers, was constructed along the coastal mountain ranges. Their hold was always tenuous as they were a minority and could only survive if the Muslim states remained weak and divided, which in fact they remained until the 12th century.

Nureddin (literally, 'light of the faith'), son of a Turkish tribal ruler, was able to unite all of Syria not held by the Franks and defeat the Crusaders in Egypt. His campaign was completed by Saladin (the Arabic, Salah ad-Din, means 'righteousness of the faith'), who overthrew the Fatimid rulers of Egypt in 1171 and recaptured Palestine and most of the inland Crusader strongholds. European rule was restored to the coast for another century with the Third Crusade.

Prosperity returned to Syria with the rule of the Ayyubids, members of Saladin's family, who parcelled up his empire on his death. They were succeeded by the Mamluks, the freed slave class of Turkish origin that had taken power in Cairo in 1250, just in time to repel the onslaught from the invading Mongol tribes from central Asia in 1260. The victorious Mamluk leader, Baibars I, ruled over a reunited Syria and Egypt until his death in 1277. By the beginning of the 14th century, the Mamluks had finally managed to rid the Levant of the Crusaders by capturing their last stronghold – the fortified island of Ruad (Arwad) – off the coast of Tartus in Syria.

However, more death and destruction was not far off and in 1401 the Mongol invader Timur (Tamerlaine) sacked Aleppo and Damascus, killing thousands and carting off many of the craftsmen to central Asia. His new empire lasted for only a few years but the rout sent Mamluk Syria into a decline for the next century.

The Ottoman Turks

By 1516, Palestine and Syria had been occupied by the Ottoman Turks and would stay that way for the next four centuries. Most of the desert areas of modern Syria and Jordan, however, remained the preserve of Bedouin tribes.

Up until the early 19th century, Syria prospered under Turkish rule. Damascus and Aleppo were important market towns for the surrounding desert as well as being stages on the desert trade routes to Persia. Aleppo also became an important trading centre with Europe, and Venetian, English and French merchants established themselves there.

For almost the whole of the 1830s the Egyptians once again gained control, led by Ibrahim Pasha, son of the Egyptian ruler Mohammed Ali. The high tax burdens and conscription imposed by Ibrahim were unpopular and the Europeans, fearful that the decline of Ottoman power might cause a crisis in Europe, intervened in 1840 and forced the Egyptians to withdraw.

The Muslim Arabs had accepted Turkish rule and the Ottoman Empire as the political embodiment of Islam, but already in the 19th century groups of Arab intellectuals in Syria and Palestine (many of them influenced by their years of study in Europe) set an Arab reawakening in train. After the Young Turk movement of 1909, power was in the hands of a military group whose harsh policies encouraged opposition and the growth of Arab nationalism.

WW I

During WW I, the area of Syria and Jordan was the scene of fierce fighting between the Turks, who had German backing, and the British based in Suez. By the end of 1917, British and Empire troops occupied Jerusalem and, a year later, the rest of Syria. Their successes would have been impossible without the aid of the Arabs, loosely formed into an army under Emir Faisal, son of Hussein, who was Sherif (ruler) of Mecca and had taken up the reins of the Arab nationalist movement in 1914. The enigmatic British colonel, T E Lawrence, better known as Lawrence of Arabia, helped coordinate the Arab Revolt and secure supplies from the Allies under General Allenby's command.

Under the Sykes-Picot agreement of 1916, Syria and Lebanon were to be placed under French mandate, and Palestine (including what was to be called Transjordan) would go to the British. By the Balfour Declaration of 1917, Britain pledged support for the ambiguously phrased 'Jewish homeland'.

In March 1920, Emir Faisal was proclaimed king of Syria but the Allied powers refused to recognise him. At the Conference of San Remo, the Allied supreme council confirmed France's mandate over Syria and

Lebanon, and the British got Transjordan and Palestine.

Out of this mess emerged the modern states of Syria, Lebanon, Jordan and, later, Israel. The histories of the modern states of Syria and Jordan from 1920 on are dealt with under their respective sections.

ARTS

Art

Islam forbids the depiction of human or animal life, and art throughout the Arab world has been dominated by these precepts. Although artists in Syria and Jordan have developed figurative painting and portraiture in the commonly accepted fashion of the West over the past 100 years, it is still the intricate geometrical designs adorning everything from mosques to illuminated manuscripts, and the extravagant calligraphy of the Arabic language itself, that impress Western visitors most by their elaborate grace.

Bedouin Crafts

The Bedouin continue to produce the most colourful textiles. Women's clothing in particular can capture the eyes with its vivid design and colours, all of which can change from region to region and tribe to tribe.

Another Bedouin speciality is the production of knives – and in certain parts of Jordan now they produce the stuff like there is no tomorrow – for the tourists of course.

Music

Arab music reflects a successful synthesis of indigenous harmony and taste, not to mention instruments, with some traits and instruments of the West. The popular music takes some time to get used to, and for many its attraction remains a mystery. Others however, are eventually caught up by its own particular magic – which is probably a good thing, because you'll hear it in one form or another wherever you go!

Literature

Modern literary genres such as the novel are a relatively new and unexperimented area in the Arab world, with such works only beginning to emerge in the late 19th century. Dominated by a highly structured and complex tradition of verse, and the undoubted beauty of the Koran, modern Arab writers come from a very different literary background to their Western counterparts.

Egyptians (such as Nobel Prize-winning Naguib Mahfouz), Lebanese and, to a lesser extent, Palestinians seem to dominate the scene. Increasingly, Arabic work is coming to be known through translation to Westerners. Many Arabs have also written principally in French or English, rather than in their indigenous tongue.

Repression in Syria has tended to hold literary production at a banal level. One exception is the self-taught Zakariya Tamir, who has lived in exile in London since 1978. His work deals much with everyday city life, marked by a frustration and despair born of social oppression - which probably explains why he ended up in London.

RELIGION

Islam

Islam is the predominant religion in both Jordan and Syria. Muslims are called to prayer five times a day and no matter where you might be, there always seems to be a mosque within earshot.

In the early 7th century in Mecca, Mohammed received the word of Allah (God) and called on the people to turn away from pagan worship and submit to the one true God. His teachings appealed to the poorer levels of society and angered the wealthy merchant class. By 622 life had become sufficiently unpleasant for Mohammed and his followers for them to migrate to Medina, an oasis town some 300 km to the north. This migration – the Hijra – marks the beginning of the Islamic Calendar, year 1 AH or 622 AD. By 630 they had gained a sufficient following to return and take Mecca.

With seemingly unlimited zeal and ambition, the followers of Mohammed spread the word, using force where necessary, and by 644 Islam had spread to Syria, Persia, Iraq,

Egypt and North Africa. In the following decades its influence would extend from the Atlantic to the Indian Ocean.

Islam is the Arabic word for submission and underlies the duty of every Muslim to submit themselves to Allah. This profession of faith (the *shahada*) is the first of the Five Pillars of Islam, the five tenets in the Koran that guide Muslims in their daily life:

shahada – the profession of faith, 'There is no God but Allah and Mohammed is his prophet', is the fundamental tenet of Islam. It is to Islam what the Lord's prayer is to Christianity, and it is often quoted, eg to greet the newborn and farewell the dead.

salat – the call to prayer. Five times a day (dawn, noon, mid-afternoon, sunset and nightfall) Muslims must face Mecca and recite the prescribed prayers.

zakat – this was originally the act of giving alms to the poor and needy. It was later developed by modern states into an obligatory land tax that goes to help the poor.

sawm – or fasting. Ramadan, the ninth month of the Muslim calendar, commemorates the month when the Koran was revealed to Mohammed. All Muslims are supposed to fast from dawn to dusk during Ramadan.

hajj – the pilgrimage to Mecca, the holiest place in Islam. It is the duty of all Muslims who are fit and can afford it to make the pilgrimage at least once in their life. On the pilgrimage, the pilgrim *(hajji)* wears a white seamless robe and walks around the *kaaba*, the black stone in the centre of the mosque, seven times.

To Muslims, Allah is the same God that the Christians worship in the Bible and the Jews in the Torah. Adam, Abraham, Noah, Moses and Jesus are all recognised as prophets by Islam. Jesus is not, however, recognised as the son of God. According to Islam, all of these prophets partly received the word of God, but only Mohammed received the complete revelation.

In its early days, Islam suffered a major schism that divided the faith into two streams: the Sunnis (or Sunnites) and the Shi'ites. The latter later split into further groups. The prophet's son-in-law and, more importantly, the father of Mohammed's sole male heirs, Ali, became the fourth caliph following the murder of Mohammed's third successor, Othman. He in turn was assassinated in 661 after failing to bend the rebellious governor of Syria, Mu'awiya, to his rule. Mu'awiya, a relative of Othman who had revolted against Ali over the latter's alleged involvement in the killing of Othman, then set himself up as caliph. The Sunnis, who comprise the majority of Muslims today, are followers of the succession from the caliph, while the Shi'ites follow the successors of Ali. The majority of Shi'ites believe in 12 imams, the last of whom will one day appear to create an empire of the true faith.

Islam & the West Unfortunately, Islam has been much maligned and misunderstood in the West in recent years. Any mention of it usually brings to mind one of two images: the 'barbarity' of some aspects of Islamic law such as flogging, stoning or the amputation of hands; or the so-called fanatics out to terrorise the West.

For many Muslims, however, and particularly for those in the Middle East, Islam is stability in a very unstable world. Many of them are keenly aware that Muslims are seen as a threat by the West and are divided in their own perceptions of the West. Not without justification, they regard the West's policies, especially towards the Arab world, as aggressive and often compare its attitudes to them with those of the medieval Crusaders. Despite this and the growing influence in Muslim countries of religious groups opposed to the West, many still admire the West. It is common to hear people say they like it, but that they are perplexed by its treatment of them. Many view Western culture as dangerous to Muslim values, but that view is by no means shared by all.

If the West is offended by the anti-Western rhetoric of the radical minority, the majority of Muslims see the West, especially with its support of Israel, as a direct challenge to their independence.

Although the violence and terrorism associated with the Middle East is often held up by the Western media as evidence of blind, religiously inspired Muslim blood-thirstiness, the efficient oppression by Israeli security forces of the Palestinian Arabs has until fairly recently barely rated a mention. The sectarian madness of Northern Ireland is rarely held up as a symbol of Christian 'barbarism' in the way political violence in the Middle East is summed up as simple Muslim fanaticism. It is worth remembering that while the 'Christian' West tends to view Islam with disdain, if not contempt, Muslims accord Christians great respect as 'People of the Book' and believers in the same God.

Just as the West receives a distorted view of Muslim society, so too are Western values misread in Islamic societies. The glamour of the West has lured those able to compete (usually the young, rich and well educated) but for others, it represents the bastion of moral decline – so it is easier for them to reassert their faith in Islam than to seek what they cannot attain. Often what is being accepted or rejected by Muslims is a mishmash of impressions, mainly received from American soap operas and film, which may bear little relation to life in the West.

These misunderstandings have long contributed to a general feeling of unease and distrust between nations of the West and the Muslim world, and often between individuals of those countries. As long as this situation persists, Islam will continue to be seen in the West as a backward and radical force bent on violent change, rather than as simply a code of religious and political behaviour that people choose to apply to their daily lives, and which makes an often difficult life tolerable for them.

Islamic Customs When Muslims go to pray, they must follow certain rituals. The first is that they must wash their hands, arms, feet, head and neck in running water before praying. All mosques have a small area set aside for this purpose. If they are not in a mosque and there is no water available, clean sand suffices, and where there is no sand, they must just go through the motions of washing.

Then they must cover the head, face

Mecca (all mosques are orientated so that the mihrab, or prayer niche, faces the right way) and follow a set pattern of gestures and genuflections – the photos of rows of Muslims kneeling with their heads touching the ground in the direction of Mecca are legion. Apart from in the mosques, Muslims can pray anywhere, and you regularly see them praying by the side of the road or in the street. Many keep a small prayer rug handy for just such moments.

In everyday life, Muslims are prohibited from drinking alcohol, eating pork (as the animal is considered unclean) and must refrain from fraud, usury, slander and gambling.

Islamic Minorities In Syria, the Shi'ites and other Muslim minorities, such as the Alawites and Druze, account for about 16% of the population.

The Druze religion is an off-shoot of Shi'ite Islam and was spread in the 11th century by Hamzah ibn Ali and other missionaries from Egypt who followed the Fatimid caliph, Al-Hakim. The group derives its name from the name of one of Hamzah's subordinates, Muhammad Darazi. Darazi had declared Al-Hakim to be the last imam and God in one, but most Egyptians found the bloody and, many believe, demented ruler to be anything but divine. When he died in mysterious circumstances, Darazi and his companions were forced to flee Egypt.

Most members of the Druze community now live in the mountains of Lebanon, although there are some small Druze towns in the Hauran, the area around the Syria-Jordan border. Their distinctive faith has survived intact mainly because of the secrecy that surrounds it. Not only is conversion to or from the faith prohibited, but only an elite, known as *'uqqal* (knowers), have full access to the religious doctrine, the *hikmeh*. The hikmeh is contained in seven holy books which exist only in hand-written copies. One of the the the codes it preaches is *taqiyyeh* (caution), under which a believer living among Christians, for example, can outwardly conform to Christian belief while still being a Druze at heart. They believe that God is too sacred to be called by name, is amorphous and will reappear in other incarnations. Although the New Testament and the Koran are revered, they read their own scriptures at *khalwas* (meeting houses) on Thursdays.

In Syria, the Alawites, an extreme Shi'ite sect, are considered by some to be heretics as they worship Ali as a god. They live mostly around Lattakia or in the Hama-Homs area. They are usually found tilling the poorest land or holding down the least skilled jobs in the towns. A smaller group goes by the name of Ismaelis, another splinter Shi'ite group that believes in seven imams.

Jordan has a 25,000-strong community of non-Arab Sunni Muslims known as Circassians. They fled persecution in Russia in the late 19th century and settled in Turkey, Syria and Jordan. Inter-marriage has made them virtually indistinguishable from their Arab neighbours.

The Chechens are another group of Caucasian origin in Jordan and are similar to the Circassians.

There is also a tiny Shi'ite minority in Jordan.

Christianity

Statistics on the number of Christians in Jordan and Syria are hard to come by and often wildly contradictory. They are believed to account for about 6% of Jordan's and 13% of Syria's population. There is a bewildering array of churches representing the three major branches of Christianity – Eastern Orthodox, Catholic and Protestant.

Eastern Orthodox This branch of Christianity is represented by the Greek Orthodox, Armenian Orthodox and Syrian Orthodox churches.

Greek Orthodox has its liturgy in Arabic and is the mother church of the Jacobites (Syrian Orthodox), who broke away in the 6th century, and the Greek Catholics, who split in the 16th century.

Armenian Orthodox (also known as the Armenian Apostolic Church) has its liturgy in classical Armenian and is seen by many to be the guardian of the Armenian national identity.

Syrian Orthodox uses Syriac, closely related to the Aramaic spoken by Christ. The patriarch lives in Damascus and the see (where the patriarch lives) has jurisdiction over foreign communities such as the Syrian Malankars in Kerala, India, and Syrian Orthodox in the USA.

Coptic Orthodox, with their pope and most coreligionists in Egypt, have a small community in Jordan.

Catholic These churches come under the jurisdiction of Rome and are listed from largest to smallest.

Greek Catholics, or Melchites, come under the authority of the patriarch who resides in Damascus, but his jurisdiction includes the patriarchates of Jerusalem and Alexandria. The church observes the Byzantine tradition, where married clergy are in charge of rural parishes and the diocesan clergy are celibate.

Armenian Catholics form a tightly-knit community. They fled from Turkish massacres in 1894 to 1896, and 1915 to 1921. They have their liturgy in classical Armenian. The patriarch resides in Beirut, and more than half their members are from Aleppo.

Syrian Catholics have Syriac as the main liturgical language although some services are in Arabic. They are found mainly in the north-east of Syria and in Homs, Aleppo and Damascus.

The Maronites trace their origins to St Maron, a monk who lived near Aleppo and died around 410. Their liturgy is in ancient

West Syrian, although the commonly used language is Arabic. They are found mainly in Lebanon (about one million), where their patriarch is based, but there are sizeable numbers in Aleppo. As with the other Christian groups of the Middle East, the majority live outside their countries of origin: there are estimated to be about three million living in Europe, North and South America, and Australia.

Latin (or Roman) Catholics live in western Syria and Aleppo. Rome recently restored the patriarchate of Jerusalem, and a patriarch was elected there in 1987.

Chaldean Catholics, who have preserved the ancient East Syrian liturgy which they practise in Syriac, are found mainly in eastern Syria, Aleppo and Damascus. Their patriarch resides in Baghdad, the Iraqi capital.

Jews

There is a small Jewish population still left in Damascus, estimated at 3000 to 4000. The Jews have been a constant tool of propaganda for the Assad regime, regularly wheeled out for pro-government demonstrations carrying approving signs in Hebrew. The reality is grimmer, with many wanting to migrate to Israel or the USA but unable to do so. In an attempt to curry favour with the USA, President Assad promised in early 1992 to ease restrictions and allow Jews to leave the country, which they in fact began to do by the middle of the year.

LANGUAGE

Arabic is the official language in Jordan and Syria. English is widely spoken in Jordan and, to a lesser extent, French in Syria, where English is also rapidly gaining ground, but any effort to communicate with the locals in their own language will be well rewarded. No matter how far off the mark your pronunciation or grammar might be, you'll often get the response (usually with a big smile): 'Ah, you speak Arabic very well!' Greeting Syrian officials, who are generally less than helpful, with the usual greeting, *salaam*

alaykum (peace be upon you), will often work wonders.

Learning the basics for day-to-day travelling doesn't take long at all, but to master the complexities of Arabic would take years of constant study.

It is worth noting here that transliteration from the Arabic script into English – or any other language for that matter – is at best an approximate science.

The presence of sounds unknown in European languages and the fact that the script is 'defective' (most vowels are not written) combine to make it nearly impossible to settle on one method of transliteration. A wide variety of spellings is therefore possible for words when they appear in Latin script – and that goes for place and people's names as well.

The whole thing is further complicated by the wide variety of dialects and the imaginative ideas Arabs themselves often have on appropriate spelling in, say, English (and words spelt one way in Jordan may look very different again in Syria, heavily influenced by French) – not that even the most venerable of Western Arabists have been able to come up with a satisfactory solution.

While striving to reflect the language as closely as possible and aiming at consistency, this book generally spells place, street and hotel names and the like as the locals have done. Don't be surprised if you come across several versions of the same thing!

T E Lawrence, when asked by his publishers to clarify 'inconsistencies in the spelling of proper names' in *Seven Pillars of Wisdom*, his account of the Arab Revolt in WW I, wrote back:

Arabic names won't go into English...There are some 'scientific systems' of transliteration, helpful to people who know enough Arabic not to need helping, but a washout for the world. I spell my names anyhow, to show what rot the systems are.

Pronunciation

Much of the vocabulary that follows would be universally understood throughout the Arab world, although some of it, especially where more than one option is given, reflects the region's dialects. Arabic pronunciation is not easy, and to reflect sounds unknown in English, certain combinations of letters are used in transliteration:

gh like French 'r' in Paris
kh 'ch' as in Scottish loch
u 'oo' as in look
ay as in stay
dh 'th' as in them – pushes the preceding vowel to the back of the throat, as if when gargling. A sound rarely mastered by non-Arabs.

Greetings & Civilities

Arabs place great importance on civility and it's rare to see any interaction between people that doesn't begin with profuse greetings, enquiries into the other's health and other niceties.

Arabic greetings are more formal than in English and there is a reciprocal response to each. These sometimes vary slightly, depending on whether you're addressing a man or a woman. A simple encounter can become a drawn-out affair, with neither side wanting to be the one to put a halt to the stream of greetings and well-wishing. As an *ajnabi* (foreigner), you're not expected to know all the ins and outs, but if you come up with the right expression at the appropriate moment they'll love it.

The most common greeting is *salaam alaykum* (peace be upon you), to which the correct reply is *wa alaykum as-salaam* (and upon you be peace). If you get invited to a birthday celebration or are around for any of the big holidays, the common greeting is *kul sana wa intum bi-kheer* (I wish you well for the coming year).

After having a bath or shower, you will often hear people say to you *na'iman*, which roughly means 'heavenly' and boils down to an observation along the lines of 'nice and clean now, huh'.

Arrival in one piece is always something to be grateful for. Passengers will often be greeted with *al-hamdu lillah 'al as-salaama* – 'thank God for your safe arrival'.

Hi.	*marhaba*
Hello.	*ahlan wa sahlan*
(literally, welcome)	or just *ahlan*
Hello. (response)	*ahlan beek*
Goodbye.	*ma'a salaama*
	or *Allah ma'ak*
Good morning.	*sabah al-khayr*
Good morning. (response)	*sabah an-noor*
Good evening.	*masa al-khayr*
Good evening. (response)	*masa an-noor*
Good night.	*tisbah ala khayr*
Good night. (response)	*wa inta min ahalu*
Please. (request)	*min fadlak* (m)
	min fadlik (f)
Please. (formal, eg in restaurants)	*law samaht* (m)
	law samahti (f)
Please. (come in or go ahead)	*tafadal* (m)
	tafadali (f)
	tafadalu (pl)
Thank you.	*shukran*
Thank you very much.	*shukran jazeelan*
You are welcome.	*afwan* or *ahlan*
How are you?	*kayf haalak?* (m)
	kayf haalik? (f)
	also dialect
	shlonak? (m)
	shlonik? (f)
Fine. (literally, thanks be to God)	*al-hamdu lillah*
Pleased to meet you. (departing)	*fursa sa'ida*
Pardon/Excuse me.	*afwan*
Sorry!	*assif!*
Congratulations!	*mabrouk!*

Small Talk

What is your name?	*shu-ismak?* (m)
	shu-ismik? (f)
My name is...	*ismi...*
I	*ana*
you	*inta* (m)
	inti (f)
he	*huwa*
she	*hiyya*
we	*nahnu, ehna*
you	*intu*
they	*humma*
Where are you from?	*min wayn inta?*
I am...	*ana...*
Australian	*ustraali* (m)
	ustraaliyya (f)
American	*amreeki* (m)
	amreekiyya (f)
Canadian	*kanadi* (m)
	kanadiyya (f)
English	*ingleezi* (m)
	ingleeziyya (f)
Do you speak	*btahki ingleezi?*
English?	or *hal tatakallam*
	ingleezi?
I speak...	*ana bahki...*
	or *ana atakallam...*
English	*ingleezi*
French	*faransi*
German	*almaani*
What do you want?	*matha tureed?* (m)
	matha tureedi? (f)
I understand.	*afham*
I don't understand.	*ma bifham*
	or *la afham*
What does this mean?	*yaanee ay?*
I want an interpreter.	*ureed mutarjem*
Yes.	*aiwa* or *na'am*
No.	*la*
No problem.	*mish mushkila*
	or *mu mushkila*
Never mind.	*malesh*
	ana mareeda (f)
I like...	*ana bahib...*
	or *ana uhib...*

I don't like...	*ana ma bahib...*
	or *ana la uhib...*
I am sick.	*ana mareed* (m)

Questions like 'Is the bus coming?' or 'Will the bank be open later?' generally elicit the inevitable response: *in sha' Allah* – God willing – an expression you'll hear over and over again. Another less common one is *ma sha' Allah* – God's will be done – sometimes a useful answer to probing questions about why you're not married yet!

Getting Around

to/from	*illa/min*
bus station	*mahattat al-baas*
railway station	*mahattat al-qitaar*
airport	*al-mattar*
bus	*al-baas*
car	*as-sayara*
plane	*at-tayara*
train	*al-qitaar*
1st class	*daraja awla*
2nd class	*daraja thani*
here/there	*hon/honak*
left/right	*yasaar/yameen*
straight ahead	*'ala tuul* or *sawa*
fast	*bi-sura'*
slow	*mish bi-sura'* or
	shwayya

Around Town

Where is the...?	*wayn...?*
bank	*masraf* or *bank*
bridge	*jisr*
castle, palace	*al-qasr*
church	*al-kaneesa*
customs	*al-jumruk*
hotel	*fundooq*
market	*as-souq*
Mohammed St	*shari'a*
	Mohammed
mosque	*al-jaama'* or
	al-masjid
museum	*al-mathaf*
passport &	*maktab al-jawazaat*
immigration	*wa al-hijra*
office	
pharmacy	*as-sayidiliyya*

police	ash-shurta
post office	maktab al-bareed
restaurant	al-matta'am
ruins,	al-athaar
historical site	
temple	al-ma'abad
tourist office	maktab as-siyaha

Accommodation

Do you have...?	fi...?
a room	ghurfa
a single room	ghurfa mufrada
a double room	ghurfa bi sareerayn
a shower	doosh
hot water	mai harr
a toilet	twalet, mirhad
	or hammam
soap	saboon
air-con	kondishon
electricity	kahraba

Shopping

What is this?	shu hadha?
How much?	qaddaysh?
	or bikam?
How many?	kam wahid?
How much money?	kam fuloos?
How many km?	kam kilometre?
Is there...?	fi...?
There isn't (any).	ma fi

money	fuloos or masaari
big	kabeer
small	sagheer
bad	mish kwayyis
	or mu kwayyis
good	kwayyis
excellent	mumtaz
finished	khalas
cheap/expensive	rakhees/ghaali
cheaper	arkhas
closed	maghlooq or
	musakkar
open	maftooh
hot/cold	harr/baarid

Time & Dates

When?	mataa, emta?
yesterday	imbaarih, 'ams
today	al-yum

tomorrow	bukra/ghadan
minute	daqiqa
hour	sa'a
day	yum
week	usbu'a
month	shahr
year	sana

What is the time?	as-sa'a kam?
5 o'clock	as-sa'a khamsa
How many hours?/	kam sa'a?
How long?	
five hours	khams sa'at

Monday	al-itneen
Tuesday	at-talata
Wednesday	al-arbi'ad
Thursday	al-khamees
Friday	al-juma'
Saturday	as-sabt
Sunday	al-ahad

Months

The Islamic year has 12 lunar months and is 11 days shorter than the Western (Gregorian) calendar, so important Muslim dates will fall 11 days earlier each (Western) year.

There are two Gregorian calendars in use in the Arab world. In Egypt and westwards, the months have virtually the same names as in English (January is yanaayir, October octobir and so on), but in Jordan, Syria and eastwards, the names are quite different. Talking about, say, June as 'month six' is the easiest solution, but for the sake of completeness, the months from January are:

January	kanoon ath-thani
February	shubaat
March	azaar
April	nisaan
May	ayyaar
June	huzayran
July	tammooz
August	'ab
September	aylool
October	ishreen al-awal
November	tishreen ath-thani
December	kanoon al-awal

The Hijra months, too, have their own names:

1st	Moharram
2nd	Safar
3rd	Rabi' al-Awal
4th	Rabei ath-Thani
5th	Jumada al-Awal
6th	Jumada al-Akhira
7th	Rajab
8th	Shaaban
9th	Ramadan
10th	Shawwal
11th	Zuul-Qeda
12th	Zuul-Hijja

Numbers

Arabic numerals are simple enough to learn and, unlike the written language, run from left to right.

¼	*ruba*
½	*nuss*
¾	*talata ruba*

0	•	*sifr*
1	١	*wahid*
2	٢	*itneen/tinteen*
3	٣	*talata*
4	٤	*arba'a*
5	٥	*khamsa*
6	٦	*sitta*
7	٧	*saba'a*
8	٨	*tamanya*
9	٩	*tisa'a*
10	١٠	*ashara*

11	*hid-ashr*
12	*itn-ashr*
13	*talat-ashr*
14	*arba'at-ashr*
15	*khamast-ashr*
16	*sitt-ashr*
17	*saba'at-ashr*
18	*tamant-ashr*
19	*tisa'at-ashr*
20	*ashreen*
21	*wahid wa ashreen*
22	*itneen wa ashreen*

30	*talateen*
40	*arba'een*
50	*khamseen*
60	*sitteen*
70	*saba'een*
80	*tamaneen*
90	*tisa'een*
100	*mia*
101	*mia wa wahid*
125	*mia wa khamsa wa ashreen*
200	*miateen*
300	*talata mia*
400	*arba'a mia*
1000	*alf*
2000	*alfeen*
3000	*talat-alaf*
4000	*arba'at-alaf*

Body Language

Arabs gesticulate a lot in conversation, and some things can be said without uttering a word. Certain expressions also go together with particular gestures.

Jordanians and Syrians often say 'no' merely by raising the eyebrows and lifting the head up and back. This is often accompanied by a 'tsk tsk' noise and it can all be a little off-putting if you're not used to it – don't take it as a snub.

Shaking the head from side to side (as Westerners would to say 'no') means 'I don't understand'. Stretching out the hand as if to open a door and giving it a quick flick of the wrist is equivalent to 'what do you want?', 'where are you going?' or 'what's your problem?'

If an official holds out his hand and draws a line across his palm with the index finger of the other hand, he is not pointing out that he has a long life-line but that he wants to see your passport, bus ticket or any other document that may seem relevant at the time.

Guys asking directions should not be surprised to be taken by the arm or hand and led along. It is quite natural for men to hold each other by the hand and, despite what you may think, rarely means anything untoward is happening. Women should obviously be more careful about such helpfulness.

A right hand over your heart means 'no, thanks' when you are offered something. When you've had enough tea, Turkish coffee or anything else to drink, you put your hand over the cup. The polite thing to say is *da'iman* ('always', more or less meaning 'may it ever be thus'). Arabic coffee has its own rituals, see the Food section in the Facts for the Visitor chapter.

As the left hand is associated with toilet duties it is considered unclean and so you should always use the right hand when giving or receiving something.

Facts for the Visitor

WHAT TO BRING

A hat, sunglasses and water bottle are essential in summer. A few other handy items are: a Swiss army knife, a torch (flashlight), a few metres of nylon cord, a tennis ball cut in half to use as a universal sink plug, earplugs, a medical kit and a sewing kit.

Toilet paper is hard to find in Syria, although small packets of tissues are sold by street vendors everywhere. Tampons are not widely available. You should also bring your own contraceptives or any special medication you need.

If you're going to be in the region in winter, make sure you have some warm clothes and a wind & waterproof jacket.

ISLAMIC HOLIDAYS

As the Hijra calendar is 11 days shorter than the Gregorian calendar, each year Islamic holidays fall 11 days earlier than in the previous year. For example, 1 January 1992 was 26 Jumada ath-Thani 1412 AH. The precise dates are known only shortly before they fall, as they depend upon the sighting of the moon. The main Islamic holidays are the following (for the equivalent Western calendar dates, see the Table of Holidays):

Ras as-Sana
New Year's Day, celebrated on 1 Moharram.
Mulid an-Nabi
The Prophet Mohammed's birthday, celebrated on 12 Rabi' al-Awal.
Eid al-Fitr
Also known as the *Eid as-Sagheer* (small feast), it starts at the beginning of Shawwal to mark the end of fasting in the preceding month of Ramadan.
Eid al Adhah
Known commonly as the *Eid al-Kabeer* (big feast), it is the time when Muslims fulfil the fifth pillar of Islam – the pilgrimage to Mecca. This period lasts from 10 to 13 Zuul-Hijja.

Ramadan

Ramadan is the ninth month of the Muslim calendar, when Muslims fast during daylight hours to fulfill the fourth pillar of Islam. There are no public holidays but it is difficult to deal with officialdom because of unusual opening hours.

During this month of fasting, pious Muslims will not allow *anything* to pass their lips in daylight hours.

Although many do not follow the injunctions to the letter, most conform to some extent. Foreigners are not expected to follow suit, but it is generally impolite to smoke, drink or eat in public during Ramadan. In the bigger cities it is less of a problem, but it remains sensible to avoid flaunting your kebabs.

Business hours tend to become more erratic and usually shorter, and in out-of-the-way places you may find it hard to find a restaurant that opens before sunset.

The evening meal during Ramadan, called *iftar* (breaking the fast), is always a bit of a celebration. Go to the bigger restaurants and wait with fasting crowds for sundown, the moment when food is served – it's quite a lively experience.

TIME

Jordan and Syria are two hours ahead of GMT in winter (October to February) and three hours ahead in summer (March to September). When it's noon in Amman and Damascus, the time elsewhere is:

Paris, Rome	1 am
London	10 am
New York	5 am
Los Angeles	2 am
Perth, Hong Kong	6 pm
Sydney	8 pm
Auckland	10 pm

Time is something that Arabs always seem to have plenty of – something that should take five minutes will invariably take an hour. Trying to speed things up will only lead to frustration. It is better to take it philosoph-

Table of Holidays

Hejira Year	New Year	Prophet's Birthday	Ramadan Begins	Eid Al-Fitr	Eid Al-Adha
1413	02.07.92	10.09.92	23.02.93	26.03.93	01.06.93
1414	21.06.93	30.08.93	12.02.94	15.03.94	21.05.94
1415	10.06.94	19.08.94	01.02.95	04.03.95	10.05.95
1416	31.05.95	09.08.95	22.01.96	22.02.96	29.04.96
1417	19.05.96	28.07.96	10.01.97	10.02.97	18.04.97
1418	09.05.97	18.07.97	31.12.98	31.01.98	08.04.98
1419	28.04.98	07.07.98	20.12.99	20.01.99	28.03.99
1420	17.04.99	26.06.99	–	–	–

ically than try to fight it. A bit of patience goes a long way when dealing with the Arabs.

HEALTH

There are no inoculations needed for entry to Jordan or Syria, unless you're coming from a disease-affected area, but it's a good idea to have preventive shots for polio, tetanus and typhoid. If you are coming from an infected area cholera shots may also be useful, although the World Health Organisation tends to discourage them, as having the shots does not guarantee you are not carrying the disease. Some border officials may not be aware of which countries are disease-affected, so you could save yourself some hassle if you have a duly stamped International Health Card.

The medical services in both countries are well developed in the larger towns and cities and many of the doctors have been trained overseas and speak English. Your embassy will usually be able to recommend a reliable doctor or hospital if the need arises. For minor complaints, pharmacies can usually supply what you need, although you will probably have to use sign language in out-of-the-way places. Drugs normally sold only on prescription in the West are available over the counter in Syria, and to a lesser extent in Jordan. The price of antibiotics in Jordan can be outrageous, so bring a supply with you.

Pay special attention to what you are sold in pharmacies, as the advice and drugs you get may not be what you need. If possible, know exactly what kind of medication you need in advance. You should bring any special medication you take regularly in with you as it may not be available in Syria or Jordan.

Travel Health Guides

There are a number of books on travel health:

Staying Healthy in Asia, Africa & Latin America, Moon Publications. Probably the best all-round guide to carry, as it's compact but very detailed and well organised.
Travellers' Health, Dr Richard Dawood, Oxford University Press. Comprehensive, easy to read, authoritative and also highly recommended, although it's rather large to lug around.
Travel with Children, Maureen Wheeler, Lonely Planet Publications. Includes basic advice on travel health for younger children.

Pre-Departure Preparations

Travel Insurance Don't leave home without it! Hopefully you will never need it, but if you do, you'll be glad you've got health insurance. There are literally dozens of policies around and good travel agents such as STA should be able to put you on the right track. Most travel insurance packages include baggage and life insurance. Read the fine print and find one that suits your needs and covers the countries you will be visiting. While some policies pay doctors and hospitals direct, others require you to pay and claim the costs back on your return. Some make it a condition that you call a reverse charges number so that they can assess your needs immediately.

If you are planning to go scuba-diving in Jordan, check that the policy covers you in case of accident. Some policies will consider diving a dangerous activity requiring a higher premium.

Check also whether or not the policy covers ambulances and/or emergency flights home.

Medical Kit It would be an unwise traveller who didn't carry at least a basic medical kit. Items worth taking include: Band-Aids, sterile gauze bandage, antiseptic cream or liquid, cotton wool, thermometer, tweezers, scissors, antibiotic cream, a course of broad-spectrum antibiotics (check with your doctor), insect repellent, anti-malarial tablets and multi-vitamins.

Some medication for diarrhoea can be handy in emergencies – Lomotil, Imodium and Pepto-Bismol are popular – and some paracetamol or codeine for aches and fevers. A rehydration mixture might be a good precaution in case of severe diarrhoea – particularly if you are travelling with children.

It is not a bad idea to carry around a couple of new syringes. If you need an injection for any reason, especially when you are away from the main centres, you may feel more confident about 'bringing your own'.

Getting hold of malarial prophylactics in Syria is next to impossible; apparently they are only available through the Health Ministry.

Health Preparations If you wear glasses, bring a spare pair and a copy of the prescription. You should carry prescriptions of any medicaments you may need as well – make sure you have the generic name, as your specific brand may well not be available. Contraceptives are hard to come by, so bring your own.

Although available in Jordan, tampons, pads and the like appear to be nonexistent in Syria.

Immunisations Tetanus boosters are needed every 10 years and are highly recommended. Typhoid shots give protection for three years and may cause side-effects, such as pain at the injection site, fever, headache and a general unwell feeling.

For protection against hepatitis A, a shot of gamma globulin should be administered – preferably just before departure, as the antibody (it is not a vaccination) only lasts for six months. A vaccine called Haurix has recently become available for hepatitis A. Two shots give a year's protection. A third shot within a year gives another 10 years' protection.

Basic Rules
Food & Water Tap water in the major towns is safe to drink, but if your stomach is a bit delicate there is bottled water available everywhere. Chances are that if you have just come from Turkey or Egypt and survived you shouldn't have any trouble here. If you are buying bottled water, make sure that the seal is unbroken or you may be paying for plain old tap water. If bottled water is unavailable, the locally made soft drinks are fine and have a surprisingly low sugar content.

When it comes to food, there are a few common-sense precautions to take. Never eat unwashed fruit or vegetables and steer clear of stalls where the food doesn't look fresh. When eating in restaurants, cooked vegetables are safest, but generally the salads are OK too. Contaminated food and water can give you all sorts of weird and not-so-wonderful diseases such as hepatitis A, typhoid, cholera, dysentery, giardia and polio but you can minimise the risks of catching any of them by being selective about where and what you eat and by exercising meticulous care with your personal hygiene. Always wash your hands before eating (restaurants provide a basin for this purpose) and, needless to say, after using the toilet.

Milk and cream should be avoided in

Syria. Jordan has its own dairy industry and its products are pasteurised. Yoghurt is always OK and some people swear by it if you have a dose of the shits. Ice cream in Syria rarely contains dairy products, so it is OK unless your stomach is having problems coping with the water.

Meat is always all right to eat as long as it is thoroughly cooked. In stews it's never a problem but when you are buying *shawarma* – lamb cooked on a vertical spit, usually on the street – go for one that looks overdone rather than underdone.

It is not a bad idea to supplement your diet with multi-vitamins and/or iron, especially if you are avoiding certain foods or your diet is for whatever reason inadequate. Vegetarians can find the going a little tough, particularly in restaurants, where explanations that you don't eat meat often result in little more than the larger chunks being removed from any given dish.

Climatic & Geographical Considerations

It gets stinking hot during the summer in Jordan and Syria and you should take care to protect yourself. Wear a hat, keep plenty of sun lotion handy and, when it's practical, keep out of the sun altogether during the real heat of the day.

Sunburn Working on your tan is not always the best idea, particularly in the desert where you can get badly burned quickly. Use strong sunscreen on unprotected parts of the body, and preferably do as the locals do and keep covered up.

Prickly Heat Prickly heat is an itchy rash caused by excessive perspiration trapped under the skin. It usually strikes people who have just arrived in a hot climate and whose pores have not yet opened sufficiently to cope with greater sweating. Keeping cool by bathing often, using a mild talcum powder or even resorting to air-conditioning may help until you acclimatise.

Heat Exhaustion Dehydration or salt deficiency can cause heat exhaustion. Take time to acclimatise to high temperatures and make sure you get sufficient liquids. Salt deficiency is characterised by fatigue, lethargy, headaches, giddiness and muscle cramps, and in this case salt tablets may help. Vomiting or diarrhoea can deplete your liquid and salt levels.

Anhydrotic heat exhaustion, caused by an inability to sweat, is quite rare. Unlike the other forms of heat exhaustion, it is likely to strike people who have been in a hot climate for some time rather than newcomers. You will stay cooler by covering up with light, cotton clothes that trap perspiration against your skin than by wearing brief clothes.

Heat Stroke This serious, sometimes fatal, condition can occur if the body's heat-regulating mechanism breaks down and the body temperature rises to dangerous levels. Long, continuous periods of exposure to high temperatures can leave you vulnerable to heat stroke. You should avoid excessive alcohol or strenuous activity when you first arrive in a hot climate.

The symptoms are feeling unwell, little or no sweating and a high body temperature ($39°C$ to $41°C$). Where sweating has ceased, the skin becomes flushed and red. Severe, throbbing headaches and lack of coordination will also occur, and the sufferer may be confused or aggressive. Eventually the victim will become delirious or convulse. Hospitalisation is essential, but meanwhile get patients out of the sun, remove their clothing, cover them with a wet sheet or towel and fan continually.

Fungal Infections Hot weather fungal infections are most likely to occur on the scalp, between the toes or fingers (athlete's foot), in the groin (jock itch or crotch rot) and on the body (ringworm). You get ringworm (a fungal infection, not a worm) from infected animals or by walking on damp areas, like shower floors.

To prevent fungal infections wear loose, comfortable clothes, avoid artificial fibres, wash frequently and dry carefully. If you do get an infection, wash the infected area daily with a disinfectant or medicated soap and water, and rinse and dry well. Apply an antifungal powder like the widely available Tinaderm. Try to expose the infected area to air or sunlight as much as possible and wash all towels and underwear in hot water as well as changing them often.

Diseases of Insanitation

Diarrhoea It's inevitable that at some stage you'll be struck down with diarrhoea, maybe just as a result of a change of food or water, but more often because of a bug of some sort.

Don't go pumping yourself full of antibiotics at the first sign of trouble. This is not a good way to treat your stomach and you can often do more harm than good by destroying all the useful intestinal flora in your gut as well as the nasties that are giving you problems.

The best course of action is to starve the little bastards out. Rest, eat nothing and drink only unsweetened tea, flat soft drinks and clean water. Make sure you drink plenty of fluids, as diarrhoea can dehydrate you very quickly. It is also important to take salt to help your body retain water. If you must eat, stick to simple foods such as boiled vegetables, plain bread or toast, and yoghurt. Keep away from dairy products (other than yoghurt), anything sweet and non-citrus fruits.

If you have to be moving on and it's not practical to stick to this regimen, you may have to take something to block you up for a while. Lomotil and Imodium are effective and handy – take two tablets three times daily. Codeine phosphate tablets or a prescribed tincture of opium are other alternatives. Antibiotics can do the trick in severe cases. Ampicillin, a broad-spectrum penicillin, is recommended. Two 250 mg tablets taken every four hours over three days should be sufficient for an adult. Children between eight and 12 should take half this and kids below eight half again.

If at the end of all this you are still suffering, you may have dysentery and should see a doctor.

Dysentery It's not all that difficult to get dysentery and the first sign that something is seriously wrong is blood and/or mucus in the stools – indications that the bowel wall has started to break down. There are two types: bacillary dysentery, the most common variety, is short, sharp and nasty but rarely persistent and responds well to antibiotics; amoebic dysentery, which is caused by amoebic parasites rather than bacteria, is harder to treat, often persistent and can do permanent damage to your intestines if left unattended. A stool test has to be done to determine which one you have.

The prescribed treatment for amoebic dysentery is metronidazole. The adult dosage is a 750-mg capsule three times daily for five days. Half the adult dose for children between eight and 12 and one third of the adult dose for children under eight. Tetracycline is recommended for bacillary dysentery – a 250-mg pill four times a day for adults, half for children aged eight to 12 and one third for those below eight. Children should only have it administered if absolutely necessary. In all cases, medical help should be sought before trying to treat the problem yourself.

Cholera Cholera usually occurs in epidemics and can be extremely dangerous. Symptoms are bad diarrhoea, vomiting, shallow breathing, wrinkled skin, stomach cramps, dehydration and a fast, faint heartbeat. If you think you have it, see a doctor immediately as you cannot treat it yourself. Cholera vaccinations are generally discouraged unless you are going into a known area. Even then they are only about 50% effective.

The best way to prevent the disease is to avoid the water.

Hepatitis This is a liver disease caused by a virus and again there are two types. Infectious hepatitis (type A) is the one you are most likely to catch. It is highly contagious and you pick it up from drinking water, eating food or using utensils contaminated by an infected person. Serum hepatitis (type B) can only be contracted by having sex with a type B carrier or using a needle previously injected into a carrier.

Symptoms start to appear three to five weeks after infection and consist of fever, loss of appetite, nausea, depression, lethargy and pains around the base of your rib cage (ie the liver). The usual telltale sign is when the whites of your eyes start turning yellow and your urine turns a deep orange or brown.

The only cure for hepatitis is complete rest, non-fatty food and giving your liver a sporting chance by laying off the alcohol. You should be over the worst in about 10 days but it can last for months, so it might be time to cash in your medical insurance and fly home.

Typhoid This is a dangerous infection that starts in the stomach and spreads throughout the body. The main symptom is high fevers and it can be caught from contaminated food and water. Vaccination is recommended. If you do get it, medical help is essential.

Diseases Spread by People & Animals

Tetanus This potentially fatal disease is found mainly in tropical areas, so should not be a problem. It occurs when a wound becomes infected by a germ that lives in the faeces of animals or people, so clean all cuts, punctures or animal bites. Tetanus is known as lockjaw, and the first symptom may be discomfort in swallowing, or stiffening of the jaw and neck; this is followed by painful convulsions of the jaw and whole body.

Rabies Rabies is caused by a bite or scratch from an infected animal. Dogs are a noted carrier. Any bite, scratch or even lick from a mammal should be cleaned immediately and thoroughly. Scrub with soap and running water, and then clean with an alcohol solution. If there is any possibility that the animal is infected, medical help should be sought immediately.

Sexually Transmitted Diseases Sexual contact with an infected sexual partner spreads these diseases. While abstinence is the only 100% preventative, using condoms is also effective. Gonorrhoea and syphilis are the most common of these diseases; sores, blisters or rashes around the genitals, discharges or pain when urinating are common symptoms. Symptoms may be less marked or not observed at all in women. Syphilis symptoms eventually disappear completely but the disease continues and can cause severe problems in later years. The treatment of gonorrhoea and syphilis is by antibiotics.

There are numerous other sexually transmitted diseases, for most of which effective treatment is available. However, there is no cure for herpes and there is also currently no cure for AIDS. Using condoms is the most effective preventative.

AIDS can be spread through infected blood transfusions; most developing countries cannot afford to screen blood for transfusions. It can also be spread by dirty needles – vaccinations, acupuncture and tattooing can potentially be as dangerous as intravenous drug use if the equipment is not clean. If you do need an injection it may be a good idea to buy a new syringe from a pharmacy and ask the doctor to use it.

Insect-Borne Diseases

Malaria Malaria in the desert? Surprising as it may seem, there is a small risk of catching malaria in Jordan and Syria. Doctors generally do not recommend anti-malarial tablets to people travelling in the region, but they might not be a bad idea if you intend to spend a while along the Euphrates River in the north of Syria. The disease is spread by mosquitoes which, fortunately, are few in number. Also, unlike in many places, the strains of malaria here are not resistant to chloroquine. The period of highest risk is from May to October. Mosquitoes appear after dusk. Avoid getting bitten by covering bare skin and using an insect repellent.

Cuts, Bites & Stings

Cuts & Scratches Cuts of any kind can easily become infected, especially in the hot months, and should always be treated with an antiseptic solution. Dive instructors will discourage walking on the coral along

Jordan's Red Sea coast, but if you must, wear shoes – coral cuts are notoriously slow to heal as the coral injects a weak venom into the wound.

Bites & Stings Trekkers in desert areas should keep an eye out for scorpions which often shelter in shoes and the like and pack a powerful sting. Snake bites are also a possibility. Wrap the bitten limb tightly, immobilise it with a splint and seek medical help (if possible with the dead snake). Tourniquets and sucking out the poison are now comprehensively discredited.

Bedbugs & Lice Bedbugs live in various places, but particularly in dirty mattresses and bedding. Spots of blood on bedclothes or on the wall around the bed can be read as a suggestion to find another hotel. Bedbugs leave itchy bites in neat rows. Calamine lotion may help.

All lice cause itching and discomfort. They make themselves at home in your hair (head lice), your clothing (body lice) or in your pubic hair (crabs). You catch lice through direct contact with infected people or by sharing combs, clothing and the like. A powder or shampoo treatment will kill the lice and infected clothing should then be washed in very hot water.

Women's Health
Gynaecological Problems Poor diet, lowered resistance due to the use of antibiotics for stomach upsets and even contraceptive pills can lead to vaginal infections when travelling in hot climates. Keeping the genital area clean, and wearing skirts or loose-fitting trousers and cotton underwear will help to prevent infections.

Yeast infections, characterised by a rash, itch and discharge, can be treated with a vinegar or even lemon-juice douche, or with yoghurt. Nystatin suppositories are the usual medical prescription.

Trichomonas is a more serious infection; symptoms are a discharge and a burning sensation when urinating. Male sexual partners must also be treated, and if a vinegar-water douche is not effective medical attention should be sought. Flagyl is the prescribed drug.

Pregnancy Most miscarriages occur during the first three months of pregnancy, so this is the most risky time to travel. The last three months should also be spent within reasonable distance of good medical care, as quite serious problems can develop at this time.

Pregnant women should avoid all unnecessary medication, but vaccinations and malarial prophylactics should still be taken where possible. Additional care should be taken to prevent illness and particular attention should be paid to diet and nutrition.

Toilets
Toilets are almost always the hole-in-the-floor variety and are in fact far more hygienic than sit-on toilets as only your covered feet come into contact with anything.

It takes a little while to master the squatting technique without losing everything from your pockets. Always carry your own toilet paper or adopt the local habit of using your left hand and water. There is always a tap at a convenient height for this purpose – whether any water comes out is something else again!

Toilet paper is widely available in Jordan, and although in Syria the familiar rolls may be hard to come by, most street vendors sell small packets of tissues that do just as well. Remember, for the sake of those who come after you, that the little basket usually provided is for your toilet paper. Trying to flush it will soon clog the system.

FOOD
Food in Syria and Jordan ranges from the exotic to the mundane. Unfortunately for the budget traveller, exotic food comes with exotic prices, so it's mostly the mundane you'll be relying on. The food is tasty as a rule but the lack of variety can be monotonous.

Snacks

Felafel, hummus and, to a lesser degree, *fuul* are the staple foods of the region and are eaten for breakfast, lunch or dinner. Fuul is a paste made from fava beans, garlic and lemon and is served swimming in oil – a bit hard to handle first thing in the morning. If you've arrived from Egypt, you will need no introduction.

Felafel is deep-fried balls of chickpea paste with spices and served in a piece of unleavened bread *(khobz)* with varying combinations of pickled vegetables, tomato, salad and yoghurt. This is one of the cheapest ways to eat and chances are you'll be thoroughly sick of felafels by the time you leave. Hummus is cooked chickpeas ground into a paste and mixed with tahini (a sesame-seed paste), garlic and lemon. It is available in virtually every restaurant and is usually excellent.

Baba ghanouj is another of the dips eaten with bread and is made from mashed eggplant and tahini.

The meat equivalent of the felafel is the *shawarma*, and you'll probably have your fair share of these too as they are cheap and convenient. Slices of lamb are carefully arranged on a vertical spit and are topped with a few big chunks of fat, which drips down the meat as it cooks, and a tomato for decoration.

When you order a shawarma, more commonly known as a *sandweech*, the vendor will slice off the meat (usually with a great flourish and much knife sharpening and waving), dip a piece of flat bread in the fat that has dripped off the meat, hold it against the gas flame so it flares, then fill it with the meat and fillings similar to those for felafels. Chicken shawarmas are quite common too.

On the same stall you will usually find *kibbih* – deep-fried balls made of a mixture of meat and cracked wheat and stuffed with more meat fried in onions. Shops selling shawarma nearly always have the spit set up out by the footpath so you can just pick one up as you walk along.

In Syria, particularly in Aleppo, you'll come across bakeries selling what look like small pizzas. They are a type of bread topped with spices, cheese and sometimes meat. You can occasionally find these as far south as Amman in Jordan.

The Arabic bread, khobz, is eaten with absolutely everything and is sometimes called *eish* (life), its common name in Egypt. It is round and flat and makes a good filler if you are preparing your own food. There is a variety of tastes and textures, depending on how it is baked, but the basic principle remains the same. On the streets of Amman, stalls sell *ka'ik*, which are round sesame rings and tastier than plain old khobz.

Other sandweech stalls specialise in offal of various kinds (liver, kidneys, brains, etc) and they are probably quite OK to eat if you can stomach that sort of thing.

Main Dishes

For main dishes, you'll be eating either chicken, kebabs or meat-and-vegetable stews most of the time.

Chicken *(farooj)* is usually roasted on spits in large ovens out the front of the restaurant. The usual serving is half a chicken *(nuss farooj)* and it will come with bread and a side dish of raw onion, chillies and sometimes olives. Eaten with the optional extras of salad *(salata)* and hummus, you have a good meal.

Kebabs are another favourite available everywhere. These are spicy minced lamb pressed onto skewers and grilled over charcoal. They are usually sold by weight and are also served with bread and a side plate.

Stews are usually meat or vegetable or both and, although not available everywhere, make a pleasant change from chicken and kebabs. *Fasooliya* is bean stew, *biseela* is peas, *batatas* is potato and *mulukiyyeh* is a kind of spinach stew with chicken or meat pieces. They are usually served on rice *(ruz)* or more rarely macaroni *(makarone)*, which are extra.

In Jordan you can eat the Bedouin speciality *mensaf*. It is traditionally served on special occasions and consists of lamb on a bed of rice and pine nuts, topped with the gaping head of the lamb. The fat from the cooking is poured into the rice and is considered by some to be the best part.

The men sit on the floor around the big dishes and dig in (with the right hand only), while the women eat elsewhere in the town or camp. Traditionally, the delicacy is the eyes, which are presented to honoured guests! Don't worry if you miss out – there are other choice bits like the tongue. It is not always so easy to refuse if offered. Once all have had their fill, usually well before it's all been eaten, you move off to wash your hands while young boys take away the leftovers and tuck in. The meal is eventually followed by endless rounds of coffee and tea and plenty of lively talk.

If you stay with the Bedouin you may be lucky enough to eat mensaf this way, but you can also buy a serve in restaurants in Amman. It is not cheap but should be tried at least once. A tangy sauce of cooked yoghurt mixed with the fat is served with it.

Another Jordanian specialty is *mezze*, which is actually a selection of appetisers but makes a meal in itself. Served on a tray with tea, you get hummus, baba ghanouj, sardines, cucumbers, tomato, liver and kidneys, fried eggs, spice and oil.

Fish *(samak)* is not widely available and is usually so heavily salted and spiced that it tastes more like a large anchovy. Decent fish can be had in Aqaba, Jordan's Red Sea port, and occasionally in Syria's Mediterranean towns.

Desserts

Arabs love their sugar and their desserts are no exception – they are horrendously sweet. There are pastry shops in every town which sell nothing but these sickly sweets. Just wander in and have a look at the selection. The basic formula is pastry drenched in honey or syrup. Many of them, however different they look, fall into the general category of *baqlawa*. Buy only a small quantity as more than one of anything is too much.

In Syria, many of the pastry shops are sit-down places. You walk in, make a selection and take a seat. They serve you your order, some water to swig between each

sweet and sometimes a coffee or tea as well. You pay on the way out. The most popular desserts are:

mahalabiyya – milk pudding
mahalabiyya wa festaq – milk pudding with pistachio nuts
baqlawa – layered flaky pastry with nuts, drenched in honey
kinaafa – shredded wheat over goat cheese baked in syrup
zalabiyya – pastries dipped in rose-water
mushabbak – lace-work shaped pastry drenched in syrup
isfinjiyya – coconut slice
halawat al-jibna – a soft doughy pastry filled with cream cheese and topped with syrup & ice cream
booza – ice cream

Soup

| soup | *shurba* |
| lentil soup | *shurbat al-'adas* |

Vegetables

cabbage	*kharoum*
carrot	*jazar*
cauliflower	*arnabeet*
eggplant	*bazinjan*
green beans	*fasooliya*
lentils	*'adas*
okra	*baamiya*
peas	*biseela*
potatoes	*batatas*
turnip	*lift*
vegetables	*khadrawat*

Salad

cucumber	*khiyaar*
garlic	*tum*
lettuce	*khass*
onion	*basal*
salad	*salata*
tomato	*banadura*

Meat

camel	*lahm jamal*
chicken	*farooj*
lamb	*lahm danee*
liver	*kibda*
kidney	*kelaawi*
meat	*lahm*

Fruit

apple	*tufah*
apricot	*mish-mish*
banana	*moz*
date	*tamr*
fig	*teen*
fruit	*fawaka*
grape	*'inab*
lime	*limoon*
orange	*burtuqaal*
pomegranate	*rumman*
watermelon	*batteekh*

Miscellaneous

bread	*khobz* or *eish*
butter	*zibda*
cheese	*jibna*
eggs	*beid*
milk	*haleeb*
pepper	*filfil*
salt	*milh*
sugar	*sukar*
water *mayy*	
yoghurt	*laban*

DRINKS
Tea & Coffee

Tea *(shay)* and coffee *(qahwa)* are the national obsessions and are drunk in copious quantities. They are also extremely strong and when your body is not used to them, drinking either in the evening is usually a recipe for a sleepless night.

The main pastime for men is sitting in a café sipping on a tea or coffee, sucking on a water pipe *(narjileh)* and chatting or playing cards or backgammon. Every town has at least one of these places and they are good for meeting local people. Arab women don't frequent cafés but it is no problem for Western women to enter, although in the smaller towns you may get a few strange looks.

Tea is served in small glasses and is incredibly sweet unless you ask for only a little sugar *(shwayya sukar)* or medium *(wassat)*. If you want no sugar at all, ask for it *bidoon sukar* (without sugar), but it is bitter and has a strong tannin after-taste.

Coffee, usually Turkish, is served in small cups and is also sweet. It is thick and muddy so let it settle a bit before drinking. Don't try to drink the last mouthful (which in cups this size is only about the second mouthful) because it's like drinking silt.

The traditional Arabic or Bedouin coffee is heavily laced with cardamom and drunk in

cups without handles that hold only a mouthful. It is poured from a silver pot and your cup will be refilled until you make the proper gesture that you have had enough – hold the cup out and roll your wrist from side to side a couple of times. It is good etiquette to have at least three cups although you are unlikely to offend if you have less. Coffee is then followed by tea *ad infinitum*.

Juice

All over the place, you will find juice stalls selling delicious freshly squeezed fruit juices *(aseer)*. In Syria these stalls are instantly recognised by the string bags of fruit hanging out the front.

Popular juices include lemon, orange, banana, pomegranate and rockmelon, and you can have combinations of any or all of these. Some stalls put milk in their drinks which, in the case of Syria at least, you'd be well advised to stay away from.

In Syria, you can be pretty sure you will get pure juice every time, but in Jordan, particularly in Amman, it pays to keep an eye on what's going on behind the counter – if indeed you can see. Diluting the juice with tap water or, worse, a sickly cordial, is a common enough and irritating practice. Often they seem to have plenty of the stuff ready, which they then top up with a couple of pieces of freshly squeezed fruit when you order.

Soft Drinks

Syrian soft drinks *(gazoza)* are cheap (about 10 cents) and not too sweet. The orange drinks are called Mirinda and the coke, regardless of what it is, generally goes by the name of Pepsi. If you take a drink away from the stall or shop you will have to pay a small deposit on the bottle. Cans of imported Canada Dry soft drinks are also available at three times the price of a bottle.

Jordan has Pepsi, 7-Up and a local product

called Viva in bottles. They and others are also available in cans but are a little more expensive. In mid-1992, Safeway (yes, the department store) started selling Coca-Cola in its Amman store.

Alcohol

Despite the fact that Islam prohibits the use of alcohol, it is widely drunk and readily available.

Beer Both countries brew their own local beers. Syria has Al-Chark in Aleppo and Barada in Damascus, and both are quite palatable and cheap. In Damascus, the black-marketeers sell cans of Amstel smuggled over the border from Lebanon.

Jordan has Amstel and Henninger beer brewed under licence from the parent European company. In Amman and Aqaba, you can buy beer imported from all over the world – everything from Guinness to Fosters.

Liquor *Araq* is the indigenous firewater and should be treated with caution. It is similar to Greek *ouzo* and is available in shops in Syria and Jordan. It is usually mixed with water and ice and drunk with food. The best araq is said to come from Lebanon. In Damascus, contraband imported liquor, like so much else smuggled in from Lebanon, is sold on the black market.

In Jordan, you can find all sorts of imported liquor in Amman and Aqaba, but you'll need a fat wallet if you are going to make a habit of it. Even the average 750ml bottle of araq will cost you US$3 to US$4.

Wine Various wines like Latroun, St Catherine and Cremisan, mostly imported from the Occupied West Bank, can be had in Jordan from US$2.50 to US$5 a bottle. They don't compare with Western wines but are still quite palatable.

Jordan

Facts about the Country

HISTORY SINCE WW I

The Arabs joined the British drive to oust the Turks in June 1916, after British assurances that they would be helped in their fight to establish an independent Arab state. This was one month after the British and French had concluded the secret Sykes-Picot agreement, whereby 'Syria' (modern Syria and Lebanon) was to be placed under French control and 'Palestine' (a vaguely defined area including modern Israel, the Occupied Territories and Jordan) would go to the British.

This betrayal was heightened by the Balfour Declaration in 1917. It was actually a letter written by the British Foreign Secretary, Arthur Balfour, to a prominent British Jew, Lord Rothschild. It stated that:

His Majesty's Government view with favour the establishment in Palestine of a National Home for the Jewish people, and will use their best endeavours to facilitate the achievement of this object, it being clearly understood that nothing shall be done which may prejudice the civil and religious rights of existing non-Jewish communities in Palestine, or the rights and political status enjoyed by Jews in any other country.

At the end of the war, Arab forces controlled, to a greater or lesser degree, all of modern Saudi Arabia, Jordan and parts of southern Syria. The principal Arab leader, Emir Faisal, set up an independent government in Damascus at the end of 1918, a move at first welcomed by the Allies. But his demand at the 1919 Paris peace conference for independence throughout the Arab world was not so kindly greeted. He and his elder brother, Abdullah, were declared kings of Syria and Iraq in March 1920, but shortly afterwards the League of Nations awarded Britain a mandate over Palestine, separating it from Syria, where the French quickly forced Faisal to flee.

The British later came to an accommodation with Faisal, handing him Iraq and having Abdullah proclaimed ruler of the territory known as Transjordan (formerly part of the Ottoman province of Syria), lying between Iraq and the East Bank of the Jordan River. This angered the Zionists, as it effectively severed Transjordan from Palestine and so reduced the area of any future Jewish National Home.

Abdullah made Amman his capital, Britain recognised the territory as an independent state under its protection in 1923 and a small defence force, the Arab Legion, was set up under British officers, the best known of whom was Major J B Glubb (Glubb Pasha). A series of treaties between 1928 and 1946 led to almost full independence, and Abdullah was proclaimed king that year. A further treaty in 1948 reserved Britain privileges only in military affairs.

Palestinian Dilemma

Transjordan's neighbouring mandate of Palestine now became a thorn in Britain's side. The Balfour Declaration and subsequent attempts to make the Jewish National Home a reality were destined for trouble from the start. Arabs were outraged by the implication that they were the intruders and the minority group in Palestine, when in fact it is estimated that at the end of WW II they accounted for 90% of the population.

Jewish immigration in the 1920s caused little alarm, although there was some violence between the two groups. The situation deteriorated sharply with the rise of Hitler and the persecution of Jews in Germany and Europe in the 1930s. Jewish immigration accelerated, fuelling Arab fears of the creation of a Jewish state in which they would be the losers.

Fighting between the two groups and anti-British riots increased, prompting a series of proposals to partition Palestine that culminated in a White Paper in 1939. It called for the creation of a bi-national state within 10 years and joint Arab-Jewish participation in administration in the meantime. It also limited Jewish immigration to 75,000 over five years. Both sides rejected this, although the plan had found some favour with the Arabs. The conflict was muted by the onset of war, during which both sides cooperated with the British.

The crisis reached its high point in the years immediately following the war. After various plans had been rejected, the UN voted for the partition of Palestine in November 1947. More than half the territory, including much of the valuable coastal strip, had been allotted to the Jews. The Arabs were shocked, and conflict was inevitable. The State of Israel was proclaimed on 14 May 1948 and the next day the British mandate finished. As British troops withdrew from the area, Arab armies marched into Palestine. However, highly trained and organised Israeli forces proved much too strong for the poorly led and ill-equipped volunteers from other Arab countries who had flocked to Palestine to support the Arab cause. Israel was soon well in control of its alloted area as well as entrenching itself in some strategic areas allotted to the Arabs. After a massacre of an entire village of Arabs by Israeli forces, a mass exodus of nearly one million Arabs followed, giving the Jews their much needed majority and at the same time placing strain on Jordan.

Fighting continued but by mid-1949 armistices had been signed between the new Israeli state and its Arab foes.

Jordan's Role

King Abdullah harboured dreams of a 'Greater Syria' to include all of the modern states of Syria, Lebanon, Transjordan and what was now Palestine and Israel in a single Arab state, later to include Iraq as well. For this, he was suspected by his Arab neighbours of pursuing quite different goals from them in their fight with the new state of Israel.

At the end of hostilities, Jordanian troops were in control of East Jerusalem and the West Bank. In response to the establishment of an Egyptian-backed Arab Government in Gaza in September 1948, King Abdullah had himself proclaimed King of All Palestine in Jericho in December. In April 1950, he formally annexed the territory, despite paying lip service to Arab declarations backing Palestinian independence and expressly ruling out territorial annexations. The new Hashemite Kingdom of Jordan won immediate recognition from Britain and the USA.

One of the effects of the mass migration of Palestinians was that Jordan's population effectively doubled and refugee camps were set up in the Jordan Valley and near Amman.

King Abdullah was assassinated outside the Al-Aqsa Mosque in Jerusalem in July 1951, and after his son Talal ruled for a year and was declared mentally unbalanced, his grandson Hussein came to power at the age of 17. With great skill and a good deal of luck he has managed to stay there ever since. In 1956 he sacked Glubb Pasha (by now Chief of Staff of the Jordanian Army) because of his taunts that Hussein was only a British puppet. After elections that year, the newly formed pro-Nasser government broke ties with the UK and the last British troops left Jordanian soil by mid-1957. With US support, Hussein staged a coup against his own pro-Nasser government, partly because it had tried to open a dialogue with the Soviet Union.

With the union of Egypt and Syria in 1958, King Hussein feared for his own position and tried a federation with his Hashemite cousins in Iraq. This lasted less than a year as the Iraqi monarchy was overthrown and British troops were sent in to Jordan to protect Hussein from a Nasserist takeover led by discontented Palestinian refugees.

The PLO

In February 1960, Jordan offered its citizenship to all Arab refugees wanting it. In defiance of the wishes of the other Arab states for an independent Palestine, Jordan continued to insist that its annexation of Palestinian territory be recognised.

Despite Jordan's opposition, the Palestine Liberation Organisation, with its own army, was formed in 1964 with the blessing of the Arab League to represent the Palestinian

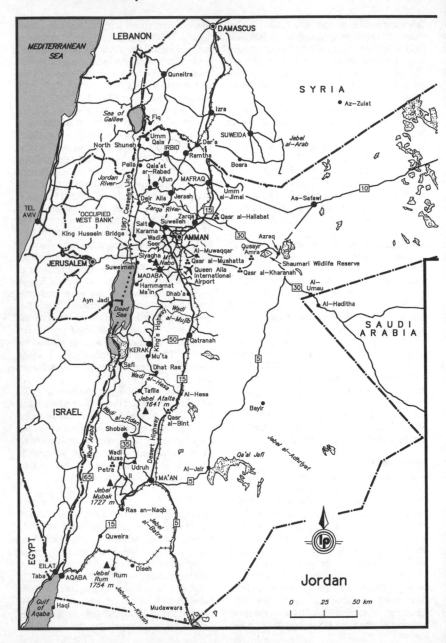

To Baghdad

IRAQ

Ar—Ruwayshid

people. The Palestine National Council (PNC) was established within the PLO as its executive body – the closest thing to a Palestinian government. It included representatives from many Arab countries, various guerrilla organisations, student bodies and trade unions.

At about the same time, an organisation called the Palestine National Liberation Movement was set up. It was known as Al-Fatah (the reversal of its Arabic initials, making up the word 'conquest'). One of the stated aims of both the PLO and Al-Fatah was to train guerrillas for raids on Israel.

A power struggle for control of the guerrilla organisations saw Al-Fatah become the dominant force within the PLO and its leader, Yasser Arafat, became chairman of the executive committee of the PLO in 1969.

After the disaster of the Black September hostilities in Jordan in 1970, the PLO concentrated its activities in Lebanon.

In 1974, the PLO made a major gain in its bid for international recognition. At the UN General Assembly it was invited to take part in a debate on the 'Palestine question' and the vote favoured the PLO as the legitimate representative of the Palestinians.

The Six-Day War

The early 1960s saw Jordan's position improve dramatically with aid from the USA and a boom in tourism, mainly in Jerusalem's old city, but it lost out badly in the Six-Day War of 1967.

The build-up to the war had seen severe Israeli warnings against increasingly provocative Palestinian guerrilla raids into Israel from Syria. With President Nasser of Egypt promising to support Syria in the event of an Israeli attack, the Syrians stepped up the raids and in May '67 announced that Israel was amassing troops in preparation for an assault. Egypt responded by asking the UN to withdraw its Emergency Force from the Egypt-Israel border, which it did. Nasser then closed the Straits of Tiran (the entrance to the Red Sea), effectively nullifying the Israeli port of Eilat, and within five days of Jordan and Egypt signing a mutual defence pact, the Israelis knew they were alone and surrounded.

On 5 June 1967, the Israelis dispatched a pre-dawn raid that wiped out the Arabs' only real fighting force. They completely destroyed the Egyptian Air Force on the ground and in the following days clobbered Egyptian troops in the Sinai, Jordanian troops on the West Bank and stormed up the Golan Heights in Syria.

The outcome for Jordan was disastrous. Not only did it lose the whole of the West Bank and its part of Jerusalem, which together supplied Jordan with its two principal sources of income – agriculture and tourism – but it saw the influx of another wave of Palestinian refugees.

On 22 September 1967, the United Nations passed Resolution 242, which called on Israel to withdraw from the areas it had taken in the recent war, and for all countries in the Middle East to respect the rights of others 'to live in peace within secure and recognised boundaries'. Jordan was among the Arab countries to accept it but Syria and Iraq would not, as it implied recognition of Israel.

After the defeat of 1967, the Palestinians became more militant and although there was tacit agreement with the Jordanian Government that they would operate freely out of their bases in the Jordan Valley, they also expected immunity from Jordan's laws. The country became increasingly unsettled and by 1970 the Government had virtually become just one of many other factions vying for power.

Clearly this couldn't last and the showdown came in September of that year in an incident that came to be known as the 'Black September' hostilities. The Palestinians, in their most daring deed to date, hijacked four commercial aircraft and flew three of them to the north of Jordan and held passengers and crew hostage. Acting on orders from King Hussein, the army moved in and in a brief civil war ending in July 1971 wiped out all resistance here and throughout the country. Many of the leaders were deported. A Syrian force sent in to support the guerrillas was also beaten off. The guerrillas were thus forced to recognise Hussein's authority and the Palestinians had to choose between exile or submission.

Camp David

Jordan was not directly involved in the October War of 1973 but did send a small number of troops to assist Syria.

In October 1974, King Hussein reluctantly agreed to an Arab summit declaration recognising the PLO as the sole representative of the Palestinians and its right to set up a government in any liberated territory, effectively nullifying Jordan's own claims to the West Bank.

The Camp David accords of 1978 were a result of a peace initiative by Egypt's President Sadat, and saw a peace agreement reached between Egypt and Israel. Hussein, along with most Arab leaders, rejected the results and isolated Egypt because the agreement neither required the Israelis to withdraw from occupied territories nor asserted Arab sovereignty over them.

Gulf Wars

Attention switched from the Arab-Israeli conflict to the Persian Gulf when Iraq invaded Iran in 1980. Jordan's backing for Iraq in the eight-year slogging match put a constant strain on its already poor relations with Syria, which backed Iran.

But Jordan's Gulf woes did not really begin until Iraq decided to annex Kuwait in August 1990. Dependent on Iraq for a quarter of its trade and most of its oil imports, Jordan found itself caught between a rock and a hard place. Support among Palestinians in his country for Saddam Hussein, who promised to link the Kuwait issue to their own and force a showdown, was at fever pitch. King Hussein had little choice but to side with Saddam, against the majority of the Arab states and the multinational force sent to eject Saddam from Kuwait.

Fearing economic catastrophe, massive waves of refugees, Israeli intervention across his territory after Iraqi Scud missile attacks and Palestinian militancy, King Hussein played the game with typical dexterity. Although tending to side publicly with Baghdad, he maintained efforts to find a peaceful solution and complied with the UN embargo on trade with Iraq. This last step won him the sympathy of Western financial bodies and, although US and Saudi aid was temporarily cut, along with Saudi oil, loans and help were forthcoming from other quarters, particularly Japan and Europe.

The West Bank

In August 1986, King Hussein unveiled a US$1300 million investment programme over five years for the West Bank, with Israeli approval. Palestinians reacted badly, saying this was a sign that Israel and Jordan were coming to some kind of arrangement at their expense. It also appeared to give the lie to Hussein's avowed support for the PLO and de facto renunciation of claims to the West Bank.

In July 1988, however, seven months after the beginning of the *intifada* – the not always so passive Palestinian revolt in the Occupied Territories – King Hussein announced that all administrative and legal ties with the West Bank were being cut, along with the development programme. West Bank Palestinians would no longer be considered Jordanian citizens, although they could still carry Jordanian passports for travel purposes. Some observers still believe, however, that the king could reverse this decision if the time looked right.

Jordan Today

In November 1989, the first full elections since 1967 were held in Jordan, with no seats for the West Bank. Women were allowed to vote for the first time.

In mid-1992, as part of a democratisation process, laws were put before Parliament that would legalise political parties, end remaining martial law provisions and reduce pressure on the media to follow the government line. The law legalising political parties was passed in September 1992.

The pressures on Jordan remain enormous. When King Hussein announced his West Bank decision in 1988, there was a flight of Palestinian capital from Jordan. The situation stabilised but showed to what extent Jordan depends on its Palestinian population. For the non-Palestinians and the king, it's a case of 'can't live with 'em, can't live without 'em'. While not wanting the Palestinians in such great numbers as could threaten his line, the king is said to be no keener on seeing them all return to an eventual Palestinian state. It is occasionally claimed that he and the Israelis would both prefer to avoid the emergence of a fully independent Palestine, and that they are cooperating to that end. Whatever the truth of that, Jordan is on better terms now with the Palestinians and the PLO than it had been for a long time, and they are cooperating closely in the painful US-brokered Middle East peace talks that have resulted from the 1991 Madrid conference.

Democratisation is fraught with dangers. The Muslim Brotherhood and other extreme religious groups constitute the most powerful bloc in Parliament and their popularity is growing. Riots in April 1989 against price hikes, mostly by non-Palestinians, forced the king to appoint a new government. He has pointed to the fundamentalist rumblings in Algeria when applying to the West for economic help and warned that, without sufficient aid, Jordan could go the same way.

GEOGRAPHY & CLIMATE

Jordan is really a tiny country with a very curious shape. Its total area, including the West Bank, is about 98,000 sq km or about the same size as Portugal. The strange kink in the Jordan-Saudi Arabia border is known as 'Winston's hiccup' because the story goes that the British Secretary of State, Winston Churchill, drew the boundary after having had a more than satisfactory lunch in Jerusalem one day back in 1920. Since King Hussein renounced claims to the West Bank (about 8000 sq km) in 1988, the country has the same boundaries of the former Transjordan.

Distances are short – it's only about 430 km from Ramtha in the north to Aqaba in the south. From Aqaba to the capital, Amman, it is 396 km. From Amman to the furthest point of interest in the east, Azraq, is just 103 km.

Jordan can easily be divided up into four major regions: the Jordan Valley, the West Bank plateau (territory annexed by Jordan in 1950 and under Israeli occupation since the 1967 war), the East Bank plateau, and the desert.

Jordan Valley

The dominant physical feature of the country is the fertile valley of the Jordan River. Forming part of the Great Rift Valley of Africa, it rises just inside Lebanon and runs the full length of the country from the Syrian border in the north to the salty depression of the Dead Sea, and south to Aqaba and the Red Sea. The river itself, 251 km long, is fed from the Sea of Galilee (Lake Tiberias), the Yarmouk River and the valley streams of the high plateaux to the east and west.

The Dead Sea, at 394 metres below sea level, is the lowest point on earth, and the soils of this central area of the Jordan Valley are highly saline and support no vegetation. The sea's water itself is loaded with salt and related chemicals, and in fact is chemically saturated at a depth of 110 metres.

South of the Dead Sea, the Wadi Araba is a desolate region with absolutely no attraction. Potash is mined at Safi and it is hoped the area contains other minerals as it is useless for anything else. On the western side of the Dead Sea are Israeli *kibbutzim* on the occupied West Bank which are fertile havens in the desert.

The only town of any size in the valley is Jericho on the western side.

The weather in the valley is oppressive in summer – it feels like you're trapped in an airless oven. Daily temperatures are well in excess of 36°C and have been recorded as high as 49°C. Rainfall is low, at only 200 mm annually.

West Bank Plateau

West of the Jordan Valley, the desolate hills of the Judaean and Samarian Mountains (famous in Biblical times) rise to about 1000 metres above sea level. ('Jebel' is the Arabic word for any natural hill or mountain.)

The plateau is broken by long, shallow valleys running west to the Mediterranean and short steep ones draining into the Dead Sea. This is the Holy Land, where Jerusalem and Bethlehem are located.

The weather is milder and less stuffy on the plateau than in the valley, but expect daily temperatures of 30 to 35°C in summer. The winters are short but things get mighty unpleasant with rain, cold winds and temperatures of around 7°C. Average annual rainfall is about 400 mm.

East Bank Plateau

The East Bank plateau is broken only by the gorges cut by the streams of the Wadi Zarqa, Wadi al-Mujib and Wadi al-Hesa, which flow into the Jordan River. ('Wadi' is the Arabic word for a valley formed by an often dry watercourse. Some, but not all, wadis begin to flow again when there has been substantial rainfall.)

This area contains the main centres of population: Amman, Irbid, Zarqa and Kerak. It's also the region with the sites of most interest: Jerash, Kerak, Madaba and Petra.

The climate is similar to that of the West Bank plateau. Snow in Amman is not unheard of and even Petra gets the occasional fall. A group of 300 European tourists had to be rescued from Petra in January 1992 after being trapped there by the heaviest snow recorded in 40 years. Average daytime temperatures in Amman range from 12.6°C in January to 32.5°C in August.

The plateaux end at Ras an-Naqb from where a fairly rapid drop leads down to the Red Sea and the port town of Aqaba. This area south of the plateaux has much warmer, drier weather, with average daytime temperatures of 22°C in January and 40.4°C in August.

The Desert

All the rest of the East Bank, or about 80% of it, is desert or desert steppe stretching into Syria, Iraq and Saudi Arabia. It is part of what is often called the Greater Syrian or North Arab desert. The volcanic basalt of the north (the bottom end of the Hauran in Syria) gives way to the south's sandstone and granite, which sometimes produce amazing sights – the area of Wadi Rum is one of the most fantastic desert-scapes in the world.

The climate is extreme with summertime temperatures to bake your brains, and days in winter when cold winds howl down from central Asia. Rainfall is minimal – less than 50 mm annually.

FLORA & FAUNA

The pine forests of the north give way to the cultivated slopes of the Jordan Valley where cedar, olives and eucalyptus are dominant. South towards the Dead Sea the vegetation gives way to mud and salt flats.

Animals found in the desert regions include the camel (of course), desert fox, sand rat, hare and jerboa (a small rodent). The hills to the north-east of the Dead Sea are home to boars, badgers and goats.

It is possible to see gazelle and oryx (a large antelope), once a common feature of the Jordanian desert, at the nearby Shaumari Wildlife Reserve, where they have been reintroduced. Outside the reserve, and despite the apparent diversity of the wildlife, you'll be lucky to see anything more exotic than camels and goats.

For parts of the year, the Azraq Oasis is home to hundreds of species of birds migrating from Europe and the Middle East, although the number has dropped steeply as exploitation of the wetlands has destroyed much of the environment.

In the Gulf of Aqaba, there's a huge variety of tropical fish and coral that makes for some of the best scuba-diving in the world.

GOVERNMENT

The constitution of 1952 states that Jordan is a constitutional monarchy with representative government. The National Assembly (*majlis al-umma*) is bicameral, the Senate having half the number of members as the House of Representatives.

The king is vested with wide-ranging powers – he appoints and can dismiss judges, approves constitutional amendments, declares war and is the commander of the armed forces. He approves and signs all laws, although his power of veto can be overridden by a two-thirds majority of both the houses of the National Assembly.

The 80-member lower house is elected by all citizens over the age of 18 years, but the prime minister is appointed by the king, as are the 40 members and president of the Senate. The prime minister, or the king through him, appoints a Council of Ministers that is subject to the approval of Parliament.

The council is responsible for general policy and coordination of the work of various departments.

Although elections are supposed to take place every four years, polls in November 1989 were the first held since Jordan lost the West Bank in the 1967 war. Since then, Jordan has in effect remained under martial law, although most of its provisions have now been rolled back. The remainder are supposed to go if and when a huge parcel of new laws, presented from mid-1992 on, are passed. These include, among other things, further easing restrictions on the press.

In 1974 the king dissolved the House; it was replaced four years later by a National Consultative Council, its 60 members appointed by the king. This in turn was later dissolved and the House reassembled in 1984. There were no full direct elections, made impossible anyway by the continued Israeli occupation of the West Bank, which accounted for half the seats, and King Hussein's earlier recognition of the PLO as the sole representative of the Palestinians.

On 30 July 1988 the House was again dissolved. The following day the king announced Jordan was cutting all administrative ties with the West Bank. New electoral laws paving the way for elections on the East Bank and increasing the number of deputies from 60 to 80 preceded the 1989 elections.

For administrative purposes the country is divided into five *muhafazat* (governorates). Until 1988, when Jordan threw in its administrative claims over the West Bank, the total had been eight muhafazat.

ECONOMY

One of the main economic victims of the Gulf war in 1990-91, Jordan has managed to weather the storm better than many expected. One UN assessment put the total cost of the Gulf crisis to Jordan, in the 12 months from August 1990, at more than US$8 billion.

Until the UN imposed a trade embargo on Iraq in August 1990, Jordan had been selling almost a quarter of its exports to that country. It had also reaped the rewards of Iraq's growing dependence on the port of Aqaba as an import/export point that had resulted from its 1980-88 war with Iran. Similarly, Saudi Arabia had long since ceded its place as Jordan's principal oil supplier to Iraq, which at the outbreak of hostilities was meeting about 80% of Jordan's requirements. All trade came to a halt, and Jordan was forced to ration petrol and seek alternative, more expensive sources of oil in Yemen and Syria.

At the time of writing the UN embargo was still in place, but Iraqi oil was again reaching Jordan as debt repayment. It is refined by the Jordanian Refining Company at Zarqa. The UN allowed this as no money was changing hands. Accusations that Jordan was permitting sanctions-busting became louder in mid-1992, and judging by the heavy traffic on the roads to and from Iraq, the claims were well founded.

Until the war an important source of income had been remittances from Jordanians and Palestinians working in the Gulf. By early 1992 most had left the Gulf states – 300,000 of them for Jordan where some have started businesses, but many are unemployed. Although the loss of remittances is a blow, the 'returnees' brought US$500 million home with them.

With US$8.5 billion foreign debt, around 30% unemployment and an estimated 25% to 30% living below the poverty line, a difficult time lies ahead for Jordan. As a condition of debt rescheduling and more loans, the International Monetary Fund has demanded a tighter economy. Amman is trying to deliver, but memories of the 1989 riots, sparked by price rises and austerity measures, are never far away.

The Gulf crisis came at an already awkward moment for Jordan, whose economic growth in the late 1980s had slowed to little more than 1% after an earlier consistent rate of 4% to 6%. Between 1987 and 1989, the dinar halved in value.

In spite of all this, and the earlier blows to the economy caused by civil disturbances in 1970-71, the loss of the West Bank in 1967 and the outcome of the 1948 war, Jordan's prospects are not all bad.

Agriculture makes up 10% of GDP (gross domestic product) and is increasingly concentrated in the Jordan Valley, where ambitious irrigation schemes like the East Ghor (now called the King Abdullah) Canal and several dam projects make cultivation possible on thousands of hectares. Modern: methods ('plasticulture' and greenhouses) have greatly increased productivity, and Jordan exports much of the fruit, vegetables and cereals that are its most important crops. On the highlands that form the eastern edge of the Jordan Valley, crops such as tobacco, wheat, barley and beans are grown. Scarce water supplies, however, are a constant threat and farmers are sometimes ordered not to plant crops because there is not enough water to go around.

The various industries account for about 25% of GDP. Phosphate mining is carried out from vast reserves at Wadi al-Hesa and is a major export. Potash is another important export. Copper from Wadi Araba, south of the Dead Sea, is also exported. Manufacturing ranges from cement and batteries to toys, beer and matches.

Although oil is yet to be found in commercially viable quantities, the government is placing greater hope in natural gas. Big reserves were found in the north-east of the country around Ar-Risha in 1987-88 and now meet 15% of Jordan's energy needs.

Tourism in Jordan took a long time to recover after the loss of Jerusalem but, aided by the 1974 decision to allow tourists to cross into the West Bank, it had begun to exceed pre-1967 levels when the Gulf crisis started. In 1989 there were more than two million visitors (but Jordanian figures include *all* entries, not just tourists) contributing about US$500 million to the economy. Tourism officials are doing everything they can to restore that situation.

POPULATION & PEOPLE

The population of Jordan (including the almost 800,000 Palestinian Arabs living on the West Bank) was estimated in 1990 by the United Nations to be just over 4 million, of whom 900,000 were registered as refugees from the wars of 1948 and 1967 with the United Nations Relief & Works Agency (UNRWA) on the East Bank and a further 400,000 on the West Bank.

About 1.2 million live in the capital, Amman, and a further 390,000 in neighbouring Zarqa and suburbs. Next comes the northern city of Irbid, with about 270,000 inhabitants.

Ethnic & Religious Groups

The majority of Jordanians are Arabs descended from various tribes that have migrated to the area over the years from all

A	C
	D
B	E

Jordanian people: A (DS); B-E (HF)

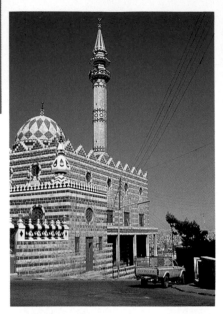

Left: Abu Darwish Mosque, Amman (HF)
Right: Strolling in Amman (HF)
Bottom: Friday prayers, King Hussein Mosque, Amman (DS)

directions. In addition, there are 25,000 Circassians, descendants of migrants from the Caucasus in the 19th century and a much smaller group of Chechens. Jordan also counts a small Armenian population.

More than 92% are Sunni Muslims and about 6% are Christians who live mainly in Amman, Madaba, Kerak and Salt. There is a tiny Shi'ite population too.

There is a small Druze population and a few hundred Bahais, another subsect of the Shi'ites. The Circassians, who first settled in Jordan in Wadi Seer and Na'ur in about 1878 and trace their heritage back to Indo-European Muslim tribes in the 12th century, form the most important non-Arab minority. Related to them is the small Shi'ite community of Chechens.

The majority of Christians belong to the Greek Orthodox Church, but there are Greek Catholics, a small Roman (Latin) Catholic community, Syrian Orthodox, Coptic Orthodox and, among the non-Arabs, Armenian Orthodox and Catholics.

Many of the Christians live on the West Bank, with which Jordan cut all administrative ties in 1988. Also on the West Bank are a few hundred Samaritans, who live near Nablus and believe that only the first five books in the Bible are authentic. There is also a Nestorian (Assyrian) Church community of little more than 1000 on the West Bank.

Palestinians

About 60% of the population are Palestinians, many of them (see above) still registered as refugees. They fled fighting, mostly from the West Bank during the wars of 1948 and 1967. All were granted the right to Jordanian citizenship and many have exercised that option, playing an important part in the political and economic life of Jordan.

Occupying high positions in government and business, many Palestinians continue to dream of a return to an independent Palestine. It is partly because of this that so many continue to live in difficult conditions in the 30 or so camps that dot the East and West banks. UNRWA is responsible for the welfare of the refugees, and also provides health and education services.

The Bedouin

These desert dwellers, the *bedu* (the name means nomadic), number about 40,000 in Jordan, although only a few thousand can still be regarded as truly nomadic. Many have, voluntarily or otherwise, settled down to cultivate crops rather than drive their animals across the desert in search of fodder. Some combine the two, and a few retain the old ways.

They camp for a few months at a time in one spot and graze their herds of goats, sheep or camels. When the sparse fodder runs out, it is time to move on again. All over the east and south of the country you'll see the black goat-hair tents *(bayt ash-sha'ar –* 'house of hair') set up; sometimes just one, often three or four together.

The Bedouin family is a close-knit unit. The women, as usual, do most of the domestic work, the men are the providers and the children are put to work tending the herds from an early age.

Often the only concession these people make to the modern world is the acquisition of a Land Rover or pick-up truck, plastic water containers and occasionally a kerosene stove.

The Bedouin are renowned for their hospitality and it is part of their creed that no traveller is turned away.

The Jordanian government provides services such as education and housing, both of which are often passed up by the bedu in favour of the lifestyle that has served them so well over the centuries.

EDUCATION

Jordan is one of the better educated of the Arab countries, with under 20% illiteracy and 97% of children attending primary school. There are three kinds of schools – government, private and missionary. UNRWA runs schools for refugee children. School is compulsory to the age of 14 and 70% of pupils attend government schools.

There are three government universities –

Jordan University in Amman, Yarmouk University in Irbid and the military Mo'ata University in Kerak. Fees tend to be in excess of US$1,000 a year – exorbitant for many. There are also expensive private institutions. They all have difficult entrance requirements, forcing some students to look abroad for a place to study.

About 90,000 people were in some form of higher education in 1987, according to a UNESCO survey. An oversupply of professionals, such as engineers, has been exacerbated by the return of many Jordanians and Palestinians from the Gulf states since the war in 1991.

Interestingly, Jordan became the only Arab country to scrap compulsory military service at the end of 1991.

CULTURE

For the predominantly Muslim population, religious values still greatly inform Jordanian social life. Although more Westernised than most Arab countries, women still tend to take a back seat to men in the professions, with the emphasis on family. Although contact between Westerners and locals,

including women, may be less fraught in some circles of Amman society than elsewhere in the Arab world, the barriers remain high. Some of the better off and well educated use social events hosted by Westerners as a chance to bend the norms a little – Jordanians can be seen to be partying in a more Western sense on occasions like the Hash House Harriers (see the Activities section in the Amman chapter) evening runs and barbecues.

Jordanians, as with most Arabs, can become vociferous at the drop of the hat, but never more so than over football (soccer to some). It doesn't matter, for instance, that Jordan might not have a team competing in the World Cup – the men will be glued to their television sets no matter who is playing.

The old tribal structure of the Bedouin remains more or less intact, but the number of true nomads is shrinking as most settle in towns. Traditional wedding chants, which bear little resemblance to better known genres of Arab music (what Westerners generally associate with belly-dancing) can still be heard wafting across the desert at night. Here the strictly observed division of the sexes and feminine modesty are at their most obvious.

Dress & Behaviour

Although fairly used to the odd ways of Westerners, immodest dress is still a source of irritation and can be an invitation for trouble for women.

Men can get around in shorts without getting much of a response, particularly in Aqaba. Women, too, can probably relax a bit in Aqaba but otherwise are advised to wear at least knee-length dresses or pants and cover the shoulders. Both sexes should be well covered when entering mosques.

Although getting your hands on a drink is not a problem in Jordan, moderation is the rule of thumb. Drunkenness in the streets is not a common sight, and trying to start a trend might have unpleasant consequences – use your common sense.

Facts for the Visitor

VISAS & EMBASSIES

Visas are required by all foreigners entering Jordan. These are issued at the border or airport on arrival, or can be obtained from Jordanian consulates outside the country.

Tourist visas are valid for one month and cost anything from nothing for Australians to more than US$50 for Canadians. For an indication of what visas can cost, Jordan's London embassy issues visas free to US citizens and Australians. It charges Canadians £30, Britons £22, and £8 for Germans and New Zealanders.

Visas are considerably cheaper in Turkey. In Istanbul or Ankara, UK citizens are charged 77,000TL (about US$10), Canadians about US$35 and New Zealanders, Germans and French just over US$3. The hitch in Turkey is that, like the Syrians, the Jordanians will often ask for a letter of recommendation from your embassy or consulate. If they insist, remember that some consulates charge for the privilege of providing such a letter, and some consulates in Istanbul don't issue them at all. The letter can cost more than the visa! If you plan on going to both Syria and Jordan from Turkey and want to get all your visas in one go, save yourself time and money and ask for more than one copy of the letter.

Better still, wait until you're on the Jordanian border itself where, despite what consular officials may tell you, visas can be obtained with little trouble and reasonably cheaply. Britons, for example, pay JD10.500 (about US$15).

Except for Canadians, who pay S£1100 (about US$26), visas obtained in Damascus are generally more expensive than in Turkey. However, the Jordanian embassy there does not ask for a letter of recommendation and is willing to issue multiple-entry and 24-hour transit visas at no extra cost. The same is true in Cairo, but elsewhere they seem less prepared to issue anything but the single entry jobs.

Any evidence of a visit to Israel will disqualify you from entering Jordan, despite the apparent contradictions in the regulations for crossing the King Hussein (Allenby) Bridge to and from the West Bank and Israel. One American traveller wrote in to say she managed to cross into Jordan despite having Israeli stamps in her passport, but that should not be interpreted as a matter of policy.

If you plan on travelling to the West Bank and further on into Israel, it's possible to return to Jordan within one month of crossing into the West Bank, as long as your visa is still valid. See the Getting There & Away chapter for details of this crazy crossing.

Jordanian Embassies

Visas can be obtained from Jordanian diplomatic missions in countries around the world.

Australia
  20 Roebuck St, Redhill, Canberra, ACT 2603 (☎ (62) 959951)
Canada
  100 Bronson Ave 701, Ottawa, Ontario (☎ (613) 238-8090)
Egypt
  6 Al-Juhaini St, Doqqi, Cairo (☎ (2) 349-9912)
France
  80 Blvd Maurice Barres, 92200 Neuilly-Seine, Paris (☎ (1) 46.24.51.38)
Germany
  Beethovenallee 21, 5300 Bonn 2 (☎ (228) 354052)
Japan
  Chiyoda House 4A-4B, 17-8 Nacata-Cho, 2-Chome, Chiyoda-Ku, Tokyo 100 (☎ (3) 35805856)
Saudi Arabia
  Diplomatic Area, Riyadh (☎ (1) 660-7633)
Syria
  Al-Jala'a Ave, Damascus (☎ (11) 234642)
Turkey
  Mesnevi, Dede Korkut Sokak No 18, Cankaya, Ankara (☎ (4) 440-2054)
  (consulate) 63 Valikonagi Caddesi, Nistansi, Istanbul (☎ (1) 230-1221)

UK
    6 Upper Phillimore Gardens, London, W8 7HB
    (☎ (071) 937-3685)
USA
    3504 International Drive NW, Washington DC
    20008 (☎ (202) 966-2675)

Jordan has no diplomatic representation in
New Zealand or Ireland. New Zealand and
Irish citizens can get a visa on arrival (as
indeed just about everybody can in practice),
although Irish citizens can obtain one
through the London embassy if they wish.

Visa Extensions
Visas can be extended for two months, and
then again for up to three months, at no cost
and with a minimum of fuss, but only at the
Directorate of Foreigners & Borders, in Suleiman al-Nabulsi St in Amman. You need
only your passport. Further extensions are
possible.

The Directorate of Foreigners & Borders
is open from 8 am to 2 pm every day except
Friday. It's right on the No 7 service-taxi
route, up past the blue King Abdullah
Mosque. It is the fourth big gateway after the
side street by the mosque.

Technically, you are supposed to register
with the police within the first month of your
arrival, but this seems to be little more than
a reminder to apply for an extension if you
want to stay that long.

Foreign Embassies in Jordan
Most of the foreign embassies and consulates are in Amman. Egypt also has a
consulate in Aqaba.

Australia
    Between 4th & 5th Circles, Wadi Seer Rd, Jebel
    Amman (☎ 673246)
Canada
    Shmeisani (☎ 666124)
Egypt
    3rd Circle, Jebel Amman (☎ 641376)
    (for visas) 1st Circle, Jebel Amman
France
    Mutanabi St, Jebel Amman (☎ 641273)
Germany
    31 Benghazi St, 4th Circle, Jebel Amman
    (☎ 689351)

Iraq
    1st Circle, Jebel Amman (☎ 621375)
Ireland
    Honorary-Consul, Jordan Insurance Co building,
    King Hussein St (☎ 625632)
Japan
    Between 4th & 5th Circles, Al-Aqsa St, Jebel
    Amman (☎ 672486)
Lebanon
    2nd Circle, Jebel Amman (☎ 641381)
New Zealand
    Khalas Building, 99 King Hussein St (☎ 636720)
Saudi Arabia
    1st Circle, Jebel Amman (☎ 814154)
Syria
    Haza al-Majali, 4th Circle, Jebel Amman
    (☎ 641076)
UK
    Abdoun (☎ 823100)
USA
    Between 2nd & 3rd Circles, Jebel Amman
    (☎ 820101)

Visas for Neighbouring Countries
Syria The Syrian embassy is past 3rd Circle
in a side street off to the right. Take a No 3
service-taxi and get out at the Ministry of
Foreign Affairs. This is a much better place
to get a Syrian visa than, say, Turkey.

In Amman, the cost of the visa ranges from
nothing for Australians and Canadians to
JD9.750 for Americans, JD17 for Japanese
and a whopping JD37.500 for Britons! The
consolation for Her Majesty's subjects is
supposed to be that their visa is valid for six
months, whereas the others are only valid for
one month. You don't get one month in the
country, but must arrive within that month to
get in for up to 15 days. After that you need
to apply for extensions.

You need a letter of recommendation from
your embassy, for which there may be a fee
(if you intend to go to Lebanon too, pick up
a couple of letters at once) and one passport
photo. Applications are accepted between 9
am and 11 am Sunday to Thursday and visas
can be picked up on the same day at 1.30 pm.

It is no problem getting multiple-entry
visas, which cost about double and are not a
bad idea if you are going to Lebanon. Syria
has no diplomatic representation in Lebanon
and, although you are supposed to be given
some kind of permit to allow you back into

Syria when you cross over, a multiple-entry visa would be good insurance.

Egypt The Egyptian consulate is just off Zahran St above 1st Circle. Do not confuse it with the embassy over the road from the InterContinental. It can be a real shitfight here. Try and catch the attention of one of the officials who will then lead you through the hordes and take care of your application. Visas cost JD40 for UK citizens, JD31 for Canadians and JD12 for the rest. The consulate is open for applications from 9 am to noon and visas can be picked up on the same day at 3 pm. You need a passport photo. Visas are valid for presentation for three months and get you one month in Egypt. Unless you really need to get it here, the consulate in Aqaba is much quieter and easier to deal with.

Iraq Close by is the Iraqi embassy, but at the time of writing no visas of any description were being issued to non-Arabs.

Lebanon The Lebanese embassy is now issuing tourist visas again, but the crowds and chaos in the tiny consular office are almost enough to put you off! It is open from 8 to 10 am for applications, except on Fridays and Sundays. Visas may be ready on the same day but there is no guarantee. You need a letter of recommendation from your embassy, a photocopy of your passport details, a passport photo and JD14 (all nationalities). The visa is valid for a month.

DOCUMENTS & PERMITS

It is a good idea to keep your passport with you when travelling around the country, particularly along the Jordan Valley. Military road blocks and checks are a common occurrence in the area because of its proximity to Israel or Israeli-held territory.

A permit is required to proceed south of Kerak along the Dead Sea to Safi or further beyond, down the Wadi Araba to Aqaba. Strangely enough, a permit is not required for the trip up the other way from Aqaba.

You need a permit to enter the West Bank.

In Amman, the Ministry of the Interior (*wizarat ad-dakhiliyya*) is at the roundabout known as Ministry of the Interior Circle (*duwaar ad-dakhiliyya*). Take a No 6 service-taxi from Cinema al-Hussein St to the end of the line near the Housing Bank Centre. If you take a taxi, you might have more luck using the Arabic names when asking for the ministry or Circle.

Permits are no longer issued to visitors wanting to sleep overnight in Petra, who do so now at the risk of an uncomfortable brush with the local constabulary.

International Driving Permits are not required in Jordan; a driver's license from your own country is enough.

CUSTOMS

You can import 200 cigarettes and a litre of wine or spirits into Jordan duty free. There are no restrictions on the import and export of Jordanian and foreign currency.

MONEY
Currency

The currency in Jordan is the dinar (JD) – known as the *jaydee* among hip young locals – which is made up of 1000 fils. You will also often hear *piastre* or *girsh* used, which are both 10 fils, so 10 girsh equals 100 fils. Often when a price is quoted to you the ending will be omitted, so if you're told that something is 25, it's a matter of working out whether it's 25 fils, 25 girsh or 25 dinar! Just to complicate things a little further, 50 fils is commonly referred to as a *shilling*, 100 fils (officially a *dirham*) as a *barisa* and a dinar as a *lira*. In fact, Jordanians rarely use the word fils at all, except for the benefit of foreigners.

The coins in circulation are 5, 10, 25, 50, 100, 250 and 500 fils. The values of the coins are written in English; the numerals are only in Arabic.

Notes come in JD0.500, 1, 5, 10 and 20 denominations. For everyday travelling, the JD5 note is about as large as you want to carry. Changing 10s and 20s can be a nuisance.

Exchange Rates

A$1	=	JD0.480
C$1	=	JD0.500
E£1	=	JD0.190 (Egypt)
F10	=	JD1.247
DM1	=	JD0.419
Y100	=	JD0.523
S£10	=	JD0.141 (Syria)
UK£1	=	JD1.231
US$1	=	JD0.678

JD1	=	A$2.08
JD1	=	C$2.00
JD1	=	E£5 (Egypt)
JD1	=	F8.30
JD1	=	DM2.38
JD1	=	Y192
JD1	=	S£52.9 (Syria)
JD1	=	UK£0.81
JD1	=	US$1.47

There is little trouble changing money in Jordan, with most hard currencies being accepted (you will get nowhere with the New Zealand dollar and the Irish punt, however). Most banks will change travellers' cheques, and the British Bank of the Middle East (there is a branch in Downtown Amman) will accept Eurocheques. American Express has an office in Amman.

The British Bank of the Middle East and the Jordan Bank accept MasterCard for cash advances, but only at selected branches.

Visa is more widely accepted for cash advances, but again only at selected branches of the following banks: the Housing Bank, the Cairo-Amman Bank, the Arab Banking Corporation, the Jordan Arab Investment Bank and the Jordan Investment & Finance Bank. The first two each have a branch in Aqaba that will give cash advances on Visa, as will a branch of the Jordan Arab Investment Bank in Irbid.

If you have problems with Visa, its head office is the Jordan Payment Services Co, on the 7th floor of the Housing Bank Centre in Amman (☎ 680570).

Credit cards can also be used for a range of purchases in Jordan. Foreign cards can't be used yet in any of the automated teller machines springing up around the country.

You can buy Jordanian currency before you leave home and take as much in with you as you like, but you will gain little by it. It is possible to change dinars into foreign (including hard) currencies, but you will need to show receipts proving you changed your currency into dinars in Jordan.

Changing & Commissions There are no local charges on credit card cash advances but the maximum daily withdrawal amount is JD500.

Cheques are another story, and it pays to shop around. All branches of all banks appear to charge at least JD2 per transaction. Some want a fee and commission, so that even a small transaction can cost around JD4, more than US$5. The commission usually rises with each lot of US$100.

One of the most irritating demands made by many banks is to see the sales receipts for the cheques before changing them – directly contradicting the standard instructions to keep them separate. Sometimes they will relent, sometimes they won't.

In Amman, the best place to go seems to be the 1st Circle branch of the Jordan Bank (sometimes also called the Bank of Jordan), which is reasonably efficient, does not ask to see sales receipts, and only charges more than JD2 at US$200 and above. It obviously will save you money to make larger transactions less frequently.

Cash is no problem, but if you are asked for commission go elsewhere.

There are bank branches at Amman's Queen Alia airport where you can change cash or cheques or get a cash advance on Visa. Beware when changing at the border, as some travellers have reported being charged US$6 and above as commission.

You can also change cash and cheques in the bigger hotels, but the rates vary greatly (US$1 at anything from JD0.600 to JD0.680) and often are lower than those offered by the banks.

In February 1989, privately-run exchange houses were shut down amid government accusations that speculation by the money-changers was pushing the currency down. There were 68 of the houses on the books, concentrated in Amman, Aqaba and Irbid, but in mid-1992, the Jordanian parliament was considering allowing them to reopen.

Changing on Holidays Banks close on Fridays and holidays, so if you get stuck, you may have to settle for changing in one of the big hotels. Many small hotel owners and shopkeepers will change cash, but not at a favourable rate.

There are two exceptions to the rule. You can change money at one of the airport bank branches seven days a week. If you are in Aqaba, try the Cairo-Amman Bank at the Arab Bridge Maritime Co. Because it sells ferry tickets to Egypt in US dollars, the bank branch in the same building is open on holidays to change money.

Black Market At the time of writing, what can only be described as a black market was operating in Amman, usually outside the closed offices of the moneychangers, but the rates offered were generally inferior to bank rates. Its only advantage was being available when the banks were closed.

Costs

Jordan is not the cheapest country in the area to travel in, but not nearly as expensive as it used to be. The most basic accommodation will cost at least US$2 to US$3, and if you've come from Egypt (or even Syria), you'll find the food and transport generally more expensive too.

With careful budgeting, US$10 per day or even less is possible as long as you don't mind eating felafel and shawarma all day and staying in the cheapest of the cheapies. Having your own tent will bring the cost down a little but the camping sites are limited.

The cheapest hotels range from JD1.500 to JD2.500, and the shower often costs another 500 fils.

Snacks like felafels and shawarmas usually cost 100 fils and 200 fils, respectively. All over the bigger cities you'll see perfectly good ice creams on sale for 50 to 100 fils, depending on their size.

A cup of tea will normally set you back 50 fils; Turkish coffee is more expensive at 100 fils. Bottles of soft drink will be 100 to 200 fils, and cans a little more. Large bottles of mineral water come at about 400 fils, fresh juices from juice stands 200 to 250 fils. A 650 ml bottle of Amstel beer costs around JD1, plus a returnable deposit of anything up to 500 fils.

Tipping & Bargaining

Tips of 10% are generally expected in the better restaurants. Bargaining, especially when souvenir-hunting, is essential but shopkeepers are less likely than their Syrian and Egyptian counterparts to shift a long way from their original asking prices.

WHEN TO GO

The best time to visit Jordan is in spring or autumn when the daytime temperatures aren't going to knock you flat and the winds aren't too cold.

If you find Amman too cool in winter, head down to Aqaba on the Red Sea; it enjoys fine weather and is something of a winter resort.

WHAT TO BRING

For details of what to bring to Jordan see the regional Facts for the Visitor chapter.

TOURIST OFFICES
Local Tourist Offices

Tourist information is sparse in Jordan although the Ministry of Tourism & Antiquities does put out a few glossy brochures and posters and a reasonable map of Jordan and Amman. There are tourist offices in Amman, Petra, Jerash and Aqaba, and although they seem to exist mainly to keep a few people employed, they can occasionally be helpful with local information.

Overseas Reps

Royal Jordanian Airlines' sales offices double as tourist offices all over the world, so don't bother trying to extract any information from Jordan's diplomatic missions. You won't get much more joy than in Jordan itself, but the glossies, along with some information on the more expensive hotels and the standard map of Jordan and Amman, are better than nothing.

If you buy a ticket at Trailfinders (☎ (071) 938-3366) in London, ask to see the library in the basement of their office at 194 Kensington High St, London W8 7RG. They have a collection of old brochures, travel articles and the like.

Also in London is Stanford's bookshop (☎ (071) 836-2121), 12-14 Long Acre, London, WC2E 9LP, which probably has the best map collection available in London. They carry a few Jordanian road and city maps, although most were produced in Jordan or Lebanon and are cheaper on the spot.

BUSINESS HOURS

Government departments are open from 8 am to 2 pm daily except Friday. Banks are open from 8.30 am to 1 pm and again from 4 to 6 pm in summer (3.30 to 5.30 pm in winter) every day except Friday. Businesses keep similar hours but are more flexible.

Small shops are open long hours, from about 9 am to 8 or 9 pm. Some close for a couple of hours in mid-afternoon. Fridays are pretty dead, although a few shops are open, and you can still change money at the airport.

The souqs and street stalls are open every day and in fact Friday is often their busiest day.

During Ramadan, the Muslim month of fasting, business hours are shorter and because of the restriction on eating or drinking during the day, it can be difficult to find a place that's open in daylight hours, particularly in out-of-the-way places.

Museums are generally open every day except Tuesday, but opening hours sometimes vary.

HOLIDAYS

Holidays are either religious (Islamic or Christian) or celebrations of important events in Jordanian or Arab history. For Islamic holidays see the Table of Holidays on page 28.

Christian Holidays

Most Christians in Jordan (and the occupied West Bank) use the Eastern (Julian) calendar to determine holidays; this can be as much as one month behind the Gregorian, which is used by the Latins and Protestants. Easter is the main festival in the Eastern Church.

Other Holidays

The following holidays all relate to the Gregorian calendar and are fixed.

January
    Tree Day (Arbor Day) (15th)
March
    Arab League Day (22nd)
May
    Labour Day (1st)
May
    Independence Day (25th)
June
    Army Day & Anniversary of the Great Arab Revolt (10th)
August
    King Hussein's Accession (11th)
November
    King Hussein's Birthday (14th)

CULTURAL EVENTS

Jordan's best known cultural event used to be the annual Jerash music festival, which generally took place in late summer or autumn. It was not held in 1991 because of the Gulf war and was not scheduled for 1992.

The foreign cultural centres have regular films, lectures and exhibitions, such as the French film festival. Enquire at the centres. Since 1989, an annual European Film festival has been held in Amman around May.

The Royal Cultural Centre, now under a bit of a financial cloud and looking ragged around the edges, still quite regularly holds music recitals and the like. Occasionally, concerts are held in Amman's Roman theatre as well.

POST & TELECOMMUNICATIONS
Postal Rates
Letters to the USA and Australia cost 320 fils, postcards 240 fils. To Europe, letters are 240 fils and postcards 160 fils.

Sending a parcel is ridiculously expensive. A five to seven-kg parcel to Australia or the USA costs JD50.770 (!) by sea mail and can take up to six months to arrive. For a similar package to the UK, they want JD22.900!

Sending Mail
Letters posted from Jordan take up to two weeks to Australia and the USA. There is no postal service between Jordan and Israel, which in this case includes the West Bank. If you tell any Jordanians that you are going to the West Bank they may well ask you to take letters to post to relatives living there.

Receiving Mail
The postal service is generally efficient and letters arriving from Europe can take as little as three or four days.

Telephone
The local telephone system isn't too bad. Calls cost 50 fils and most shopkeepers and hotels will let you use their phone, which is better than trying to use the few noisy public telephones.

Overseas calls can be made easily from offices in Amman and Aqaba but cost the earth, at up to JD2.750 per minute with a three-minute minimum. It may take up to 30 minutes or so to get the connection. It is not possible to make collect calls from Jordan.

You can make calls from hotels, too, but they cost substantially more than from the offices. The smaller hotels will take about JD3 per minute for a call to Europe; the bigger ones, like the InterContinental in Amman, charge JD6.500 per minute to Australia and JD5 per minute to Europe. The three-minute minimum always applies.

As with the postal service, there are, officially at least, no connections between Jordan and Israel. In early 1992, a furore developed over direct-dial calls routed by Israel via

satellite in the USA to 12 Arab countries. Although Jordan claimed the satellite calls had been blocked, hundreds of lines are believed to have been used to receive calls from Israel and the West Bank.

The local telephone codes are:

Amman	06
Irbid	02
Jerash & Mafraq	04
Ma'an, Petra,	
Kerak & Aqaba	03
Zarqa	09

There is a telephone directory in English, but it has not been updated since 1983 and is hard to come by. The guy at reception in the British Council has one stashed away.

Fax, Telex & Telegram
The post offices in Amman and Aqaba will send telegrams, and the telephone offices will send telexes. Five-star hotels will also send telexes and faxes for guests – for a fee. Even some smaller hotels will send faxes.

TIME
For details on Jordanian time see the regional Facts for the Visitor chapter.

ELECTRICITY
Jordan's electricity supply is 220 volts, 50 AC. Sockets are generally of the European two-pronged variety. Those taking electrical appliances with different plugs should buy an appropriate adapter. If you use a radio or walkman a lot in your room, it will work out cheaper than buying tons of batteries, which often turn out to have less life in them than expected.

Power is generated by the two large oil-fired generating plants in Zarqa and Aqaba. Supply is reliable and uninterrupted, although oil shortages mean it is sometimes a close run thing. Saudi Arabia cut Tapline oil to Jordan during the war, making it more dependent on Iraqi fuel.

LAUNDRY
In the bigger cities, especially Amman, there are plenty of places, often displaying a sign

saying 'Dry Cleaning' where you can have your laundry done. Ask your hotel. You can be charged around 400 fils to have a shirt cleaned, and 600 fils for a pair of trousers. It is hardly cheap and often takes a few days.

WEIGHTS & MEASURES
Jordan uses the metric system. There is a standard conversion table at the back of the book.

BOOKS & MAPS
History
A couple of general histories of the Arabs to be recommended are Philip Hitti's *History of the Arabs* (MacMillan paperback), which has become something of a classic. A more recent and widely acclaimed work is *A History of the Arab Peoples*, by Albert Hourani (Faber, 1991). On Jordan's recent history, there is the somewhat gushing *Hussein of Jordan* by James Lunt (Fontana).

Travel Guides
The locally produced *Travellers' Guide to Jordan* (Josephine Zananiri, Al-Shourok, Beirut-Amman, 1983) is not a lot of use, but the Franciscan friars' *Guide to Jordan*, compiled in 1953, has some interesting odds and ends in it.

Fodor's *Jordan & the Holy Land* (Kay Showker, 1986) is mainly for the group tourist, or those with a vehicle, and lists only up-market establishments. The Harvard *Let's Go* guide to Israel and Egypt includes a reasonable but slim section on Jordan.

Archaeological Sites
For a detailed look at the main archaeological sites, there are a number of books available.

Petra and *Jerash & the Decapolis* by Iain Browning are well illustrated and detailed guides (Chatto & Windus, latest edition 1991, JD14).

If you want something smaller, a couple of excellent guides by Rami Khouri, former editor of the Jordan Times, are titled *Petra – A Guide to the Capital of the Nabataeans* and *Jerash – A Frontier City of the Roman East*

(Longmans UK, 1986, available for JD4.800 from the Jordan Distribution Agency, Amman). They give full details of the two sites and have excellent maps and plans.

The same author is largely responsible for a series of booklets, published by Al-Kutba, to most of the sites, great and small, in Jordan. They are available for JD2.

Written in 1959, *The Antiquities of Jordan* (G Lankester Harding, Jordan Distribution Agency, 1984, JD8) is a bit dated but is still the most comprehensive guide to archaeological sites in Jordan and includes those on the West Bank. The author was Director of the Department of Antiquities in Jordan for 20 years.

Living in Jordan
If you want more practical information on everything from road rules to how to track down a plumber, *Welcome to Jordan* (American Women of Amman, Amman, 1986) might be for you. Produced mainly with expatriates in mind, it does have some information that could be of use to the short-term visitor. It is not easy to find, so try at the American Centre or British Council libraries.

Trekking & Climbing
For rock-climbing and walking, *Treks & Climbs in the Mountains of Rum & Petra* by Tony Howard (Jordan Distribution Agency, Cicerone Press, 1987) is an excellent handbook full of walks, climbs, and 4WD and camel treks. A new edition was due in 1993 with over 250 routes. *Walks & Scrambles in Rum* (Al-Kutba Publishers) is a useful pocket guide by Tony Howard.

Photography
High Above Jordan, an officially sanctioned book of aerial photographs by Jane Taylor, is not a bad coffee-table book of the place, but a little pricey at JD20.

Maps
There are a couple of maps available but none are terribly good. The Royal Jordanian Geographic Centre puts out a map of the

country for JD1.500, but although it comes with extra details such as distances between major towns, it is the same as the free map you can get at the Ministry of Tourism.

Beirut's GEOprojects produces a similar map for JD2, with small plans of Jerash and Petra, but it's little better.

MEDIA

The press in Jordan is given a surprisingly free reign, but according to some journalists in the country, pressure is still exercised from time to time on those thought to be out of line. They also say that the bulk of newspapers all too often push an editorial line curiously similar to the government's position. By the region's standards, however, the controls are loose.

Newspapers

The daily English-language newspaper, the *Jordan Times*, has a reasonably impartial outlook and gives good coverage of events in Jordan, elsewhere in the Middle East and worldwide. It also has a What's On listing that includes films, exhibitions, flight information, emergency telephone numbers and even the latest market prices of fruit and vegetables.

The *Star* is a weekly tabloid with more feature articles, a section in French and some great cartoons (*The Far Side* by Gary Larson).

Radio & TV

Radio Jordan transmits in Arabic and English. The English station is on 855 kHz AM and 99 kHz FM in Amman and Aqaba. It's mostly a music station.

The Hebrew transmissions on both the radio and TV are aimed at Israelis, in the hope that they might see the Arab point of view.

The BBC World Service broadcasts into the Middle East on a variety of frequencies. In Jordan, programmes can be picked up during most of the day on 1323 kHz or 227 mHz on medium wave. It also broadcasts less frequently on 639 kHz and medium wave 469 mHz. The BBC alters its programming every six months or so, and the British Council in Amman usually has the latest information.

Jordan TV broadcasts on two channels; the first in Arabic, and Channel 2 in a combination of English, French, Hebrew and Arabic. Jordanians are avid TV watchers and you can see them in the tea shops glued to the sets following the latest developments in American soaps. (Wrestling also draws big audiences.) The standard of television is much higher than in neighbouring Arab countries, and the foreign channel sometimes screens excellent movies and TV series.

In the north of the country you can pick up Syrian TV as far down as Azraq. Israeli TV can be seen in places like Aqaba and Kerak, not too far from the Israeli border. The locals have no qualms about tuning in to Israeli TV, especially if movies are being shown that would be cut to ribbons by Jordanian censors. In Aqaba, you can watch (why would you want to, though?) Egyptian TV.

FILM & PHOTOGRAPHY

Kodak and other brands of film, including slide, are widely available at the tourist sites in Jordan and in Amman itself, but don't expect to pay less than you would at home (anything up to JD7 for a roll of 36 slides). Check the use-by dates before buying.

Getting your film developed in Amman and Aqaba is easy but fraught with danger. Even the best equipped Kodak stores seem to have a tendency to ruin a good batch of photos. You've been warned!

Always ask permission before photographing anyone, particularly women, and be careful when taking pictures in and around Aqaba as Israel is just 'over there' and the Saudi border is only 20 km away. Photography in military areas is forbidden.

HEALTH

For general information on how to stay healthy in Jordan and how to treat any medical problems that do arise, see the Health section in the Facts for the Visitor chapter at the beginning of the book.

WOMEN TRAVELLERS

Women travelling alone in Jordan will find that Jordanian men are a little less hung-up about Western women and sex than a lot of men in other Middle Eastern countries, but it still pays to dress and behave modestly. Walking the streets of Amman in shorts and a singlet would be as embarrassing for the locals as for you.

There are some activities, such as sitting in the tea shops, that are usually men-only activities and although it's quite OK for Western women to enter, in some places the stares may make you feel a little uncomfortable.

Staying in the budget hotels can be problematic. You'll often have to take a room for yourself, and it's not a bad idea to look around for holes in interesting places. Some women swear they feel better with some tissue stuffed into key holes and the like.

Women travelling alone should think carefully before hitching to avoid unwelcome proposals.

DANGERS & ANNOYANCES

Jordan is a safe and friendly country to travel in. The military keep a low profile and you would be unlikely to experience anything but friendliness, honesty and hospitality here. The closest you'll come to being kidnapped is someone dragging you into their house to drink tea or stay the night! If this happens, don't hesitate to accept – Arabs pride themselves on their hospitality.

It is generally safe to walk around anywhere day or night in Amman and other towns.

Theft

Theft is usually no problem for people who take reasonable care with their gear. Leaving your bag in the office of a bus station or hotel for a few hours should be no cause for concern. Shared rooms in hotels are also quite OK as a rule, but don't take unnecessary risks.

WORK

Work in Jordan is probably not an option for most foreigners passing through. Teaching English is the most obvious avenue, but the top two schools, the British Council and the American Language Centre (☎ 659859) mainly recruit in the UK and the USA, respectively. Two other possibilities are the Yarmouk Cultural Centre in Shmeisani (☎ 671447) and the Modern Language Center in Jebel al-Weibdeh (☎ 625582). There are also a couple of fly-by-night organisations that would take time to track down and be dubious to sign up with.

You may be able to get work on archaeological digs, but it is usually unpaid. If the Department of Antiquities is no help, try the British Institute for Archaeology & History (☎ 841317) or the American Center of Oriental Research (ACOR; ☎ 846117).

If you are a diving instructor, you could always try your luck at one of the three dive centres in Aqaba. Overall, though, the prospects are not bright.

ACTIVITIES
Diving

The coast south of Aqaba port up to the Saudi border is home to one of the world's better diving spots, with plenty of coral and colourful fish life. There are three dive centres in Aqaba. A single dive will cost from about JD10, depending on the gear you have with you and the centre you dive with. All three run PADI and CMAS courses for beginners and beyond, for which you'll be looking at up to US$300.

There are fears that pollution from the port will damage the sea life at Aqaba – thousands of tons of phosphates are dropped into the water during loading every year. Nevertheless, the diving offers great variety and is relatively easy. Egypt's Ras Mohammed is thought by most to be better, but requires deeper dives in more dangerous circumstances.

Hiking & Climbing

Wadi Rum and Petra are ideal places for long day walks, or in the case of Wadi Rum, treks that could last days, on foot or by camel. Rock climbing is also a possibility in Wadi Rum, but only basic gear is available on the site.

Language Courses

For those taken enough by the mystery of the Arab world to want to learn something of the language, there are several possibilities. Jordan University, in University Street, Amman (☎ 843555, fax 832318) offers summer courses in Modern Standard Arabic as well as more leisurely courses through the rest of the year. Enquiries should be made to the director of the Language Centre in the Arts Faculty. On occasion they can help find accommodation with Jordanian families.

The British Council (☎ 636147) offers very low-level classes of just four hours a week in Jordanian colloquial. Some of the other cultural centres sometimes offer similar language courses.

Another option might be Kelsey College, not far from the British Council in Amman. It is run by an Evangelical priest and caters mainly to non-lay people. The courses, run over two semesters of 400 hours, are respected but have a religious content. Lay people happy to accept that may be able to join classes. Enquire at the council or the American Centre.

HIGHLIGHTS
Archaeological Sites

For the traveller with little time to spend in Jordan, there is a handful of places that should not be missed, all of which could be seen in as little as five days. Heading north to south, the Roman Decapolis city of Jerash is an easy day trip from the capital, Amman, and is one of the best preserved Roman provincial cities in the region. Excavations and restoration continue to reveal more of its impressive array of buildings. These include the Artemis Temple, two theatres, the strange Oval Forum and a number of churches.

Only 118 km south of Amman is the impressive Crusader fortress of Kerak. It can be visited on the way down to Jordan's main attraction, Petra, the city hewn into rock by the ancient Nabataeans. Although it really deserves at least a couple of days, you can still cover some of its more remarkable features, like the Khazneh (remember *Indiana Jones & the Last Crusade*?), the theatre and Roman city centre, the tombs, and at a pinch the Monastery. If you only had a day in Jordan, this is where it should be spent.

Natural Attractions

To the south-east of Petra are the sandstone and granite rockscapes rising out of the sandy desert at Wadi Rum, made famous by *Lawrence of Arabia*. Finally, you could do worse than spend a day diving off the Red Sea port town of Aqaba.

ACCOMMODATION

There are no youth hostels so it's a matter of shelling out for a room. A bed in a shared room in a cheap hotel will not cost under JD1.500 and, generally, will be more like JD2 to JD2.500 without shower. It's sometimes possible to sleep on the roof, which in summer is a good place to be, but this will still cost at least JD1.

Especially in Amman, the cheap places can be incredibly noisy because of traffic and the hubbub of the cafés and shops, so try to get a room towards the back of the building.

The most surprising thing about accommodation in Jordan is that there are towns, some of them quite large like Jerash and Madaba, that have no hotel at all. Other towns, like Ajlun and Azraq, offer little or nothing in the bottom end of the market, and you may find yourself obliged to shell out up to JD20 for a single room.

The cheap hotels may insist on hanging on to your passport to put in the 'safe', which is usually the drawer in the desk at the front. If you want to keep it with you (where else is there to have it?), a little friendly persuasion usually works.

There is a reasonable range of middle-range hotels in Amman, Aqaba and Petra, where a single may cost from JD8 to JD20. Beyond that, there is no shortage of the top-end stuff, where rooms nudge close to the JD100 mark.

FOOD & DRINKS

For information on the food and drink you will have in Jordan, see the Food and Drinks sections in the regional Facts for the Visitor chapter at the beginning of the book.

ENTERTAINMENT

Jordan is not exactly thumping with night life. The big hotels offer the usual expensive and often dull discos and nightclubs and occasionally present Arab musicians and belly dancing. The smart set and generally better off of Amman hang around the restaurants and cafés in Shmeisani, which can be quite busy, but everything is shut by about 11pm.

The bars in the bigger hotels are one exception to the rule and sometimes stay open quite late.

Amman also has a few reasonable cinemas where you can catch comparatively recent movies that haven't been too badly mauled by the censors.

THINGS TO BUY

Jordan doesn't have a lot to offer the souvenir hunter. Most things are overpriced and many, such as the inlaid backgammon boards and boxes, come from Syria anyway.

Bedouin rugs and tapestries done by Palestinian women are popular but you need to look carefully to make sure they are actually handmade.

Brass and copper coffee pots are one of the better buys but are difficult to transport and usually come from Syria where you can pick them up for less. Small bottles of coloured sand from Petra, skilfully poured into the bottle to form intricate patterns, are sold for anything from 500 fils upwards. Natural, coloured sand was originally used, but these days the sand is often artificially coloured (what else is new?).

In Amman and Aqaba there are a few low-key souvenir shops which have all this stuff. Fleecing the tourist has not been developed into the fine art that it is in many countries and it is possible to pick up the occasional bargain.

Getting There & Away

Jordan can be reached by air, overland from Israel, Syria, Iraq or Saudi Arabia and by sea from Egypt. Royal Jordanian, the country's flag carrier, flies to places such as Europe, the USA, Indonesia and Singapore.

AIR
To/From the USA & Canada
The *New York Times*, the *LA Times*, the *Chicago Tribune* and the *San Francisco Examiner* produce weekly travel sections in which you'll find any number of travel agents' ads. Council Travel and STA Travel have offices in major cities nationwide.

The magazine *Travel Unlimited* (PO Box 1058, Allston, Mass 02134) publishes details of cheap air fares.

In Canada, Travel CUTS has offices in all major cities. The *Toronto Globe & Mail* and the *Vancouver Sun* carry travel agents' ads. The magazine *Great Expeditions* (PO Box 8000-411, Abbotsford BC V2S 6H1) is useful.

The cheapest way from the USA or Canada to the Middle East is a return flight to London and a bucket-shop deal from there.

Royal Jordanian fly direct from New York. The full quoted economy fare is US$1083 one way and US$2166 return. They also have flights from Toronto and Montreal. The quoted fare from Toronto to Amman is C$1855 one way and C$3710 return. Local reductions and special fares are available.

To/From the UK
Discount fares are big business in London and you can get some of the best deals to just about anywhere. Bucket shops dealing in these tickets abound and a hunt around a few of them will give you an idea of what's available. Two of the more reliable ones are STA, 74 Old Brompton Rd, London SW7, and Trailfinders at 46 Earls Court Rd, London W8 (with another office around the corner at 194 Kensington High St, London W8). Check *Time Out, City Limits, Exchange & Mart,* the Sunday papers and London's free magazines (usually found around the main railway and tube stations).

Most British travel agents are registered with ABTA (Association of British Travel Agents). If you have paid for your flight to an ABTA-registered agent who then goes out of business, ABTA will guarantee a refund or an alternative. Unregistered bucket shops are riskier but also sometimes cheaper.

The Globetrotters Club (BCM Roving, London WC1N 3XX) publishes a newsletter called *Globe* which covers obscure destinations and can help in finding travelling companions.

One of the cheapest return excursion (maximum 35-40 days) fares available is £260 with Rumania's Tarom, stopping at Bucharest en route. Travellers should be warned that transfers from Bucharest can be chaotic. A small desk littered with scraps of paper serves as the transfer desk, and the wait for the onward flight can be long. It is not unknown with booked onward flights to be told that Tarom knows nothing about it.

Other fares include a Yugoslav Airlines' return excursion at £290, via Belgrade (perhaps not a good idea at present), or one-way tickets from £230 to £248 with EgyptAir, KLM and Air France, or up to £486 return (EgyptAir, one year, with a stop-over in Cairo).

To/From Europe
Athens is another good discount centre. Royal Jordanian and Cyprus Airways each fly twice a week, the latter stopping in Larnaca. Some agents have one-way fares for Dr27,000 (about US$150) and returns for around Dr60,000.

Hunting around the Sultan Ahmet area of Istanbul will turn up similar offers.

In Amsterdam, NBBS is a popular travel agent.

To/From Australia & New Zealand
There are no direct connections between Australia or New Zealand and Jordan but STA Travel offers a fare of A$1260 return and A$928 one way from the east coast of Australia with Qantas and Royal Jordanian. The fare can change depending on the date of travel.

The full economy fare quoted by Royal Jordanian is A$6064 return and A$3600 one way.

Along with STA, Flight Centres International are a major dealer in cheap air fares. Check the travel agents' ads in the Yellow Pages and ring around. The cheapest way to get there may be to fly to a nearby destination

Air Travel Glossary

Apex Apex, or 'advance purchase excursion' is a discounted ticket which must be paid for in advance. There are penalties if you wish to change it.

Baggage Allowance This will be written on your ticket: usually one 20 kg item to go in the hold, plus one item of hand luggage.

Bucket Shop An unbonded travel agency specialising in discounted airline tickets.

Bumped Just because you have a confirmed seat doesn't mean you're going to get on the plane – see Overbooking.

Cancellation Penalties If you have to cancel or change an Apex ticket there are often heavy penalties involved. Some airlines impose penalties on regular tickets as well, particularly against 'no show' passengers. Insurance can sometimes be taken out against these penalties.

Check In Airlines ask you to check in a certain time ahead of the flight departure (usually 1 to 2 hours on international flights). If you fail to check in on time and the flight is overbooked, the airline can cancel your booking and give your seat to somebody else.

Confirmation Having a ticket written out with the flight and date you want doesn't mean you have a seat until the agent has checked with the airline that your status is 'OK' or confirmed. Meanwhile you could just be 'on request'.

Discounted Tickets There are two types of discounted fares – officially discounted (see Promotional Fares) and unofficially discounted. The lowest prices often impose drawbacks like flying with unpopular airlines, inconvenient schedules, or unpleasant routes and connections. A discounted ticket can save you other things than money – you may be able to pay Apex prices without the associated Apex advance booking and other requirements. Discounted tickets only exist where there is fierce competition.

Full Fares Airlines traditionally offer first class (coded F), business class (coded J) and economy class (coded Y) tickets. These days there are so many promotional and discounted fares available from the regular economy class that few passengers pay full economy fare.

Lost Tickets If you lose your airline ticket an airline will usually treat it like a travellers' cheque and, after inquiries, issue you with another one. Legally, however, an airline is entitled to treat it like cash and if you lose it then it's gone forever. Take good care of your tickets.

No Shows No shows are passengers who fail to show up for their flight, sometimes due to unexpected delays or disasters, sometimes due to simply forgetting, sometimes because they made more than one booking and didn't bother to cancel the one they didn't want. Full fare passengers who fail to turn up are sometimes entitled to travel on a later flight. The rest of us are penalised (see Cancellation Penalties).

On Request An unconfirmed booking for a flight, see Confirmation.

like Egypt, Turkey or even Greece and to go from there.

To/From Asia

Hong Kong is the discount air ticket capital of the region, although Singapore, Penang and Bangkok can also be good places to look for cheap fares. Jordan is a bit off the beaten track, however, and there is not much discounting on these routes.

STA has branches in Hong Kong, Tokyo, Singapore, Bangkok and Kuala Lumpur.

Royal Jordanian fly to Singapore, Jakarta and New Delhi. The quoted economy fare from New Delhi to Amman is Rs 12,404 one way and Rs 22,552 return. The quoted fare

---

Open Jaws A return ticket where you fly out to one place but return from another. If available, this can save you backtracking to your arrival point.

Overbooking Airlines hate to fly empty seats and since every flight has some passengers who fail to show up (see No Shows), airlines often book more passengers than they have seats. Usually the excess passengers balance those who fail to show up but occasionally somebody gets bumped. If this happens, guess who it is most likely to be? The passengers who check in late.

Promotional Fares Officially discounted fares like Apex fares, available from travel agents or direct from the airline.

Reconfirmation At least 72 hours prior to departure time of an onward or return flight, you must contact the airline and 'reconfirm' that you intend to be on the flight. If you don't do this the airline can delete your name from the passenger list and you could lose your seat. You don't have to reconfirm the first flight on your itinerary or if your stopover is less than 72 hours. It doesn't hurt to reconfirm more than once.

Restrictions Discounted tickets often have various restrictions on them – advance purchase is the most usual one (see Apex). Others are restrictions on the minimum and maximum period you must be away, such as a minimum of 14 days or a maximum of one year. See Cancellation Penalties.

Standby A discounted ticket where you only fly if there is a seat free at the last moment. Standby fares are usually only available on domestic routes.

Tickets Out An entry requirement for many countries is that you have an onward or return ticket, in other words, a ticket out of the country. If you're not sure what you intend to do next, the easiest solution is to buy the cheapest onward ticket to a neighbouring country or a ticket from a reliable airline which can later be refunded if you do not use it.

Transferred Tickets Airline tickets cannot be transferred from one person to another. Travellers sometimes try to sell the return half of their ticket, but officials can ask you to prove that you are the person named on the ticket. This is unlikely to happen on domestic flights, on an international flight tickets may be compared with passports.

Travel Agencies Travel agencies vary widely and you should ensure you use one that suits your needs. Some simply handle tours, while full-service agencies handle everything from tours and tickets to car rental and hotel bookings. A good one will do all these things and can save you a lot of money but if all you want is a ticket at the lowest possible price, then you really need an agency specialising in discounted tickets. A discounted ticket agency, however, may not be useful for other things, like hotel bookings.

Travel Periods Some officially discounted fares, Apex fares in particular, vary with the time of year. There is often a low (off-peak) season and a high (peak) season. Sometimes there's an intermediate or shoulder season as well. At peak times, when everyone wants to fly, not only will the officially discounted fares be higher but so will unofficially discounted fares or there may simply be no discounted tickets available. Usually the fare depends on your outward flight – if you depart in the high season and return in the low season, you pay the high-season fare. ∎

from Singapore to Amman is S$2426 one way and S$4852 return.

From Karachi in Pakistan there are flights with PIA and the fare is Rs 15,370 or JD415 for an excursion return ticket. A one-way ticket is JD239.

To/From North Africa

There are regular flights with Royal Jordanian and EgyptAir between Amman, Cairo and/or Tunis, but there is no discounting and it can be quite an expensive business. Amman-Cairo is JD80 one way and double return; Amman-Tunis with Royal Jordanian is JD325 one way and JD410 return!

Unless you are really pushed for time, the route through the Sinai via the Nuweiba-Aqaba ferry is a more interesting (and cheaper) alternative than flying from Cairo.

There are expensive small planes that now fly from Aqaba to Sharm ash-Sheikh and Hurghada in Egypt. See the Aqaba section for more details.

Buying a Ticket

The plane ticket will probably be the single most expensive item in your budget, and buying it can be an intimidating business. Although the number of airlines flying to Jordan is limited, it is worth putting aside a few hours to research the state of the market and check around the many travel agents hoping to separate you from your money, particularly if you don't plan to fly direct to Jordan. Start early: some of the cheapest tickets have to be bought months in advance, and some popular flights sell out early.

Talk to other recent travellers – they may be able to stop you making some of the same old mistakes. Look at the ads in newspapers and magazines, consult reference books and watch for special offers. Then phone round travel agents for bargains. (Airlines can supply information on routes and timetables; however, except at times of inter-airline war they do not supply the cheapest tickets.) Find out the fare, the route, the duration of the journey and any restrictions on the ticket. Then sit back and decide which is best for you.

You may discover that those impossibly cheap flights are 'fully booked, but we have another one that costs a bit more...' Or the flight is on an airline notorious for its poor safety standards and leaves you in the world's least favourite airport mid-journey for 14 hours. Or they claim to have only two seats available for that country for the whole of July, which they will hold for you for a maximum of two hours. Don't panic – keep ringing around.

Use the fares quoted in this book as a guide only. They are approximate and based on the rates advertised by travel agents at the time of going to press. Quoted airfares do not necessarily constitute a recommendation for the carrier.

If you are travelling from the UK or the USA, you will probably find that the cheapest flights are being advertised by obscure bucket shops whose names haven't yet reached the telephone directory. Many such firms are honest and solvent, but there are a few rogues who will take your money and disappear, to reopen elsewhere a month or two later under a new name. If you feel suspicious about a firm, don't give them all the money at once – leave a deposit of 20% or so and pay the balance when you get the ticket. If they insist on cash in advance, go somewhere else. And once you have the ticket, ring the airline to confirm that you are actually booked onto the flight.

You may decide to pay more than the rock-bottom fare by opting for the safety of a better known travel agent. Firms such as STA, which have offices worldwide, Council Travel in the USA or Travel CUTS in Canada are not going to disappear overnight, leaving you clutching a receipt for a nonexistent ticket, but they do offer good prices to most destinations.

Once you have your ticket, write its number down, together with the flight number and other details, and keep the information somewhere separate. If the ticket is lost or stolen, this will help you get a replacement.

It's sensible to buy travel insurance as early as possible. If you buy it the week before you fly, you may find, for example, that you're not covered for delays to your flight caused by industrial action.

Air Travellers with Special Needs

If you have special needs of any sort – you've broken a leg, you're vegetarian, travelling in a wheelchair, taking the baby, terrified of flying – you should let the airline know as soon as possible so that they can make arrangements accordingly. You should remind them when you reconfirm your booking (at least 72 hours before departure) and again when you check in at the airport. It may also be worth ringing round the airlines before you make your booking to find out how they can handle your particular needs.

Airports and airlines can be surprisingly helpful, but they do need advance warning. Most international airports will provide escorts from check-in desk to plane where needed, and there should be ramps, lifts, accessible toilets and reachable phones. Aircraft toilets, on the other hand, are likely to present a problem; travellers should discuss this with the airline at an early stage and, if necessary, with their doctor.

Guide dogs for the blind will often have to travel in a specially pressurised baggage compartment with other animals, away from their owner, though smaller guide dogs may be admitted to the cabin. All guide dogs will be subject to the same quarantine laws (six months in isolation, etc) as any other animal when entering or returning to countries currently free of rabies, such as Britain or Australia.

Deaf travellers can ask for airport and in-flight announcements to be written down for them.

Children under two travel for 10% of the standard fare (or free, on some airlines), as long as they don't occupy a seat. They don't get a baggage allowance either. 'Skycots' should be provided by the airline if requested in advance; these will take a child weighing up to about 10 kg. Children between two and 12 can usually occupy a seat for half to two-thirds of the full fare, and do get a baggage allowance. Push chairs can often be taken as hand luggage.

LAND

Bringing Your Own Vehicle

It's no problem bringing your own vehicle to Jordan, although you will need a *carnet de passage en douane* and your own insurance. The UK Automobile Association requires a financial guarantee for the carnet, which effectively acts as an import duty waiver, as it could be liable for customs and other taxes if the vehicle's exit is not registered within a year. The kind of deposit they are looking at can be well in excess of US$1000. It is essential to ensure that the carnet is filled out properly at each border crossing or you could be up for a lot of money. The carnet may also need to have listed any more expensive spares that you're planning to carry with you, such as a gearbox.

Obviously, you will need the vehicle's registration papers, but you do not need an International Driving Permit – your national licence is sufficient.

You may be obliged to take out local insurance of JD6, with a JD1 charge for the paperwork.

To/From Syria

Bus The only border crossing between Syria and Jordan is at Ramtha/Der'a and, as the traffic is heavy, it gets extremely crowded during the day.

Twice a day air-conditioned JETT (Jordan Express Tourism Transport) and Karnak buses (respectively the Jordanian and Syrian government bus companies) run between Amman and Damascus. The trip takes about seven hours depending on the border formalities and is the easiest way to make the crossing. It costs JD4.500 from Amman but only JD4 (!) or US$5 from Damascus. You can't pay in Syrian pounds either way and you need to book 48 hours in advance as demand often exceeds supply.

For more details see the Getting There & Away section in the Amman and North of Amman chapters.

Train There is a railway line from the Syrian border in the north to the Saudi border in the south. This is the Hejaz railway line built early this century to take the pilgrims from Damascus to Mecca.

At the time of writing there were no scheduled passenger services along it but there was talk in Amman and Damascus of reviving the run between the two capitals at any time. Narrow gauge railway buffs should check out the latest situation at either end of the line. For years it has been an on again, off again proposition.

Service-Taxi The *servees* are slightly faster than the buses and run at all hours, although it gets harder to find one in the evening. They usually get a far more thorough search at the border, so you often save no time at all. They leave from around the Abdali bus station in Amman – you can't miss the distinctive American-made yellow taxis – and from next to the Karnak bus station in Damascus. It costs JD4 or S£300 (pay in dinars, it works out a little cheaper) to cross the border.

There are competing service-taxi companies down in Shabsough St that go to Damascus and other destinations. They also operate between Damascus and Irbid in northern Jordan for the same price.

Hitching It is possible to cross the Jordan-Syria border with a combination of local bus, walking and hitching. See the Irbid (Jordan) and Der'a (Syria) sections for details.

To/From Iraq
Bus In the wake of the Gulf war, and with the USA unleashing its bombers again from time to time, Iraq, even if you could get a visa, is probably not a sensible place to go at the moment. The simmering state of revolt and crackdown in the south and Kurdish north-east add to the danger.

However, there are two daily JETT buses between Amman and Baghdad. They cost JD12, depart at 10 and 11 am and take about 14 hours.

Hijazi buses, which are much the same as JETT's buses, leave each day from the Abdali bus station. They cost JD8.

Service-Taxi The service-taxis are faster than the buses, but over a long distance the bus is probably more comfortable. You'll find taxis for Baghdad around Abdali bus station and in Shabsough St in Downtown Amman.

Hitching If you are determined to go, the steady stream of trucks heading to Baghdad used to make hitching fairly easy, although drivers may be reluctant to be seen with foreigners now. From Amman, ask for a town bus from Raghadan bus station that will drop you near the highway to Azraq.

To/From Saudi Arabia
Bus There are three JETT buses a week to Jeddah and Riyadh, ranging in price from JD25 one way to JD40 return. The journey can take up to 24 hours, depending on your destination. Transport can also be arranged to destinations beyond, such as Abu Dhabi and Kuwait. Hijazi also has buses to Saudi Arabia for similar prices. Unless you are a Muslim or doing business in Saudi Arabia, the hard part is getting a visa. The only ones dished out to tourists are transit visas, which sometimes allow you to travel along the Tapline (Trans Arabia Pipeline) in three days, but sometimes only let you fly in and out and spend a day in Riyadh.

The entry to Saudi Arabia for the land route is from Azraq, 103 km east of Amman. There are two other crossing points, one down on the coast of the Gulf of Aqaba at ad-Durra, the other further east via Al-Mudawwara.

Hitching This may be possible on the route from Azraq, but from Aqaba can be difficult as the cars are often full to bursting with people and their goods and chattels.

To/From Israel & the West Bank
West Bank Permit This is one of the crazier results of international conflict. The Jordanians insist that in going to the West

Bank you are not leaving Jordan (despite having declared in 1988 that Jordan no longer has any legal ties with the West Bank), so they don't stamp you out of the country but give you a permit. The Israelis, on the other hand, reckon that by entering the West Bank you are entering Israeli territory and will stamp you in (generally on a loose sheet, but you'd better ask to be sure), so theoretically you are in two countries at once!

First you need a permit from the Ministry of the Interior in Amman. They take about three days to issue so get things moving as soon as you get to Amman if you don't want to be held up. You don't have to leave your passport, so you can travel around for a while and come back to collect the permit.

The ministry is near the Housing Bank Centre in Shmeisani, one of the city's landmarks. *Don't* ask for a permit to visit Israel or tell them that you intend going further than the West Bank. You will be directed to a small prefab-style building in the back of the ministry where you will be given two forms to fill out. You also need a passport photo and will be asked to buy a 100 fils stamp at tables set up outside the building. When the forms are filled out, you hand them back in to a guy in a little office behind the main counter. This is where you pick the permit up, usually ready and waiting for you two or three days later. It is simply a list of people going across, with your name ticked off.

The permit technically allows you a one-month stay on the West Bank. Of course, once you are across the King Hussein Bridge, as far as the Israelis are concerned you are in Israel and free to travel anywhere around the country. You can return to Jordan as long as your Jordanian visa is still valid and your passport hasn't got an Israeli stamp in it. Even if you don't intend returning to Jordan, make sure you ask for the stamp on a separate sheet of paper when you cross the bridge as Israeli stamps are bad news when travelling in the Arab world.

Entry into Jordan is prohibited if there's any evidence of a visit to Israel in your passport, but believe it or not, it is possible to cross from Israel. To do this you must have a Jordanian visa before you get to Israel because, for obvious reasons, they are not available there.

Once in Jordan, you would have to follow the above procedure to get a permit if you wanted to return to the West Bank or Israel.

King Hussein (Allenby) Bridge The King Hussein Bridge is the only place where people can cross the Jordan River (although some officials have claimed it is possible to cross by the Prince Mohammed and King Abdullah bridges). It is only open from about 8 am until noon Sunday to Thursday, from 8 to 10 am on Fridays, and it is closed altogether on Saturday (the Jewish *shabbat* – Sabbath).

JETT minibuses are the only vehicles allowed to take passengers across and there's a terminal on either side. It's not possible to walk, hitch or take a private car across.

The most expensive way to cross the border from Amman is the JETT bus for JD5. It leaves daily, except Saturdays, at 6.30 am and takes you as far as the foreigners' terminal. There your permit is stamped and you are transferred to a minibus which continues to the bridge for another permit check. There is usually a stop for baggage and body searches.

Taking a service-taxi or local bus from the southern end of Abdali bus station in Amman is cheaper, but you won't save much time as everyone goes across on the same minibuses.

The bridge itself is narrow and only about 30 metres long, a bit of a disappointment if you're expecting something large and imposing. Once across the bridge there is an Israeli passport check before you arrive at the immigration terminal on the West Bank. Here everything is super efficient and the Israeli officials are polite and thorough. You must present any electrical goods for inspection, and if you have film in the camera, you'll be asked to shoot a frame to show it is what it appears to be.

There are money changing facilities (the rate is OK, US$1 gets 2.40 new Israeli shekels) and you are supposed to pay an entry tax of NIS4.5, although it seems quite easy to slip by without paying. Take note that the exit tax from the West Bank to Jordan is a whopping NIS59.50, although some travellers have reported being able to get through without paying.

From the West Bank terminal, share taxis *(sheruts)* run to Jericho (NIS5.50), Jerusalem (NIS26) and other places on the West Bank. Ignore their claims that there are no buses – go around the corner to the left of the main entrance and take the Arab bus (NIS2) to a rest house and bus station a few km away, from where you can get another bus to Jerusalem for NIS8. If you're counting every penny, take a bus (NIS2) or even walk the two km from the resthouse to Jericho, from where there is another bus to Jerusalem for NIS2.

Note It is important to remember that, with the sometimes unstable political climate, the slightest disturbance on either side can see the bridge close without notice for days on end. When this happens, no-one seems to know when it is likely to reopen so you just have to sit it out. If in doubt, check the *Jordan Times*, which usually reports if the bridge is to be closed for any reason.

Bus There are several local buses leaving from the south end of Abdali bus station for JD1. The disadvantage is you have to wait until they fill up. On the other hand, everyone has to wait at the Jordanian terminal until JETT minibuses start making the run across the bridge anyway, and it's more interesting travelling with the locals. The minibus across the bridge costs JD1.5 for those who don't take the JETT bus from Amman.

JETT Bus From Amman there is a JETT bus daily, except Saturday, at 6.30 am. It costs JD5. The bus takes you right across the bridge to the Israeli side. On a good day you can be in Jerusalem by 10 am.

Service-Taxi You can take a service-taxi from the south end of Abdali bus station for JD1.500 a head. They're not much faster

than the buses, and again you pay another JD1.500 to get across the bridge.

SEA
To/From Egypt
Ferry There are car ferries between Aqaba and Nuweiba in Sinai. There used to be a service to Suez, too, but this was stopped in 1990. The Nuweiba service started up in April '85 and has proved very popular.

There is an Egyptian consulate in Aqaba and visas are issued with relatively little fuss on the same day. It's a lot easier than doing battle at the crowded consulate in Amman. Beware of buying ferry tickets in Amman, as you may be charged for nonexistent 1st-class places.

The trip is meant to take three hours but can often take much longer. Occasionally, a southerly wind blows up that can oblige ferries coming to Nuweiba to wait until it subsides, but the problem is more likely to be chaos at one port or the other. Although some travellers have reported the luxury of travelling on a near-empty boat, the more common experience is of ferries packed beyond capacity. Be prepared for a trip that could last as long as eight hours.

The worst time to travel is just after the Hajj, when Aqaba fills up with hajjis (pilgrims) returning home from Mecca to Egypt and all points west with their overloaded cars. At the peak, they sometimes put on two extra boats, and although foot passengers should have little problem getting a ticket, the delays and confusion are a rude introduction to the bureaucratic frustrations that await in Egypt.

For details on ticket prices and departure tax see the Aqaba section.

Bus You can book a ferry and bus right through to Cairo at the JETT bus office. The ticket costs US$43, but you can pick up Cairo-bound buses on arrival at Nuweiba anyway.

To/From Saudi Arabia
Before the Gulf war it was possible to travel between Aqaba and Jeddah by boat, but this

service had not been resumed at the time of writing.

TOURS

If money is not an object and time is, a number of organisations offer various guided tour possibilities to Jordan. For English speakers, there are quite a few based in the UK, although travel agents or Royal Jordanian offices in other countries should be able to put you on the trail of local operators. To get an idea, Prospect Art Tours Ltd (☎ (081) 995-2151/2163), 454-458 Chiswick High Rd, London W4 5TT, organises nine-day guided tours from £975 (about US$1800). The Imaginative Traveller, which has offices around the world including the USA, the UK, Australia, Canada, New Zealand and South Africa, offers various programmes of differing duration in Jordan. Costs vary depending on season and country of departure. Jasmin Tours (☎ (0628) 531121), High St, Cookham, Maidenhead, Berks SL6 9SQ,

runs combined tours to Syria and Jordan for around £1300. The programmes on such trips are usually fairly tight, leaving little room for roaming around on your own, but they take much of the hassle off your plate. As there are quite a few tour operators, it pays to shop around to see what suits you. Check itinerary details, accommodation, who does the ticketing, visa and other documentation footwork, insurance and tour conditions carefully.

LEAVING JORDAN

You will be stamped out and, if you have a single-entry visa and wish to return, will require a new visa, regardless of how long you have been in Jordan. This, however, does not apply to the West Bank.

Departure Tax

There are three departure taxes from Jordan: JD4 across land borders (except to the West Bank); JD6 from Aqaba by sea; and JD10 by air.

Getting Around

AIR

The modern Queen Alia International Airport is about 35 km south of Amman and there are regular connections to Europe, the Middle East and Asia.

There are banking facilities open seven days a week from 7 am to 8 pm (the times should be taken with a pinch of salt). You will also find postal, telephone and telex facilities.

Local Air Services

Being such a small country there is hardly any need for an internal air network. Royal Jordanian connects Amman to the Red Sea port and resort town of Aqaba. For details see the Amman and Aqaba Getting Around sections.

BUS
JETT Bus

The enormous blue-and-white buses belonging to the JETT bus company run on limited routes within the country and run charter tours. Buses run from Amman to Aqaba, King Hussein's Bridge, Petra and Hammamat Ma'in.

See the Getting There & Away section of The Amman chapter for details of destinations, transport routes and ticket prices.

Bus/Minibus

Large private buses, usually air-conditioned, run north from Amman to Irbid (850 fils) and south to Aqaba (JD2).

All smaller towns are connected by 20-seat minibuses. These leave when full and on some routes operate infrequently. The correct fare is nearly always posted in Arabic somewhere inside the front of the bus. If you can see a sign with (for most shorter trips) a three-digit figure, you've probably found the price in fils, so it literally pays to learn the Arabic numerals. Ask the other passengers what to pay, although if you *are* being ripped

off – it happens rarely – they may side with the bus operators.

You sometimes have to pay full fare even if you are not going to the end of the line, or you pick the ride up along its route. However, they usually work out a lower rate based on the distance you're travelling. As a rule, it's sensible anyway to establish the fare before taking the ride.

TRAIN

Goods trains use the Hejaz railway line and the new line built to take the phosphate from Al-Hesa to Aqaba. There are no internal passenger services.

SERVICE-TAXI

By far the most popular mode of transport is the service-taxi. These are usually Peugeot 504 or 505 station wagons with seven seats or Mercedes sedans with five seats.

They operate on all routes and because of the limited number of seats, it usually doesn't take long for one to fill up. They cost up to twice as much as the minibuses but are faster as they stop less along the way to pick up or set down passengers.

CAR
Road Rules

Vehicles drive on the right-hand side of the road in Jordan. Rules are not always given great attention by locals, and the police tend to be fairly indulgent towards foreigners so long as they do nothing serious. The prudent driver should have little trouble, but take particular care in built-up places, where people and cars tend to jostle for space.

Rental

Most things in Jordan are expensive and hire cars are no exception. If there are four or more of you to split the cost it can be a good way of seeing a bit of the country, especially the desert castles, some of which are not serviced by public transport.

There are a dozen or more rental agencies in Amman and a couple in Aqaba. The smaller companies are a lot cheaper than the international crowds like Budget and Avis. See the Amman and Aqaba sections for details.

You'll be lucky to find a small car with unlimited km for under JD25 a day with a three-day minimum. Limited-km deals work out to be much more expensive if you're going to be doing more than 100 km per day. They cost from about JD20 per day plus 50 to 60 fils for every km over 75.

Note that although insurance is usually included, you will generally be liable for JD200 as an excess charge in case of accident. You may also be asked for a deposit of up to JD200, sometimes not until you've all but signed on the dotted line. If you spoke on the phone before arranging anything and no mention was made of it, tell them you haven't got that kind of money and that you'll go elsewhere; sometimes they will relent.

Some hire-car places will drop the car at your hotel. You can also hire cars with drivers if you want, although the roads aren't too bad and the driving relatively easy.

Petrol

There is no trouble getting petrol in the towns, but stations are scarce even along main roads. *Benzin* (normal) is about 230 fils (about US35c) a litre, but *mumtaz* (super) is not so widely available. Forget about unleaded petrol.

BICYCLE

Cycling is an option in Jordan but not necessarily a fun one. The desert in summer is not a good place to indulge in any kind of movement. Cycling north or south (most travelling will be done in those directions) can be hard work too. There is a strong prevailing wind from the west that can wear you down. Bring plenty of spare parts.

Bicycles can travel by air. You *can* take them to pieces and put them in a bike bag or box, but it's much easier simply to wheel your bike to the check-in desk, where it should be treated as a piece of baggage. You may have to remove the pedals and turn the handlebars sideways so that it takes up less space in the aircraft's hold; check with the airline well in advance, preferably before you pay for your ticket.

HITCHING

Hitching is definitely feasible in Jordan. The traffic varies a lot from place to place but you generally don't have to wait long for a lift.

Some drivers will pick someone up as a way of subsidising their own trip. If you want to avoid a possibly unpleasant situation when you get out, ask beforehand if payment is expected and if so, establish how much they want. Otherwise, simply offer a small amount when you get out. Nine times out of 10 this courtesy alone will be appreciated and payment refused. If you are adamant about not paying, you may have to knock back a couple of rides before getting a lift.

Make sure you have a hat and some water to fight the heat if you have to wait a while for a lift. Hassles when hitching are rare, but women travelling alone should definitely not hitch. Even one single male traveller wrote in to warn about the truck drivers who may have 'designs on your body'.

LOCAL TRANSPORT
To/From the Airport

You can reach central Amman by local bus and taxi, or rent a car at the Budget or Avis desks at the airport.

Bus

Amman has an efficient and cheap public bus network but none of the buses have the destination in English (although some have the number), so unless you can read Arabic or know which one to catch, their usefulness is limited.

Service-Taxi

Amman is well served by service-taxis which, like buses, run along set routes through the city, and these are by far the best way of getting around. They too have nothing posted in English but are a lot easier to track down than the buses.

The city service-taxis are generally white, but the important feature is the *white* panel on the driver's and front passenger's door with the number and route in Arabic. They wait until full at their terminus stop and will drop you wherever you want along their route and pick up other passengers along the way. You pay the full fare wherever you alight.

Irbid also has a couple of service-taxi routes.

Taxi

In all other places you'll have to walk, which poses no problems, or take one of the many regular taxis. The regular taxis tend to be yellow but are distinguished from the service-taxis by the *green* panel on the front doors. These are equipped with meters and the drivers usually speak a fair amount of English, especially in Amman. Late at night they will probably charge more than is shown on the meter.

TOURS

The only scheduled tours are operated by JETT to Petra and Hammamat Ma'in. They are really only for those who have limited time in Amman and want to see something of these two sites. The drive to Petra takes three hours each way, which doesn't leave much time for sightseeing.

Only a few of the multitude of travel agents in Downtown Amman will try to help you put together your own tour; some of those are in or near the big hotels. Beware of the latter. Royal Tours (☎ 644267), a subsidiary of Royal Jordanian with offices in the InterContinental Hotel in Amman, will put you in a chauffeur-driven car for a few days and work out an itinerary (as hectic as you please) to cover sites from Jerash in the north to Petra and Wadi Rum in the south. They book you (and your driver) into hotels and take into account a mile of 'extras'. A typical tour like this lasting three or four days and finishing up at, say, King Hussein Bridge for the West Bank crossing would set you back about US$400! Don't count on having the car to yourself either – you're likely to find yourself sharing with other tourists who have as little time as you.

Another one of these tour organisers is Grand Travel, just by the Amman Marriott. A sample of their quoted prices for car hire from Amman with an English-speaking driver is: US$50 for a half-day in Jerash; US$50 for a half-day at the Dead Sea; US$78 for a day in Jerash, Ajlun and Umm Qais. If you're with other people, you can bring the price per head down.

A reasonable daily rate for car and driver seems to be about JD40. You might try Jerusalem Express Travel (☎ 685196) in Abdali, Amman, or Jordan Regular Transport (☎ 622652), also in Abdali. If you just organise the car through the agent, you can then settle on hotels and so on of your choice, and save yourself a lot of money along the way.

There is another option – bargain with regular taxi drivers. You can sometimes convince them to go just about anywhere for the day for about JD25.

Amman

Amman is certainly never going to win any prizes for being the most interesting city in the world and in fact has very few attractions. The Downtown area is a busy, noisy, chaotic jumble of traffic – human and motorised – and just crossing the street on foot successfully is a major achievement. In fact, the town council seems bent on making the situation as difficult as possible, erecting barriers along footpaths too narrow to cope with the human squeeze. Nevertheless, Amman is the hub of all roads in Jordan so it's highly unlikely that a visitor to the country will not pass through it.

A village of about 2000 people at the turn of the century, Amman has grown incredibly in recent years and now sprawls over a large area. Standing on top of one of the seven main *jebels* (hills) that the city is built on and surveying the scene, it's easy to get the impression that it is nothing more than thousands of concrete blocks with little greenery to break up the glaring monotony. On closer inspection, the situation is not quite so dire. There are some leafy, agreeable areas in the city and, although there is no feeling of being in one of the ancient metropolises of the Muslim world (since Roman times it had never been much more than a village), the Downtown area is a lively, bustling place.

Unfortunately, modern Middle-Eastern, low-budget architecture is extremely boring and Amman is no exception. Most houses and buildings are built with the same materials from about half a dozen different designs, so most buildings look remarkably alike.

Having condemned Amman in that respect, it must be said that it's one of the friendliest cities you're likely to visit. Many of the residents are Palestinians who fled from the area west of the Jordan River during the wars of 1948 and 1967. They are generally well educated, friendly, speak a fair amount of English and are eager to chat with a foreigner. In almost every encounter a Jordanian (or Palestinian – although most hold Jordanian passports, those citizens who are Palestinians are proud of their separate identity) will say to you 'Welcome in Jordan', and you get the feeling that they really mean it.

The shops in Downtown Amman are full of Western goods – from cameras to cuddly toys – and if it were not for the chaotic traffic and the wailing of the muezzin from the mosques, you could almost be somewhere in Europe.

HISTORY

Excavations in and around Amman have turned up finds from as early as 3500 BC. Occupation of the town, called Rabbath Ammon in the Old Testament, has been continuous and objects found in a tomb dating back to the Bronze Age show that the town was actively involved in trade with Greece, Syria, Cyprus and Mesopotamia.

Biblical references are many and reveal that by 1200 BC Rabbath Ammon was the capital of the Ammonites. During David's reign, he sent Joab at the head of the Israelite armies to besiege Rabbath, after having been insulted by the Ammonite king Nahash.

It seems David was not the most benevolent of rulers. After taking Rabbath he burnt the inhabitants alive in a brick kiln (II Samuel 12) and, before the town had been taken, he sent Uriah the Hittite 'in the forefront of the hottest battle' (II Samuel 11) where he was bound to be killed, simply because David had taken a liking to Uriah's wife Bethsheba.

The town continued to flourish and supplied David with weapons in his ongoing wars. His successor, Solomon, erected a shrine in Jerusalem to the Ammonite god Molech. From here on, the only Biblical references to Rabbath are prophecies of its destruction at the hands of the Babylonians, who did in fact take over but did not destroy the town.

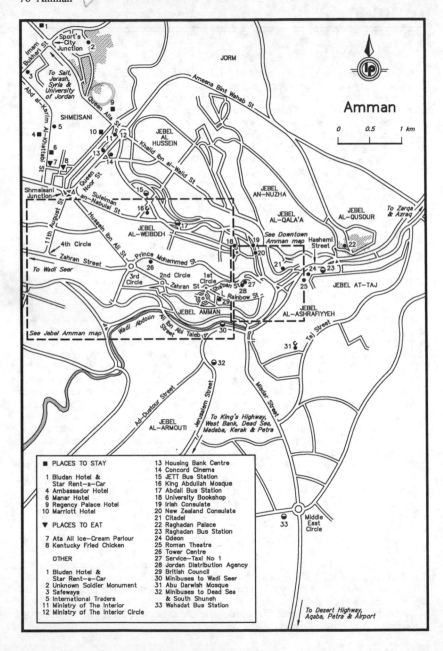

Amman

0   0.5   1 km

PLACES TO STAY

1 Bludan Hotel &
  Star Rent-a-Car
4 Ambassador Hotel
6 Manar Hotel
9 Regency Palace Hotel
10 Marriott Hotel

PLACES TO EAT

7 Ata Ali Ice-Cream Parlour
8 Kentucky Fried Chicken

   OTHER

1 Bludan Hotel &
  Star Rent-a-Car
2 Unknown Soldier Monument
3 Safeways
5 International Traders
11 Ministry of The Interior
12 Ministry of The Interior Circle

13 Housing Bank Centre
14 Concord Cinema
15 JETT Bus Station
16 King Abdullah Mosque
17 Abdali Bus Station
18 University Bookshop
19 Irish Consulate
20 New Zealand Consulate
21 Citadel
22 Raghadan Palace
23 Raghadan Bus Station
24 Odeon
25 Roman Theatre
26 Tower Centre
27 Service-Taxi No 1
28 Jordan Distribution Agency
29 British Council
30 Minibuses to Wadi Seer
31 Abu Darwish Mosque
32 Minibuses to Dead Sea
   & South Shuneh
33 Wahadat Bus Station

The history of Amman between then (circa 585 BC) and the time of the Ptolemies of Egypt is unclear. Ptolemy Philadelphus (283-246 BC) rebuilt the city during his reign and it was named Philadelphia after him. The Ptolemy dynasty was succeeded in turn by the Seleucids and, briefly, by the Nabataeans, before Amman was taken by Herod around 30 BC and so fell under the sway of Rome. The city, which even before Herod's arrival had felt Rome's influence as a member of the semi-autonomous Decapolis (a kind of loose commercial union that included Jerash and Gadara, the present day Umm Qais), was totally replanned and rebuilt in typically grand Roman style.

Philadelphia was the seat of Christian bishops in the early Byzantine period, but the city declined and fell to the Persian Sassanids about 614 AD. Their rule was short-lived, collapsing before the forces of Islam around 630 AD.

At the time of the Muslim invasion, the town was still alive and kicking, and living on the caravan trade. Its fortunes declined and some believe it was reduced to a prison town for exiled princes and notables. It was nothing more than a sad little village when a colony of Circassians was resettled here in 1878. It became the centre of Transjordan when Emir Abdullah made it his headquarters in the early 1920s.

In 1950 it was officially declared the capital of the Hashemite kingdom, and since then has gone ahead in leaps and bounds to become a modern bustling city, with a population of more than a million.

ORIENTATION

Amman is built on seven major jebels and it can be mighty confusing to begin with. The Downtown area is at the bottom of four of these hills, which means that wherever you want to go from there is up, and these hills are steep! The centre of Downtown is the area immediately around the King Hussein Mosque (built in 1924 and also known as the Al-Husseini Mosque). The cheap hotels cluster in this area, about a half-hour walk

downhill from the bus stations most travellers arrive at in Abdali.

The only way to make any sense of Amman in a short time is to pick out the major landmarks on the jebels. Most streets are signposted, but unfortunately the official name often means nothing to the locals. Just to note one example, Abu Bakr as-Sadiq St is so named on the street sign and official maps, but is actually known to everyone as Rainbow St. Under the circumstances, asking for directions to a street is generally useless.

From the citadel on top of Jebel al-Qala'a you have a view of the surrounds and can try to get your bearings. The main hill is Jebel Amman, where you'll find most of the embassies and some of the flash hotels. The traffic roundabouts on Jebel Amman are numbered as you leave Downtown, so you go from 1st Circle up to 7th Circle and beyond. Just to confuse matters, the circles from 4th on are not circles at all but regular junctions with traffic lights. The main landmark on Jebel Amman is the Jordan Tower Centre just below 3rd Circle – it's the high, circular white tower topped by a 'crown'.

Jebel al-Hussein is the next one to identify, as there are two major bus stations here and also the Ministry of the Interior for West Bank permits. It's north-west of the citadel and the Housing Bank Centre sticks out a

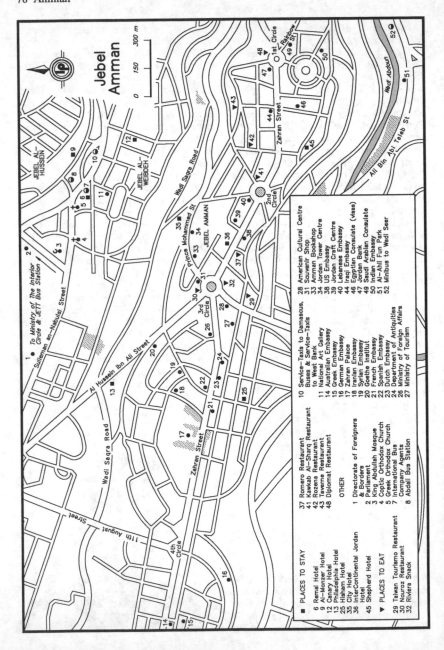

Jebel
Amman

0   150   300 m

JEBEL AL-
HUSSEIN

JEBEL AL-
WEIBDEH

JEBEL AMMAN

Wadi Saqra Road

Prince Mohammed St

Al Hussein Ibn Ali Street

Zahran Street

Wadi Saqra Road

11th August Street

4th Circle

3rd Circle

2nd Circle

1st Circle

Zahran Street

Wadi Abdun

Ali Bin Abi Taleb St

To Ministry of The Interior
Circle & JETT Bus Station
Sulieman an-Nabulsi Street

■ PLACES TO STAY

6   Remal Hotel
9   Al-Monzer Hotel
12 Canary Hotel
13 Philadelphia Hotel
25 Hisham Hotel
35 Orly Hotel
36 InterContinental Jordan
    Hotel
45 Shepherd Hotel

▼ PLACES TO EAT

29 Taiwan Tourismo Restaurant
30 Nouroz Restaurant
32 Riviera Snack

37 Romero Restaurant
41 Kawkab Al-Sharq Restaurant
42 Rozena Restaurant
43 Taverne Restaurant
48 Diplomat Restaurant

OTHER

1   Directorate of Foreigners
    & Borders
2   Parliament
3   King Abdullah Mosque
4   Coptic Orthodox Church
5   Greek Orthodox Church
7   International Bus
    Company Agents
8   Abdali Bus Station

10 Service—Taxis to Damascus,
    Buses & Service-Taxis
    to West Bank
11 National Art Gallery
14 Australian Embassy
15 Greek Embassy
16 German Embassy
17 Zahran Palace
18 Iranian Embassy
19 Syrian Embassy
20 Goethe Institut
21 French Embassy
22 Spanish Embassy
23 Dutch Embassy
24 Department of Antiquities
26 Ministry of Foreign Affairs
27 Ministry of Tourism

28 American Cultural Centre
31 Souvenir Shop
33 Jordan Bookshop
34 Jordan Tower Centre
38 US Embassy
39 Jordan Craft Centre
40 Lebanese Embassy
44 Iraqi Embassy
46 Egyptian Consulate (visas)
47 Jordan Bank
49 Saudi Arabian Consulate
50 Indian Embassy
51 Al-Ahli Fun Park
52 Minibus to Wadi Seer

mile – it's the tall, terraced building with the creepers hanging down the sides. Closer to the Downtown area, also on Jebel al-Hussein, is the big, blue dome of the spanking new King Abdullah Mosque. It's also easy to identify as it's one of the few buildings that is not grey or white! Close to the mosque are the Abdali and JETT bus stations.

To the south of Jebel al-Qala'a is Jebel al-Ashrafiyeh. It's the tallest and steepest of the jebels and has the curious Abu Darwish Mosque on the top, built in alternating layers of black and white stone. To get to the top for an excellent view, take a No 25 or 26 service-taxi from behind the Church of the Saviour.

INFORMATION
Tourist Office
There's no tourist office in Amman but you can go to the Ministry of Tourism (☎ 642311) just up from 3rd Circle. They have a few glossy brochures (sometimes) and good maps of Jordan and Amman. Unless you want a few free wall posters, it's not really worth the effort. To get there from Downtown, catch a No 3 service-taxi and get out just after 3rd Circle; the ministry is one block over to the left.

Your Guide to Amman is a free monthly booklet that lists embassies, airlines, travel agents, rent-a-car companies and has other useful and not-so-useful information. Pick up a copy at the ministry or any of the airline offices or travel agents.

Money
There are numerous banks all over the Downtown area as well as in Jebel Amman and Shmeisani. The rates don't vary but the commissions and other charges do. For travellers' cheques, the best place is probably the Jordan Bank branch on 1st Circle.

There are several places where you can use Visa card for cash advance, including the Cairo-Amman Bank in Downtown and at the InterContinental and Mariott Hotels; also at several banks in Shmeisani. You can use MasterCard and cash Eurocheques at the British Bank of the Middle East – there is a branch on King Hussein St, Downtown (see Facts for the Visitor chapter for more details).

The American Express agent is International Traders (☎ 661014) but the office is out in Shmeisani, opposite the Ambassador Hotel in Abd al-Karim al-Khattabi St. The office is open from 8 am to noon and 3 to 6 pm daily except Friday.

It is not on any public transport route, so you'll have to take a taxi or walk from the last stop on the No 7 service-taxi route.

Post
The central post office in Amman is conveniently located in the Downtown area, on Prince Mohammed St. The poste restante mail is kept in a box on the counter at Window No 1 and you can look through the lot. If there are bulky items for you, a slip is usually placed in the box for you to pick out and hand in. Some of the employees don't seem to be aware of the significance of these slips, so insist that there must be a parcel stashed away for you somewhere until someone who knows what's going on comes to your aid. The office is open from 8 am to 7 pm daily except Friday, when it closes at 1.30 pm.

The post office will also send telegrams.

You can have mail forwarded to the American Express representative in Amman, too. Technically you should be a customer, which means having cheques or a credit card, although generally they don't seem to mind one way or the other. See the Money section.

Parcels The parcel post office is in the same street as the telephone office, down near the corner of Prince Mohammed St. It looks more like a shop-front than a post office. It is right opposite a rear entrance to the main post office. The office is open from 8 am to 2 pm.

Posting a parcel is time consuming but simple enough, although their asking prices are out of this world (see the Jordan Facts for the Visitor chapter). Take the parcel *unwrapped* to the parcels office, from where you'll be directed to the customs office on the 1st floor of the main post office. After a perfunctory search they clear it and send you back to the parcel office, where the parcel is weighed and you pack it. They provide cotton to wrap it.

Telephone

The main office for international telephone calls is in the street up behind the post office, opposite the Al-Khayyam Cinema. It's open from 7.30 am to about 10.30 pm (they are definitely closed by 11 pm), seven days a week.

For details on the cost of international calls from Amman see the Jordan Facts for the Visitor chapter. From 10 pm, the rates are cheaper, JD1.810 and JD1.300 per minute, respectively. Be prepared for a bit of a crush, though.

You need to fill out a yellow sheet (that comes in Arabic only) with your name, the destination city and country, and the number you want to call. You specify a theoretical amount of time for the call and attach an appropriate sum of money. If your call goes over you pay the difference; if it goes under they give you the change – and they do, so don't worry about handing over too much.

You can also send telexes from the telephone office, but not faxes. International calls can also be made from five-star hotels.

For directory assistance for local calls, ring ☎121.

Foreign Embassies

See the Jordan Facts for the Visitor chapter for addresses of foreign embassies in Amman, and for information on permits, visas and visa extensions.

Cultural Centres & Libraries

The British Council (☎ 636147) on Rainbow St (or Abu Bakr as-Sadiq St), Jebel Amman, east of 1st Circle, has a good library, current newspapers, and regularly shows films. The library is open from 8.30 am to 1.45 pm and 3.30 to 6.30 pm Saturday to Wednesday, from 10 am to 1.45 pm on Thursday and is closed on Friday.

The American Center (☎ 641520) also has

a library (open from 8 am to 7 pm Sunday to Thursday), newspapers and occasional films. A good place to escape the heat for an hour or so, it's just across the far side of 3rd Circle, although it was planning a move to Abdoun, near the UK embassy, by the end of 1992.

The French Cultural Centre (☎ 637009) is by the roundabout at the top of Jebel al-Weibdeh, the hill directly behind the post office. It is open from 9 am to 1 pm and 3 to 7.30 pm daily except Friday and Sunday. It also has a library and organises films.

For German speakers, the Goethe Institut (☎ 641993) is the place to go. It is only open from 9 am to 12.30 pm Saturday to Wednesday and again for an hour from 5.45 pm on Saturday.

Travel Agencies

There is a plethora of travel agencies dotted around the city, with a crowd of them along the Downtown end of King Hussein St. Although some claim to organise tours within Jordan, the bulk of them appear to be little more than ticketing agents for international air travel.

It is inadvisable to book sea passage to Nuweiba (Egypt) with these agents, as some travellers have reported paying for 1st-class cabins that don't exist. If you can, simply buy a ticket in Aqaba.

For land travel you are better off going to the JETT offices (see the Jordan Getting Around chapter and the Amman Getting There & Away section). For more information on tours see the Jordan Getting Around chapter and the Amman Getting Around section.

Bookshops

There are a few bookshops in Amman worth mentioning, but don't hold your breath about any of them. The most irritating thing is that none seem to have the full range of available books on Jordan – if you want something specific, you may have to trudge around a few. Bear in mind that some of the souvenir shops in hotels and near the Amphitheatre

Top: View of Roman theatre from citadel, Amman (DS)
Left: Nymphaeum, Amman (DS)
Right: King Hussein Mosque, Amman (HF)

Top: The Forum, Jerash (TW)
Left: Dusk at the mosque in Ajlun (HF)
Right: The Golan Heights from Umm Qais (HF)

sometimes have just as a good a range of books on Jordan.

Possibly the best bookshop is the one at the InterContinental Hotel, which has a range of books on Jordan and the Middle East, not a bad selection of fiction and a good range of foreign press. It is the best of the hotel bookshops, although the Marriott's has some different material on Jordan available.

The Jordan Distribution Agency is the closest to Downtown, just by the No 1 service-taxi stop where Sha'ban and Prince Mohammed Sts meet. It has a reasonable range of books on the Middle East, a small stock of fiction and some foreign press. The University Bookshop, at the small round-about on Jebel al-Weibdeh, and the Amman Bookshop, just below 3rd Circle, have a similar but smaller range.

Medical Services

You could choose worse places to get ill, as Amman has more than 20 hospitals. Among the better are the Hussein Medical Centre in Wadi Seer (☎ 8138/32) and the Palestine Hospital in University St, Shmeisani (☎ 664171). *Your Guide to Amman* contains

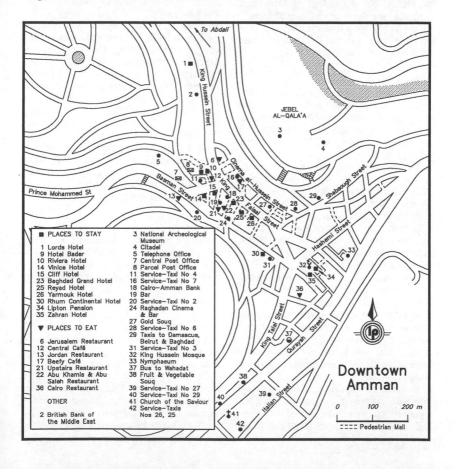

■ PLACES TO STAY
1 Lords Hotel
9 Hotel Bader
10 Riviera Hotel
14 Vinice Hotel
15 Cliff Hotel
23 Baghdad Grand Hotel
25 Reyad Hotel
26 Yarmouk Hotel
30 Rhum Continental Hotel
34 Lipton Pension
35 Zahran Hotel

▼ PLACES TO EAT
6 Jerusalem Restaurant
12 Central Café
13 Jordan Restaurant
17 Beefy Café
21 Upstairs Restaurant
22 Abu Khamis & Abu Saleh Restaurant
36 Cairo Restaurant

OTHER
2 British Bank of the Middle East
3 National Archeological Museum
4 Citadel
5 Telephone Office
7 Central Post Office
8 Parcel Post Office
11 Service—Taxi No 4
16 Service—Taxi No 7
18 Cairo—Amman Bank
19 Bar
20 Service—Taxi No 2
24 Raghadan Cinema & Bar
27 Gold Souq
28 Service—Taxi No 6
29 Taxis to Damascus, Beirut & Baghdad
31 Service—Taxi No 3
32 King Hussein Mosque
33 Nymphaeum
37 Bus to Wahadat
38 Fruit & Vegetable Souq
39 Service—Taxi No 27
40 Service—Taxi No 29
41 Church of the Saviour
42 Service—Taxis Nos 26, 25

Downtown Amman

0   100   200 m

==== Pedestrian Mall

To Abdali

JEBEL AL—QALA'A

Prince Mohammed St

Basman Street

King Hussein Street

Cinema al-Hussein Street

Shabsough Street

Hashemi Street

Faisal Street

King Talal Street

Qurayeh Street

Italian Street

a complete list of hospitals and doctors on night duty throughout the capital.

Emergency
In case of emergency, you can contact the police by telephone (☎ 192 or 621111). For an ambulance or first aid call ☎ 195. The fire department can be contacted on ☎ 622090. The number for the traffic police is ☎ 656390.

THINGS TO SEE
Amman does not have a lot to offer in terms of sights, but a handful of buildings, museums and the ruins on the citadel testify to the city's long history. One can only imagine what Roman Philadelphia must have been like in its heyday.

Roman Theatre
The restored Roman theatre, five minutes' walk east of Downtown, is the most obvious and impressive remnant of Philadelphia. It is cut into the northern side of a hill that once served as a necropolis and has a capacity of 6000 people.

The theatre is believed to have been built in the 2nd century AD in the reign of Antoninus Pius, who ruled from 138 to 161. These theatres often had religious significance, and the small structure built into the rock above the top row of seats is believed to have housed a statue of the goddess Athena, who was particularly significant in the religious life of the city.

Restoration began in 1957, but unfortunately different materials from the original were used and reconstruction was in part inaccurate. Just in front of the theatre are the remains of a colonnaded square that once formed part of the city's forum. In recent years it has once again become a place of entertainment, and productions are put on at irregular intervals.

Entrance to the theatre is free, although you will probably be accosted by 'guides' trying to rope you into a tour of the theatre and anything else you care to suggest, in and out of Amman.

Odeon
On the eastern end of what was the forum stands the Odeon, which is still being restored. Built about the same time as the Roman theatre, it served mainly for musical performances. You can't get in yet, but if you walk up the stairs behind you can get a peak inside to the rows of seats facing west. It is thought that the building, much taller in its original state, was enclosed with a wooden or temporary tent roof for performances to shield performers and audience from the elements.

Nymphaeum
Philadelphia's chief fountain stands with its back to Quraysh St, west of the theatre and not far from the King Hussein Mosque. Much of it still stands but is often missed because the interesting parts are hidden from immediate view. To get an impression of what it really looked like, you need to get around to Hashemi St and head down a lane, take a short left and right down other lanes and push open what looks like a door to someone's backyard – which it effectively is, as private houses and shops have been built right up to the decorative face of the Nymphaeum. It is thought to have been built a little later than the theatre and Odeon.

Citadel
Although much of the citadel's buildings have disappeared or been reduced to rubble, you can see evidence of Roman, Byzantine and Islamic construction. Artefacts dating to the Bronze Age show that the hill served as fortress or agora for thousands of years.

The most impressive building, which stands behind (north of) the National Archaeological Museum, is now simply known as the *qasr*, or palace. Generally believed to be the work of the Omayyad Arabs, dating back to the early 8th century, no-one seems to be able to say for certain what its function was. To the north and northeast are ruins of Omayyad palace grounds.

Closer to the museum (it is signposted) is a small Byzantine basilica, of which little is left standing. Thought to date from the 6th or 7th century, it contained mosaics that excavators have covered for their own protection.

About 100 metres south is what is commonly thought to have been a temple to Hercules. The fencing, cranes and general mess around the site is largely the work of the US team working to restore the temple to some of its former glory. By the end of the US$600,000 project, some of the columns and parts of the temple walls should again be standing. The temple dates from the reign of the emperor Marcus Aurelius (161-180 AD). The Romans also fortified the hill with defensive walls, partly restored by the Omayyads and still visible in parts today. On the northern slope of the citadel is an enormous water cistern cut into the rock.

From the southern side, near the 'Bedouin tent', where a tea can cost you JD1 (!), you get sweeping views of the theatre and the centre of town, including a lot of backyards full of washing and assorted debris.

MUSEUMS
Folklore Museum
This is one of two small museums housed in the wings of the Roman theatre. The Folklore Museum is in the right wing of the theatre and houses a collection of items showing the traditional life of the local people – a Bedouin goat-hair tent complete with all the tools and utensils, musical instruments (note the single-string *rababah*, a classic Bedouin instrument), woven rugs and a camel saddle. It's open from 9 am to 5 pm Saturday to Thursday, and from 10 am to 4 pm Fridays and holidays. Entry is 250 fils.

Traditional Jewels & Costumes Museum
This is in the left wing of the Roman theatre and has well-presented displays of traditional costumes, jewellery and utensils. The best, however, is the mosaic collection, most of it from churches in Madaba and dating back to the 6th century.

It is open from 9 am to 5 pm and, unlike its opposite number, *is* closed on Tuesdays and holidays. Entry is 250 fils.

National Archaeological Museum
Just north-west of the Hercules Temple is the Archaeological Museum. Although small, it has quite a good collection of ancient bric-a-brac ranging from 6000-year-old skulls from Jericho to artwork from the Omayyad period. There are some examples of the Dead Sea scrolls, a copy of the Mesha Stele (see the section on Madaba for details) and some odd-looking Iron Age anthropomorphic cocoon-like coffins. It's open from 9 am to 5 pm daily except Tuesday, when it closes, and Friday, when it opens from 10 am to 4 pm. Entry is 250 fils.

Jordan University Archaeology Museum
If you have a special interest in archaeology, or happen to be out at Jordan University, there is a small museum there containing artefacts found at various sites in Jordan – mostly ceramics and some statuary – from the Bronze and Iron ages, as well as the Roman, Hellenistic and Islamic periods. Entrance is free and it's open Sunday to Thursday – the hours are flexible.

LANGUAGE COURSES & WORK
It is possible to enrol for courses in Arabic in Amman. There are several choices; the best bet is probably Jordan University. Outside limited teaching possibilities, the chances of work are slim. See the Activities section in the Jordan Facts for the Visitor chapter for details.

PLACES TO STAY
Places to Stay – bottom end
The Downtown area is thick with cheap hotels. Along King Faisal St practically every building is a hotel. A lot of these places have shops on the ground floor, a tea shop on the 2nd and then rooms on the 3rd and 4th floors. They are nearly all noisy as hell; the din from the street and neighbouring buildings is penetrating and seems no better on the upper floors. For what it's worth, try to get a room at the back.

The most popular, and possibly the best, is the *Cliff Hotel* (☎ 624273), although it is not the cheapest around. It is just opposite what a lot of people call 'Seiko Corner', with the entrance up a side alley. It is clean and the managers are friendly and well used to backpackers. A bed in a double costs JD2.500 or JD2 upstairs. You can sleep on the roof (a good idea in the heat of summer, especially as the rooms don't have fans) for JD1. A hot shower costs 500 fils extra, and they sell soft drinks on the premises. You can do your own cooking and store luggage for free.

The owner, Abu Suleiman, is a mine of information on what to do and how to do it. You can have a look through a book of travellers' latest notes on Syria; a similar book on Iraq is no longer of much interest.

One lane up towards the post office is the *Vinice*, with beds in a shared room at JD2. It is quite OK, but some women have reported peeping Toms – stuff those keyholes. Hot water 'comes from the sun', which may not be much help in winter.

The *Hotel Bader* is set back slightly from the street, directly opposite the Cliff and Vinice and the entrance is along an alleyway with a small restaurant that spills onto the footpath. The rooms are generally clean, have a fan, bath and hot water. It is a little expensive at JD5/7 for singles/doubles, but they may come down, with much protesting, to about JD3 for a single. The owner says he has a fax service.

Another in this category of cheapies is the *Baghdad Grand Hotel* which is only about 30 metres down from the Cliff Hotel. They want JD4 for a basic double and will try to get you to take the whole room if you are travelling alone. It's not a bad place, but try to get a room away from the noisy front lounge.

Another lane further down towards the King Hussein Mosque is the *Reyad* (supposed to be 'Riyadh'). A bed comes for JD2.500, including shower and fan. This is an OK place and fairly quiet.

A bit cheaper still is the *Yarmouk*, a little further down again, where a bed costs JD2. Some of the rooms have big balconies overlooking the main drag.

Probably the cheapest is the *Zahran Hotel*, just by the mosque. Beds come at JD1.500 without bargaining, include a shower and you can elect to stay on the roof. You'll need to be deaf or an early riser, as you can't get much closer to the call to prayer.

The *Lords Hotel* (☎ 622167) on King Hussein St is big and cavernous and a bit gloomy but this does help to keep it cool in summer. It's a bit pricey at JD5/8 for singles/doubles with fan and hot water. It is centrally heated in winter and even has room service. This is a good place to head for if you're after a bit of privacy.

Places to Stay – middle

For something a bit better, the *Al-Monzer Hotel* (☎ 633277) by the Abdali bus station has good, clean rooms with fan and piping hot showers for JD8.500/10.500. Try to avoid the top-floor rooms which are quite stuffy. The *Cleopatra Hotel* next door wants the same prices without any of the quality – although they are quicker to drop the price by a couple of dinars.

On the other side of the road, tucked away in a side street opposite the police department, is the *Hotel Remal* (☎ 615585) which has quite comfortable, if somewhat sterile, rooms with ensuite bath at the odd prices of JD9.350/11.550. There is no air-conditioning.

Not too far away (a steep walk or taxi ride from Abdali bus station) is the *Canary Hotel* (☎ 638353) on Jebel al-Weibdeh, opposite the Terra Sancta college. Rooms come for JD14/17.500, but you can bargain JD2 off this. They are clean and quiet, and the leafy location is quite accessible – the No 4 service-taxi passes fairly close by. You can have breakfast for 750 fils.

The *Granada Hotel* (☎ 622617), which has a cosy bar that is quite popular with expats, has singles/doubles for JD14/17. It's opposite the Sri Lankan consulate near 1st Circle.

For a bit of three-star comfort, try the *City Hotel* (☎ 642251) on the road up to 3rd Circle from Downtown. The rooms have fan and bath and cost JD12.650/14.850/20 a single/double/triple.

Better still is the *Rhum Continental Hotel* (☎ 623162) – they also spell it 'Rum', as in the wadi. It's on Basman St in Downtown and has spotless rooms with air-conditioning, heating in winter, hot ensuite shower, TV and mini-bar for JD14.500/17 plus 10% tax. There is a restaurant and bar, as well as a fax service open to customers.

The *Lipton Pension* is right behind the mosque and is the only tall building there. The windows of the pokey rooms are only a stone's throw from the minaret and you get little more for your trouble than at the Zahran, only they want JD8/10. Avoid this place.

Places to Stay – top end

Amman also has its share of four and five-star international hotels. Some of those a little way out from the centre, hovering between three and four stars, aren't bad value. Up on Abd al-Karim al-Khattabi St is the *Manar Hotel* (☎ 662186) with singles/doubles for JD16.400/21.250, including breakfast and swimming pool. Further up the same road is the *Ambassador Hotel* (☎ 665161), with good rooms from JD22/26 plus 10% tax.

Among the biggies, the closest to Downtown is the *InterContinental Jordan* (☎ 641361), midway between 2nd and 3rd circles, right opposite the US embassy. Singles/doubles go for JD85/95 plus 10% tax. Along with the *Marriott* (☎ 660100), which charges JD85/92 plus 20% in taxes, it is the most expensive. The Marriott, a block behind the Ministry of the Interior, has all you would expect of such a hotel; 24-hour international telephone and fax, swimming pools, restaurants and bars.

Virtually across the main road heading out to the university is the slightly gloomy *Regency Palace* (☎ 660000), with rooms at JD70/85 plus 20% in taxes. On the north-western side of Jebel Amman is the former Holiday Inn, now called the *Philadelphia*. It charges JD75/90 plus the usual taxes. This is where important Palestinians, PLO or otherwise, tend to stay.

The *Plaza Hotel* in the Housing Bank Centre has rooms for JD82/89 plus 20% taxes.

PLACES TO EAT

Amman offers quite a range of food options, with many non-Middle Eastern cuisines represented. If you're on a tight budget though, you won't be seeing much of this kind of food. It's not as bad as it was, however, because restaurant prices have not kept pace with the devaluation of the dinar since 1988.

Cheap Eats

If you're on a fairly tight budget, your mainstay in Amman will be felafel and shawarma and, in summer at any rate, plenty of ice cream.

Breakfast is easy. Right by the Cliff Hotel are a couple of alleys with small shops that sell yoghurt, milk, fruit, butter, bread and all sorts of cheeses. Stock up with goodies and put your own breakfast together.

In the alley that leads to the Bader hotel is a good cheap restaurant for felafel, hummus and fuul or combinations of some or all of the above. A filling meal with bread and tea is only about 300 fils and it seems to be open when the rest of Amman is asleep. Just around the corner in King Hussein St are several shawarma stalls next to each other. The price of a shawarma is 200 fils, but you'll need a couple to make a halfway decent lunch. Shawarma and felafel stands like these can be found dotted about Downtown.

In the same lane as the Baghdad Grand Hotel is a place called the *Abu Khamis & Abu Saleh Restaurant* (you can also enter it from the back lane). There is no sign in English but it's a big place with a chicken-roasting oven out the front. They have a good range including chicken (800 fils for half), stuffed green peppers, potato chips, a variety of meat and vegetable stews, rice, and soup as well as salads, hummus and bread. A filling meal of chicken, chips and a Pepsi will cost you JD1.150; soup, fasooliyah, chips and Pepsi, JD1. Generally the food is not bad.

The *Jerusalem Restaurant*, on King

Hussein St, (ask for the *matta'am al-quds*) is a good place, again with no sign in English. The front window is full of sweets and pastries. The best dish here is the traditional mensaf with a delicious cooked yoghurt sauce. It's not cheap at JD2 but it is excellent. For dessert try mahalabiya wa festaq for 240 fils. Other standard meat dishes cost about JD1.400.

In much the same league is the *Al-Saha al-Hashemieh* opposite the front of the theatre. Outside you can dine under a 'Bedouin' tent roof in the company of a stuffed hyena. Most meat dishes are about JD1.400, a half chicken is JD1, and a quick glance at the menu reveals that lambs balls (sic) can be had for a very reasonable 920 fils. After that, a relaxing smoke on the hubble bubble (or narjileh) will add JD1.100 to the bill.

Cheaper, and with a similar range to the Abu Khamis, is the *Cairo* restaurant a block south-west of the King Hussein Mosque. A meal of chicken, mulukiyyeh, rice salad and a soft drink – more than one can eat – will set you back JD1.500.

There is another good place in the same lane as the Cliff Hotel. Turn right out of the hotel entrance and it's the last door on the left before you emerge on Basman St. The restaurant is up the stairs on the 2nd floor. There is no sign in English. A good meal of kebabs, salad, hummus and bread will cost about JD1. The little open terrace is a nice place for a beer in summer.

Just off Cinema al-Hussein St is the *Beefy* café, a fast-food-type place with good hamburgers, pizzas and chips. Best of all, they must do one of the best milkshakes in the region. You can sit at one of the couple of tables or by the window, or just take away. A basic hamburger is 350 fils. The pizzas (which are quite good) are a bit expensive at JD1.500. A double cheese burger, chips and milk shake come to JD1.400.

Another burger place is *Riviera Snack* up at 3rd Circle. The food isn't as good but you can sit outside and watch the traffic roar by. It charges 400 fils for a burger and JD1.200 for a 650 ml bottle of Amstel beer.

Mid-Range

A few doors down from the Amman Bookshop, before you get to the Jordan Towers building, is the *Chicken Tikka Inn* with good curries for around JD1.500. It's open from noon to 4 pm and 6.30 pm to midnight.

Right on 1st Circle, the *Diplomat Restaurant* has a good range of dishes for JD1 to JD3, including reasonable pizzas. It's open until quite late and they have tables on the footpath where you can sip on an Amstel (JD1.150). Up on 2nd Circle is a similar place called the *Kawkab al-Sharq*. The lady in green on the sign is Umm Kalthoum, the Arab world's most revered singer.

The *Nouroz* ('Nairuz' in Arabic) restaurant up on 3rd Circle, virtually opposite the Riviera, does pizzas for JD1.200/2.200, but don't waste time asking for the ham version. A bottle of Latroun wine will cost you JD7.

Up near the American Cultural Center, just behind the hospital in a side street, is the *Taiwan Tourismo*, where a filling and good Chinese meal for two can be had for JD8/10.

In Shmeisani there is a whole string of places where you won't come away with much change from JD5, except at the Western takeaways: *Pizza Hut* and *Kentucky Fried Chicken*. Popular places include *Milano*, a nice place for light Italian lunches, *La Terrasse*, which often has Arabic musicians in the evening, and *New York, New York*. These are all clustered around Queen Noor St, but the easiest thing to do is jump into a cab and ask for *Jabri* in Shmeisani.

In the same area, *Ata Ali's* ice cream parlour, before the Manar Hotel on Abd al-Karim al-Khattabi St, has a great range of ice cream flavours to take away. The sit-down section is expensive and disappointing.

Expensive

For a meal with a view, try the restaurant on the 23rd floor of the *Jordan Towers* building (known simply as the *burj*, or tower), just below 3rd Circle. It's worth the trip just for the view. Mezze is JD3.500, most main dishes JD5 to JD8 and a modest glass of draught beer in the bar a cool JD2.200.

In a side street near the US embassy, opposite the InterContinental, is the expensive Italian restaurant *Romero*. The next side street up towards the 3rd Circle has the Spanish version, the *Bonita Inn*; a meal for two in either will cost at least JD20. The *Taverne* and *Rozena* are in much the same league, and a little more difficult to find as well.

The big hotel restaurants are generally expensive and not as good as some of those outside. None have very good breakfast deals either, most charging JD4 or more for outside guests.

Cafés

Some of the Downtown cafés make good places to sit and write letters, meet the locals or read. The *Central Cafe* is right on Seiko Corner, above the Seiko sign at the corner of King Hussein St and King Faisal St. You get a good view from here and they serve hot and cold drinks. It shares an entrance with the *Hilton* bar, which is off to the right of the stairs just up King Hussein St. The café is on the left. The café on the 1st floor of the Baghdad Grand Hotel is another good one.

ENTERTAINMENT
Bars

Apart from the Hilton, there are numerous tiny little bars tucked away in the rabbit warren of alleys around the Cliff Hotel. In the first lane east of the lane where the Cliff is, you'll find one called the *Jordan Bar*. Another is up in Basman St, just next to the Raghadan Cinema. A beer at these places generally costs about JD1.200.

Up on Jebel Amman, the Hisham Hotel has a nice beer garden where a pint of draught lager will cost you JD1.800. The Granada Hotel has a bar popular with expats (the British Council and US embassy are nearby) called *After Eight*. The InterContinental bar is open until at least midnight.

Cinemas

The two best cinemas in town, which often get comparatively recent releases in a not too censored form, are the Philadelphia in the basement of the Jordan Towers complex and the Concord up near the Housing Bank Centre in Shmeisani. Tickets are JD2. The Rainbow, between 1st Circle and the British

Council, is not so good. See the *Jordan Times* for what's on.

Then there are the typical Middle Eastern cinemas, where heavily censored Chuck Connors style movies are the staple. Seats for these movies, which can occasionally be entertaining, cost JD1. The cultural centres often have films on for free. There is also a European film festival in May and a French film festival.

Exhibitions & Music
The various cultural centres regularly organise lectures, exhibitions and musical recitals. The jaded Royal Cultural Centre also occasionally puts something on, although its financial future is now in doubt.

ACTIVITIES
Hash House Harriers
If you want to meet a few of the local expatriates, the Hash House Harriers is a social jogging club where the emphasis is on the social side of things rather than the jogging. They meet every Monday night at about 6 pm and after a run of up to 10 km (you can bail out before) there's a barbecue and drinks at one of the members' homes. You bring your own meat, although first-timers are not really expected to.

Men pay JD3 and women JD2, which pays for the barbecue and copious quantities of Amstel beer. To find out where it's on, ask someone at the British embassy or British Council. First-timers be warned that they will be identified as 'virgins' and obliged to do a bit of high-speed drinking at some point in the evening.

Quiz Night
For those who are interested, the InterContinental has a quiz night in the bar every Wednesday at 9 pm. It's open to all comers and first prize is JD25 worth of their food.

Friends of Archaeology
If you are interested in archaeology, get in touch with this group which regularly organises trips to places of interest all over Jordan with an expert guide. Ask at the British Council how to track them down.

Swimming
If you want to cool off there are not many cheap options. You can try the big hotels, where you'll pay more than JD5. For an Olympic-size pool, there is Sports City (Al-Medina ar-Riyadiyya), but here too you'll be up for JD5 for pool and locker. The cheapest alternative in pools appears to be the Manar Hotel, which charges nonresidents JD3.

THINGS TO BUY
The Jordan Craft Centre (☎ 644555) is right by 2nd Circle. It looks like a normal house but has some excellent handmade articles for sale. Prices are high but this is quality stuff, a lot of it made by Palestinian refugees. It is open from 9 am to 1 pm and 4 to 7 pm every day except Fridays.

There's another good souvenir shop around the corner from the Nouroz restaurant on 3rd Circle. Some of the souvenir shops in Downtown are worth hunting around in too.

GETTING THERE & AWAY
Air
International Amman is the arrival and departure point for international flights. For details of airlines that service Jordan see the Jordan Getting There & Away chapter.

The following airlines have offices in Amman:

Aeroflot
    InterContinental Hotel, Jebel Amman (☎ 641510)
British Airways
    InterContinental Hotel, Jebel Amman (☎ 641430)
EgyptAir
    Zaatarah & Co, King Hussein St (☎ 630011)
KLM
    King Hussein St (☎ 622175)
Middle East Airlines
    King Hussein St (☎ 636104)
Royal Jordanian
    King Hussein St (☎ 639351)
Saudia
    King Hussein St (☎ 639333)
Syrian Arab Airlines
    Prince Mohammed St (☎ 622147)

Domestic The only internal air route is between Amman and Aqaba. There are at least four flights per week with Royal Jordanian. The ticket costs JD15 one way, JD18 return.

Bus

JETT Bus The JETT bus office/station is on King Hussein St, about 500 metres past the Abdali bus station. If you arrive from Syria on a Karnak bus, this is where you'll end up. To get Downtown take a No 6 service-taxi (70 fils) heading downhill and ride it to the end. It drops you in Cinema al-Hussein St right in the centre. A normal yellow taxi costs about 400 fils. If you want to walk it takes about 30 minutes. Tickets for JETT buses should be booked two days in advance.

There's one bus daily to the King Hussein Bridge for the West Bank at 6.30 am (JD5). See the Jordan Getting There & Away chapter for more details on crossing to the West Bank.

Buses for Damascus leave at 7.30 am and 3 pm (JD4.500), for Baghdad at 10 and 11 am (JD12) and there's a daily bus to Petra at 6.30 am for JD5!

There are seven daily services to Aqaba (JD3.500).

The No 6 service-taxis start running at about 5.30 am so you can catch one from Downtown for any of the early-morning departures.

Bus/Minibus The main bus stations in Amman are: Abdali for transport north and west, Wahadat for buses south, and Raghadan for local buses and Hammamat Ma'in, from where you can get buses heading east and north-east. There are also a few less well defined bus stops for certain destinations.

Abdali bus station is on King Hussein St, about 20 minutes' walk (uphill) from Downtown. A No 6 or No 7 service-taxi from Cinema al-Hussein St goes right by it. Minibuses run to Jerash (about one hour, 320 fils), Ajlun (1½ hours, 500 fils), Irbid (two hours, 530 fils), Salt (45 minutes, 175 fils),

Suweileh (20 minutes, 80 fils) and Deir Alla in the Jordan Valley (one hour, 370 fils). There's no timetable and they just leave when full, but tend to stop running at about 5 pm.

There are also air-con Hijazi buses that run every 15 to 20 minutes for the two-hour trip to Irbid (850 fils). Buy tickets from their office at the northern end of the station.

From the southern end of the station you can get one of several morning minibuses to the King Hussein Bridge (45 minutes, JD1).

Wahadat bus station is way out to the south of town by the traffic roundabout called Middle East Circle (Duwaar Sharq al-Awsat). It is connected to Abdali bus station by service-taxi (120 fils, no number), or you can get a No 27 service-taxi from Downtown near the fruit and vegie souq or even a local bus from along Quraysh St to Middle East Circle. This is where you'll arrive if you come from anywhere south by minibus.

Wahadat is the station all buses and service-taxis heading south leave from. Nothing runs to a schedule so it's just a matter of getting a seat and waiting.

There are irregular minibus departures for Kerak (750 fils), Hammamat Ma'in (JD1), Ma'an (JD1.050) and Wadi Musa/Petra (JD2). There are also large air-con buses for Aqaba for JD2, and fairly regular departures to Madaba (175 fils). The fares are generally posted at the front inside the buses in Arabic only. You may have to bargain to pay the correct amount.

From Raghadan bus station, which is a few minutes' walk further east of the Roman theatre, there are highly irregular local buses (usually No 31) to Madaba (150 fils), but the wait is sometimes so long you might be better off getting out to Wahadat and taking a bus or minibus from there. They all take about an hour. There are minibuses and local buses to Hammamat Ma'in at anything from 80 to 120 fils.

Minibuses for Wadi Seer (30 minutes, 100 fils) depart from Ali ibn Abi Taleb St, about a 10 to 15-minute walk from the King Hussein Mosque. Minibuses for South Shuneh (about one hour, 400 fils) and occasionally direct to the Dead Sea resort of Suweimeh (550 fils) leave from Jerusalem St (the area commonly known as Ras al-Ain). Take a No 29 service-taxi from Quraysh St, a little past the Church of the Saviour, and get off as it veers right off Jerusalem St.

Service-Taxi

The service-taxis are faster and more convenient than the buses but are more expensive. Because they only carry five or seven people, they fill up a lot faster than the buses and don't stop along the way. They use the same stations as the buses (Abdali, Wahadat and Raghadan).

From Abdali bus station they run to Irbid (two hours, JD1) Jerash (one hour, 650 fils), Ajlun, Salt, the King Hussein Bridge (45 minutes, JD1.500) and even occasionally to Ramtha, the Jordanian border crossing with Syria (JD1).

From Wahadat there are departures for Kerak (two hours, JD1), Madaba (30 minutes, 300 fils), Wadi Musa (three hours, JD2.500), Ma'an (2½ hours, JD2) and Aqaba (five hours, JD3.300).

With both the buses and service-taxi there are many more departures in the morning.

From Raghadan, the only one that might be of interest is the service-taxi to Marka (100 fils), which can drop you by the Hejaz railway station to the east of central Amman. Tell the driver your destination: *mahattat sikkat hadid al-Hejaz* (the Hejaz railway station).

Car Rental

One of the cheapest car rental agencies is Star Rent-a-Car (% 604904) out by Sports City Junction. The guy there is helpful and willing to do a deal. For unlimited km he charges JD25 per day with a three-day minimum. This includes insurance above the first JD200 and he'll deliver the car to you Downtown.

If you're going to be doing less than 100 km per day, Natour (☎ 627455) in Sha'ban St, Jebel Amman, is not bad. They will give you a late 1980s Corolla for JD60 for three

days. Each km above that is 45 fils. Heart (☎ 695745), near Abdali bus station, rents out a brand new Daihatsu Charriot for JD22 a day for three days, also with a three-day minimum, and 50 fils per extra km.

The international companies like Avis and Budget charge from JD32 to JD40 a day depending on the car make and whether or not you want unlimited km. See the Jordan Getting Around chapter for more information.

Hitching

To hitch you need to start out of town. For the King's Highway it's easiest to catch a town bus to Madaba and hitch from there. For the Desert Highway take an airport bus (500 fils) and get off where it turns off the highway.

If you're heading north take a minibus from Abdali bus station to Suweileh, which will put you right on the highway.

GETTING AROUND
To/From the Airport

The Queen Alia International Airport is about 35 km south of the city. Buses make the 50-minute run every half hour, at five minutes past the hour, from 6.05 am to 8.05 pm from the Abdali bus station for 500 fils. There is a small stand marked for the airport bus at the top end of the bus station, but it's none too distinct.

You can also get special airport taxis for the trip into town. They cost about JD7, but note that while most metered taxis ring up fils, these only ring qirsh (see the Money section in the Jordan Facts for the Visitor chapter for the difference).

Service-Taxi

The local bus system is hard to figure out as nothing is in English so the service-taxi are the way to go. For details on how to identify service-taxis see the Jordan Getting There & Away chapter.

There's a standard charge of 70 to 80 fils for most, depending on the route, and you pay the full amount regardless of where you get off. An exception is the Abdali-Wahadat service-taxi, which costs 120 fils.

The cars queue up and so do you. Often the queue starts at the bottom of a hill – you get into the last car and then the whole line rolls back a car space and so on. Some of the more useful routes are:

No 1 – leaves from Prince Mohammed St, near Jordan Distribution Agency, and continues up to the 3rd Circle (70 fils).
No 2 – leaves from Basman St, near the post office, for the 1st and 2nd circles (70 fils).
No 3 – leaves from Basman St for the 3rd and 4th circles (80 fils).
No 4 – leaves from the side street, near the post office, up to Jebel al-Weibdeh (70 fils).
No 6 – leaves from Cinema al-Hussein St for the Ministry of the Interior Circle, going past the Abdali and JETT bus stations (70 fils).
No 7 – leaves from Cinema al-Hussein St, continues up King Hussein St past Abdali bus station and King Abdullah Mosque, and along Suleiman an-Nabulsi St (80 fils).
Nos 25, 26 – leave from behind the Church of the Saviour Downtown and continue to the top of Jebel al-Ashrafiyyeh at the Abu Darwish Mosque for a good view (70 fils).
No 27 – leaves from near the fruit and vegie souq and continues to the Middle East Circle for Wahadat bus station (75 fils).
No 29 – leaves from near the front of the Church of the Saviour (past Dead Sea buses) for Jebel al-Armouti (70 fils).

Taxi
The guys who drive the regular taxis are keen and if you do any walking in Amman you'll get sick and tired of getting honked at as they prowl for fares. Although generally they do use the meter, keep your eyes open. The flag fare is 150 fils, and any cross-town journey you want to make should never cost more than 500 fils. Don't stand for any bullshit about having to pay extra for baggage or other extras they may feel inclined to tack on.

Late at night they will often only take you for a negotiated price and nothing will change their minds. When this is the case you just have to bargain – you know at least what the upper limit should be. (See the Jordan Getting Around chapter for further details.)

Around Amman

SALT
The village of Salt, 30 km north-east of Amman, used to be the administrative centre for the area during the time of Ottoman rule. It was passed over as the new capital of Transjordan in favour of the small village of Amman. The result is that Amman has been transformed from small village to modern city, while Salt has retained its charm.

Salt is worth a visit if you have half a day to kill. There's not really anything special here but if you wander around the town you will see some fine examples of Ottoman architecture. It's a curious sight to see a Turkish house which has had a typically modern, concrete-block upper floor added. The town is the only one in Jordan where you don't get the feeling that it has been thrown together in the last 10 or 15 years. Take a walk downhill from the bus station into Wadi She'ib, a refreshing valley with some interesting caves.

Getting There & Away
A minibus from Abdali bus station costs 175 fils for the 45-minute trip. A service-taxi will cost you 300 fils.

From Salt there are also minibuses heading down into the Jordan Valley to South Shuneh.

WADI SEER & 'ARAQ AL-AMIR
The narrow fertile valley of Wadi Seer is a real contrast to the bare, treeless plateau of Amman to the east. The ruins of the building of **Qasr al-Abd** (Castle of the Slave) and the caves, known as 'Araq (or 'Iraq) al-Amir

(Cave of the Prince), are another 10 km down the valley from the largely Circassian village of Wadi Seer.

Just outside Wadi Seer you cross a small waterway where you can see an ancient **aqueduct** on the right. Just after, on the left, is a facade cut into the rock known as **ad-deir** (the monastery), although in fact it was probably a medieval dovecot.

The caves are up to the right of the road and are in two tiers; the upper one forms a long gallery along the cliff face. The caves were apparently used as cavalry stables – the local villagers now use them to house their goats and store chaff. One of the caves, easily recognised by its carved doorway, has historians guessing, for to the right of the door the name Tobias is engraved in Aramaic. Some say it is the Jewish version of Hyrcanus.

The castle is about 500 metres down the valley and can be seen from the caves. There is still some mystery as to when and why it was built but it is believed that it was built in the 2nd century BC by Hyrcanus of the powerful Jewish Tobiad family. The 1st century historian, Josephus, in his book *Antiquities of the Jews*, talks of a castle of white stone which was decorated 'with carvings of 'animals of a prodigious magnitude'.

Today, reconstruction of the palace is complete. A French archaeologist spent three years making detailed drawings of the fallen stones. He then made cardboard cutouts of each stone and tried to piece it all together. He has spent a further seven years on the actual reconstruction. The result is a fine monument which, up until now, has been completely ignored by tourists.

The best part is the north entrance with one of the original carved beasts, an enormous lion, in place over the north-west corner. The building was once covered in such figures. Note the lion on ground level on the east facade, which was used as a fountain. The whole place is unique in that it was built out of the largest blocks of any building in the Middle East. The largest measures seven by three metres but as they were only 20 cm or so thick, the whole construction was quite flimsy and the earthquake of 362 AD completely flattened it.

Getting There & Away

A minibus from Ali bin Abi Taleb St takes half an hour and costs 100 fils. There are also minibuses from Suweileh and local town buses.

From Wadi Seer you catch a minibus for 100 fils that will take you right to the end of the road at 'Araq al-Amir. You might have to wait a while for this bus to fill up, although on Fridays it's a little quicker as a lot of people head down to various parts of the wadi for picnics.

North & West of Amman

The area to the north of Amman is the most densely populated in Jordan, with the major centres of Irbid and Jerash as well as dozens of small towns dotted in amongst the rugged and relatively fertile hills. In this area lie the ruins of the ancient Decapolis cities of Jerash and Umm Qais (Gadara), and the 12th-century castle of Ar-Rabad.

North of Irbid, the country flattens out to the plains of the Hauran (and the strange black basalt town of Umm al-Jimal) which stretch away to the Syrian border. To the west lies the Jordan Valley, one of the most fertile patches of land in the Middle East.

JERASH
Situated 51 km north of Amman, Jerash is one of Jordan's major attractions, second only to Petra. Lying in the Gilead Hills right on the road that leads to Ramtha and on to

North & West of Amman

Syria, it is the best example in the Middle East of a Roman provincial city and is remarkably well preserved.

The modern town of Jerash, which lies on the east bank of a small tributary of the Zarqa River, has a sizeable population of Circassians who were settled here by the Turkish authorities late last century.

The main ruins of Jerash are on the west of the same stream and were rediscovered in 1806 by a German traveller, Ulrich Seetzen. Restoration work began in 1925 under the British Mandate, and three years later the first excavations were carried out. Prior to that most of the city was buried under sand, which accounts for the good condition of many of the buildings.

In its heyday it is estimated that Jerash had a population of around 15,000 and, although it wasn't on any of the main trade routes, its citizens prospered from the good corn-growing land which surrounds it. The ancient city preserved today was the administrative, civic and commercial centre of Jerash, the bulk of the inhabitants lived on the east side of Wadi Jerash.

Excavations have revealed two theatres, an unusual oval-shaped forum, temples, churches, a market place and baths. Restoration work continues on various parts of the site. Despite its importance, there's usually not more than a handful of people there at any one time, including a few locals flogging 'antiquities' – exercise the usual sceptical caution. It's open daily, except Friday, from 9 am till dark and entry is 500 fils.

History

Although there have been finds to indicate that the site was inhabited in Neolithic times, it was from the time of Alexander the Great (332 BC) that the city really rose to prominence.

In 63 BC the Roman emperor Pompey conquered the region and Jerash became part of the Roman province of Syria and, soon after, one of the cities of the Decapolis. Over the next two centuries trade was established with the Nabataeans and the city became extremely wealthy. Local agriculture and iron-ore mining in the Ajlun area contributed to the city's economic wellbeing. A completely new plan was drawn up in the 1st century AD and it centred on the typical feature of a colonnaded main street intersected by two side streets.

With Emperor Trajan's exploits around 106 BC, which saw the annexation of the Nabataean kingdom and even more wealth finding its way to Jerash, many of these new buildings were torn down to be replaced by even more imposing structures.

In 129 AD, when the emperor Hadrian visited and stayed for some time, the town administration went into top gear again. To mark a visit of such importance, the Triumphal Arch at the southern end of the city was constructed.

Jerash reached its peak in the beginning of the 3rd century when it was bestowed with the rank of Colony, but from then on it went into a slow eclipse. With the overland caravans now defunct because of the sea trade and disturbances in the area such as the destruction of Palmyra in 273 AD, the decline continued steadily. The only respite was during the reign of Diocletian (circa 300 AD), which saw a minor building boom.

By the middle of the 5th century, Christianity had become the major religion of the region and the construction of churches proceeded at a startling rate. During the reign of Justinian (527-565 AD) no less than seven churches were built, mostly out of stones filched from the earlier pagan temples and shrines. No more churches were built after 611.

With the Persian invasion of 614 and the Muslim conquest of 636, followed by a series of earthquakes in 747, Jerash was

Triumphal Arch

really on the skids and its population shrunk to about 25% of its former size.

Apart from a brief occupation by a Crusader garrison in the 12th century, the city was completely deserted up until the arrival of the Circassians in 1878. Conservation and restoration begun in 1925 continue today.

Information

There's a Visitors Centre with a souvenir shop and post office, and a Government Rest House which sells refreshments. There used to be a nightly sound & light performance at 8.30 pm, but at the time of writing it was not being put on. There are several souvenir stands just outside the South Gate. Prices for maps and books are fairly standard.

The Ruins

Approaching from Amman, the **Triumphal Arch** is first to come into view. Although its present height is daunting, it was twice as high when it was first built. One unusual feature of the construction is the wreaths of carved acanthus leaves above the bases of the pillars, which look like they'd be more at home on the top.

Behind the arch is the **hippodrome**, the

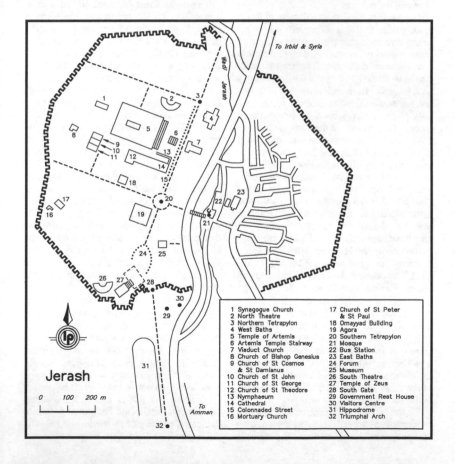

Jerash

0   100   200 m

To Irbid & Syria

To Amman

1 Synagogue Church
2 North Theatre
3 Northern Tetrapylon
4 West Baths
5 Temple of Artemis
6 Artemis Temple Stairway
7 Viaduct Church
8 Church of Bishop Genesius
9 Church of St Cosmos
   & St Damianus
10 Church of St John
11 Church of St George
12 Church of St Theodore
13 Nymphaeum
14 Cathedral
15 Colonnaded Street
16 Mortuary Church
17 Church of St Peter
   & St Paul
18 Omayyad Building
19 Agora
20 Southern Tetrapylon
21 Mosque
22 Bus Station
23 East Baths
24 Forum
25 Museum
26 South Theatre
27 Temple of Zeus
28 South Gate
29 Government Rest House
30 Visitors Centre
31 Hippodrome
32 Triumphal Arch

old sports field that used to be surrounded by seating that held up to 15,000 spectators. Some of the seating has been restored in ongoing conservation work. The 244 by 50 metre pitch hosted mainly athletics competitions and, as its name suggests, horse races.

The entrance to the main site is from behind the Government Rest House which is about 50 metres outside the **South Gate**. The gate, originally one of four in the 3500-metre-long city wall (little of which remains to be seen), also bears the acanthus leaf decoration of the Triumphal Arch. It is thought that a new city quarter was planned between the two gates.

Once inside the gate, the **Temple of Zeus** is the ruined building on the left. It is being restored to its former glory, when a flight of stairs supported by vaults led up to it from a lower sacred enclosure. The temple itself was built in the latter part of the 2nd century on a holy site from earlier times. The lower level or *temenos* had an altar and served as a holy place of sacrifice. Of the temple itself, there is little to see but the outer walls.

The **Forum** is unusual because of its oval shape, and some attribute this to the desire to link gracefully the main north-south axis *(cardo* – the standard Roman main street) with the existing Hellenistic sacred site of the Zeus temple or its predecessor. In fact, some historians dispute that it was a forum (market place) in the strict sense, suggesting it too may have been a place of sacrifice connected to the temple. The reconstructed Ionic columns surrounding it are an impressive sight. The centre is paved with limestone and other softer blocks. It is believed the podium in the centre was the base for a statue.

The **South Theatre**, behind the Temple of Zeus, was built in the 1st century and could once hold 5000 spectators. The back of the stage was originally two storeys high and has now been rebuilt to the first level. From the top of the seats you can get an excellent view of the ruins with the modern town of Jerash in the background.

On the far side of the Forum the cardo, or **colonnaded street**, stretches for more than 600 metres to the North Gate. The street is still paved with the original stones and the ruts worn by thousands of chariots over the years can be clearly seen. The columns on the west side are of uneven height and were built that way to complement the facades of the buildings that once stood behind them.

At the two main intersections ornamental *tetrapyla* were built. The **Southern Tetrapylon** consisted of four bases, each supporting four pillars topped by a statue. Only the bases have been rebuilt, of which the south-eastern one is the most complete. The intersection was made into a circular plaza at the end of the 3rd century.

The cross street *(decumanus)* runs east, downhill to a bridge spanning the small river and on to the **Eastern Baths**, just behind the present bus station, and west to a gate in the city wall. On the left, before this cross street, is the city's recently restored **Agora**. There was a fountain in the middle.

The steps of the 4th century **cathedral** (so-called, although there is little proof it was more than another church) are on the left, about 100 metres after the intersection. The gate and steps actually cover the remains of an earlier temple to the Nabataean god Dhushara.

Behind the Cathedral lies the **Church of St Theodore**, built in 496 AD, and between the two a large courtyard with fountain. Just south of the church lies an **Omayyad Building**, the existence of which supports the theory that the newly arrived Muslims lived in reasonable harmony with the city's earlier, largely Christian inhabitants.

Next along the cardo is the **Nymphaeum**, the main ornamental fountain of the city and a temple to the Nymphs. Built in 191 AD, the two-storey construction was elaborately decorated and faced with marble slabs on the lower level and plastered and painted on the upper level. Water used to cascade over the facade into a large pool at the front and the overflow from this went out through carved lions' heads to drains in the street below.

Next on the left is the most imposing building on the site, the **Temple of Artemis**, dedicated to the patron goddess of the city. After the Great Gate of the temple come two flights of stairs leading up to the courtyard where the temple stands. Large vaults had to be built to the north and south of the temple to make the courtyard level. Originally, the temple was surrounded by pillars but only the double rows at the front remain, as they and much of the material of which the temple was built were taken and reused in later buildings, such as the churches. The temple was fortified by the Arabs in the 12th century, but this work was destroyed by the Crusaders. The grand entrance off the cardo is now being restored by an Italian team.

Back on the main street, opposite the Great Gate, is the **Viaduct Church** built over what was once the road leading up to the Temple of Artemis. Further up the main street is the second major intersection and the **Northern Tetrapylon**, dedicated to the Syrian wife of the Emperor Septimus Severus. This was different from the southern one in that it consisted of four arches surmounted by a dome.

The **West Baths** are just downhill from the northern tetrapylon. Dating back to the 2nd century, they represent one of the earliest examples of a dome being put on a square room. It's all a bit of a jumble today.

The **North Theatre**, just to the west of the tetrapylon, is smaller than the south theatre and is only beginning to look itself after much restoration that is still to be completed. From the Northern Tetrapylon it is about 200 metres to the **North Gate** but this stretch is now just a mass of stones and weeds.

Just to the south of the Temple of Artemis lie the ruins of a number of **churches**. In all, 13 have been uncovered and it is widely believed that there are more to be found. To the west of the church of St Theodore are the churches of St Cosmos & St Damianus, St John and St George. They were all built around 530 AD and opened on to one another. The floors of all three were finely decorated with mosaics, some of which you can still see in St Cosmos and St Damianus and also in the Traditional Jewels & Costumes Museum in Amman. Little remains of the other churches.

In the tiny **museum** just to the east of the

Forum is a good selection of artefacts from the site, ranging from pottery theatre tickets to jewellery, glass and Mamluk coins such as the *tetradrachma*. The main attraction is the gold jewellery and coins found in a family tomb near the Triumphal Arch. The staff are friendly and will show you around if you want.

The whole site takes a good few hours to wander around and absorb and one can only imagine what it would be like if the other 90% of it were excavated!

Places to Stay & Eat

Surprisingly perhaps, there is no hotel in Jerash. However, its proximity to Amman makes it an easy day trip or you could go on to stay at Ajlun, but be warned that the cheapest single on offer there is JD7.

The *Government Rest House* by the entrance has an expensive restaurant but it costs nothing to sit in the air-con cool and have a glass of cold water. Do not eat here if you can avoid it. A piece of meat on a slice of khobz, with chips and a cooked tomato constitute a hamburger – and costs JD1.100! A soft drink goes for 350 fils.

The bus station has the usual collection of cafés selling the usual felafel and shawarma.

For something a bit better, try the *Lebanese House Restaurant* – head to the southern end of town on the road that skirts the site, go right at the roundabout and take a left at the sign to the restaurant, another km or so.

Getting There & Away

The minibus and service-taxi station is right by the Eastern Baths. From Amman, take a service-taxi (45 minutes, 650 fils) or minibus (350 fils) from Abdali bus station, or hitch from the Suweileh roundabout.

From Jerash, there are minibuses to Irbid (290 fils), Mafraq (270 fils) and Ajlun (170 fils), 25 km to the west.

If you're staying at Jerash after about 5 pm, be prepared to hitch back to Amman as all transport stops running soon after that. The Tourist Police, who for the most part hide in the air-con Visitors Centre, may help by flagging down a car for you.

AJLUN

The trip to Ajlun, 22 km to the west of Jerash, goes through some beautiful small pine forests and olive groves.

The attraction of the town is the **Qala'at ar-Rabad**, built by the Arabs as protection against the Crusaders. The castle is a fine example of Islamic military architecture. It stands on a hill two km to the west of the town and from the top you get fantastic views of the Jordan Valley to the west. It's a tough uphill walk but there are minibuses (in this case called service-taxis) to the top for 50 fils or you can take a taxi for 500 fils one way.

It was built by one of Saladin's generals and nephews, 'Izz ad-Din Urama bin Munqidh, in 1184-85 and enlarged in 1214. It commands not only the Jordan Valley but three wadis leading to it – the Kufranjah, Rajeb and Al-Yabes – making it an important strategic link in the defensive chain against the Crusaders, and a counter to their fort Belvoir on the Sea of Galilee (Lake Tiberias). With its hill-top position it was one in a chain of beacons and pigeon posts that allowed messages to be transmitted from the Euphrates to Cairo in the space of a day.

After the Crusader threat subsided, it was largely destroyed by Mongol invaders in 1260, only to be almost immediately rebuilt by the Mamluk Sultan Baibars. An Ottoman garrison was stationed there in the 17th century, after which it fell into disuse. Earthquakes in 1837 and 1927 damaged it badly, but it has since been partly restored.

The castle is quite well preserved and open seven days a week. There is no entry fee and the Jordanian Department of Antiquities rep is more than happy to show you around.

In the town of Ajlun itself, the only thing of interest is the mosque in the centre. Its minaret is said to date back some 600 years.

Places to Stay & Eat

There are two hotels along the way up from the town to the castle. The first and more expensive is the *Al-Rabad Castle Hotel* (☎ 462202), about 500 metres before the castle. It has very comfortable rooms (no fans though) and commanding views of the valley and town but the prices are just as stunning – JD14/17.800 for singles/doubles with bath and balcony. The manager is willing to come down a few dinars. There is a pleasant restaurant and pergola at the front.

About 100 metres further up is the more austere *Ajlun Hotel & Restaurant* (☎ 462524). Rooms go for JD7/12 with bath, heating and balcony. They know the competition and aren't much interested in bargaining on price.

It may be possible to stay at the Christian college two km back towards Jerash but don't count on this.

If you have your own tent, it is possible to camp in the small patch of forest just to the west of the castle. Take the track to the right 50 metres before the castle, pass the Al-Rabadh restaurant and after the second concrete shed, there's a small track off to the right. Watch out for old gaping cisterns and the occasional ant nest.

It's good advice to pass by the *Al-Rabadh* restaurant. They have the nerve to ask 500 fils for a coke and the only food on offer is a tomato and egg salad! If you bring your own food, join the locals for a picnic around the base of the castle. There is a drinks stand by the entrance.

The *Green Mountain Restaurant*, by the traffic roundabout in the centre, has – surprise, surprise – roast chicken, hummus, salad and bread. Next door is the *Abu 'Az* café. There are a couple of felafel and shawarma joints around the bus station.

The *Ajlun Tourist Park*, where you can sit down for a meal of kebabs and a beer, is on the left-hand side of the road about one km on the Jerash side of Ajlun. It has a beautiful view of the castle across the valley.

Getting There & Away

There are regular minibuses from Jerash for 170 fils (25 km and about half an hour) or direct from Amman for 500 fils (1½ hours). At a push it would be possible to go from

Amman to Jerash and Ajlun and on to Irbid in one day.

To get to Irbid, minibuses costs 250 fils for the 45-minute trip. On working days there are also large air-con buses, for which competition is keen in the mornings with all the students heading off to Yarmouk University in Irbid.

IRBID

Although artefacts and graves in the area show Irbid has been inhabited since the Bronze Age, it has little to offer the visitor. However, it is a handy base for making the trip out to Umm Qais and Al-Hemma, right up on the Syrian border with views of the Golan Heights and the Sea of Galilee, as well as to Pella.

The university on the south of town was the scene of some unrest in early 1986, when students demonstrated against the lack of student participation in the running of the university. In the ensuing clash with police, three of the demonstrators were trampled to death. The riot was seen as part of a growing resentment in the country at the lack of participation in government, which culminated in the price-hike riots of April 1989. The country's first full general elections with universal suffrage were held in November 1986.

Information

Money There is no problem changing money as most of the big banks are represented in the centre of town. You can get Visa cash advances at the Jordan Arab Investment Bank on the 1st floor of the same building as the Al-Umayya Hotel on Palestine St.

Things to See

Not much is the short answer, but there are two museums at the university. From the main entrance walk straight up the main thoroughfare about 200 metres. Off to the right is the **Museum of Jordanian Heritage**, open from 10 am to 5 pm in winter, to 3 pm in summer, daily except Tuesdays. It is considered the best archaeological museum in the country, with modern displays far

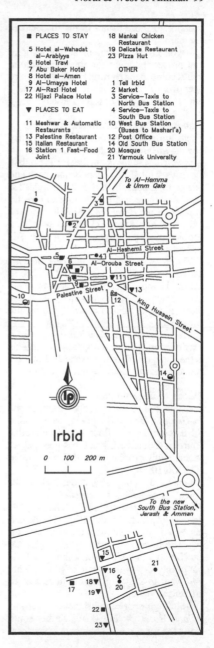

■ PLACES TO STAY	18 Mankal Chicken Restaurant
5 Hotel al-Wahadat al-Arablyya	19 Delicate Restaurant
6 Hotel Travl	23 Pizza Hut
7 Abu Baker Hotel	
8 Hotel al-Amen	OTHER
9 Al-Umayya Hotel	1 Tell Irbid
17 Al-Razi Hotel	2 Market
22 Hijazi Palace Hotel	3 Service-Taxis to North Bus Station
▼ PLACES TO EAT	4 Service-Taxis to South Bus Station
11 Meshwar & Automatic Restaurants	10 West Bus Station (Buses to Mashari'a)
13 Palestine Restaurant	12 Post Office
15 Italian Restaurant	14 Old South Bus Station
16 Station 1 Fast-Food Joint	20 Mosque
	21 Yarmouk University

Irbid

0   100   200 m

To Al-Hemma & Umm Qais

Al-Hashemi Street
Al-Orouba Street
Palestine Street
King Hussein Street

To the new South Bus Station, Jerash & Amman

superior to those found in the museum in Amman.

If you go back to the main thoroughfare and proceed straight towards the stadium, you'll come to the **Natural History** museum, open from 8 am to 5 pm in winter and to 3 pm in summer, daily except Tuesdays.

Places to Stay – bottom end

There are a few sleazy hotels in the busy downtown area. The best is the *Hotel al-Wahadat al-Arabiyya*, but the sign in English just says 'Hotel'. It's friendly and clean and you can get beds for JD1.500 or singles for JD3. A shower is 500 fils. Almost directly opposite is the *Hotel Travl* (sic). It offers the same deal but is not as clean and even local shopkeepers point you back to the Al-Wahadat.

The *Hotel al-Amen* (pronounced 'ameen') has basic rooms, again for JD1.500 a bed in a shared room. There are hot showers (500 fils), some rooms have fans and you can use their fridge and stove. The staff are also quite friendly.

The entrance to the *Abu Baker Hotel* is up a stairway with a Jordan Bank sign on it. This is the cheapest place in town at JD1.500 for bed and shower. Some rooms have fans.

Places to Stay – middle

For something a bit more up-market, try the *Al-Umayya Hotel* (☎ 245955) on Palestine St. It is on the 2nd floor above the Jordan Arab Investment Bank and has good, clean rooms with ensuite bath, TV and fan at JD8.500/10.

Out by the university, about 100 metres down a side street opposite the mosque, is the *Al-Razi Hotel* (☎ 275515). It has singles/doubles/triples for JD12/16/20 plus 10% tax, but they may come down with some bargaining. The rooms are clean and airy, with TV and fan. It's in a nice spot, although a little out of the way (if the centre of Irbid is what you want to see), and mostly houses more affluent students.

Irbid's premier establishment, the *Hijazi Palace Hotel* (☎ 279500) is further south along the main road. It has three to four-star service with rooms for JD30/48 a single/double.

Places to Eat

There is a huddle of felafel and shawarma stands around the Hotel Travl. For something different, the *Meshwar Restaurant* near the roundabout by the post office does all sorts of filled sandwiches for 250 fils. Some look a little off-putting, but for a tasty change from felafel and shawarma, try their 'fish sandwich'. This bright and cheery place also sells fresh juices for 100 fils.

Next door is the more conventional *Automatic Restaurant* where you can get the usual kebabs, half chicken and salad. You can also get a beer. The *Al-Saadi* across the road from the Al-Umayya Hotel is similar.

If it's just a drink you want, there is not a bad bar around the corner from the Meshwar. The *Palestine* does fairly standard fare and doubles as a tea room.

Out by the university there is a plethora of eateries, and the area seems to be the liveliest part of Irbid. Turn left when leaving the university's main entrance and you hit a main road. On the corner is an *Italian restaurant* and there are a few more places heading north. On the corner turning south is *Station 1*, a fast-food joint just by the mosque. For chicken, try the *Mankal*, across the road and a bit further south. Next door is a pizza place – the *Delicate*! If this sounds dubious but it's a pizza you want, walk on down past the Hijazi Palace and you'll find a Western favourite – *Pizza Hut*.

Getting There & Away

Bus/Minibus Irbid has four bus stations. The northern one is about a 20-minute walk from the centre; alternatively, a service-taxi runs past it from near the souq for 60 fils. There are minibuses from this bus station to Umm Qais (45 minutes, 220 fils) and Al-Hemma (one hour, 280 fils).

The old south bus station is no longer of much interest to travellers, servicing only a few local destinations, and should not be confused with the main bus station to the south-east of town.

From the new south bus station (ask for the *mujama' Amman al-jadeed)* there are air-con Hijazi buses to Amman's Abdali bus station. They leave every 15 to 20 minutes until about 6.30 pm for 850 fils. You buy seated tickets at the office and the trip takes about 1½ hours, depending on the traffic. Alternatively, there are minibuses till about 8.30 pm (about two hours, 530 fils) and service-taxis (two hours, JD1). There are also minibuses to Ajlun (45 minutes, 250 fils), Ramtha (see below) and Mafraq.

From the west bus station, off Palestine St and near the town centre, there are minibuses to Al-Mashari'a (1½ hours, 300 fils), within walking distance of the Roman city of Pella in the northern Jordan Valley. From Al-Mashari'a you can also get to any other Jordan Valley destination.

To/From Syria If you want to go direct to Damascus there are Syrian service-taxis operating out of the new south bus station. The trip takes three to four hours depending on border formalities and costs JD4 or S£300.

To cross on your own, take a minibus from the same bus station to Ramtha (or Ar-Ramtha), the last town before the Jordanian border post, for 100 fils. You can then hitch the couple of km to the border post, and after the formalities the soldiers will flag down a vehicle to take you to the Syrian side. Once you're through there, it's a three or four-km walk or hitch to Der'a, the first town, from where there are buses to Damascus and Bosra.

Alternatively, you can get a service-taxi from Ramtha to Der'a for JD2 or S£125.

If you're coming from Syria, you can follow the same options in reverse. Once in Ramtha, you can take the minibus to Irbid and another to Amman, or a minibus to Hammamat Ma'in via Mafraq for 500 fils. From Hammamat Ma'in there are town buses and minibuses (80 to 120 fils) that take you the 20 km to Downtown Amman. If it doesn't stop at Raghadan bus station, jump out at the King Hussein Mosque.

Getting Around
Many people may want to use Irbid as a staging post for heading elsewhere (it is quite possible to get to Umm Qais and Al-Hemma via Irbid in one long day), and you can get from one bus station to the other without getting caught up in the town at all. There are service-taxis (often in the form of minibuses) that run between all the stations and the middle of town. Service-taxis leave from near the souq to the north bus station for 60 fils.

From the main drag, Al-Hashemi St, there are service-taxis to the new south bus station (that normally run past the old one, too) for 80 fils. There are also taxis and minibuses to Yarmouk University from near the same spot for 50 fils. The north, west and new south bus stations are all linked by the same kind of service-taxi (the ride costs 100 fils), so you need never stop in town itself.

UMM QAIS
Right in the corner of Jordan, 30 km northwest of Irbid, is Umm Qais, with views over the Golan Heights and the Sea of Galilee (Lake Tiberias) to the north and the Jordan Valley to the south.

This is the site of the ancient Graeco-Roman town of Gadara, one of the cities of the Decapolis and, according to the Bible, the place where Jesus cast out the devil from two men into a herd of pigs (Matthew 8: 28-34).

The city was captured from the Ptolemies by the Seleucids in 198 BC, and the Jews under Hyrcanus captured it from them in 100BC. When the Romans (led by Pompey) conquered the East and the Decapolis was formed, the fortunes of Gadara, taken from the Jews in 63 BC, increased rapidly and building was undertaken on a typically large scale.

The Nabataeans controlled the trade routes as far north as Damascus. This interference with Rome's interests led Mark Antony to send Herod the Great to conquer them. The Nabataean king was finally overcome in 31 BC. Herod was given Gadara following a naval victory and he ruled over it until his death in 4 BC, much to the disgust of the locals who had tried everything, in vain, to put him out of favour with Rome. On his death, the city reverted to semi-autonomy as part of the Roman province of Syria.

Gadara continued to flourish with the downfall of the Nabataean kingdom at the hands of Trajan in 106 AD, and was the seat of a bishopric until the 7th century. By the time of the Arab conquest, however, it was little more than a small village. Since 1974, German and Danish teams have been excavating and restoring the site.

Things to See

Just after the town, on the way down to Al-Hemma, turn off on a dirt track pointing to the Government Rest House. On a rise to the left (once the acropolis?) stands an old Ottoman building, Bayt Rusan, now converted into a small **museum**. Open from 8 am to 5 pm (4 pm in winter) and closed on Tuesday (entrance free), it contains artefacts and mosaics from the area. One of the mosaics, a 4th century example found in one of the town's mausoleums, is one of the most interesting exhibits, overshadowed perhaps by the headless, white marble statue of a goddess that was found sitting in the front row of the **Western Theatre**.

The theatre, in a sorry state of repair, can be found on the other side of the Government Rest House, further past the museum down the track that shows signs of better days as a Roman road. It has incredible views out over the Sea of Galilee.

Next to it is a **colonnaded street** that was once probably the town's commercial centre. The theatre and some of the columns are made of black basalt, as indeed are many of the modern homes in the area, built by vandalising the ancient ruins. Further west along what's left of the main Roman street, are a **mausoleum** and then **baths** on the right and, further along still, another mausoleum on the left. A few hundred metres more take you to the barely visible contours of what was once a hippodrome.

Al-Hemma

The baths of Al-Hemma are a further 10 km from Umm Qais, down the hill towards the Yarmouk River and Golan. The area near the river and springs is a lush green, in stark contrast to the bare, steeply rising plateau of the Israeli-occupied Golan to the north, where you can see the occasional jeep patrol on the other side.

The baths were famous in Roman times for their health-giving properties and are still used today, but you have to be keen to want to jump into the smelly water. If you do, there are separate timetables for men and women.

Places to Stay & Eat

There is nowhere to stay in Umm Qais, and precious few places to eat outside the expensive *Government Rest House* and a few small shops. In Al-Hemma, there is a hotel by the baths with rooms for JD7, and a terrace café.

Getting There & Away

There are regular minibuses to Umm Qais from Irbid for 220 fils (45 minutes) and to Al-Hemma for 280 fils (one hour). From Umm Qais, just wait by the side of the road for a passing minibus or hitch a ride with another vehicle. You need your passport for the trip down as there's a military control point on the edge of Umm Qais and at least one other closer to Al-Hemma.

UMM AL-JIMAL

Comparatively little is known about this strange, black city in the south of the Hauran (also called Jebel Druze), only about 10 km from the Syrian border and about 20 km east of Mafraq.

It is thought to have been founded in about the 2nd century AD and formed part of the defensive line of Rome's Arab possessions. Roads lead north to Bosra (in present-day Syria) and south-west to Amman (Philadelphia) and it served as an important trading station for Bedouins and passing caravans. The town, which may have had as many as 10,000 inhabitants in its heyday, continued to flourish into Omayyad times, but was destroyed by an earthquake in 747 and never recovered.

Things to See

Much of what remains, some of it more interesting for archaeologists than tourists, is simple urban architecture – ordinary peoples' houses and shops. When you enter the site, the first big building with a square tower has been identified as a **barracks** and **church** combined. The most easily identifiable building, with its four arches, is the **western church**. Between the two is a **cathedral** on the right (looking towards the western church) and what has been called the **Praetorium** on the left.

Getting There & Away

It is possible to do the trip in a day from Amman, from where you would take a local bus or minibus to Hammamat Ma'in (80 to 120 fils), a minibus from there to Mafraq (350 fils) and from there another for 200 fils. By car, you head away from Mafraq on Highway 5 towards As-Safawi where the other main road east from Amman via Azraq joins up on its desolate way to Baghdad. There is little reason for heading out this way, but should you want to, a minibus from Mafraq to as-Safawi costs 800 fils.

The Jordan Valley

Forming part of the Great Rift Valley of Africa, the fertile valley of the Jordan River was of great significance in Biblical times and is now the food bowl of Jordan.

The river rises from several sources, mainly the Anti-Lebanon Mountains in Syria, and flows down into the Sea of Galilee (Lake Tiberias), 212 metres below sea level, before draining into the Dead Sea which, at 392 metres below sea level, is the lowest point on earth. The actual length of the river is 360 km, but as the crow flies the distance between its source and the Dead Sea is only 200 km.

It was in this valley some 10,000 years ago that people first started to plant crops and abandon the nomadic lifestyle for permanent settlements. Villages were built, primitive water-harnessing schemes were undertaken and by 3000 BC, produce from the valley was being exported to neighbouring regions. The river itself is highly revered by Christians because Christ was baptised by St John the Baptist in its waters.

Since 1948, the Jordan River has marked the boundary between Israel and Jordan from the Sea of Galilee to the Yarbis River. From there to the Dead Sea the river marks the 1967 cease-fire line between the two countries.

In the 1967 war with Israel, Jordan lost the land it had annexed in 1950, the area known as the West Bank. The population on the east bank of the valley dwindled from 60,000 before the war to 5000 by 1971. During the '70s new roads and fully serviced villages were built and the population has now soared to over 100,000. There are no cities along the river course although the Roman city of Pella (Tabaqat Fahl) used to occupy a commanding position on the eastern bank.

Ambitious irrigation projects such as the East Ghor (now King Abdullah) Canal, which was extended in the late '80s and early '90s, have brought substantial areas under irrigation. Plans are under way to construct a new dam at Karameh, 50 km from Amman, which would irrigate another large area of new agricultural land. The giant Al-Wahda dam project with Syria on the Yarmouk River has been stalled because international investors won't chip in without Israeli approval of the project.

The hot dry summers and short mild winters make for ideal growing conditions and two or even three crops a year are grown. Thousands of tons of fruit and vegetables are produced annually, with the main crops being tomatoes, cucumbers, melons and citrus fruits. The introduction of portable plastic greenhouses saw a seven-fold increase in productivity and this has meant that Jordan can now afford to export large amounts of produce to surrounding countries.

Apart from the Dead Sea and Pella, there

is little to attract the visitor to the valley today, although Deir Alla might also be of interest to budding archaeologists.

DEIR ALLA

The site of Deir Alla, 35 km north of South Shuneh, is to the left of the main road heading north. Although there is little to see today, the site is of historical importance. According to the Old Testament book of Joshua, Jacob is said to have rested here after wrestling with an angel and named the place Succoth – some archaeologists have cast doubt on this claim.

An impressive sanctuary was built on the small *tell* (hill) around 1500 BC. It was in use up until 1200 BC when it was abandoned after being destroyed, some say by earthquake, others by Egyptian troops. Dutch archaeologists excavating the site have found figurines and incense burners on the site which appears to have been a temple.

Deir Alla was a Persian settlement in the 3rd century BC, but it was later abandoned until the Arab era when it served as a cemetery for nearby villages. There is a sign up at the base of the tell indicating what there was to see.

Places to Eat

Even if you are disappointed by the site, the friendly old couple in the dusty restaurant over the road will serve up a filling meal of felafel, salad, eggs, bread and a couple of Pepsis for just 500 fils for two.

Getting There & Away

There is a direct minibus from Abdali bus station in Amman, but it doesn't leave very often (370 fils). Failing that, catch another minibus heading for Suwalha (370 fils – not to be confused with Suweileh), which is an important minibus interchange along the valley, a few km south of Deir Alla. From here you can get buses to any destination (you may have to change once or twice along the way) north or south along the valley.

If you're coming from South Shuneh, take the Al-Karama minibus (70 fils) and change

there for Deir Alla (200 fils). You can also make the trip down from Al-Mashari'a.

PELLA

Another 30 km north of Deir Alla, near the village of Al-Mashari'a, are the ruins of the ancient city of Pella (Tabaqat Fahl), two km east of the road. It is a steep walk up to the site, and the heat can be punishing in summer, so get some water at one of the shops in Al-Mashari'a before heading up.

Although the site was inhabited from as early as 5000 BC, and Egyptian texts make several references to it in the 2nd millennium BC, it was during the Graeco-Roman period that Pella flourished. The city's original name, Pehel, appears to have been altered to that of the birthplace of Alexander the Great. Pella followed the fate of many other cities in the region, coming successively under the rule of the Ptolemies, the Seleucids and the Jews who largely destroyed Pella in 83 BC because its inhabitants were not inclined to adopt the customs of their conquerors.

Pella was one of the cities of the Decapolis, the commercial league of 10 cities formed by Pompey after his conquest of Syria and Palestine in 64 BC. It was to Pella that Christians fled persecution from the Roman army in Jerusalem in the 2nd century AD.

The city reached its peak during the Byzantine era and by 451 AD there was a Bishop of Pella. Its population at this time is estimated to have been about 25,000. It was a popular bathing place, and the locals still enjoy a splash around in the cool springs of Wadi Al-Jirm. The defeat of the Byzantines by the invading Arab armies near the city in 635 was quickly followed by the knockout blow at the Battle of Yarmouk the next year.

There is strong evidence that, until the massive earthquake that shook the whole region in 747, the city of Fahl (its Arabic name) continued to prosper under Omayyad Arab rule. Archaeological finds show that even after the earthquake the city remained inhabited on a modest scale. The Mamluks occupied it in the 13th and 14th centuries, but afterwards the town was all but abandoned until the 19th century.

In 1967 American excavations began. They were joined by an Australian team in 1978, which has since taken over the bulk of the work. Although it will never throw up classical monuments to the extent of, say, Jerash, it is a far more important site as it has revealed evidence of life from the Stone Age through to medieval Islam.

Things to See

The first building on the site you'll see emerges on the left of the track. Dubbed the **West Church**, it was built in the 6th century – you'll know it by its three standing columns. After passing through an area still under excavation, you'll pass the archaeologists' dig house on the left before coming to a graveyard and the remains of a 14th century Mamluk mosque. Further off to the left is a Byzantine cistern which was capable of holding 300,000 litres of water.

You then approach an area known drily as the 'main mound'. Here is a maze of houses, shops, store houses and the like. If you look across the valley, you can see a new building with three arches – the new Government Rest House (what else?). Down below to the right lies a concentration of Byzantine and Roman structures, the most important of the city's public buildings.

Right next to the imposing **Civic Complex Church**, built in the 6th and 7th centuries, is a small 1st century *odeon* or **Theatre**, which sits on the Wadi Al-Jirm. Just east of the church are the remains of a Roman **Nymphaeum**, or baths, and further east again, perched up on a rise, is the **East Church**. To the south is **Tell Hosn**, on top of which was a Byzantine fort. To the west of the cathedral rise up imposing remnants of Bronze Age city walls.

Getting There & Away

From Irbid you can catch an Al-Mashari'a minibus from the west bus station. From Amman, take a minibus for Suwalha and change for Al-Mashari'a. You can also catch a series of minibuses up the valley from South Shuneh or down from North Shuneh.

Hitching is also a possibility.

THE DEAD SEA

The Dead Sea (Al-Bahr al-Mayit or Bahr Lut – the Sea of Lot) is 75 km long and from six to 16 km wide and has no outlet. The name becomes obvious when you realise that the high salt content (33%) makes any plant and animal life impossible. The concentration of salt has nothing to do with it being below sea level but comes about because of the high evaporation rate which has, over the years, led to the build up of salts. Despite the fact that the Jordan River flows into the sea, the actual level of the sea is falling as more and more water is diverted from the river each year for irrigation.

Whatever the reason for the salt build up, it certainly makes for an unusual swimming experience. The higher density of the water makes your body more buoyant, so drowning or sinking is virtually impossible. Swimming is also just about impossible as you're too high in the water to be able to stroke properly, but of course you can always float on your back while reading the newspaper and get your picture taken. While swimming you will probably discover cuts

that you never knew you had as the water gets into them and stings like crazy, and if any water gets into your eyes, be prepared for a few minutes of agony. After a dip in the Dead Sea you are left with a mighty uncomfortable, itchy coating of salt on your skin which you can't get off quick enough – don't swim where there are no showers or freshwater springs.

At the southern end of the sea the Jordanians have started to exploit the high potash content of the mineral-rich water. Vast evaporation ponds covering some 10,000 hectares were built and each day over one million tons of water are pumped into them. The concentrated potash salts are then refined at the processing plant south of Safi.

The project is now producing more than 1.4 million tons of potash annually, making Jordan one of the world's largest producers. However, with world prices failing to reach the levels predicted in feasibility studies, the project has not been the money spinner that had been hoped for. In 1990, however, the Arab Potash Company made a profit of US$60 million and paid its first dividend. It is planning expansion of its projects and hopes to push production up to 1.8 million tons by the end of 1993.

Places to Stay & Eat

The 'resort' at Suweimeh is where most people go for a float on the east (Jordanian) bank of the Dead Sea. The government-owned *Dead Sea Rest House* here provides day-trippers with showers, changing rooms and an air-con restaurant. The prices in the restaurant are high so bring something to eat if you are staying for the day.

Entry to the resort costs 500 fils; it's another 250 fils for a shower (bring your own soap) and yet another 250 fils if you want a cabin to change in. The resort gets crowded

on Fridays and Sundays, and there are no showers after sunset.

An all-body Dead Sea mud pack, which is supposed to do wonders for your skin, will cost you JD1. Women are advised to insist on applying their own mud.

If you have your own vehicle there is a better place to swim about 10 km south of Suweimeh. Here there are hot, freshwater springs gushing out by the shore, so you can have a swim and then sit under a hot waterfall or in the tepid pools.

Although you may be able to doss down for the night at the Suweimeh resort, the only hotel option is the *Dead Sea Spa Hotel*, not far from the springs. It costs JD6 just to walk in and use their bit of beach and pool, and another JD8 for lunch. The rooms are well beyond the average traveller's budget.

Getting There & Away

You can get to the Dead Sea direct from Amman by the minibus (550 fils) that leaves from Jerusalem St. There are not many of these, and the last one back to Amman leaves about 4 pm. They go right to the resort.

There are more frequent buses to South Shuneh (ash-Shuneh al-Junubiyyeh) for 400 fils. From there another minibus leaves about every half an hour for Suweimeh. The trip costs 200 fils, which for some odd reason they like you to pay in 100 fils instalments, the second of them about halfway. This drops you about one km away – follow the sign to the rest house. You can also get to South Shuneh from Salt.

Fridays and Sundays are the best days for hitching as families head down to the sea on their day off, although many of the cars are full.

If you are going to be visiting Israel, the resorts on the western side at Ein Feshka (Occupied West Bank) and Ein Gedi (Israel) are far more accessible.

East of Amman

To the east of Amman, the stony desert plain rolls on to Iraq and Saudia Arabia. It is cut by the Trans Arabia Pipeline and the highway to Iraq, and if not for these, east Jordan would be left alone to the Bedouin. Apart from Azraq and As-Safawi, there are no towns to speak of and no points of interest except for the desert castles and a small wildlife reserve.

The Desert Castle Loop

A string of what have become known as 'castles' lies in the desert east of Amman. Most of them were built or taken over and adapted by the Damascus-based Omayyad rulers in the late 7th and early 8th centuries. Two of the castles, Azraq and Hallabat, date back to Roman times and there is even evidence of Nabataean occupation.

There are various theories about their use. The early Arab rulers were still Bedouin at heart and it is thought their love of the desert led them to build or take over these pleasure palaces, which appear to have been surrounded by artificial oases teeming with wild animals to hunt and growing fruit and vegetables.

Here they pursued their habitual pastimes of hawking, hunting and horse-racing for a few weeks each year. The evenings were apparently spent in excessive festivities with plenty of wine, women, poetry and song. Some historians believe that the caliphs only felt comfortable here about so flouting the Koran. Others say they came to avoid epidemics in the big cities or even to maintain links with, and power over, their fellow Bedouin, the bedrock of their support in the conquered lands.

The castles can be visited in a loop from Amman via Azraq and are never more than a couple of km off the road. With the exception of Qasr al-Mushatta, it is quite feasible to see all the main castles in one day using a combination of public transport and hitch-

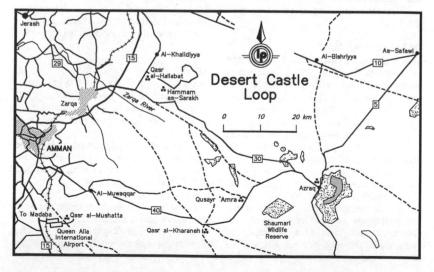

ing. There are several so far off the beaten track that only 4WDs and experienced guides will do. A private car would simplify matters.

From Amman take the road for Hammamat Ma'in and then turn off to Azraq. Qasr al-Hallabat and Hammam as-Sarakh are signposted off to the left after about 20 km. It is another seven km to Hallabat, and then a further three km to the Hammam. From here follow the same road eastwards back onto the main highway to Azraq, a further 70 km. From here an excellent new road heads back to Amman going right past the castles of Qusayr 'Amra and Qasr al-Kharanah, before joining the Desert Highway on the southern outskirts of Amman.

At one stage this road widens out and has runway markings on it! Don't panic – you haven't strayed into the airport, it's just an emergency strip should the Queen Alia International Airport be put out of action at any time. This road is incredibly busy and was built to carry the enormous trucks that (in spite of the UN embargo) still ply this backdoor route into Iraq from Aqaba, allowing them to bypass Amman. Because of the Gulf wars, most of Iraq's supplies go by this route, as did its exports and imports prior to August 1990.

QASR AL-HALLABAT

This was originally a Roman fort built during the reign of Caracalla (198-217 AD) as a defence against raiding desert tribes, although there is evidence that Trajan before him had established a post on the site of a Nabataean emplacement. During the 7th century it became a monastery and then the Omayyads further fortified it and also converted it to a pleasure palace.

Today it is a jumble of crumbling walls and fallen stone, and many of them bear Greek inscriptions. The site is sometimes locked but the custodian will wander over if you wait by the gate and let you in. He will also point out the sites of interest among the ruins. Usually though, you can just pull the bolt back and enter yourself.

HAMMAM AS-SARAKH

A few km down the road heading east is this bathhouse and hunting lodge built by the Omayyads. It has been almost completely reconstructed over the years and you can see the channels that were used for the hot water and steam. These baths often had a hot (caldarium), lukewarm (tepidarium) and cold bath (frigidarium). Here, the latter is absent.

This site is fenced off but not locked. Just use a bit of force on the stiff gate lock to get it to open. If you wait at the gate for any length of time, a self-appointed guide will appear expecting handsome payment for extremely little.

Getting There & Away

From Amman take a minibus to Hammamat Ma'in, from where you can get another to Hallabat (230 fils). The same bus drives right by the two sites. For reference's sake, the Qasr is in west Hallabat (Hallabat al-Gharbi) and the Hammam in east Hallabat (Hallabat ash-Sharqi). From the Hammam it's probably easiest to hitch to the Azraq highway and on to Azraq.

There is a minibus running between Hammamat Ma'in and Azraq for 450 fils. The trip takes about 1½ hours. You can either catch the Hallabat minibus back to Hammamat Ma'in and start again from there, or simply wait to pick up an Azraq minibus on its way past.

AZRAQ

The oasis town of Azraq is 103 km east of Amman and is the junction of the roads heading north-east to As-Safawi and on to Iraq, and the road south-east into Saudi Arabia.

To the south the wide shallow valley of the Wadi Sirhan stretches away to Saudi Arabia. This was a major caravan route and was used by T E Lawrence on his trips between Aqaba and his headquarters in the castle here.

Azraq has the only water in the whole of the eastern desert and used to be one of the most important oases in the Middle East for birds migrating between Africa and Europe. It is also home to water buffalo and other wildlife. In the past 10 years or so, the water level in the swamps has fallen drastically because of the large-scale pumping of water from wells to supply Amman with drinking water. In the 1960s the swamp in and around Azraq covered some 10 sq km; today it has been reduced to little more than a pool. The number of birds stopping here has been reduced by 95% – they now settle on the shores of the Sea of Galilee in Israel – and it has been suggested that it will cease to be an oasis if pumping is not reduced dramatically.

The water that gives the oasis life originates in Syria, filters slowly through underground streams and surfaces at Azraq. It is estimated that this process takes 10,000 years. It is not being replenished at anything like the rate that it is being used. There are plans, however, to revive the wetlands by pumping in water from northern aquifers.

The area was once home to various species of deer, bear, cheetah, ibex, oryx and gazelle. In the Shaumari Wildlife Reserve to the south-west of Azraq, an attempt is being made to reintroduce some of these animals to the area.

Qasr al-Azraq

The large castle here is built out of black basalt and in its present form dates back to the beginning of the 13th century. It was originally three storeys high, but much of this crumbled in an earthquake in 1927. Greek and Latin inscriptions date earlier constructions on the site to around 300 AD – about the time of the reign of Diocletian. The Omayyads followed and maintained it as a military base, as did the 13 century Ayyubids. In the 16th century the Ottoman Turks stationed a garrison there.

After the 16th century, the only other recorded use of the castle was during WW I when T E Lawrence made it his desert headquarters in the winter of 1917, during the Arab Revolt against the Turks. He set up his quarters in the room immediately above the southern entrance. His men used other areas of the fort and covered the gaping holes in the roof with palm branches and clay. They were holed up here for months in crowded

conditions with little shelter from the cold, of which more than one man died.

The southern door is a single massive slab of basalt and Lawrence describes how it 'went shut with a clang and crash that made tremble the west wall of the castle'. Some of the paving stones inside the door have small indentations. These were carved by former gatekeepers who played an old board game using pebbles to pass the time.

In the middle of the courtyard is a small mosque that is possibly Omayyad. Opposite the entrance are store rooms and stables, and in the north-west corner what is thought to have been a prison. The old caretaker will tell you that the remaining three-level structure in the west wall housed a Roman general.

The caretaker is a great old character, the son of one of Lawrence's Arab officers. Not only is he keen to show you around but he will also pull out some old snaps of Lawrence and a few old magazine stories about his good self.

The site is open daily and entrance is free, but this guy is really worth a tip.

Shaumari Wildlife Reserve

Established in 1975, the reserve is an attempt to reintroduce wildlife into the region that had long since disappeared. They have gone from nothing to 128 wild oryx, about 30 gazelle, 14 ostriches and other less visible bird life. There are plans to move half the oryx to a new reserve in Wadi Rum and so expand the project.

Unfortunately, you may not see much apart from the ostriches which tend to stick close to an enclosure not far from the entrance to the park. The gazelle and oryx largely roam free and, it seems, out into the desert, so although you can borrow binoculars from the park attendants and climb up a viewing tower, don't expect to see hundreds of animals – the odd gazelle and oryx may be the limit. There are also some enclosures where sick animals are kept under observation.

Entrance costs 300 fils, or 100 fils for students. They have some brochures and a tiny natural history museum in the office.

The only way to this quite small reserve, about 10 km south of the old junction in Azraq, is by car or hitching. Travel five km down the road to Saudi Arabia and turn right. After about five km what appears to be a eucalyptus copse in the stony desert rises up on the left.

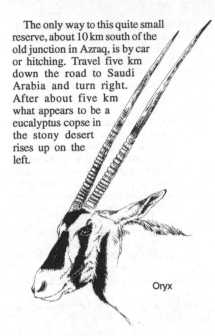

Oryx

Places to Stay & Eat

All of Azraq seems to be in the process of being dug up to lay out new roads, so getting around the small town is remarkably confusing. However, just south of the Qasr (and north of the old junction) is the *Hotel Al-Sayad*. The main road used to simply pass by the hotel and castle, now it's impossible to tell which unmade roads lead to what.

You may see signs for the *Hunter Hotel* too – they are one and the same, *sayad* is Arabic for hunter. It's quite flash and has a pool. The singles/doubles with ensuite bath (loo paper provided!) and non-functioning air-conditioning come for JD15/19, although they'll come down on the price.

Quite a way outside the town is the *Government Rest House*, also known as the Azraq Tourist Resort. If you're coming from Amman, turn left at the new intersection before reaching the old junction in town, and turn left again at an unsignposted tree-lined avenue that looks oddly out of place. At JD20/30, the rooms come with most mod

cons. Like the Al-Sayad, the rest house has a restaurant. It's a little sterile, and without a car a huge pain to get to.

The best deal by far is the *Al-Zoubi Hotel*, about one km south of the old junction on the road to Saudi Arabia. Doubles go for JD10 (bargain down to JD8), and they don't seem to deal in singles. They even have a honeymoon suite. The employees are friendly, the place is immaculately clean and the bathrooms are sheer luxury. One hitch is the constant noise of trucks on the highway nearby.

There is a bunch of small restaurants on the one-km stretch south of the old junction. These guys are all keen for your money, so it is advisable to find out what you'll be paying before eating. The big *Lebanon Restaurant* will charge you JD6 for a very average meal of kebabs, fasooliya, salad, hummus and soft drinks for two.

Getting There & Away

There is a minibus from near the post office (north of the Qasr) to Hammamat Ma'in (1½ hours, 450 fils).

QUSAYR 'AMRA

Heading back towards Amman on Highway 40, the Qusayr (little castle) 'Amra, built during the reign of caliph Walid I (705-715 AD), appears on the right 25 km after the fork in the road that leads to Hammamat Ma'in. This is the best preserved of the desert castles and the walls of the three halls are covered with frescoes. The plain exterior belies the beauty that lies within. It is believed the building was part of a greater complex that served as a caravanserai, and which was probably in existence before the arrival of the Omayyads.

You first enter the audience hall with walls covered in frescoes, many badly damaged but partly restored by a Spanish team in the '70s. Note on the right (west wall) the depiction of a nude woman bathing. What makes such a fresco remarkable is that under Islam any kind of illustration of living beings, let alone nudes, was all but prohibited! To her left stand six great rulers, of whom four have been identified – Caesar, a Byzantine emperor, the Visigoth king Roderick, the Persian emperor Chosroes, and the Negus of Abyssinia. The fresco either implies that the present Omayyad ruler was their equal or better, or is simply a pictorial list of Islam's enemies.

The small room with the dome was the steam room and had benches at either end. The dome is of special interest because it has a map of the heavens on it.

The two rooms at the back of the main hall have fine mosaic floors.

QASR AL-KHARANAH

This castle is a further 16 km along the road to Amman, stuck in the middle of a treeless plain to the left of the highway. It seems it was the only one of the castles built solely for defensive purposes, although no-one really knows what its purpose was. Another popular explanation was that it was one of the first Islamic *khans*, or caravanserais, for travelling traders. The date of construction is uncertain but a painted inscription above one of the doors on the upper floor puts it at 710 AD. The presence of stones with Greek inscriptions in the main entrance frame suggests it was built on the site of a Roman or Byzantine building.

The affable Bedouin caretaker will wander over from his hut and show you around. The long rooms either side of the entrance were used as stables. It is built around a central courtyard and in it are pillars that used to support a balcony. Right in the centre of the courtyard was a basin for collecting rain water.

The castle is remarkably well preserved and most of the rooms, particularly those of the upper level, are decorated with carved plaster medallions set around the top of the walls. There are also Kufic inscriptions scattered around the upper level. Stairs in the south-east and south-west corners lead to the 2nd floor and the roof.

From Qasr al-Kharanah it is also possible to visit Qasr al-Mushatta. There are tracks from the main road that cut across the desert to the airport, but these should not be attempted without a guide. The other alternative is to take the highway to the outskirts of Amman and then take the road to the airport.

QASR AL-MUSHATTA

Qasr al-Mushatta is 35 km south of Amman near the airport. It was the biggest and most lavish of all the Omayyad castles (its name means winter camp or residence) but for some unknown reason it was never finished. It is believed to have been begun under the caliph Al-Walid II, and that he also intended to establish a city in the area. Arab historians recount that he was assassinated by angry forced labourers, many of whom had died

Qusayr 'Amra

during the building because of a lack of water in the area.

Today it looks far from grand, especially as the elaborate carving on the facade was stripped and shipped off to a museum in Berlin after the palace was given to Kaiser Wilhelm, just before WW I, by Sultan Abd al-Hamid of Turkey. Some pieces of this are still lying around the site and they give some idea of how it must have once looked.

One unusual feature of the building is that the vaults are made from burnt bricks – an uncommon material in buildings of this style.

This site is kept locked at night but is opened each day by the soldiers who are part of the airport security.

Getting There & Away

The Qasr al-Mushatta is not more than two km from the airport but can no longer be reached on foot, as security guards will not allow you to walk past the control tower to get to it. The only option is to drive the 10 km around the airport perimeter: turn right at the roundabout by the Alia Gateway Hotel as you approach the airport and the road will take you past two checkpoints and on to the castle. You must leave your passport with the guard at the second checkpoint and pick it up on the way back.

If you take the airport bus as far as the turn-off, you might be able to hitch around, although little traffic heads out that way. You might also bargain with a taxi to take you.

Top: Enjoying the Dead Sea (HF)
Bottom: Sea-level marker in the Jordan Valley (HF)

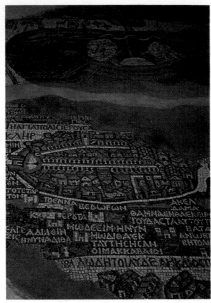

Top Left: Qala'at ar-Rabba (DS)
Top Right: Floor mosaic in St George's Orthodox Church, Madaba (HF)
Bottom Left: Qusayr 'Amra (HF)
Bottom Right: Qasr al-Kharanah (HF)

South of Amman

The King's Highway

There are two routes south of Amman to Aqaba: the Desert Highway and the King's Highway.

If you only have limited time the Desert Highway is the road to use, but by far the more interesting route is the picturesque King's Highway (known as At-Tariq as-Sultani, the Sultan's Rd), which twists and winds its way south, connecting the historic centres of Madaba, Kerak, Tafila, Shobak and Petra. Transport along the route is reliable but infrequent.

Hitching is the quickest way to go as you don't have to wait for minibuses (which you can pick up on the road anyway) to fill up at bus stations, but be prepared for waits of an hour or two on deserted stretches. Towns along the way are connected by a series of minibuses, except at Wadi al-Mujib where you'll have no choice but to hitch if you don't have a private car.

There's also a road running along Wadi Araba from South Shuneh to Aqaba. Minibuses from Kerak make that run, but you need a permit from the military to use it or take the bus. See the Kerak section for details.

MADABA

This easygoing little town 30 km south of Amman is perhaps best known for its mosaics, including the famous 6th century map of Palestine.

History

Madaba is the Moabite town of Medeba of the Bible (Isaiah 15:2, Joshua 13:9,16) and it was one of the towns divided among the 12 tribes of Israel. It is also mentioned on the famous Mesha Stele, or Moabite Stone, which was an inscribed stone set up in about 850 BC by the Moab king Mesha, detailing his battles with the kings of Israel.

The Ammonites had retaken Madaba by 165 BC, but it was taken by Hyrcanus I of Israel in about 110 BC. It was promised to the Nabataeans by Hyrcanus II if they would help him recover Jerusalem. Under the Romans it became a prosperous provincial town with the usual colonnaded streets and impressive public buildings.

During the Byzantine period up until the Persian invasion in 614 AD, Madaba continued to prosper and most of the mosaics are from this time.

Further damage was inflicted after the Persians by a devastating earthquake in the middle of the 8th century, which led to the town's abandonment. It wasn't until the late 19th century that the mosaics were uncovered when 2000 Christians from Kerak migrated here and started digging foundations for houses.

Information

The tourist office is right opposite St George's Church and the staff here are helpful. It is open daily from 8 am to 2 pm except Fridays. Next door is the Government Rest House which sells food and drink.

Things to See

The most interesting **mosaic** is in the Greek Orthodox St George's Church. It is a clear map of Palestine and lower Egypt and although it is now far from complete, many features can still be made out, including the Nile River, the Dead Sea and the map of Jerusalem showing the Church of the Holy Sepulchre. It was made around 560 AD and originally measured a staggering 25 by five metres and was made from over two million pieces.

The **museum** is tucked away at the end of a small alley and houses mosaics from churches and private homes in the Madaba area, jewellery, traditional costumes, a small

113

South
of
Amman

0   10   20 km

archaeological display – mostly pottery, seals and the like – and a copy of the ubiquitous Mesha Stele. The most interesting mosaics are the 6th century 'Banche & Satyrs' in a room marked **Old Madaba House** (50 years old), and one depicting Paradise and its fruits in a room marked **Byzantine Floor Mosaics**. The museum is open from 9 am to 5 pm daily (10 am to 4 pm on Fridays and holidays) except Tuesday, and entry is 250 fils.

In the **Church of the Apostles** down by the King's Highway was an enormous mosaic dedicated to the 12 Apostles. The church now looks like a building site as a US-financed reconstruction and restoration project goes ahead. The mosaic is in storage in the museum, away from prying eyes, until the project is finished. Completion was due in November 1992.

Madaba is also famous for its colourful rugs; in a couple of small shops in town you can see them being woven on large hand looms.

Places to Stay & Eat
There's nowhere to stay so it's a case of making a day trip from Amman or seeing Madaba en route between Amman and Kerak.

Along the King's Highway there are a few cheap restaurants. The *Madaba Modern Restaurant* does a half chicken and salad for JD1. The *Somer Restaurant* over the road from St George's Church does similar food, and there are a couple of other nondescript places to eat near the banks in the centre of town.

Getting There & Away
Madaba is served by Amman town buses and minibuses from Wahadat bus station. The No 31 bus from Raghadan costs 150 fils but is mighty irregular. It probably works out quicker and is less frustrating to get out to Wahadat and take a bus or minibus from there for 175 fils.

In Madaba, the bus station is just off the King's Highway, a few minutes' walk from the main intersection. The last buses for

Amman leave about 7.30 pm. You can get minibuses to Dhiban (250 fils), the last stop before Wadi al-Mujib. You have to hitch to the other side to continue south. There are also occasional minibuses to South Shuneh.

Just south of the bus station along the highway are minibuses to Muqawir (250 fils, about an hour). From there you can go on to Macharaeus.

Minibuses for Mt Nebo (Fasaliyyeh) can be flagged down at the roundabout just past the tourist office, at the bus station or just by the Jordan Bank.

For Hammamat Ma'in, 35 km from

Madaba, the bus stop is near the town centre. There is only one bus, supposedly at about 11 am (500 fils), but it appears to be at the driver's discretion whether he goes or not. If there's not enough interest, he'll only do the run to Ma'in. There are more regular services to Ma'in, leaving 15 km to hitch on a very deserted road, although Fridays and Sundays are not so bad.

MT NEBO
This is an area about 10 km west of Madaba on the edge of the plateau. There are actually three peaks, the first is called Nebo and the last is Siyagha ('monastery' in Aramaic), which is right on the edge of the eastern plateau and is supposedly one of the sites of the tomb of Moses. On a clear day it is possible to see the Dead Sea and the spires of the churches in Jerusalem.

The Franciscan Fathers bought the site at Mt Nebo in the 1930s and have excavated the ruins of a church and monastery. The existence of the church was reported by a Roman nun, Etheria, in 393 or 394 AD, and by the 6th century it had expanded to a large Byzantine church and baptistry. Although little remains of the buildings that housed them, the mosaics from this period can be seen today, protected by a modern structure erected by the Franciscans.

The main mosaic is stunning. Measuring some three by nine metres, it is well preserved and depicts scenes of wine-making as well as hunters and an assortment of animals, such as a panther, bear, fox, lion, sheep and hens.

When you arrive you may have to hunt around to find someone to open the place up for you. There is a shop selling souvenirs and an interesting guide to Jordan written by the Franciscan Fathers. There is a rest house, but at the time of writing it was closed. The Franciscan monastery is out of bounds for tourists.

Getting There & Away
From Madaba take a minibus from the traffic roundabout (near the tourist office) or by the Jordan Bank heading for Mt Nebo

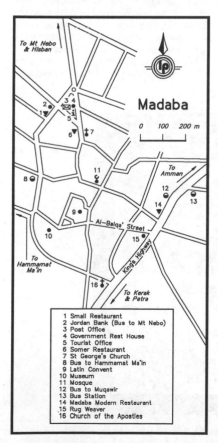

Madaba

0   100   200 m

1 Small Restaurant
2 Jordan Bank (Bus to Mt Nebo)
3 Post Office
4 Government Rest House
5 Tourist Office
6 Somer Restaurant
7 St George's Church
8 Bus to Hammamat Ma'in
9 Latin Convent
10 Museum
11 Mosque
12 Bus to Muqawir
13 Bus Station
14 Madaba Modern Restaurant
15 Rug Weaver
16 Church of the Apostles

(Fasaliyyeh) for 100 fils. From there it's about a four-km walk. There are a few vehicles along this section so it may be possible to hitch.

HAMMAMAT MA'IN

The hot springs and resort of Hammamat Ma'in lie 35 km south-west of Madaba. The serpentine road crosses some of the most spectacular territory around the Dead Sea and drops fairly steeply to the springs after the first 30 km. There is a hot waterfall and natural spa baths and saunas along with an expensive resort complex.

Hammamat Ma'in should not be confused with the town of Ma'in, 15 km short of the springs. Nor is it the Biblical Callirhoe, another 10 or so km west on the Dead Sea coast where Wadi Zarqa Ma'in ends up. A road connection is planned between Hammamat Ma'in and the famous springs of Zarqa Ma'in, and it may be possible to get to them along the road from South Shuneh if the military will let you that far south.

The therapeutic value of Callirhoe's waters was made famous by figures such as Herod the Great. The source of the Callirhoe springs is the same as that of the springs at Hammamat Ma'in, whose value has also been known since ancient times.

Before you even get into the place, they hit you for money. It's a minimum JD1.100 just to approach it. They'll try to ask you for JD3.300, but this includes use of a swimming pool, which you can pay for inside if you decide to use it. As you walk down to the Ashtar Hotel, you'll see a 25-metre waterfall fed by warm spring water. You can go across the stream and, if you can find a vaguely dry spot, drop your stuff and splash around.

For a free sauna and spa, walk along the road passing under part of the hotel and after

Mosaic floor, Siyagha

a few hundred metres you'll reach a mosque. Continue past this another 50 metres and you'll come to a natural sulphur spa bath. The cave to the right is as good a sauna as you'll ever have. Women should be aware that this is, unfortunately, generally a male-dominated activity – the usual warnings apply and going alone is not a good idea.

Places to Stay & Eat

There is no cheap accommodation here, unless you search for a spot to camp around the stream. The cheapest is the *Safari Caravans* park just behind the Drop & Shop 'supermarket' on your left shortly after entering the site. These claustrophobic little sweat boxes are JD11 for two a night. To the right of these are 'chalets', self-contained flatettes that go for JD90.800 for two per day.

In the *Ashtar Hotel*, the heart of the resort, singles/doubles are US$70/US$90. The hotel has spa and health facilities for guests only. It also has an expensive restaurant. The only alternative is the poolside restaurant which doesn't have much to offer anyway. Or you can buy some biscuits at the so-called supermarket.

There is a drink stand by the mosque, and like everyone else, they feel entitled to charge over the odds.

Getting There & Away

From Amman you can catch the JETT bus from Abdali for JD2 one way, or pay JD7.200 for the round trip, which includes entry and lunch. From Wahadat there are up to four minibuses in the morning for JD1. Be early and be patient.

From Madaba there *may* be one minibus about 11 am to Hammamat Ma'in (500 fils). Otherwise the best you can do is catch one to Ma'in (150 fils) and hitch – sometimes easier said than done. Returning, there is the JETT bus to Amman (JD2), which leaves from the pool at around 5 pm. There may also be a minibus or service-taxi back to Madaba (JD1). The Drop & Shop supermarket seems to be the best place to pick something up, but be there about 4.30 pm and keep your eyes peeled.

MACHAERUS

Perched on a 700-metre high hill about 50 km south-west of Madaba are the ruins of Herod the Great's fortress Machaerus, where John the Baptist was beheaded by his successor, Herod Antipas. The hill, which has commanding views over the Dead Sea to the west and surrounding valleys, was first fortified about 100 BC and expanded by Herod the Great in 30 BC. From here, Jewish troops were supposed to keep the Nabataeans in check.

Herod Antipas feared John the Baptist's popularity and did not take kindly to criticism of his second marriage to Herodias, but whether or not he really wanted him killed is not entirely clear. One night he promised Salome, Herodias' daughter, anything she wanted for her dancing and she, on her mother's prompting, asked for the head of John the Baptist.

The king was sad, but because of the promise he had made in front of all his guests he gave orders that her wish be granted. So he had John beheaded in prison. The head was brought in on a plate to the girl, who took it to her mother (Matthew 14: 9-12).

Things to See

The fort, known to the locals as **Al-Meshneq**, is approached up a set of stairs. Excavations are still going on. There's not an awful lot to see, but as you pass the workers' hut you come upon **baths** and around them to the east and north are vestiges of Herod Antipas' **palace**. On the west side are parts of the fortress **wall** and defensive **towers**. From here you can see clearly across the Dead Sea into the West Bank. Bring your own food and water as there is nowhere to buy anything here.

Getting There & Away

From Madaba take a Muqawir minibus (about one hour, 250 fils), which follows the King's Highway to Libb and turns right. This is not a heavily touristed spot, so tell the driver what you want and he'll let you out at an appropriate place. You can see the hill and fort to the west.

It is about half an hour's walk directly across a goat path and down to an unfinished road that will take you to the stairs. On the way along the road you'll see some artificial caves (tombs?). The minibuses back to Madaba are infrequent and finish at about 5 pm, so keep a watch out.

KERAK

The town of Kerak (often spelled Karak) can be reached from the Desert Highway, but if you go this way you'll miss one of the most spectacular sights in Jordan, the canyon of Wadi al-Mujib, about 50 km north of Kerak on the King's Highway. The canyon is over 1000 metres deep and the road winds precariously down one side and up the other. At the bottom, there is only a bridge over the wadi and a post office looking totally out of place. This canyon is the Arnon of the Bible and formed a natural boundary between the Moabites in the south and the Amorites in the north. There is no public transport across the wadi.

The greater part of the town of Kerak lies within the walls of the old Crusader town and is dominated by the fort – one in a long line built by the Crusaders, which stretched from Aqaba in the south right up into Turkey in the north.

History

Kerak lies on the routes of the ancient caravans that used to travel from Egypt to Syria in the time of the Biblical kings, and were also used by the Greeks and Romans. It is mentioned several times in the Bible as Kir, Kir Moab and Kir Heres and later emerges as a provincial Roman town, Characmoba.

The arrival of the Crusaders launched the town back into prominence and the Crusader king, Baldwin I of Jerusalem, had the castle built in 1132 AD. This site was chosen because it was strategically placed midway between Shobak and Jerusalem and had a commanding position. It became the capital of the Crusader district of Oultrejourdain and, with the taxes levied on the passing caravans and the food grown in the district, helped Jerusalem prosper.

After holding out for years against the attacking Arab armies, it finally fell to the forces of Saladin in 1188 AD. The governor of the fort at the time, Renauld de Chatillon, who was killed by Saladin shortly after the Crusaders' defeat at the Battle of Hittin, had the charming habit of throwing his enemies over the battlements of the castle into the valley 450 metres below. He even went to the trouble of fastening a wooden box over their heads so they wouldn't lose consciousness before hitting the bottom!

The Mamluk Sultan Baibars strengthened the fortress in the late 13th century, but three towers later collapsed in an earthquake. In the 1880s, local infighting compelled the Christians of Kerak to flee north to Madaba and Ma'in, and peace was only restored after thousands of Turkish troops were stationed in the town.

Fort

The fort itself has been partially restored and is a jumble of rooms and vaulted passages. It is still possible to see the cisterns where water was stored, but not much else. A torch (flashlight) would be useful for poking around some of the darker places, but watch your step as there are gaping light shafts and collapsed ceilings all over the place.

When you enter, turn left. Stairs lead down to the museum, or you can veer up to the right and double back to find yourself in the lower of two long vaulted rooms, probably used as stables or dining halls. The multi-storeyed building at the southern end was the *donjon* (dungeon).

Ask the museum caretaker to show you the underground vaulted rooms entered by a locked door about 30 metres opposite the museum. This is the best preserved and deepest part of the castle. The hall is 150 metres long and divided by a larger room with four *iwans* (vaulted halls). On the west side of the iwan room is the original entrance to the castle. Stacked up any old how in the southern end are piles of ancient and medieval pottery and other artefacts.

Museum

The museum is down a flight of stairs on the right as you enter the castle. Apart from a selection of Neolithic tools and Bronze and Iron Age pottery, it also has one of the many copies of the Mesha Stele and a translation of its text.

The original stele was found by a missionary at Dhiban, just north of Wadi al-Mujib, in 1868. It was a major discovery because, not only did it give historical detail of the battles between the Moabites and the kings of Israel, but it was also the earliest example of Hebrew script to be found. After surviving intact from about 850 BC to 1868 AD, it came to a rather unfortunate end.

After finding the stele, the missionary reported it to Charles Clermont-Ganneau at the French Consulate in Jerusalem who then saw it, made a mould of it and went back to Jerusalem to raise the £60 which he had offered the locals for it. While he was away the local families argued over who was going to get the money and some of the discontented lit a fire under the stone and then poured water on it causing it to shatter. Although most pieces were recovered, inevitably some were lost. The remnants were gathered together and shipped off to France and the reconstructed stone is now on display in the Louvre in Paris.

The castle is open daily during daylight hours and there is no entrance charge. Entry to the museum is 250 fils and it's open from 8 am to 5 pm daily except Tuesdays.

Places to Stay & Eat

Of the two cheapies in town, the *Castle Hotel* (☎ 352489) is the best. Apart from the smelly loo and loud call to prayer, it is comfortable if basic. They have a small restaurant downstairs and will bring drinks up to your room. A bed in a shared room costs JD3 or a double costs JD7.

The *New Hotel* (☎ 351942) is in the centre of town, further away from the castle. You

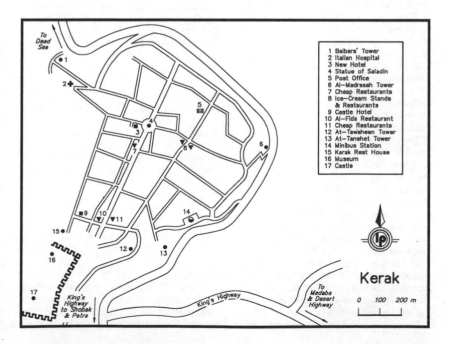

1 Baibars' Tower
2 Italian Hospital
3 New Hotel
4 Statue of Saladin
5 Post Office
6 Al–Madrasah Tower
7 Cheap Restaurants
8 Ice–Cream Stands
  & Restaurants
9 Castle Hotel
10 Al–Fida Restaurant
11 Cheap Restaurants
12 At–Tawaheen Tower
13 At–Tanshet Tower
14 Minibus Station
15 Karak Rest House
16 Museum
17 Castle

Kerak

0   100   200 m

To Dead Sea

King's Highway to Shobak & Petra

King's Highway

To Madaba & Desert Highway

can cook in the kitchen, which you have to pass through to get to the shower. You can get a bed for JD3 or a room (double or triple) for JD5. The hotel is cheap but basic and a little too cramped.

Next to the castle is the *Karak Rest House* (☎ 351148) which charges JD13.500/17 for singles/doubles. The rooms are comfortable and the views excellent, as it is right on the edge of the escarpment.

From the restaurant there are good views over the Dead Sea on a clear day, but the prices are high. A small can of Amstel beer costs JD2, although you can get a simple cream cheese sandwich for 150 fils.

Apart from the rest house there are a few other cheap eateries around, but after 8 pm it can be difficult to find one that's open. Of these the *Al-Fida* restaurant, just down the road from the Castle Hotel, is one of the best. For JD3.500 you will get a reasonable combination of chicken, omelette, salad and drinks for two. They have an extensive menu, but little on it is actually available.

There are a couple of other cheapies a block east of the Al-Fida, and a small group of cheap-food places and ice-cream stands a block east of the central roundabout, where a statue of Saladin now stands instead of a Roman column.

Getting There & Away

From the bus station there are minibuses and service-taxis for Amman along the Desert Highway. Minibuses depart until 6 pm and cost 750 fils. They also run north along the King's Highway as far as Ariha (just before Wadi al-Mujib) for 300 fils and south to Tafila (500 fils, 1½ hours). Public transport along the King's Highway is infrequent and you're better off hitching. That way you can jump on a minibus if one comes and also have the chance of getting a lift with a truck or private car.

If you are heading north to Ar-Rabba, Madaba and beyond, the turn-off is four km east of Kerak along the road that runs to the Desert Highway, so you have to get yourself out there either on foot or by hitching.

There is an occasional bus to Aqaba down

Wadi Araba, the last leaving about 2.30 pm (JD1.750, three hours), and to Safi for the Dead Sea, but you need to get a military pass in Kerak before setting off (see below for details). Strangely, you need no such pass to make the reverse journey.

AROUND KERAK
The Dead Sea

It is possible to visit the Dead Sea from Kerak, but it's a bit pointless as there's nothing to see and nowhere to wash the salt off after a swim. If you still want to do it, it's necessary to get a military permit in Kerak. The office that issues them is not, as you might expect, on the road to the Dead Sea but outside Kerak, about two km back towards Amman after the Madaba turn-off – all up a six km hike out of the centre of town! There is a sign pointing off the road to the left as you head north, and the office is just past a hospital. You need your passport, but getting the permit itself is painless.

Once you've got the permit find a minibus heading for the phosphate-mining town of Safi. This will drop you at a road junction in the Wadi Araba. From here it's about a five-km walk to the water. The whole bloody trip is more hassle than it's worth.

Ar-Rabba

About 20 km north of Kerak, this small town boasts a Roman temple and other Roman and Byzantine remains just west of the highway. The two niches in the temple contained statues of the Roman emperors Diocletian and Maximian. The local authorities thought it would be a good idea to place chunks of Roman columns at regular intervals along the median strip down the length of the town.

Getting There & Away You can reach Ar-Rabba by any northbound minibus from Kerak.

Dhat Ras

The crumbling ruins of a Nabataean and Roman settlement can be seen in this small village about 25 km south of Kerak. The remains of a wall and column belonging to a

2nd century temple lean at a crazy angle and look set to tumble down.

Getting There & Away The village is five km east of the King's Highway and a minibus runs between it and Kerak (30 minutes, 250 fils).

Tafila
Second only to Wadi al-Mujib, the deep gorge of Wadi al-Hesa bisects the King's Highway about 45 km south of Kerak. Some 32 km further on lies Tafila, a busy market centre where surrounding fruit and olive growers bring their produce.

Tafila was part of the Crusaders' line of bases; a large, squat building a couple of hundred metres west of the highway, about halfway into the town, probably dates from then. It's locked and the keeper seems to keep out of sight. You can see in through the gate anyway, which will satisfy most visitors. Tucked in among sprawling houses, it overlooks valleys that fall away steeply from the town's edge.

Getting There & Away Minibuses from Kerak cost 500 fils and take about 1½ hours.

SHOBAK
This is yet another Crusader castle/fort in the chain and, like Kerak, has a commanding position over some incredibly desolate land. The fortress, called Mons Realis (Montreal), stands 60 km south of Tafila and was built by Baldwin I in 1115. It suffered numerous attacks from Saladin before it finally fell to him in 1189. It owes much of its present form to the Mamluk restoration from the 14th century.

Today the place looks more impressive from the outside, as it is built on a small knoll right on the edge of the plateau. The inside is in a decrepit state, although restoration work is under way. There are two churches in the castle, the first of them on the left of the entrance and up the stairs. There is evidence of baths, cisterns and rainwater pipes. The caretaker will happily point out a well reached by 365 steps (about an hour's walk)

cut into the rock. The Arabic inscriptions on the walls of the castle were left by Saladin.

At the foot of the hill you can see abandoned Bedouin houses.

Getting There & Away
A side road leads to the castle from the King's Highway, about two km north of the small village. It is marked by two signs and is hard to miss. From there it is another four km to the castle, although it comes into view on the right after about 2½ km. If you are on foot head straight for it as soon as you see it and you'll cut off a km or so.

There's not much transport to Shobak village and, again, hitching is probably the best option. Minibuses linking Wadi Musa and Ma'an, up the Desert Highway to the north-east, pass through Shobak. There are irregular connections to Tafila.

PETRA
If you are only going to see one place in Jordan, or the whole Middle East for that matter, make it Petra. It's worth going a long way to see and it certainly is the number one attraction in Jordan. Petra is the ruined capital of the Nabataeans – Arabs who dominated the Transjordan area in pre-Roman times – and they carved elaborate buildings and tombs out of the solid rock.

So many words have been written about Petra (which means 'rock' in Greek), including the much overworked 'rose-red city half as old as time' (from Dean Burgen's poem, *Petra*), but these can hardly do the place justice. You have to spend at least a couple of days walking around in the silence and getting the feel of the place.

Much of Petra's fascination comes from its setting on the edge of the Wadi Araba. The sheer and rugged sandstone hills form a deep canyon easily protected from all directions. The easiest access is through the Siq, a narrow winding cleft in the rock that is anything from five to 200 metres deep. Although the sandstone could hardly be called rose-red, it is still a deep rust colour and is banded with grey and yellow and every shade in between.

There are few free-standing buildings in Petra, the rest are all cut into the rock, and there are hundreds of them. Up until the mid-1980s many of these caves were home to the local Bedouin. At that time they were moved to a 'new village' to the north – an arrangement they are less than happy with. You can see the village north of the Colonnaded Street from a vantage point up by the Pharaon column. There are still a few families who have the black tents set up and live in the caves. They make their money from Pepsi stands, handicrafts and other artefacts – usually scraps of the distinctive pottery and 'old' coins – which they sell to the tourists.

Not so long ago it was an arduous journey from Amman to Petra, only affordable by the lucky few. Now Petra is connected to Amman and Aqaba by good bitumen roads and can be reached in only three hours via the Desert Highway and Shobak, or five hours down the historic King's Highway. When you arrive there are all types of accommodation, ranging from the five-star Forum Hotel to a Bedouin cave.

The number of people visiting Petra is growing and the main sights can be quite busy in the middle of the day. However, most of them rush Petra. They spend a couple of hours taking happy snaps and then zoom off to the next place on their itinerary, which is great because it means that for the best parts of the day, early morning and late afternoon, the place is almost deserted. Spend a couple of days exploring and soak up the atmosphere.

History

Excavations carried out in the 1950s in the region unearthed a Neolithic village at Beidha, just to the north of Petra, which dates back to about 7000 BC. This puts it in the same league as Jericho on the West Bank as one of the earliest known farming communities in the Middle East.

Between that period and the Iron Age (circa 1200 BC), when it was the home of the Edomites, nothing is known. The Edomite capital Sela in the Bible (II Kings 14:7, Isaiah 16:1) was, probably mistakenly, once thought to have been the massif Umm al-Biyara – the Mother of Cisterns – which is part of the western wall of the canyon. The actual site of Sela appears in fact to lie to the north, about 10 km south of Tafila. Sela (which also means 'rock'), was where the Judaean king Amaziah, who ruled from 796 to 781 BC, threw 10,000 prisoners to their deaths over the precipice.

The Nabataeans were a nomadic tribe from western Arabia who settled in the area somewhere around the 6th century BC and became rich, first by plundering and then by levying tolls on the trade caravans for safe passage through the area under their control. The Seleucid ruler Antigonus, who had come to power in Babylonia when Alexander the Great's empire was parcelled up, rode against the Nabataeans in 312 BC and attacked one day when all the men were absent. His men killed many of the women and children and made off with valuable silver and spices. The Arabs retaliated immediately, killing all but 50 of the 4000 raiders. Antigonus tried once more to storm Petra but his forces, which were led by his son Demetrius, were driven off.

Petra then became the sophisticated capital of a flourishing empire which extended well into Syria. The term empire is used loosely, for it was more a zone of influence. As the Nabataeans expanded their territory, more caravan routes came under their control and their wealth increased accordingly. It was principally this, rather than territorial acquisition, that motivated them.

The Roman emperor Pompey, having conquered Syria and Palestine in 63 BC, tried to exert control over the Nabataean territory but the Nabataean king Aretas III was able to buy off the Roman forces and remain independent. Nonetheless, Rome exerted a cultural influence and the buildings and coinage of the period reflect the Graeco-Roman style.

The Nabataeans weren't so lucky when they chose to side with the Parthians in the latter's war with the Romans. Petra had to pay tribute to Rome after the defeat of the Parthians. When the Nabataeans fell behind

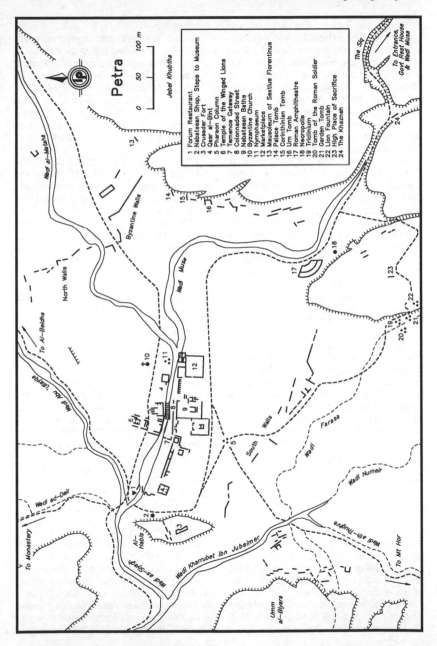

Petra

0 50 100 m

1 Forum Restaurant
2 Nabataean Shop, Steps to Museum
3 Crusader Fort
4 Qasr al-Bint
5 Pharaon Column
6 Temple of the Winged Lions
7 Temenos Gateway
8 Colonnaded Street
9 Nabataean Baths
10 Byzantine Church
11 Nymphaeum
12 Marketplace
13 Mausoleum of Sextius Florentinus
14 Palace Tomb
15 Corinthian Tomb
16 Um Tomb
17 Roman Amphitheatre
18 Necropolis
19 Triclinium
20 Tomb of the Roman Soldier
21 Garden Tomb
22 Lion Fountain
23 High Place of Sacrifice
24 The Khazneh

in paying this tribute, they were invaded twice by Herod the Great. The second attack, in 31 BC, saw him gain control of a large slice of territory. Finally in 106 AD, the Romans took the city and set about transforming it with the usual plan of a colonnaded street, baths and the rest of the trappings of modern Roman life.

With the rise of Palmyra in the north and the opening up of the sea-trade routes, Petra's importance started to decline. During the Christian era there was a Bishopric of Petra and a number of Nabataean buildings were altered for Christian use. By the time of the Muslim invasion in the 7th century, Petra had passed into obscurity and the only activity in the next 500 years was when the Crusaders moved in briefly in the 12th century and constructed a fort.

From then until the early 19th century, Petra was a forgotten city known only to the local Bedouin inhabitants. These descendants of the Nabataeans were not inclined to reveal its existence because they feared the influx of foreigners might interfere with their livelihood.

Finally in 1812, a young Swiss explorer and convert to Islam, Johann Ludwig Burckhardt, while en route from Damascus to Cairo, heard the locals tell of some fantastic ruins hidden in the mountains of Wadi Musa. In order to make the detour to Wadi Musa without arousing local suspicions, he had to think of a ploy. As he says:

I, therefore, pretended to have made a vow to have slaughtered a goat in honour of Haroun (Aaron), whose tomb I knew was situated at the extremity of the valley, and by this stratagem I thought that I should have the means of seeing the valley on the way to the tomb.

This is exactly what happened and he was able to examine very briefly only a couple of sites, including the Khazneh (Treasury) and the Urn Tomb, which aroused the suspicions of his guide. He managed to bluff his way through and report to the outside world that 'it seems very probable that the ruins at Wadi Musa are those of the ancient Petra'.

Information

There is a Visitors Centre near the entrance, but the Tourist Police staffing the desk don't seem to have much knowledge to impart. The place looks like everyone's moved out. There is a branch of the Arab Bank in the same building, but whether or not it opens seems a matter of chance. If not, and you have to change money, you can do so at an unfavourable rate in the nearby Forum Hotel.

There is a small post office at the site, although it too is unreliable. There are several souvenir stands selling various guide books to Petra, but everything is at least JD2 more expensive than in Amman.

Those wanting to stay overnight in Petra do so at the risk of an altercation with the local police. People are still doing it without hassles, but permits are no longer issued at Petra or by the Department of Antiquities in Amman.

In the town of Wadi Musa there is another post office and a small medical centre.

'Ain Musa

The first thing you come across as you enter Wadi Musa from Amman or Aqaba is a small building on the right with three white domes. This is not a mosque but 'Ain Musa (Moses' Spring), where Moses supposedly struck the rock and water gushed forth. The road then winds down the two km to the village of Wadi Musa (formerly Elji), and a further three km to the site entrance at the Government Rest House.

The Ruins

From the entrance, where you pay your JD1 entry, the track leads down to the Siq – the narrow winding wadi that leads in to Petra. The gate here is supposedly only open from 6 am to 6 pm but these hours are flexible. There are dozens of Bedouin with horses eager to take you the three km or so to the Khazneh. You're not allowed to do anything much but walk the horses, which is fine, but the locals can be a real pain, clattering up and down the Siq at high speed and throwing up clouds of dust.

Off to the left is the **Brooke Hospital for Animals,** a haven for doctoring local wildlife and where some of the horses end up after being given too hard a time. The officially sanctioned prices are JD4.500 for the horse ride there and back (you arrange that with the owner), JD9 for horse and cart, and JD5 for a guide (plus JD4.500 for *his* horse) to the lower city for two hours. So when bargaining, use these as the upper limit.

It's more interesting to walk through the ruins anyway, and this gives you time to look at the first of the monuments – three square freestanding tombs on the right. No evidence of bones has been found and it may be that, rather than tombs, they are a kind of outsize tombstone.

Further on to the left is the **Obelisk Tomb,** which originally reached seven metres high. Five graves were found inside the monument, four represented by the pyramid-shaped pillars and the last by a statue between the middle pillars.

Just past the Obelisk Tomb a path leads up to the left to what was a place of religious worship called Al-Madras (signposted). This is not the most spectacular of Petra's offerings, but is full of small memorials, inscriptions, and niches for making offerings. A similar area people rarely bother to poke around in is just opposite the Obelisk Tomb – just scramble up and you can't help stumbling on to tombs and memorials hewn from the stone.

After a party of 23 tourists was drowned in a flash-flood in the Siq in 1963, the entrance was blocked by a dam that diverts the intermittent flow of water into an ancient tunnel on the right and into Petra the long way. During construction, engineers working on the project found the foundations of a Nabataean dam and used them as the base for the new one.

Once inside the Siq, the path narrows to about five metres and the walls tower up to 200 metres overhead. The original channels cut in the walls to bring water into Petra are visible and in some places the 2000-year-old terracotta pipes are still in place. In Roman times the path was paved and one section is still intact. The niches in the walls used to hold figures of the Nabataean god Dushara.

The Siq is not a canyon, a gorge carved out by water, but rather is one block that has been rent apart by tectonic forces. You can see at various points that the grain of the rock on one side continues on the other. The entrance to the Siq was once topped by an arch built by the Nabataeans. It survived until the late 19th century, but you can still see remains of it as you enter the gorge.

The walls close in still further and at times almost meet overhead, shutting out the light and seemingly the sound as well. Just as you start to think that there's no end to the Siq, you catch glimpses ahead of the most impressive of all Petra's monuments – the Khazneh.

Khazneh (Treasury) Being in such a confined space, the Khazneh is well protected and has not suffered the ravages of the elements, and it must be from here that Petra gained its 'rose-red' reputation. Although it was carved out of the solid iron-laden sandstone to serve as a tomb, the Treasury gets its name from the story that pirates hid their treasure here, in the urn in the middle of the second level. The locals obviously believe this story for the 3.5-metre-high urn is pockmarked by rifle shot, the result of vain attempts to break open the solid-rock urn.

Like all the rock-hewn monuments in Petra, it is the facade that captivates (the final scenes of *Indiana Jones & the Last Crusade* were shot here); the interior is just an unadorned square room with a smaller room at the back. The Khazneh, which is 40 metres high, is at its best between about 9 and 11 am (depending on the season) when it is in full sunlight, or late in the afternoon when the rock itself seems to glow.

Barely distinguishable reliefs on the exterior of the monument have aroused much speculation, little of it conclusive, about their identification, although it is felt they represent various gods. The Khazneh's age has also been a subject of speculation, and estimations range from 100 BC to 200 AD.

From the Khazneh, the Siq turns off to the

right, and diagonally opposite is a sacred hall, which may have had ritual connections with the Treasury. It features the most characteristic expression of this Nabataean architecture, the 'crow-step' decoration, which is like a staircase on the top of the facade.

As you head down towards the city, the number of niches and tombs increases, becoming a virtual graveyard in rock arching around the back of the amphitheatre, so that it has in fact become known as the Theatre Necropolis.

Amphitheatre The 8000-seat amphitheatre, thought to hold only 3000 until it was fully excavated, comes into view ahead and to the left. Originally assumed to have been built after the Roman defeat of the Nabataeans in 106 AD, it is now felt the Nabataeans themselves cut it out of the rock around the time of Christ, slicing through many caves and tombs in the process. Under the stage floor were store rooms and a slot through which a curtain could be lowered at the start of a performance. Through this slot an almost-complete statue of Hercules was recovered.

Not all the caves around the theatre served as tombs; some of them were houses. Just before the theatre on the left is a staircase leading up to the High Place of Sacrifice – an interesting 1½-hour climb (detailed in the High Places section).

Royal Tombs The wadi widens right out after the theatre and after passing a few Pepsi-and-souvenir stalls you come to the main city area covering about three sq km. Up to the right, carved into the face of Jebel Khubtha, are the three most impressive tombs, known as the Royal Tombs. The whole rock facade sometimes goes by the name of the Kings' Wall, although who the 'kings' were, no-one knows.

The first is the **Urn Tomb** with its open terrace built over a double layer of vaults. The room inside is enormous, measuring 20 by 18 metres, and the patterns in the rock are striking. It's hard to imagine how the smooth walls and sharp corners were carved out with

such precision. A Greek inscription on the back wall details how it was used as a church in Byzantine times.

The next in the line is the **Corinthian Tomb**, a badly weathered monument similar in design to the Khazneh. Next to it is the **Palace Tomb**, a three-storey imitation of a Roman palace and one of the largest monuments in Petra. The top left-hand corner is built out of cut stone as the rock face didn't extend far enough to complete the facade. The four doors lead into small uninteresting rooms.

Further north and little visited is the **Mausoleum of Sextius Florentinus**, a Roman administrator under emperor Hadrian, which his son had made in 130 AD. There is plenty of room here for wider exploration of still more graves and religious sites.

North of Jebel Khubtha is one of Petra's important artificial water channels, which carried water from Moses' Spring into city aqueducts.

The Colonnaded Street A few of the columns have been re-erected in the colonnaded street which runs alongside the wadi. The slopes of the hills either side are littered with the debris of the ancient city.

The street follows the standard Roman pattern of the east-west decumanus. What is puzzling is that there is no evidence of a cardo, or north-south axis, which traditionally was always the main street. In Petra it would probably have had to be as much staircase as street, but no trace of it has been found, although little excavation has been done.

Coming from the direction of the ampitheatre, a **marketplace** lay to the left and on the other side of the street a **nymphaeum**, or public fountain. Little remains to be seen today. Further along on the left is a Nabataean bath, possibly used for ritual cleansing of believers. The street finishes at the **Temenos Gateway**, which was originally fitted with wooden doors and marked the entrance to the temenos, or courtyard, of the Qasr al-Bint.

Qasr al-Bint Firaun This is Nabataean and dates from around 30 BC. The Qasr al-Bint (Castle of the Pharaoh's Daughter, the picturesque Bedouin title for it) is also known as the Temple of Dushara, after the god who was worshipped there, and was probably the main place of worship in the Nabataean city. It is the only freestanding structure in Petra and has been partially restored, which the building was in need of as it seemed close to toppling over.

Temple of the Winged Lions Up on the rise to the east of the Temenos Gateway is the recently excavated Temple of al-'Uzza-Atargatis or Temple of the Winged Lions, named after the carved lions that topped the capitals of the columns. The temple was dedicated to the fertility goddess, Atargatis, who was the partner to the main male god, Dushara.

The excavation of the temple, started in 1975 by an American group and still continuing, soon revealed that this was a building of great importance and had a colonnaded entry with arches and porticoes that extended right down to and across the wadi at the bottom. Fragments of decorative stone and plaster found on the site and now on display in the small museum suggest that both the temple and entry were handsomely decorated.

Byzantine Church To the north-east of the Temple of the Winged Lions, an American team is excavating a Byzantine church and preparing to carry out restoration on what the Americans believe may be the oldest Byzantine mosaic ever discovered. It is planned to have it open to public viewing, protected by a roofing structure to be erected when the restoration work is complete.

Al-Habis Just beyond the Qasr al-Bint is the small massif of Al-Habis (The Prison). In the old cave dwellings at the base are a couple more of the small souvenir-and-Pepsi shops found dotted around the whole city. Steps to the left of the Nabataean Shop lead up the face of Al-Habis to the small, free **museum**, which has a collection of artefacts found here over the years.

A track to the right leads across the wadi past the fancy Forum Restaurant and up to the monastery (or *deir* in Arabic), another 'High Place' that takes a good hour to slog your way up to but shouldn't be missed.

High Places

There are a number of things well worth seeing that require a bit of hard sweat to reach but the effort is repaid by the spectacular views. As well as the following climbs, if you're really keen you can make the six-hour climb to the top of **Mt Hor** and **Aaron's Tomb**, passing the **Snake Monument** (a stone reptile on a rock pedestal overlooking the dead buried in the area) on the way. Collect the keys from the Bedouin in the tent at the bottom.

Crusader Castle The easiest of these climbs is up to the Crusader castle on top of Al-Habis. With so many other fine monuments around, the ruins of the castle itself are of little interest. The steps leading to the top start from the base of the hill on the rise behind the Qasr al-Bint. A track goes all the way around Al-Habis, revealing still more caves on its western side.

Monastery The climb to the monastery is quite long but the ancient rock-cut path is easy to follow and not steep. Not far along the path, a sign points the way left to the **Lion Tomb** set in a small gully. The two lions that give it its name are weather-beaten but can still be made out facing each other at the base of the monument.

The monastery itself is similar in design to the Khazneh but, at 50 metres wide and 45 metres high, it is far bigger. You don't really appreciate the size until you see someone standing in the eight-metre-high doorway. As usual, the inside is very plain.

The monastery was built in the 3rd century BC and crosses carved on the inside walls suggest that it was later used as a church. On the left of the facade, through a small gap in the rock where a lone tree grows, is a rough staircase that takes you right up to the rim of the urn on top. From there you can just make out the layout of a forecourt in front of the monastery down below.

Opposite the monastery, there's a strategically placed stall in a cave with a row of seats outside where you can sit and contemplate the monastery. The views from the area around the monastery are stunning. The village of Wadi Musa can be seen right over the top of the Siq to the south-east; to the west and about 1500 metres below is the Wadi Araba, which stretches from the Dead Sea to Aqaba; and to the south-west is the peak of Mt Hor (Jebel Haroun) topped by the small white dome that marks the traditional site of the tomb of Aaron, the brother of Moses.

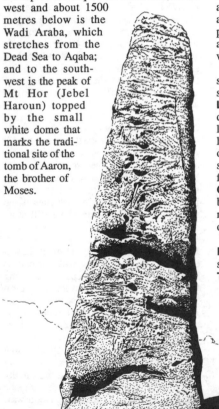

High Place of Sacrifice The third climb is up to the High Place of Sacrifice near the Siq. This 1½-hour climb is best done in the early morning so you have the sun behind you. Coming from the Khazneh, the steps head up to the left just as the theatre comes into view. At the top the track cuts sharply back to the right.

The top of the ridge has been quarried flat to make a platform and large depressions with drains show where the blood of the sacrificial animals flowed out. There are also altars cut into the rock and just to the south are obelisks and the remains of buildings, probably used to house the priests. Once again the views over the ruined city to the west and Wadi Musa to the east are excellent.

The path then continues down the other side between the obelisk and the ramshackle souvenir-and-Pepsi shop and leads to the **Lion Fountain**, where the water used to run down the rock from above and out of the lion's mouth. The lion is about 4.5 metres long and 2.5 metres high. A stone altar diagonally opposite suggests the fountain had some religious function. The steps wind further down the side of the cliff to the **Garden Tomb**, although archaeologists believe it was more probably a temple. To its right can be seen remains of a high wall, part of what was once a water reservoir.

A little further on is the **Tomb of the Roman Soldier**, so named because of the statue over the door. Opposite this is the **Triclinium** (hall for religious feasts held for

High Place Obelisk

the dead of the Tomb of the Roman Soldier), unique in Petra for its decorations on the interior walls. A bit past this on the right are two less interesting classic facades, one with the appearance of two columns either side of the entrance. The path then flattens out and follows the Wadi Farasa, the site of the ancient rubbish dumps, and ends up at the **Pharaon Column**, the only surviving column of another temple. A few drums of other columns that once stood next to it lie around the Pharaon Column.

Umm al-Biyara The hike up to the top of Umm al-Biyara, once thought to be the Biblical Sela, is tough-going and takes two to three hours. It is certainly not for the faint-hearted or vertigo sufferers! The path up the rock face starts from next to the largest of the rock-cut tombs at the base. Climb up the rock-strewn gully to the left of this tomb for 50 metres or so and you'll find the original path cut into the rocks; just keep following it. At times the steps are indistinct and have been almost completely eroded. Once on top there is not much to see on the site itself, other than some 8000-year-old piles of stones and some rock-cut cisterns, but the views over Petra and the surrounding area are the best you'll get from anywhere.

Al-Beidha

Eight km north of the Forum Hotel are the ruins of the ancient village of Al-Beidha. These date back some 9000 years and, along with Jerich, it is one of the oldest archaeological sites in the Middle East. It was excavated by Diana Kirkbride from 1958 to 1983 and the excavations have shown that it was occupied for at least 500 years during the 7th century BC.

On the various levels are the ruins of houses of different design, fireplaces and workshops. The ruins can be reached by road from outside Petra itself. On the way you can see the vestiges of a Crusader fort to the left, **Al-Wueira**, of which only some of the outer walls remain intact. You can also take a two-hour walk from the centre of Petra – just keep heading north.

Places to Stay

Wadi Musa The owner of the *Mussa Spring Hotel* (☎ 83310) seems to have a deal going with a lot of the local transport, as it is not uncommon for travellers to be dropped off here on arrival. He has the advantage of being the first hotel you come across, right after 'Ain Musa. Singles/doubles go for JD1.500/3, but he'll probably try for more – just say you'll walk down the road to the next place. It is JD1 on the roof. The rooms are basic, the showers clean, and for JD2 he does a very reasonable evening meal. You also get to see a scratchy video of *Indiana Jones & the Last Crusade*, starring Petra's Treasury in the final scenes. They can also give you a lift down to Petra early in the morning, coming back about 5 pm – this saves you the hour's walk you'd have to do otherwise.

A few hundred metres down the road is the *Al-Anbat Hotel* (☎ 83265). The name is Arabic for 'the Nabataeans'. These guys have a feud going with the Mussa Spring Hotel and will match its prices, including meals, lifts to the site and so on (they don't show any movies though). They have a range of accommodation of varying quality ranging from JD1 to camp and JD2 for a bed in a shared room to JD15 for a triple with bath in high season.

In the town itself, just past the main square and off to the right, is the *Rock City Hotel* (☎ 83440). The rooms are expensive with singles/doubles/triples for JD9/12/17. They have heating, TV and mini-bar, but some of the singles are airless cubbyholes.

A few hundred metres before you reach Petra itself is the *Petra Palace Hotel* (☎ 83066). The rooms are attractively furnished, but without air-con or any of the other extras like TV, and are too expensive at JD13/26.

Virtually next door is probably the best deal in Petra. The *Sunset Hotel* (☎ 83579) has beds for JD4, but you can bargain down a little. You can also sleep on the roof for JD1.500. The rooms are spacious and clean, you are a quick walk from the entrance and as a bonus, the hotel keeps big travellers' notebooks on Egypt, Syria, the West Bank and Jordan itself.

Petra The *Petra Rest House* (☎ 83011), right by the entrance gate, has good rooms and a strange tariff system. Singles are JD20.900 with breakfast and dinner or JD15 without, but are only available in August-September. Doubles (you can get one all year round) are JD41 with meals or JD30.900 without. Part of the hotel is built around an old Nabataean tomb, and a fairly ugly 45-room extension is being built.

The *Petra Forum Hotel* (☎ 634209, fax 634201) is the premier hotel with singles/doubles for JD50/60 plus 20% tax. From the poolside bar there is a nice view over the rocky terrain north of the Siq, but if you were thinking about stopping for lunch, the price of a beer should put you off – JD2.650 for a can of Amstel. You can camp near the carpark for JD4 per person plus taxes. Not surprisingly, it's rare to see any campers there.

Ideally, the best place to stay in Petra is a cave inside the site. However, permits are no longer available to do this and the authorities take a dim view of those who do stay.

Places to Eat

The Petra Rest House and Forum Hotel both have expensive restaurants, and all the other hotels have restaurants attached. The cheapest being those at the Mussa Spring and Al-Anbat hotels. There dinner is JD2 and breakfast an expensive JD1.

The last small building on your right after the Sunset Hotel, but before the entrance, houses a small felafel joint where you can get a pretty decent sandwich for 150 fils and tea for the same price. In the town are two places, the *Al-Wadi* café on the town square and the *Al-Furat*, about 100 metres down the road heading right off the square as you approach from Petra. Both sell the usual kebabs, rice and occasional stew and close early. The Al-Wadi seems cleaner.

There are a couple of shops selling bread, cheese and vegetables so you can stock up and put your own food together. There's no bread available after 5 pm so if you're preparing for the next day's lunch in the ruins, buy it early.

In the ruins themselves there is the expensive *Forum Restaurant*, where a can of beer alone will cost you JD2.400. At the nearby Nabataean Shop, you can get a lunch bag containing a cheese sandwich, yoghurt, a tomato, cucumber, orange and a Pepsi for JD2. The Pepsi stands scattered around the site generally want 500 fils for the drink, but may drop to 400 fils.

Getting There & Away

JETT Bus There is one JETT bus daily from Amman, leaving at 6.30 am. It is mainly for day trippers who don't have the time to spare for a longer stay and the JD25.500 price reflects this. The fare includes lunch at the Government Rest House, entry to the site, horses and guide. As the drive from Amman is three hours each way, it doesn't leave much time for exploring the ruins. To take the bus one way without entry fee or extras is still JD5 – a blatant rip-off. It returns to Amman about 4 pm.

Three days a week, there is a similar tour departing from Aqaba at 8 am for JD18.500, returning at 5 pm. You can catch the bus one way with no frills for JD3.500.

Minibus/Service-Taxi Public transport connections to Petra are irregular. There are supposed to be four daily departures for Amman (Wahadat bus station) from the Visitors Centre that also pass through the town, the first at 6 am, the last around 1 pm (JD1.500 without luggage, JD2 with). There are two early departures (about 6 and 7.30 am) for Aqaba (JD1.200 without luggage, JD1.500 with).

Occasional service-taxis run to and from Wahadat bus station in Amman for JD2.500, and often charge up to JD1 for luggage. Don't expect to find anything in the afternoon going either way.

The most frequent connection is the minibus to Ma'an (500 fils), which is supposed to leave about once an hour. From Ma'an you can get another minibus or service-taxi to Amman or Aqaba, or just get off on the highway and hitch.

If you're staying at the Mussa Spring or Al-Anbat hotels, ask the managers to arrange for one of the minibuses to keep you a place and stop by on their way out. If you're not up when they arrive, they won't wait.

Occasionally, you might be able to find a pick-up willing to do the run to Wadi Rum – JD2 to JD3 is not unreasonable, but don't be surprised by a stop in Quweira or Ma'an to pick up stores. For the driver, it's a case of killing two birds with one stone.

Hitching Hitching is easy enough if you get yourself up to the junction by Moses' Spring. Allow five hours to get to Kerak and three to Aqaba.

A lot of the traffic coming out of Wadi Musa is only going as far as Ma'an, 50 km to the south-east on the Desert Highway, but from here there's plenty of traffic in both directions.

The Desert Highway

The Desert Highway is exactly that – a strip of bitumen running through the monotonous desert for the 300 km from Amman to Ras an-Naqb, where it then winds down off the plateau to Aqaba. It used to be a bit of a nightmare stretch in parts, but its development into a dual carriageway and the UN embargo on Iraq have combined to reduce many of the hazards. However, it can still be pretty hairy around Amman and Aqaba, and eventually truck traffic will probably again reach the crazy proportions of before the invasion of Kuwait in the summer of 1990.

At the time of writing, traffic was already pretty heavy in spite of the embargo and sparked accusations in the USA that Jordan was allowing large-scale sanctions-busting. These guys have scant regard for the niceties of road etiquette – they work and drive hard to scrape together a living and don't worry too much about taking regulation rest breaks.

MA'AN

There's nothing of interest in Ma'an, the biggest town in southern Jordan and the administrative centre of the region, but you may find yourself coming through here en route from Amman to Aqaba and Petra.

The Desert Highway skirts the west side of the town so if you are hitching through there's no need to go into Ma'an itself.

Places to Stay & Eat

Petra and Aqaba offer far better accommodation alternatives, but there is a couple of hotels here if you get stuck. Don't bother going into the centre of town. People will direct you to the Hotel el-Jezira, which has been closed for years.

Head west for the feeder road onto the highway (it branches east off the Desert Highway at points north and south of Ma'an, meeting at a roundabout in the middle that has a third road heading into the centre of town). North of the roundabout is the *Hotel Shaweekh* (just 'Hotel' in English) where a bed costs JD2 or a double room with ensuite bath costs JD6. The front rooms have plants all over the balconies and inside. It is marginally better than the *Hotel Tabok*, just up the road, which charges JD3 to JD5 for singles/doubles.

Both hotels have restaurants attached, and there are some more of the usual felafel, chicken and kebab places in the centre of town.

If there is an attraction in Ma'an, it's the *Khoury Rest House*, about 500 metres along the feeder road when you come off the Desert Highway from the north. If you're driving down, it's worth stopping there for a drink. The owner looks and talks like someone still well entrenched in the '60s, and his bar (he no longer runs the hotel or restaurant) is a truly psychedelic experience – stuffed with what seems like hundreds of clocks, assorted weapons, coloured lights and crazy sounds. You can hardly see the bar for 'the collection', and if he were in New York, London or Sydney, he'd make a mint.

At the southern exit is a popular truckies' stop where you can get an acceptable fish & chips.

Getting There & Away

The minibus and service-taxi station in Ma'an is awkwardly placed on the south-eastern side of town. It's about a 20-minute walk into the centre and another 20 minutes out to the hotels. However, it can be a useful place to pick up transport north or south if you're coming from Petra.

Minibuses to Amman cost JD1.050 and service-taxis JD2. Minibuses to Aqaba cost 750 fils. There are a few minibuses to Wadi Musa for 500 fils.

QUWEIRA

From Ma'an the Desert Highway continues to Ras an-Naqb and then descends tortuously down through the hills. It's one of the most dangerous sections of road and tankers sometimes get out of control and explode. The antics of the trucks as they jockey for position makes for some hair-raising entertainment.

Quweira is the only town between Ma'an and Aqaba and is the nearest town to Wadi Rum, 35 km to the south-east. The turn-off for Wadi Rum is five km south of town; the sign just says 'Rum' and there's a couple of little restaurants at the intersection.

WADI RUM

Many people are put off going to Wadi Rum because it takes some effort to get there and there is no hotel, but it has some of the most spectacular desert scenery you'll ever see and is well worth a visit. Along with Petra, this is a 'must' in Jordan.

During the Arab Revolt in 1917-18, it was one of the stamping grounds of the enigmatic T E Lawrence, and the desert shots in the film *Lawrence of Arabia* were taken around here. In his book, *Seven Pillars of Wisdom*, he describes his approach by camel from the south:

(The hills) drew together until only two miles divided them: and then, towering gradually till their parallel parapets must have been a thousand feet above us, ran forward in an avenue for miles...The Arab armies would have been lost in the length and breadth of it, and within the walls a squadron of aeroplanes could have wheeled in formation. Our little caravan grew self-conscious, and fell dead quiet, afraid and ashamed to flaunt its smallness in the presence of the stupendous hills.

Jebel Rum is in fact closer to 6000 feet (5788 feet or 1754 metres to be exact) above sea level.

The rusty jebels of Wadi Rum rise sheer from the two-km-wide valley floor and are capped with smooth, pale sandstone. They completely dominate the tiny settlement of Rum, which is a collection of about 20 Bedouin families in their black goat-hair tents, a few concrete houses, a school, a shop and the 'Beau Geste' fort, headquarters of the much-photographed Desert Patrol Corps.

The camel-mounted Desert Patrol was originally set up to keep dissident tribes in order and patrol the border. Today, they have exchanged their camels for blue armoured patrol wagons, with heavy machine guns mounted at the back and specially adapted for the desert. They can achieve speeds of over 100 km/h through the desert as they pursue their prey (usually drug smugglers on

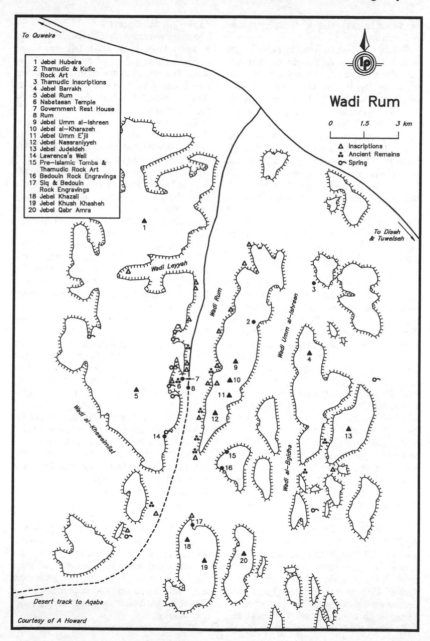

To Quweira

1 Jebel Hubeira
2 Thamudic & Kufic
  Rock Art
3 Thamudic Inscriptions
4 Jebel Barrakh
5 Jebel Rum
6 Nabataean Temple
7 Government Rest House
8 Rum
9 Jebel Umm al–Ishreen
10 Jebel al–Kharazeh
11 Jebel Umm E'jil
12 Jebel Nassraniyyeh
13 Jebel Judeideh
14 Lawrence's Well
15 Pre–Islamic Tombs &
   Thamudic Rock Art
16 Bedouin Rock Engravings
17 Siq & Bedouin
   Rock Engravings
18 Jebel Khazali
19 Jebel Khush Khasheh
20 Jebel Qabr Amra

Wadi Rum

0   1.5   3 km

△ Inscriptions
⚘ Ancient Remains
❍ Spring

To Diseh
& Tuweiseh

Wadi Leyyah

Wadi Rum

Wadi Umm al–Ishreen

Wadi al–Khawelmlat

Wadi al–Bgicha

Desert track to Aqaba

Courtesy of A Howard

the Saudi border), and occasionally rescue lost tourists.

The men of the patrol can be quite a sight in their traditional full-length khaki robes, bandoleer, dagger at the waist, pistol and rifle slung over the shoulder, but mostly they wear khaki uniforms like anywhere else. Even their value as a tourist attraction seems unable to halt the tide of modernisation. Inside the compound, the officer and men on duty (often from as far away as Irbid) sit under the shady eucalyptus trees and while away the time entertaining visitors with traditional Arabic coffee, heavily spiced with cardamom, followed by sickly-sweet tea.

Things to See

It costs JD1 to enter Wadi Rum, and there seems little way of avoiding this. Payment entitles you to a cup of coffee and precious little else.

There are a few things of interest in the immediate vicinity of the village. **Lawrence's Well** is a spring about two km south-west of Rum, about halfway up the slope. If you scrabble up, the disappointment in finding little more than a stagnant pool will be compensated by the startling views across to Jebel Khazali and beyond. A more beautiful spring is tucked away at the base of Jebel Rum, only 500 metres from the rest house. Just follow the white paint the army splashed on the rocks, while playing war games, to a clump of small trees.

This spring is the largest of many in the area and supplied the settlement with water before the Government laid a water pipeline from Diseh. There are many Nabataean inscriptions by Lawrence's Well, as well as some written by the camel drivers of the Thamud tribe in Saudia Arabia.

Between the Government Rest House and the face of Jebel Rum are the ruins of a 1st century **Nabataean temple** which was a square courtyard surrounded by rooms on three sides. On the north side of Jebel Khazali there is a narrow siq (gorge) with Bedouin rock carvings. The whole area is dotted with examples of Thamudic and Kufic inscriptions and rock art.

Exploring the Desert

The main attraction of a visit to Wadi Rum, however, is the desert, and to fully appreciate it you need to get out of the village. There are a few alternatives here: Land Rover, camel and your own two feet. The local Bedouin population have the monopoly on the first two and know it.

To hire a Land Rover will cost you anything from JD5 just to get down to Lawrence's Well and back to JD30 for a full day. If you want a guide, they hope to get JD5 an hour out of you. The prices are posted in the rest house. You can try to use them as the upper limit in bargaining, but bargain they are loathe to do – if you don't have much time, you can cover a lot of ground this way, but you don't escape the noise.

Camels are a better choice from this point of view. You can hire them to certain destinations or for several days, say to Aqaba by the desert track, at JD12 a day, staying with Bedouin families camped in the desert on the way.

The best way to do it is on your own, although care must be taken as this is inhospitable country and it is easy to get lost. For any treks longer than a day that take you far from Rum itself, you should consider hiring a guide or at least getting Tony Howard's book on trekking and climbing in the area (see Rock-Climbing below). It should not be attempted in summer as the temperatures are extreme and dehydration and exhaustion are real dangers.

The only gear you need is a sleeping bag, hat, good shoes and adequate food and water. Five-litre water containers can be bought at the shop in Rum and this should be enough water for one person for two days.

Once you're prepared, just head off south down the wadi and camp the night somewhere. There is enough small dead wood around for a fire and the experience of a sunset in the desert is unbeatable. At night the silence is so strong that it rings in your ears, unless you hear the strange sounds of Bedouin traditional singing wafting down the valleys.

There are the occasional Bedouin camps

dotted around and you'll always be welcomed, but don't just waltz in – wait for an invitation. The Bedouin are incredibly hospitable people and will never turn away a stranger.

Rock-Climbing
If rock-climbing is your thing Wadi Rum offers some very challenging routes, equal to just about anything in Europe. Little has been done towards catering to the climber so you need to have your own gear.

In the 1980s the Ministry of Tourism commissioned a British climber, Tony Howard, to explore the area and map the climbs he did. The result is the excellent and detailed book *Treks & Climbs in the Mountains of Wadi Rum & Petra*, available from the Ministry of Tourism and in some bookshops. The 2nd edition due out in 1993 has over 250 walks, 4WD routes, camel treks and rock climbs of all standards. He has also done a book called *Walks & Scrambles in Rum* (Al-Kutba Publishers).

You might also want to ask for a guy called Salah when you get to Rum. He is supposed to know climbing routes and have some basic gear.

Places to Stay & Eat
There's nothing much in the way of hotels or hostels in Wadi Rum. The *Government Rest House* was reopened in early 1992 and has quite reasonable two-person tents out the back for JD2 a head. Or you can sleep on the roof (they provide mattress and blankets) for JD1. Take note that even in summer it gets pretty cool in the evenings. The rest house has showers, kitchen and luggage storage.

If this doesn't appeal, head out into the desert and sleep under the stars. You may be asked in by Bedouins to sleep under their tents instead – but don't turn up uninvited.

The rest house has an overpriced restaurant. The cheapest item on offer is a basic cheese sandwich for JD1.100, while a 1.5 ml bottle of mineral water costs 550 fils, and a Pepsi 750 fils.

The best advice is to bring your own food or hang on until you find the general store, just past the Desert Patrol's 'fort' and behind an animal enclosure. The same bottled water costs 400 fils, and the Pepsi 150 fils. It also sells canned foods and some vegetables. Bread you can probably get for nothing at the rest house.

Getting There & Away
Public transport into Wadi Rum is nonexistent, so it's a matter of sticking out your thumb. The turn off for Wadi Rum is five km south of Quweira and the 30-km road from there is surfaced. From Aqaba take a Quweira minibus (350 fils) or a Ma'an minibus (750 fils) to the turn-off.

After about 15 km, the road to Rum forks to the right another 12 km. The left fork goes to the Bedouin towns of Diseh and Tuweiseh. Traffic along the Rum road is infrequent and you may well have to wait a couple of hours. When leaving Wadi Rum, be by the road early in the morning as nothing much goes out after 9 am. Some drivers ask for ridiculous payments – like JD5 – but 500 fils is reasonable for the ride to the Desert Highway or Quweira.

Occasionally you may be able to get a ride all the way to Petra, for which you shouldn't have to pay more than JD3.

The only other possibility is to ask the drivers of tour buses that sometimes arrive in the afternoon and stay for an hour or so – just long enough for the tourists to ride a camel and take a few snaps – and then head back to Amman or Aqaba.

DISEH & TUWEISEH
If you find the number of tourists at Wadi Rum is too much, you could do worse than follow up with an excursion out to the towns of Diseh and Tuweiseh, about 12 km northeast of Rum. The terrain is not quite as breathtaking as Wadi Rum, but still more deserted.

There is no formal accommodation here at all, nor are there any places to eat, although there are a few basic shops in Diseh. The local Bedouin are keen to get some of the tourist biscuit and will happily drive you out into the desert area north of the Aqaba railway line. The place is dotted with old Nabataean and Roman dams, at least three artificial rock bridges, and assorted rock carvings and inscriptions, but unless you are somewhat of an expert in these things, they are a bit thin on interest for the average traveller.

There are several hitches, too. You should not head off into the desert without a local guide. However, few of them speak any English, making their sometimes dubious explanations of points of interest, such as one of the big camping grounds of Lawrence of Arabia and the Arab rebels during WW I, less than satisfactory.

Bargain hard for the Land Rover ride – these guys are friendly but will take what they can get. You should certainly not pay more than JD30 per car for a full day. Ask around when you get there; people will soon understand why you have arrived. If all else fails, ask for Sheikh Awad Nasser az-Zuweibdeh in Tuweiseh, a few km further east from Diseh. You might end up being invited to lunch and he and his men know most of the sights, such as they are.

Places to Stay & Eat

There are only two possibilities – camping out in the desert or being invited to stay with one of the local families, which is not as unlikely as it may sound. If you want to camp out, the Bedouin will help out with food and the like, but nothing is free, so make sure you know what you are paying. There are a couple of small shops in Diseh, but about all you can buy in Tuweiseh is Pepsi and dry biscuits.

Getting There & Away

It is easier to get to/from Diseh and Tuweiseh than from Rum. A minibus heads from Tuweiseh to the Desert Highway via Diseh at about 7 am (300 fils). Or you can hitch, as there is a much steadier stream of traffic from these towns than from Rum.

Aqaba

The balmy winter climate and idyllic setting on the Gulf of Aqaba make this Jordan's aquatic playground. While Amman shivers with temperatures around 5°C and the occasional snowfall, the mercury hovers steadily around 25°C in Aqaba. The water is clear and warm and as an added bonus offers some excellent diving for the underwater enthusiast. In summer, the weather is uncomfortably hot with daytime temperatures around 35°C and higher.

The town itself is of little interest but with the beaches, good cheap hotels and restaurants that offer something a bit different, it's not a bad place to stay for a few days.

The bulk of Jordan's exports and imports go through the port to the south of town, which also became Iraq's principal export outlet during its war with Iran until 1988. From August 1990 until the end of the Allied assault on Iraq's forces in January-February 1991, activity at the port was effectively choked off by Allied warships. At the time of writing it had largely recovered, although the amount of merchandise to and from Iraq was officially reduced to medical and other humanitarian supplies. It is also probable that a lot of goods were flowing both ways in contravention of the UN sanctions.

Day and night there's a steady stream of road tankers into and out of Aqaba, but the activity is not as great as it was prior to August 1990, and fortunately the trucks are kept out of the town centre and directed to the enormous truck park three km north of town.

HISTORY
And King Solomon made a navy of ships in Ezion Geber, which is beside Eloth, on the shore of the Red Sea, in the land of Edom.

This verse from the Old Testament (I Kings 9:26) probably refers to the present-day Aqaba. The name Eloth is a reference to the Israeli town of Eilat. Excavations at Tell al-Khalifa to the west of Aqaba right on the Jordan-Israel border have revealed copper smelters, held to be the site of Solomon's Ezion Geber. Smelting was carried out here from the 10th to the 5th centuryBC with the ore coming from mines in the Wadi Araba.

With the development of trade with Southern Arabia and Sheba (present-day Yemen), it became a thriving settlement. In Roman times, the great road from Damascus came through here via Amman and Petra and then headed off west to Egypt and Palestine.

At the time of the Muslim invasion in the 7th century, there was a church and even a Bishop of Aqaba, or Ayla. The Crusaders occupied the area in the 12th century and fortified the small island of Ile de Graye, now known as Pharaoh's Island, seven km offshore. By 1170 both port and island were in Saladin's hands. In 1250 the Mamluks took over and by the beginning of the 16th century had been swallowed up by the Ottoman Empire. The small fort in the town was built sometime around the 14th century and today it houses the Visitors Centre.

For the 500 years or so until the Arab Revolt during WW I, Aqaba remained an insignificant fishing village. The Ottoman forces occupied the town but were forced to withdraw after a raid by T E Lawrence and the Arab forces. From then on the British used it as a supply centre from Egypt for the push up through Transjordan and Palestine.

After the war the Transjordan-Saudi Arabian border had still not been defined, so Britain arbitrarily drew a line a few km south of Aqaba. The Saudis disputed the claim but took no action. As the port of Aqaba grew the limited coastline proved insufficient and in 1965 King Hussein traded 6000 sq km of Jordanian desert for another 12 km of coastline. This gave the port room to expand and saw the fine Yamanieh coral reef become Jordanian territory.

ORIENTATION

The main axis of Aqaba runs north-south along the coast through the centre of town and follows the gulf around to the west, ending at King Hussein's winter residence and a military buffer zone up against the Israeli border.

On the western side of the gulf, just across the border fence from Aqaba, is the Israeli resort of Eilat. Despite the hostilities between the two countries since 1948, the two towns have managed to co-exist peacefully. Depending on which side of the fence you're on, the gulf is known as either the Gulf of Aqaba or the Gulf of Eilat.

The airports serving the two towns lie close to each other either side of the border, which has led to the occasional stuff up. In 1986 a plane carrying Israeli tourists to Eilat landed. The pilot confirmed with the traffic controller that he had landed but was somewhat startled when the reply came back: 'Where? You're not on my strip.' He had in fact managed to land at the Aqaba airfield. A Jordanian official came on board, wished the passengers a happy flight and the plane took off for the two-minute flight to Eilat.

Beyond Eilat, the coast of Egypt extends down the west side of the gulf, and Saudi Arabia on the east.

The city counted 3000 inhabitants in the 1950s, but by the year 2000 could have as many as 160,000. Most of the charmless expansion is taking place in the north and west of the town, while the expanding port facilities lie about seven km south of the centre along the road to Saudi Arabia, which is 20 km from the centre. Most of the cheap hotels, restaurants, banks and post office are clustered in the centre, with the more expensive ones at the north-west end of the beach.

INFORMATION
Tourist Office

This is housed in the Visitors Centre behind the old fort by the waterfront. The office is open seven days a week from 8 am to 2 pm and the staff are quite helpful with local information. They also have a free hand-out with some useful (and useless) telephone numbers. The museum is also housed here.

Money

There are numerous banks around for changing money. If you are stuck without cash on a Friday or holiday, try the branch of the Cairo-Amman Bank at the Arab Bridge Maritime Co, which is open seven days so that people can change money to pay for ferry tickets in US dollars.

The agent for American Express is International Traders (☎ 313757) near the Municipality, just along from the Ali Baba Restaurant.

Post & Telecommunications

The post and telephone offices are next to one another right in the centre of town. The post office is open from 7.30 am to 7.00 pm every day except Friday, when it closes at 1.30 pm. The telephone office is open from 8 am to 10 pm every day.

American Express (see above) does *not* hold mail in Aqaba, but the post office has a poste restante service.

Foreign Embassies

The Egyptian consulate is in the new part of town, about 20 minutes' walk from the centre. Tourist visas are issued on the spot for JD12 with a minimum of fuss and the place is deserted – a great contrast to the shambles at the consulate in Amman. The

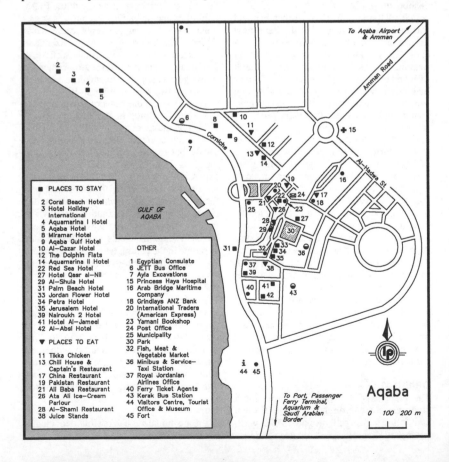

PLACES TO STAY

2 Coral Beach Hotel
3 Hotel Holiday International
4 Aquamarina I Hotel
5 Aqaba Hotel
8 Miramar Hotel
9 Aqaba Gulf Hotel
10 Al–Cazar Hotel
12 The Dolphin Flats
14 Aquamarina II Hotel
22 Red Sea Hotel
27 Hotel Qasr al–Nil
29 Al–Shula Hotel
31 Palm Beach Hotel
33 Jordan Flower Hotel
34 Petra Hotel
35 Jerusalem Hotel
39 Nairoukh 2 Hotel
41 Hotel Al–Jameel
42 Al–Absi Hotel

PLACES TO EAT

11 Tikka Chicken
13 Chili House & Captain's Restaurant
17 China Restaurant
19 Pakistan Restaurant
21 Ali Baba Restaurant
26 Ata Ali Ice–Cream Parlour
28 Al–Shami Restaurant
38 Juice Stands

OTHER

1 Egyptian Consulate
6 JETT Bus Office
7 Ayla Excavations
15 Princess Haya Hospital
16 Arab Bridge Maritime Company
18 Grindlays ANZ Bank
20 International Traders (American Express)
23 Yamani Bookshop
24 Post Office
25 Municipality
30 Park
32 Fish, Meat & Vegetable Market
36 Minibus & Service–Taxi Station
37 Royal Jordanian Airlines Office
40 Ferry Ticket Agents
43 Kerak Bus Station
44 Visitors Centre, Tourist Office & Museum
45 Fort

GULF OF AQABA

To Aqaba Airport & Amman

Amman Road

Corniche

Al–Hadwe St

To Port, Passenger Ferry Terminal, Aquarium & Saudi Arabian Border

Aqaba

0   100   200 m

visa office is open from 9 am to 1 pm daily, except Friday.

A taxi from the Municipality will cost 400 fils with bargaining.

Bookshops
The Yamani bookshop opposite the post office has a good range of books on Jordan and the Middle East as well as current local and international newspapers. However, the book prices are the most outrageous in all Jordan – up to JD6 more than you'll pay in Amman.

Radio
If you have an FM radio there's a good music station broadcasting from Eilat, and Radio Jordan is on the dial at 99.00 kHz.

Medical Services
The Princess Haya hospital is well equipped, even to the extent of having decompression chambers, and the staff are trained to deal with diving accidents.

THINGS TO SEE
Ayla
A few minutes' walk north along the main waterfront road after the Municipality is the site of old Aqaba, the early medieval port city that bore the name of Ayla (or Ailana). Signs in English and Arabic clearly pinpoint items of interest of the 120 by 160 metre city centre, including vestiges of the 80-metre-long north-western wall and towers.

The history of the Egypt Gate reflects that of the old city. From an impressive arch on columns in about 650 AD it was reduced to a small, roughly hewn doorway by 950 as the city declined, to end up filled in with just a sewage pipe poking through. The US-funded excavations are a long way from completion.

Fort
The small fort down on the waterfront is worth a quick look. The Hashemite Coat of Arms above the main entrance to this 14th century Arab construction went up during WW I after the Turks were thrown out by combined British-Arab forces in 1917. Built under one of the last Mamluk sultans, Qansah al-Ghouri, the fort has been substantially altered several times in succeeding years, and was partly destroyed by Royal Navy shelling.

The caretaker will happily show you around old barracks, kitchens and a well that still functions. His father and predecessor was quite a character and had planted two eucalyptus trees in the courtyard in 1963. He died in 1988 and, sadly, so has one of his beloved trees. Entrance is free and the fort is usually open seven days a week, although Fridays may be dodgy.

Museum
Since excavations of medieval Ayla got seriously under way in 1987, the little museum in the back of the Visitors Centre has acquired greater interest, with artefacts, plans and plenty of information on the old city. Ceramics showing Iraqi, Egyptian and Chinese influence is evidence that Ayla was a busy trading port in the Middle Ages.

Entrance is to the museum is free, but a sign inside the entrance says '250 fils per person appreciated'.

Aquarium
Located in the Marine Sciences Centre, 100 metres south of the passenger ferry terminal, the Aquarium, inaugurated in 1980, has a small but varied collection of the many-coloured and sometimes bizarre local sea life. If you can't go diving, this will at least give you a glimpse of what's down there. The staff are more than willing to explain which fish are what.

The Aquarium is open every day from 7.30 am to 2.30 pm and costs 500 fils to get in. You'll have to pay JD1 for a taxi to get there.

Pharaoh's Island
The Aquamarina Hotel is the place to go for this one-day excursion to what was once called the Ile de Graye, an island about eight km south of Taba in Egyptian waters. There is evidence that the island was inhabited as far back as the Bronze Age.

The JD20 fee includes transport, visas, lunch and a visit to Saladin's castle (actually built by the Crusaders in 1115). The trip only goes if enough people have expressed interest.

Beaches

The public beaches have been considerably improved in the past few years. The ones in town aren't bad, and stretch from south of the big hotels to the marina and again from the marina down to the Visitors Centre. There are small drink and snack stands dotted around the place. Glass-bottom boats cruise around trying to net tourists. The going rate seems to be about JD5 per boat for half an hour, but there are plenty around so take no prisoners when bargaining. There are also pedal boats for hire.

Unfortunately, in spite of all the rubbish bins, the locals seem to care little about how much litter they leave around, and the beaches can become quite mucky.

South of the port there is a cleaner beach with clearer water. You can actually stay there in the National Touristic Camp (see Places to Stay below).

Finally, there are the hotel beaches which are generally kept quite clean, but cost from JD2.200 at the Aqaba Hotel to JD6 at the Coral Sea (!). The guy at the Aqaba will drop his price in the afternoon, but the whole thing is ridiculous, as the Aquamarina I Hotel next door will usually let you onto its beach – which it shares with the Aqaba Hotel – for nothing! You can hire snorkelling gear at the Aqaba and Aquamarina hotels and deck chairs cost JD1.

It appears no private sailing is allowed in the Gulf for security reasons.

Warning A few women travellers have reported varying degrees of harassment from the local lads on the beaches, even some of those belonging to the hotels. Single Western women in bikinis on the public beaches are asking for trouble.

ACTIVITIES
Diving

Many people come to Aqaba just for the diving, and there are three centres here. Most of the best diving is just off the beach on the Yamanieh Reef north of the Saudi Arabian border, and although the general consensus is that Ras Mohammed in the Sinai is more spectacular, the diving here is still some of the best in the world.

Any of the usual dive cards is OK, but it is recommended you go down with an instructor if you haven't dived for more than six months. It is a good place for beginners, as much of the interesting stuff can be seen at fairly shallow depths. At its best, visibility is claimed to be as much as 40 metres, although it's usually closer to 20 metres. March and April are the worst times because of algae bloom.

Diving instructors are also increasingly worried about the threat to the reef from the nearby container terminal. One British instructor reckons up to 125,000 tons of phosphates, one of Jordan's biggest exports, are accidentally dumped into the sea each year during dumping.

The Royal Diving Centre (☎ 317035),

which has been going since 1987, is right down on the beach, about 12 km out of town. They charge JD10 a dive or JD17 for two in a day, including all equipment. A day's snorkelling costs JD3.500, or you can just hang around their pool for JD2. There is a cafeteria but no accommodation. A private bus does a round of the big hotels in town at about 9 am and returns at 4.30 pm. Although marginally cheaper than the other two places, particularly for courses (see below), it has had mixed reviews from divers.

The longest established and best equipped dive centre is at the Aquamarina I Hotel (☎ 316250, fax 314089). It is the most expensive, too. They take divers down along the coast by bus or boat. A dive from the boat costs JD13, snorkelling costs JD8. A dive from the beach is JD10. They also organise speed-boat hire, water-skiing (JD3 per 10 minutes), sailboarding and fishing trips.

The Aquamarina has recently seen competition grow in the form of a dive centre at the Al-Cazar Hotel (☎ 314131, fax 314133). A single dive is US$14 to US$19 or JD10 to JD13, depending on how much equipment you bring yourself. Newcomers who just want to find out what it's like can go down with an instructor holding their hand for US$40 or JD30, all inclusive. Both hotels organise night dives and deep dives of 40 metres, and have marine cameras for hire. You can use the hotel facilities too.

Courses PADI (Professional Association of Diving Instructors – sometimes known as Pay And Dive Immediately) open-water courses and the CMAS certificate, both of which take from four to seven days to complete, cost anything from about JD100 to JD125 at the Royal Diving Centre to about US$300 at the Aquamarina. All three centres can cater for more advanced courses too.

Horse-Riding
Ask at the Aquamarina Hotel (I or II) about horse-riding with the Royal Hippic Club. At JD2 a half hour it's not particularly cheap, and possibly a little frustrating as galloping is prohibited.

Hash House Harriers
Believe it or not, there is another of the worldwide running and drinking clubs here too. They take a small run and a drink or two on Monday nights. Ask at the Al-Cazar dive centre for details.

TOURS
There is a bunch of taxi agents around the centre of town with whom you can organise half and full-day trips to Petra and Wadi Rum. A full day to Petra should not cost more than JD25 for the car, JD15 for an afternoon to Rum and JD40 for a full day to both (crazy).

PLACES TO STAY
Places to Stay – bottom end
Standing alone next to a car park, the *Hotel Qasr al-Nil* is one of the cheaper places. The rooms are basic at JD1.500 a bed, but most come with balconies and reasonable views. The showers are cool.

There are three cheapies next to each other on the main street in the centre of town, and none is noticeably better than the others. The *Petra Hotel* (☎ 313746) has rooms at the front on the 3rd and 4th floors with balconies and a great view of the town, the gulf and the mountains of the Sinai. Singles/doubles with fans and hot water cost JD3/5. A bed in a shared room is JD1.500 and you can sleep on the roof for JD1.

The *Jerusalem Hotel*, or Al-Quds in Arabic, (☎ 314815) has much the same deal, while the *Jordan Flower Hotel*, or Zahrat al-Urdun in Arabic, (☎ 314377) does not offer beds in shared rooms and is pricier. Rooms go for JD5/6/7.500, but bargaining down a dinar or two is not too hard when business is slow.

The *Red Sea Hotel* (☎ 312156) is one block back from the main street, near the post office. It's a little overpriced at JD4.500/ 6.600 for small rooms with fan, but you get your own hot shower. Try not to get a room on the top floor in summer.

Next door is the *Nairoukh Hotel* (a little more upmarket) with rooms featuring TV, mini-bar, air-con and your own bath. They start at JD7.500/10, but some determined bargaining can bring them down to JD5/8.

The *Hotel al-Jameel* (☎ 314118), fronting a dirt car park, has air-con rooms for JD6/8. It's not too bad, but the air-con is a little noisy.

Camping It is possible to camp in the garden of the *Aqaba Hotel* for JD1.500, which isn't too bad and gives you free access to their beach (not that you need it, since you can get onto the beach next door for free anyway). You can also camp in the squalid little garden of the *Palm Beach Hotel* for JD2 per person.

If you want to get away from things, south of the port is the *National Touristic Camp*, where you can pitch a tent for 500 fils. There are sun shelters, showers and a cafeteria on the beach.

Places to Stay – middle

Moving up the scale, the *Palm Beach Hotel* (☎ 313551) on the waterfront is being renovated. It has 'chalets' for one to three people with a lounge for JD16, which is not bad value.

Around the corner, heading towards the waterfront from the Al-Jameel, is the *Al-Absi Hotel* (☎ 313403, fax 314620) where air-con singles/doubles go for JD15/20. Deals can be done on the room price.

Better in this price range are the *Nairoukh 2* (☎ 312980, fax 312981) on the waterfront, which opened only in 1991, and the *Al-Shula Hotel* (☎ 315153, fax 315154), just across the lane from the Shami restaurant. Of the two, the Al-Shula is a little cheaper and marginally better at JD14/17.500 plus 10% taxes. The modern rooms all have double beds, air-con, TV, mini-bar, ensuite bathroom and some have good views out over the gulf. The price includes breakfast. The Nairoukh 2 has similarly good rooms for JD15/20.

A group might like to take a self-contained, furnished flat for JD40 at *The Dolphin* (☎ 314296), just up from the Al-Cazar Hotel. Sleeping four, the flats are spacious with TV, kitchen, lounge and bathroom.

Aquamarina II has reasonable singles/doubles for JD13/17 plus 20% taxes, but don't listen to the rot about getting free passes onto the beach at its sister hotel, the *Aquamarina I* (☎ 316250, fax 314271 for both hotels), since the beach is free for all comers anyway. Depending on the degree of luxury and whether or not you want a sea view, the Aquamarina I has singles/doubles ranging from JD13/17 to JD45.

The *Aqaba Hotel* (☎ 314090, fax 314089), to the left of the beachside Aquamarina, has well-equipped bungalow-style rooms for JD30/40. They have all the mod cons and there's a seafood restaurant at the end of the pier.

Away from the beach, the *Al-Cazar Hotel* (☎ 314131, fax 314133) has reasonable rooms for US$33/44, including breakfast and taxes. The *Miramar Hotel* (☎ 314310, fax 314339) is not bad either, with singles/ doubles/triples for JD20/25/30 plus 20% taxes.

Places to Stay – top end

At the top end of the scale, only the *Aqaba Gulf Hotel* (☎ 316636, fax 318246) is not on the water front. They ask a steep US$70/90 but come down to a more reasonable JD36 for a single with remarkable speed if the place is empty.

To the right of the Aquamarina I is the *Holiday Hotel International* (☎ 312426, fax 313426). Starting prices are US$70/90 for singles/doubles, plus 20% taxes, but again a bit of persuasive bargaining in the off season will see the tariff collapse to US$36 for a single. They charge nonresidents JD6 to use their strip of beach.

Next door, the *Coral Beach Hotel* is the most expensive of the lot and won't hear of reductions: US$77/99 plus the usual taxes.

PLACES TO EAT

Aqaba has quite a few choices when it comes to food. The *Ali Baba Restaurant* is the most up-market in town and has tables set up outside. If you like your beer out of a teapot, this is the place to come. In deference to more traditional Muslim sentiments, the management feels it a good idea to hide what they are serving – you'll get a plastic cup too. Fresh fish meals go for about JD5 to JD7, and they have an unusually wide selection of other meals from spaghetti bolognese (JD1.500) to crêpes suzette (JD2).

Around the back of the post office, the *Pakistan Restaurant* has a limited range of unconvincing subcontinental food. Their version of a chicken biriani is a bed of boiled rice, with curry sauce and a chicken leg thrown on top for JD1.

Up near Grindlays ANZ Bank, the *China Restaurant* does some pretty good meat and rice dishes for around JD1.500 and great soups for 500 fils. The cook is Chinese.

By the Aquamarina II there are a few new places. The *Captain's Restaurant* does filet mignon (JD2.350), pasta, fresh fish and the usual kebabs. Next door is the American-style fast food *Chili House*. Their double hamburgers are OK for JD1.100, but the tiny Chilli hot dogs are a washout at 650 fils. If it's fast chicken you want, try *Tikka Chicken* across the road – two pieces with fries and bread for JD1.600.

Down a passageway off the main street in the centre of town is the *Al-Shami Restaurant*, with overpriced kebabs at JD2.500. There are nice views upstairs, but they are hardly worth the price of a meal.

Then of course there are the old favourites, road-side stands and cheapies with the usual stuff – you'll find a bunch of them in the centre of town.

For desert, go to *Ata Ali*, just up from the Ali Baba. They have a sugar-addict's paradise in traditional sweets and delicious ice cream. There is a couple of reasonable juice places diagonally across the road from the Jerusalem Hotel.

The shops along the main street are well stocked with all sorts of food, so if you are heading for Wadi Rum stock up with goodies like dates, cheese and bread. The souq also has plenty of fresh fruit and vegetables.

GETTING THERE & AWAY
Air
Royal Jordanian has daily flights from Amman to Aqaba at 7.15 am. The trip takes 45 minutes and costs JD15 one way or JD18 return, if the second leg takes place between two and 15 days after the original.

To/From Egypt For the jet-setter, the Egyptian al-Massria air company runs small planes from Aqaba to Sharm ash-Sheikh (US$120 one way) and Hurghada (US$180 one way) four days a week. They arrange the visas if you want. Ask at the bigger hotels or call Mr Hussein on ☎ 316570.

Bus
JETT Bus The JETT office is on the waterfront road opposite the Ayla site. The smooth and fast air-con buses run six times daily to Amman, the first at 7 am, the last at 4.30 pm. The five-hour trip costs JD3.500. Book two days in advance.

JETT also runs one-day tours to Petra for JD18.500 three days a week, leaving at 8 am. You can catch the bus one way for JD3.500. It returns to Aqaba at 5 pm.

Minibus/Service-Taxi The main bus station is just a couple of minutes' walk from the main street in the centre of town. There are a few buses for Amman in the morning (JD2) and service-taxis for JD3.300. If there's nothing around, take a bus to Ma'an (750 fils, departures until 5 pm) and try again from there. Minibuses to Quweira are 350 fils. Take either of these for Wadi Rum – tell the driver where you are going and he'll let you off at the turn-off, about five km before Quweira.

There are two daily buses to Petra (JD1.500), at 10 and 11 am, but they don't run on Fridays or holidays.

Buses leave for Kerak irregularly when full from a small bus station behind a mosque, not far from the Al-Jameel Hotel (three hours, JD1.750). The last one goes at about 2 pm. You don't need any permits for the trip up Wadi Araba, despite the fact that they are required for the reverse journey.

Car Rental
There are several car rental agencies dotted around town but, as in Amman, they are far

from cheap. Rum Rent-a-Car (☎ 313581), across the road and down a little from the Grindlays ANZ bank, will rent you a 4WD for JD28 a day (no minimum) and 65 fils a km (no free kms). They charge JD200 for a week, with 600 free km and a charge of 65 fils every extra km. Al-Manarh (☎ 318122) is cheaper at JD20 a day and 60 fils a km, but it's hardly a bargain.

If you're hiring a car for any length of time and want to cover the whole country that way, it would be cheaper to do so in Amman.

Hitching

If you arrive in Aqaba by truck, you may be dropped off at the truck park about three km north of town. A taxi into the centre shouldn't cost more than 500 fils, as you can usually find other people going into town.

For hitching north from Aqaba the truck park is also a good place to start.

Boat

To/From Egypt There is a whole stack of travel agents along the waterfront road selling ferry tickets to Nuweiba, or you can buy one from the Arab Bridge Maritime Co. The ferry terminal is south of the port, seven km from the centre. The only way to get there is to walk, or more sensibly, take a taxi, which should cost about JD1 with fierce bargaining.

There are two car-ferry departures for Nuweiba, at noon and 6 pm. The (officially) three-hour crossing costs US$18 (plus a 200 fils charge) or JD13.500, but is often hopelessly delayed and packed to the brim – especially after the hajj. Tickets can be bought on the day of departure and you only need to be at the dock about one hour before sailing (for more details see the Jordan Getting There & Away section).

You can buy a ferry and bus ticket to Cairo at the JETT bus office for US$43, although it's easy enough to pick up a local bus for Cairo in Nuweiba anyway.

From Nuweiba the fare is US$25 (you cannot pay in Egyptian pounds). For more details on the trip, visas and departure tax see the Jordan Getting There & Away chapter.

GETTING AROUND
To/From the Airport

The Aqaba airport is about 10 km north of town and a taxi costs about JD2.

Taxi

Other than walking, taxi is the only way to get around Aqaba. The only time you should need to catch one is if you want to go to the port or airport. These sharks don't use their meters and should be treated with extreme caution.

Top Left: Bedouin camp, Wadi Rum (HF)
Top Right: The 'Bedouin Supermarket', Petra (HF)
Bottom Left: First glimpse through the Siq of the Treasury, Petra (HF)
Bottom Right: Monastery, Petra (DS)

Top Left: Garden Tomb, Petra (DS)
Top Right: Wadi Rum (DS)
Bottom Left: Desert Patrolman on sentry duty, Wadi Rum (HF)
Bottom Right: The Gulf of Aqaba with Eilat in the distance, Aqaba (HF)

Syria

Facts about the Country

HISTORY SINCE 1920

In the dying days of WW I, T E Lawrence and other British officers involved with the Arab Revolt encouraged Arab forces to take control of Damascus and Emir Faisal, the leader of the revolt, to set up a government in 1918. When Arab nationalists proclaimed him king of Greater Syria (including Palestine and Lebanon) in March 1920, and his Hashemite brother, Abdullah, king of Iraq, the French, who the following month were formally awarded the mandate over Syria and Lebanon by the League of Nations, moved swiftly to force Faisal into exile.

Employing what amounted to a divide-and-rule policy, the French split their mandate up into Lebanon (including Beirut and Tripoli) where the Christians were amenable; a Syrian Republic, whose largely Muslim majority resented their presence; and two districts of Lattakia and Jebel Druze. Hostility to the French led to insurrection in 1925-26 and France twice bombarded Damascus.

A Constituent Assembly set up in 1928 to hammer out a constitution for partially independent Syria was dissolved by the French because it proposed a single state, including Lebanon, as the successor to the Ottoman province. This was unacceptable to the French.

In 1932 the first parliamentary elections were held, and although the majority of moderates elected had been hand-picked by the French, they rejected all French terms for a constitution. Finally in 1936, a treaty was signed but never ratified; under the deal, a state of Syria would control Lattakia and Jebel Druze as well as the *sanjak* (sub-province) of Alexandretta, the present-day Turkish province of Hatay. After riots by Turks in the sanjak protesting against becoming part of Syria, the French encouraged Turkey to send in troops to help supervise elections. The outcome favoured the Turks and the sanjak became part of

Turkey in 1939. This has never been recognised by the Syrians and further sharpened feeling against France. Maps printed in Syria still show the area as Syrian territory.

When France fell to the Germans in 1940, Syria and Lebanon came under the control of the puppet Vichy government until July 1941, when British and Free French forces took over. The Free French promised full independence, but this did not come for another five years, after violent clashes in 1945 had compelled Britain to intervene. Syria took full control of its own affairs when the last of the British troops pulled out in April 1946.

In Lebanon meanwhile, what was originally the mainly Christian Turkish province of Mt Lebanon became, with the annexation of some non-Christian (mainly Sunni, Druze and Shi'ite) territories, the state of Greater Lebanon. The French governor was forced to bow to Lebanese demands for self-rule and in 1926, when the new constitution was adopted, Greater Lebanon became the Lebanese Republic. As was the case in Syria, full independence was achieved only in 1946, when France withdrew the last of its troops.

United Arab Republic

Civilian rule in Syria was short-lived. In March 1949, the Kouwatli government was overthrown by the army, and successive military coups brought to power officers with nationalist and socialist leanings. By 1954, the Ba'athists in the army, who had won support among the Alawite and Druze minorities, had no serious rival.

The Ba'ath party was committed to pan-Arabism which led to Syria forfeiting its sovereignty. In a merger with Egypt under President Nasser in 1958, Syria became what amounted to the Northern Province of the United Arab Republic. In 1960, a united National Assembly came together, with 400 Egyptian and 200 Syrian deputies. It was a popular move with many Syrians, but the

Egyptians treated them as subordinates, which led to the restoration of Syrian independence following yet another military coup in September 1961. Although outwardly civilian, the new regime was under military control and it made few concessions to Ba'ath and pro-Nasser pan-Arabists, resulting in yet another change of government in March 1963.

A month before the Ba'ath takeover in 1963, which first propelled an air force lieutenant-general, Hafez al-Assad, to power, the Iraqi branch of the party seized power in Baghdad. Attempts were made to unite Iraq, Egypt and Syria but the parties were unable to agree on the tripartite federation. Syria and Iraq then tried to establish bilateral unity but these efforts also came to nothing when the Ba'ath party in Iraq was overthrown in November 1963.

Now that Syria was on its own, the Ba'athists were faced with the problem that being pan-Arabist, the Ba'ath party had branches in other Arab countries, thereby giving non-Syrians a significant say in Syrian affairs. There followed a party split, and in February 1966, the ninth coup saw a new regime set up in the name of the Syrian Ba'ath. The party's economic policy of nationalisation met with much dissatisfaction, which found expression in a bloodily repressed revolt in the city of Hama in 1964. A coup by the radical wing of the party in 1966 saw Assad lose power, but he remained in the government.

The Six-Day War

The socialist government was severely weakened by loss in two conflicts. The first was the defeat of the Syrians at the hands of the Israelis in the June 1967 war. This war, which came to be known as the Six-Day War, was partly in retaliation for raids by Syrian guerillas on Israeli settlements. Israel attacked after President Nasser, having pledged support for Syria, closed the straits of Tiran (at the entrance to the Red Sea) to Israeli shipping. The end result was a severe political and psychological defeat for the Arab states and saw vast areas of land fall into Israeli hands. Syria was the target for a furious assault; the Golan Heights were taken and Damascus itself was threatened.

The second conflict was the Black September hostilities in Jordan in 1970. In this clash, the Jordanian army moved against and defeated Syrian-supported Palestinian guerilla groups who were vying for power in Jordan.

At this point Assad, who had opposed backing the Palestinians against the Jordanian army, seized power and ousted the civilian party leadership. He was sworn in as president for seven years on 14 March 1971.

On 6 October 1973, Egypt and Syria launched a surprise attack on Israel in an attempt to recover lost territories. After initial gains, the Israelis managed to hold their ground and Egypt signed an armistice in January 1974. Fighting in the Golan Heights continued until the end of May, without Syria gaining much for its trouble.

Assad's Success

Since 1971, Assad has managed to hold power longer than any other post-independence Syrian government with a mixture of ruthless suppression and guile. His success can be attributed to a number of factors: giving disadvantaged and minority groups a better deal; stacking the bureaucracy and internal security organisations with members of his own Alawite faith (which has led to wide-scale repression and silencing of opposition both at home and abroad); and an overall desire, no doubt shared by many Syrians, for political stability. In 1992, he was elected to a fourth seven-year term with a predictable 99.9% of the vote. Assad rules through the so-called National Progressive Front, a Ba'ath-dominated body of allied parties.

Lebanon

Since civil war erupted in Lebanon in 1975, Syria's involvement in its neighbour's affairs has waxed and waned. After several Arab summits, a 30,000-strong peace-keeping force, mostly Syrians, was sent in to quell fighting in Lebanon. At the same time,

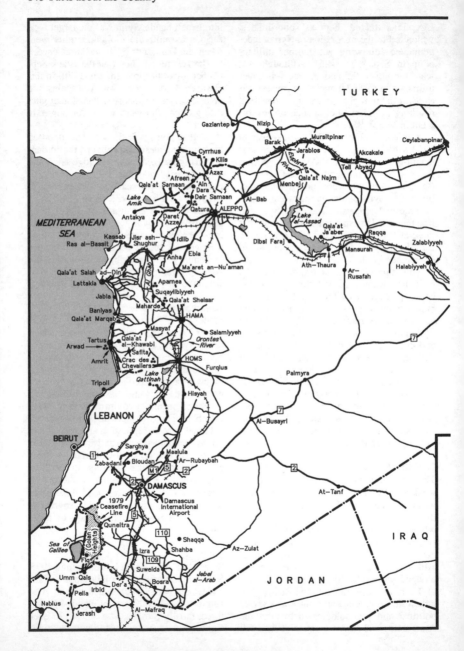

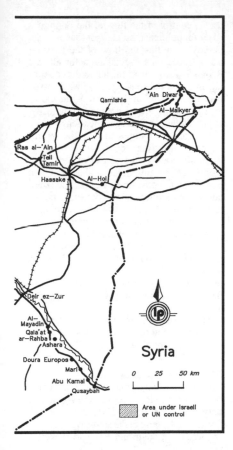

Syria

| 0 | 25 | 50 km |

Area under Israeli or UN control

Soviet military support for Syria grew – by 1983 there were about 6000 Soviet military advisers in Syria.

Israel's invasion of Lebanon in 1982 and quick advance on Beirut heightened tensions, and for a while it seemed conflict between the two was inevitable. The invasion came shortly after Israel had formally annexed the Golan Heights. In the following years, Israel and Syria, with the PLO and various Lebanese factions, faced each other off. By the end of 1985, the Israelis had withdrawn from Lebanon, maintaining control over a buffer zone in the south, and

Syria had reduced its forces in the country too.

Since then, Syria has attempted with varying degrees of success to gain control over the Lebanese mess, manoeuvring for leverage over the many Lebanese, Palestinian and other factions at large in the country. Now that peace appears to have returned to Lebanon, Syria seems to have won greater control over the country's affairs than ever. The fact that neither country has diplomatic representation in the other's capital is seen as confirmation of a Syrian policy of 'two countries, one nation', and even a prelude to moves for a 'Greater Syria'.

Opposition

In the '80s, economic difficulties helped fuel growing opposition to Assad's regime. The main opposition came from the extremist militant group, the Muslim Brotherhood, who particularly object to Alawite-dominated rule, as the Alawites account for only 11.5% of the population. Membership of the Brotherhood became a capital offence in 1981, but in 1985 the official attitude softened and exiled members of the group were pardoned and allowed to return to Syria, and it was reported that 500 members were freed from jails within the country.

The Brotherhood's opposition has sometimes taken a violent course. In 1979, 32 Alawite cadets were killed in a raid in Aleppo. Anti-Ba'ath demonstrations were held in Aleppo in 1980, and in the most serious threat to Assad yet, as many as 30,000 people were killed in the town of Hama when the army, under Assad's brother Rifa'at, moved in brutally to quash a revolt led by Sunnis who ambushed Syrian security forces and staged a general insurrection in February 1982.

Since then little has been heard of the opposition but in early 1984, when Assad was recovering from a heart attack, a vigorous internal power struggle ensued when Rifa'at apparently attempted to seize power and was effectively exiled to France. In 1986, he was allowed back and re-elected to the Regional Command, the most powerful body in the country, but has since been forced to take a back seat again. The lack of an obvious successor remains a glaring problem, but fears of growing instability have been lulled in the early '90s by Assad's astute exploitation of the Gulf War in 1990-91 and improvements in the economy, where new oil finds and the gradual relaxation of draconian laws on banking, foreign finance and imports have awakened hopes of an improvement in the business environment.

Gulf War & Peace Talks

Syria joined the Allied anti-Iraq coalition in 1990, no doubt spurred on by the collapse of the Soviet Union, its main superpower backer. Although no friend of Baghdad, having supported its enemy Iran throughout the first Gulf war, above all Assad saw in 1990 a chance to get into the good books with the West and the USA in general. In return for its modest contribution to the Allied effort, Syria hoped to be dropped from Washington's list of states supporting international terrorism, for which Syria has a well-entrenched reputation, having long been accused over the 1988 Pan-Am air explosion over Lockerbie.

Assad also loosened the reigns on Syria's small Jewish population, promising in early 1992 to make it easier for them to emigrate. The USA, although markedly warmer in its lip service, has yet to take Syria off the list, which would be a signal to Western nations to loosen aid purse strings.

Assad has, by his moves, brought Syria out of the cold, and his decision to join in the peace process begun in Madrid in 1991 was another step in the same direction. Syria's main preoccupation in its relations with Israel remains the Golan Heights, and in September 1992, at a time when Syria was virtually writing the peace talks off as useless, the recently elected Labour prime minister in Israel, Yitzak Rabin, announced for the first time since 1967 that Israel was prepared to trade at least part of the Golan Heights for a lasting peace.

Another growing source of friction is coming from the north, as Turkey appears to use its control of the flow of the Euphrates River for political reasons. Syria has accused Turkey of cutting the flow of the river on several occasions in retaliation for alleged Syrian backing for Kurdish guerillas operating in south-east Turkey. The water issue may one day bring Iraq and Syria closer together again, after a decade of animosity, as they both fear Turkey's intentions.

At home, changes are in the wind, although they may be slow in coming. Rumours grew in the course of 1992 that Assad, feeling more relaxed about his own position, was considering altering the structure of government and, more importantly, removing the Ba'ath Party's virtual stranglehold on power. As a concession to Western pressures, there were reports that many of the 6000 political prisoners in Syrian jails – many held without trial for up to 30 years under state of emergency laws – might be released, and Amnesty International confirmed about 2000 had gone free in the first months of 1992.

The question of the succession remains unsolved, but at 62, Assad may have a long innings in front of him yet.

GEOGRAPHY & CLIMATE

Syria is not a large country – it has an area of 185,000 sq km, a bit over half the size of Italy. It is very roughly a 500-km square with Lebanon intruding in the south-west, Jordan and Iraq in the south and east, and Turkey to the north.

There are four geographical regions in Syria: the coastal strip, the mountains, the cultivated steppe and the desert.

The Coastal Strip

The coastline of Syria stretches for about 180 km between Turkey and Lebanon. The Jebel an-Nusariyah (Ansariyah Mountains) almost front the coast in the north but give way to the Sahl Akkar (Akkar Plain) in the south. The fertile alluvial plains are intensively farmed year-round. The two major ports are Lattakia and Tartus and there's a large oil refining complex at Baniyas.

Average daily temperatures range from 29°C in summer to 10°C in winter and the annual rainfall is about 760 mm.

The Mountains

The Jebel an-Nusariyah form a continuous jagged ridge running north-south just inland from the coast. With an average height of 1000 metres, they form a formidable and impenetrable barrier which dominates the whole coast. Snowfalls on the higher peaks are not uncommon in winter. The western side is marked by deep ravines, while on the east the mountains fall almost sheer to the Orontes, the fertile valley of the Nahr al-Assi (the 'rebel river') that flows north into Turkey.

The Jebel Lubnan ash-Sharqiyah (Anti-Lebanon Mountains) mark the border between Syria and Lebanon and average 2000 metres in height. Syria's highest mountain, Jebel ash-Sheikh (Mt Hermon of the Bible), rises to 2814 metres. The main river to flow from this range is the Barada, which has enabled Damascus to survive in an otherwise arid region for over 2000 years.

Other smaller ranges include the Jebel Druze, which rise in the south near the Jordanian border, and the Jebel Abu Rujmayn in the centre of the country, north of Palmyra.

The Cultivated Steppe

The Fertile Crescent is, as the name suggests, Syria's main agricultural region and forms an arc in which the major centres of Damascus, Homs, Hama, Aleppo and Qamishle are found. The Euphrates and Orontes rivers provide enough water for intensive farming, while away from the water sources, dry-land wheat and cereal crops are grown. Irrigation is in fact stretching the area under cultivation, and another historically rich zone, the Jezira, is re-emerging. It literally means 'island' and is the area bounded by the Euphrates and Tigris rivers in Syria and Iraq.

Temperatures average around 35°C in summer and 12°C in winter. Rainfall varies from about 250 to 500 mm.

The Desert

The Syrian desert occupies the whole southeast of the country. It is a land of endless stony plains. The oasis of Palmyra is on the northern edge of this arid zone and along with other oases used to be an important centre for the trade caravans plying the routes between the Mediterranean and Mesopotamia.

The Bedouin are at home in this country. During the winter months they graze sheep until water and fodder becomes scarce, and then move west or into the hills.

Temperatures are high and rainfall low. In summer the days average 40°C and highs of 46°C are not uncommon.

FLORA & FAUNA

Heavy clearing has all but destroyed the once abundant forests of the mountain belt along the coast of Syria, although some small areas are still protected. Yew, lime and fir trees predominate in areas where vegetation has not been reduced to scrub. Elsewhere, vegetation is dominated by agriculture, with little or no plant life in the unforgiving stretches of the Syrian Desert.

Your chances of coming across anything more interesting than a camel are next to nil, although – officially at least – wolves, hyenas, foxes, badgers, wild boar, jackals, deer, bears, squirrels, and even polecats supposedly still roam around in some corners of the country.

GOVERNMENT

Actual power resides in the president as leader of the Arab Ba'ath Socialist Party. He has the power to appoint ministers, declare war, issue laws and appoint civil servants and military personnel. Under the 1973 constitution, approved overwhelmingly by the Syrian electorate, legislative power supposedly lies with the people and freedom of expression is guaranteed. With the constant military and political tensions, enforcement of these principles has been less than thorough to say the least.

At the time of the promulgation of the constitution, which guarantees freedom of religious thought and expression, there was outrage that Islam was not declared the state religion. Bowing, but not all the way, to the pressure, Assad and his government amended it to say that the head of state must be Muslim.

All political parties are officially affiliated through the National Progressive Front, of which Assad is also the leader. Being dominated by the Ba'ath Party, the Front is for all intents ineffective and is little more than a tool by which Assad's regime can influence the non-Ba'ath parties. There is also a 250-member People's Council, which has limited legislative powers, but just as the Ba'ath Party is the dominant force in the Front, so the Front dominates the Council.

The President has three vice-presidents, including his disgraced brother, Rifa'at, and it has been generally assumed that a successor might be chosen from among them. However, changes in the structure of government have been guardedly mooted, with suggestions that the three vice-presidents might be replaced by one deputy, that more power might be devolved onto the prime minister and the cabinet, which have had little more than rubber-stamp powers, and that the Ba'ath Party may lose its privileged position in the party structure.

The country is divided into 14 governorates, or muhafazat, which in turn are subdivided into smaller units of local government.

ECONOMY

After a particularly bad decade in the '80s, the outlook for Syria's seriously shackled economy was looking brighter in the early '90s.

One ray of hope has come from the development of petrol and gas finds in the Deir ez-Zur area along the Euphrates in the country's east. Production of the reasonably high quality light crude began in 1986 and was expected to top 400,000 barrels a day by the end of 1992. Most is produced by the Al-Furat Petroleum Company, a consortium of several foreign companies and a Syrian Government component. Until then, only a small amount of poor, heavy crude was being extracted in the north-east of the country.

As the government loosens its policy on concessions to foreign companies, more are expressing interest in various projects, from improving the disastrous telephone system to upgrading sewerage systems, along with agricultural and industrial projects.

Agriculture accounts for just over 20% of GDP and employs a quarter of the workforce, although a rural flight to the cities is slowly reducing this. Cereals and cotton are the main products of the Fertile Crescent and the Jezira. In the mountains and on the coast tobacco, various fruits, especially citrus, and olives are all intensively grown.

Industry accounts for 23% of GDP, and includes the production of phosphates and fertilizers at Palmyra and Homs, iron and steel in Hama, and cement in Tartus. Syrians are proud of their drive towards some degree of self-sufficiency, and other products include rubber, glass, paper, food processing, along with the assembly of TVs, fridges, tractors and some other vehicles.

Power generation remains a huge problem, with power cuts a regular feature of daily life. The dam built on the Euphrates River at Lake Assad was designed to solve the difficulties but has failed to meet expectations, partly because of Turkey's exploitation of Euphrates water upstream for their own Ataturk dam. According to observers in Damascus, the biggest problem is the vintage and make of most of the industrial equipment and power network. It's old, Russian and simply inadequate.

Severe strain is placed on the economy by defence, which still accounts for over 60% of total expenditure, more than five times what is spent on education. The internal security apparatus also soaks up a sizeable chunk. As a 'front-line' state, Syria was entitled to US$1850 million in aid under the Baghdad agreement, but as Jordan found, only Saudi Arabia was willing to pay its share. Syria's participation in the anti-Iraq coalition was partly calculated to win it lucrative new aid deals, not only with Gulf states, but in the West. It needs all the help it can get – national debt stands at more than US$16 billion.

In an attempt to keep valuable tourist revenue in the banking system, the tourist exchange rate has been raised to almost the same level as the black market rate. Tourism is far from a huge money-spinner. Reliable statistics are virtually impossible to find but in 1988, for instance, it seems there were fewer than 130,000 Western visitors, many of them on business.

Despite campaigns to control smuggling, the black market continues to thrive. Corruption within the government is rife and the breakdown of customs control is so widespread that goods smuggled in from Lebanon are sold openly in the street. The despair that many Syrians, particularly the businesspeople, feel about the level of corruption is voiced in an Arab saying: 'If he (Assad) knows about it, it's a disaster; if he doesn't know about it, it's a bigger disaster'.

POPULATION & PEOPLE
Syria has a population of 12.2 million, and its annual growth rate of 3.6% (one of the highest in the world) is way out of proportion with its economic growth. The two biggest cities are Damascus and Aleppo, with respectively about 1.5 million and one million inhabitants.

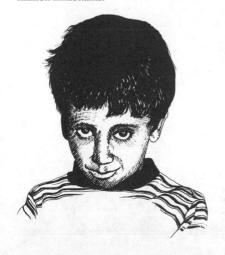

Ethnic Groups
Ethnic Syrians are of Semitic stock. About 90% of the population are Arabs, which includes some minorities such as the Bedouin (about 100,000).

The remainder is made up of smaller groupings of Kurds, Armenians, Circassians and Turks.

Of the estimated 20 million Kurds in the region, about one million are found in Syria and, along with their counterparts in Turkey, Iran and Iraq, are agitating for an independent Kurdish state – with little success so far. They have been blamed for some acts of terrorism in Syria, which were seen as part of their push for self-government. Since the late '80s, Turkey has repeatedly accused Syria of sheltering Kurdish rebels making incursions into southern Turkey, an allegation Damascus flatly denies. Syria's Kurds will often say things are just fine, but many are quick to tell outsiders, discreetly, of their desires for greater autonomy.

The Armenians, much in evidence in Aleppo where whole quarters are inhabited by them and signs in their language abound next to the Arabic, are mostly descendants of those who fled the Armenian genocide in Turkey during WW I.

Linguistic Groups
Arabic is the mother tongue of the majority. Kurdish is spoken in the north, especially towards the east, Armenian in Aleppo and other major cities, and Turkish in some villages east of the Euphrates.

Aramaic, the language of the Bible, is still spoken in two or three villages.

English is widely understood and increasingly popular as a second language, while French, although waning, is still quite common among the older people.

Religious Groups
Islam is practised by about 86% of the population – one-fifth of these are minorities such as the Shi'ite, Druze and Alawite, while the remainder are Sunni Muslims.

Christians account for most of the rest and belong to various churches including the

Greek Orthodox, Greek Catholic, Syrian Orthodox, Armenian Orthodox, Maronite, Roman Catholic and Protestant.

There are a few thousand Jews concentrated in Damascus, although most who could have emigrated to Israel or the USA. In August 1992, the Government announced that about 800 Jews had been given passports and most of these were also given exit permits. Some predicted that by the end of 1993 the entire Jewish community would have left. In the meantime, the regime makes regular propaganda use of those who remain, organising the usual spontaneous demonstrations of undying loyalty to the President.

EDUCATION

In the 1970s, the literacy rate in Syria was estimated by some at about 50%. This has been increased, but it is difficult to ascertain by how much. Officially at least, primary education from the age of six is free and compulsory. Secondary education is only free at the state schools, for places in which there is fierce competition. Although there are private schools, they follow a common syllabus.

Competition for places in the universities is also fierce. Damascus and Aleppo have the two main universities, with two smaller ones in Lattakia and Homs, and another small higher education institute recently set up in Deir ez-Zur.

UNRWA also runs schools for Palestinian refugees living in Syria, and they have the right to free places in Syrian schools as well.

About 150,000 students attend higher education institutions. Something that most young Syrians have to contend with is 2½ years' military service.

CULTURE
Avoiding Offence

Syrians are conservative when it comes to clothes and are not accustomed to the bizarre ways some tourists dress. Women should always wear at least knee-length dresses or pants and tops that keep at least the shoulders covered.

Men will have no problem walking around in shorts but will be considered a bit eccentric and should expect to get stared at a lot. To avoid unpleasant scenes, dress conservatively if you want to enter a mosque. Some, such as the Omayyad Mosque in Damascus, will provide you with a cloak if they feel you're 'indecent'.

When crossing borders or dealing with officials, there's no need to smarten yourself up specially as they seem more interested in who you are than what you look like.

Facts for the Visitor

VISAS & EMBASSIES

All foreigners entering Syria must obtain a visa. These are available at Syrian consulates outside the country, or supposedly on arrival at the border, port or airport, although there have been conflicting stories about this. To be on the safe side, get a visa before showing up at the border. If there's any evidence of a visit to Israel in your passport, you won't be allowed into Syria. Similarly, if you plan on going to Israel after Syria, don't say so. A passport with a lot of stamps in it may well slow you down at times. It can take two Syrian officials half an hour to decide that a trekking permit from Nepal has nothing to do with Israel!

A tourist visa is valid for 15 days and must be used within one month of the date of issue. On entry, you will fill out a yellow entry card (in English), which virtually replaces the former currency declaration form. Keep this, as you'll need it to get visa extensions and on leaving Syria. The cost of visas varies according to nationality and on where you get them, and it is *not* always cheaper the closer you get to Syria. There seems to be little rhyme or reason in deciding which nationalities pay what, except in the case of UK passport-holders, who *always* pay a lot.

In the UK, Australians and New Zealanders pay £28.50, while US passport-holders will only have to cough up £7.50. Germans are a little better off, at £6, and Canadians pay only £3.50. UK travellers have also been able to obtain visas for £28.50 in London (after a break of more than four years) since the two countries restored diplomatic relations in November 1990.

In Turkey, you can get visas in Ankara and Istanbul, and for some nationalities they are much cheaper. Australians and New Zealanders, for example, only pay TL40,000 (about US$6), but US, Canadian and German citizens all do worse than they would in Europe, at TL100,000, TL40,000 and TL70,000, respectively. Britons pay a whopping TL360,000. In addition, the Syrians here don't like issuing anything but single-entry visas. You need a letter of recommendation from your embassy, for which you may be charged (Australians pay A$10) and one passport photo. Visas take two working days to issue. German travellers should note that their consulate does not issue letters of recommendation in Istanbul.

It is easier and generally cheaper to get visas in Jordan. You still need a letter and photo, but visas are issued on the same day and multiple-entry visas are no problem – they cost about double. Single-entry visas are free for Australians and Canadians, JD9.75 (about US$14) for Americans, JD4 for New Zealanders, but still a hefty JD37.50 for Britons.

Although single-entry visa-holders who want to go to Lebanon are supposedly issued with re-entry permits on leaving Syria (there is no Syrian consulate in Lebanon), it would be a safer bet to get a multiple entry instead, otherwise you may find yourself having to fly out or catch a boat to Cyprus.

Syrian Embassies

Syria has no diplomatic representation in New Zealand. Nationals of New Zealand wishing to get a visa prior to leaving home are advised to contact the Lebanese embassy.

Irish citizens should contact the embassy in London.

The following countries have Syrian embassies:

Australia
41 Alexandra Ave, South Yarra, Victoria 3141 (☎ (03) 867 5131)
Egypt
Doqqi, Cairo (☎ (2) 718232)
France
20 rue Vaneau, 75007 Paris (☎ (1) 40.62.61.00)
Germany
Andreas Hermes Str 5, 5300 Bonn 2 (☎ (228) 819920)
Japan
Homatgade No19-45, Akasaka Minato-ku, Tokyo 106 (☎ (3) 35868978)
Jordan
Haza al-Majali, 4th Circle, Jebel Amman (☎ (6) 641076)
Saudi Arabia
Sharia ath-Thalatheen, muqabil (opposite) Baladiyyeh al-'Aliyya wa as-Sulaimaniyyeh, Riyadh (☎ (1) 465-2943)
Turkey
Abdullah Cevdet Sokak No 7, Cankaya, Ankara (☎ (4) 440-9657)
(consulate) 3 Silahhane Caddesi, Ralli Building, Nisantasi, Istanbul (☎ (1) 248-2735)
UK
8 Belgrave Square, London, SW1 (☎ (071) 245-9012)
USA
2215 Wyoming Ave NW, Washington DC 2008 (☎ (202) 232-6313)
(consulate) 820 Second Ave, New York, NY 10017 (☎ (212) 661-1553)

Visa Extensions

If your stay in Syria is going to be more than 15 days you have to get a visa extension. This can be done at an immigration office, which you'll find in all main cities. You can get more than one extension and their length appears to depend on a combination of what you're willing to ask for and the mood of the official you deal with.

Extensions are usually only granted on the 14th or 15th day of your stay, so if you apply earlier expect to be knocked back. If, as sometimes happens, they do extend it earlier, check that the extension is from the last day of your visa or previous extension, and not from the day of application.

The cost, number of passport photos and the time taken to issue the extension all vary from place to place. The cost is never more than US$1; you'll need anything from three (Damascus) to five (Aleppo) photos; and time taken varies from on-the-spot (most places) to 1 pm the following day (Damascus). There are also several forms to fill in, in French and/or English, usually containing questions repeated several times in slightly different ways – it is a challenge to think of sensible things to put down.

It is possible to get residence for a year or so, but you have to enrol in an approved Arabic language school or get an approved teaching job; see the Work section and Language Courses in the Activities section.

Foreign Embassies in Syria

Some of the foreign embassies and consulates to be found in Damascus are:

Australia
128a Farabi St, al-Mezzeh (☎ 665317)
Canada
Block 12, al-Mezzeh (☎ 236851)
Egypt
Mahadar al-Fursan 133, al-Mezzeh ash-Sharqiyyeh (☎ 667901)
France
Ata Ayoubi St (☎ 247992)
Germany
53 Ibrahim Hanano St (☎ 716670)
Iraq
Closed
Ireland
No diplomatic representation in Syria, see UK embassy
Japan
15 Al-Jala'a Ave (☎ 339421)
Jordan
Al-Jala'a Ave (☎ 234642)
Lebanon
No diplomatic representation in Syria
New Zealand
No diplomatic representation in Syria, see UK embassy
Saudi Arabia
Al-Jala'a Ave, Abu Roumaneh (☎ 334914)
UK
Malki Quarter, 11 Mohammed Kurd Ali St, Imm Kotob (☎ 712561)
USA
2 Al-Mansour St, Abu Roumaneh (☎ 333052)

Visas for Neighbouring Countries

Jordan Jordanian visas are available at the border, but if you want to get one in Damascus the embassy is on Al-Jala'a Ave, about five minutes' walk over the bridge from the National Museum. One-month tourist visas are issued the same day, require two passport photos and cost anything from nothing (Americans and Australians) to S£1100 (Britons and Canadians). The embassy is only open from 8 to 11.30 am and is closed on Fridays. Multiple and 24-hour transit visas are also available.

Iraq & Lebanon The Iraqi embassy is closed, and in one locally produced guide erroneously marked as the Italian embassy! There is no Lebanese diplomatic representation in Damascus, presumably a testament to the Syrian policy of 'one nation, two countries'.

DOCUMENTS

When travelling in Syria, keep your passport handy at all times. Although ID checks have become less frequent in recent years, they can still occur on any bus you board. Keep the yellow entry card you filled out at the border. You'll be issued with a new one for each visa extension you get and have to hand it in when departing.

An International Driving Permit is required if you intend to do any driving in Syria.

CUSTOMS

There is no longer any compulsory exchange (at a terrible rate) of US$100 on entering Syria, and you can bring in up to US$5000 without declaring it. Officially, you can only export US$2000 without declaring it, or S£5000 to Jordan or Lebanon.

MONEY

The banking system in Syria is entirely state-owned, although there has been talk of creating openings for private and even foreign institutions. That still looks some way off, and initially would concern investment banks alone. The Commercial Bank of

Syria is the public face of the state system and there's always at least one branch in every major town. The fun starts when there's more than one branch, because the different departments of the bank will be in its different branches, so Branch No 1 might change cheques but not cash and Branch No 2 might take neither or both!

Since late 1991, the tourist exchange rate available in the bank has been set at close to the black market rate, so although it can still take ages to actually complete the transaction in the bank (the number of forms in quintuplicate can be enough to make your head spin), you will get a reasonable rate.

You may want to buy some Syrian pounds before you leave home, and will probably get a slightly better rate for them, but it is not a currency in big demand – or supply.

If you leave by land, you can trade your leftover pounds for dinars in Jordan or for lira in Turkey with little trouble, and now that the rate inside Syria is more realistic, this does not entail the financial suicide it once did. In Turkey, it is probably best to change at the border, but in Jordan most banks should accept Syrian pounds.

When shopping, some store-owners will accept not only foreign hard currency, but travellers cheques and even some personal cheques – they will ask you to keep it quiet, though.

Currency

The currency is the Syrian pound (S£), known locally as the *lira*. There are 100 piastres (*qirsh*) to a pound. Coins in circulation are ¼ (rare), ½ and one pound. Notes are S£1 (rare), 5, 10, 25, 50, 100 and 500.

The S£500 notes are really too big for everyday use and can be a hassle, although it's surprising how often the owner of some crummy little street stall will bring out a wad of notes and change it for you.

Exchange Rates

Although things are gradually changing, the Commercial Bank of Syria still has a bewildering array of exchange rates to suit every occasion. Many concern business people alone, but there are two rates to be aware of apart from the normal tourist rate.

The hotels that charge US dollars work their room prices out at the 'official rate' of S£11.20 to the US dollar. When taking extras like breakfast, try to pay on the spot in Syrian pounds – which you will have changed in the bank at S£42 to the US dollar. Anything that goes on the room bill will be worked out at the official rate.

A$1	=	S£27.95
C$1	=	S£35.25
F10	=	S£73.50
DM1	=	S£25.25
Y100	=	S£30.60
JD1	=	S£52.85 (Jordan)
TL1000	=	S£7* (Turkey)
UK£1	=	S£78
US$1	=	S£42

S£100	=	A$3.57
S£100	=	C$2.83
S£100	=	F13.60
S£100	=	DM3.96
S£100	=	Y327
S£100	=	JD1.89 (Jordan)
S£100	=	TL14,300* (Turkey)
S£100	=	UK£1.28
S£100	=	US$2.38

*You may find it difficult to change Turkish lira in the banks. The rate given is a black market approximation.

Aviation Rate If you want to buy an air ticket in Syria, the 'aviation rate' applies to international travel, which is S£30 to the dollar. When you buy a ticket you will have to go to a bank, ask to change money at the aviation rate and get an appropriate receipt, which you will then hand over to the travel agent with payment for the ticket.

Changing & Commissions

You can leave your credit cards at home as they are virtually useless, except for paying the bill at some of the bigger hotels.

Most travellers' cheques are accepted in the banks, but a minimum commission of

S£5 is paid per transaction for every bunch of five cheques. If you change one cheque on five occasions, you'll pay S£5 every time. If you change all five at once, you'll only pay the commission once.

Occasionally you'll be asked to present sales receipts when changing travellers cheques, which of course you are not supposed to have with you. Not all branches do this, but you may find you have no choice, since in some towns there is only the one bank.

There is no commission for changing cash and, as with cheques, most major currencies are accepted. If, as in the UK, new notes are being issued, you may have trouble convincing banks in more out-of-the-way places that they are genuine.

More often than not, you'll find yourself being diddled for a pound or two, as bank employees (and others) tend to round everything off to the nearest five pounds.

Costs

Despite the end of the compulsory border exchange and more reasonable exchange rates, Syria is not much cheaper to travel in now than it was years ago. The reason is the massive inflationary heave the country experienced in November 1991, when the lid was partly lifted and prices on just about everything quadrupled. In fact, the cheaper hotels and food cost much the same as in neighbouring Jordan, where prices have stayed stable despite a devaluation of the currency by half since 1988. Transport and other items remain very cheap in Syria, however.

It is quite possible to stay within the US$10 a day mark, but only if you are prepared to stay in the cheaper hotels and stick to a diet of felafels, shawarma and juice. For more details on hotel costs, see the Accommodation section.

With some exceptions, the cheapest beds in Syrian hotels come for around S£100. In Damascus, even this is rare enough, but in some places, particularly Lattakia, you can have a perfectly adequate room to yourself for half that.

An average meal in a middle-range restaurant can cost anything from S£100 to S£200. As in Jordan, waiters in the better restaurants expect tips, and occasionally deduct them themselves when giving you change.

A felafel on the street will cost S£5 to S£10, while a shawarma will usually cost S£15. Similarly, a bottle of soft drink bought from a street vendor is S£5, while a can of imported Canada Dry is S£15. Fruit, such as apples, goes for about S£10 a piece.

Bargaining

Whatever you buy in the way of souvenirs, remember that bargaining is an integral part of the process and listed prices are always inflated to allow for it. When shopping in the souqs, bargain – even a minimum effort will see outrageous asking prices halved.

Show only a casual interest if you really want something and name a price well below what you are willing to pay. Take your time, smile and don't feel obliged to go above your intended price just because the shopkeeper is hospitable and serves tea or coffee. If after all this you can't agree on a price, try another shop – there are plenty of them. Remember that their starting price is more often than not double what they are prepared to sell for.

Black Market

The introduction of the 'rate in neighbouring countries' in late November, at the same time as massive price rises, has dealt a more effective blow to the black market in currency than a tough law introduced in 1986 providing for up to 15 years in jail for the unwarranted possession of hard currency. Officials insist that law has now fallen into disuse, and although people are still afraid of the possible consequences, they are changing more openly than a few years ago. Some will even change travellers' cheques. The difference between what you'll get in the bank and on the street is, however, probably not great enough to justify going out of your way to use the black market.

WHEN TO GO

Spring is the best time to visit as temperatures are mild and the winter rains have cleared the haze that obscures views for much of the year. Autumn is the next choice.

If you go in summer, don't be caught without a hat and water bottle, especially if visiting Palmyra or the north-east. A siesta in the heat of the afternoon is a popular habit, although when the daily power cuts leave you stranded in a hot room with no fan you may as well be outside.

Winter can be downright unpleasant on the coast and in the mountains, when temperatures drop and the rains begin.

WHAT TO BRING

For details of what to bring with you to Syria see the Regional Facts for the Visitor chapter.

TOURIST OFFICES

Syria is trying to attract more tourists and in fact the country's Fourth Five-Year Plan (1976-80) envisaged tourism becoming its third largest source of income. Like many of the plan's goals, that hope was not realised. Statistics on the number of tourists vary wildly. Official government figures put the figure in 1988 at 217,000, of whom about half were said to be Westerners. You'd probably find more tourists in London on any one day in summer than in Syria in a whole year. This becomes apparent when you visit a site or museum, as often you'll be the only one there.

Local Tourist Offices

There is a tourist office in every major town, but don't expect too much in the way of information. All they generally have is a free hand-out map of often indifferent quality, although the Damascus one isn't bad.

Many of the museums and some of the archaeological sites have small booklets on sale, usually tucked away somewhere in a hidden cupboard. Occasionally they'll have only one or two booklets – about somewhere else!

Overseas Reps

For information before arriving in Syria, contact any of the Syrian diplomatic missions overseas. It is worth being insistent as they often have a complete set of the free hand-out maps available for each town in Syria. There are no tourist bureaux outside Syria.

The library at Trailfinders (☎ (071) 938-3366), in the basement of their office at 194 Kensington High St, London, W8 7RG, has some handy scraps of information, maps and so on.

Also, if you are in London, try Stanford's bookshop (☎ (071) 836-2121), at 12-14 Long Acre, London, WC2E 9LP, for some none-too-cheap but otherwise hard-to-come-by maps (but try your best at the embassy for the freebies first).

BUSINESS HOURS

Government offices, such as immigration and tourism, are generally open from 8 am to 2 pm every day except Fridays and holidays, but the hours can swing either way by an hour or so. Other offices and shops keep similar hours in the morning and often open again from 4 to 6 or 7 pm. Most restaurants and a few small traders stay open on Fridays.

Banks generally follow the government office hours, but there are quite a few exceptions to the rule. Some branches keep their doors open for only three hours from 9 am, while some exchange booths are open as late as 7 pm.

In smaller places, the post office closes at 2 pm. In bigger cities they stay open longer; until 8 pm in Damascus and Aleppo, where they are open on Fridays too. As a rule, telephone offices are open much longer hours; in Damascus, for example, around the clock.

Museums and monuments are usually open from 8 am until 2 pm, and sometimes later in the afternoon as well. Most are closed on Tuesdays.

HOLIDAYS

Most holidays are either religious (Islamic and Christian) or are celebrations of important dates in the formation of the modern Syrian state. Most Christian holidays fall according to the Julian calendar, as in Jordan,

which can be as much as a month behind the Western (Gregorian) calendar.

For Islamic holidays see the table of holidays page 28. Other holidays are:

January
  New Year's Day (15th)
February
  Union Day (22nd)
March
  Revolution Day/Women's Day (1st)
  Arab League Day (22nd)
April
  Evacuation Day (17th)
May
  Martyrs' Day (6th)
  Security Force Day (29th)
August
  Army Day (1st)
  Marine's Day (29th)
October
  Veteran's Day (6th)
  Flight Day (16th)
November
  Correction Movement Day (16th)
December
  Peasant's Day (14th)
  Christmas (25th)

CULTURAL EVENTS

The Roman Theatre at Bosra, south of Damascus, regularly plays host to theatre and music festivals, although often they are functions for the big nobs of government.

Every year, in September, Damascus holds a two-week trade fair, itself of little interest to the traveller, which is usually accompanied by various cultural events. Check the *Syria Times* for details.

The foreign cultural centres occasionally show films and organise lectures. Notices of what's on appear in the *Syria Times* on Wednesdays and Thursdays.

POST & TELECOMMUNICATIONS
Post
Postal Rates The cost of sending a letter or postcard seems to be different every time. Letters to any destination seem to be up to S£9, postcards to Australia and the USA S£3.75, and to Europe S£2.75.

Sending Mail The Syrian postal service is

Syrian people (HF)

Top Left: Takiyyeh as-Sulaymaniyyeh Mosque, Damascus (DS)
Top Right: Damascus from Jebel Qassioun (HF)
Bottom Left: Azem Palace, Damascus (DS)
Bottom Right: Western Gate of the Temple of Jupiter, Damascus (HF)

slow but effective enough. Letters mailed from major cities take about 10 days to Europe and anything up to a month to Australia or the USA.

To send a parcel from Damascus or Aleppo, take it (unwrapped) to the parcel post office for inspection. After it's been cleared it has to be wrapped and covered with cotton. You have to buy the cotton from one guy, pay another to give you some cardboard tags for the address, and yet another to wrap it! It's basically the enforced baksheesh gravy train for unemployed Syrians, which will cost you about S£20 to S£30.

For all that, the process doesn't usually take more than about half an hour. A two-kg parcel to Australia or the USA costs S£375, to Europe S£275.

Receiving Mail The poste restante counter at the main post office in Damascus will allow you to look through alphabetically organised piles under your name and surname. Take your passport.

Telephone

International calls can be made from the telephone offices in major cities or through any of the five-star hotels. There is a three-minute minimum and you can wait up to two hours for a connection to be made. Bring your passport along, as they'll want to see it. Calls to Australia cost S£115 per minute, calls to Europe S£100. The hotels ask anything up to S£300 a minute to Australia and S£250 a minute to Europe. There are no collect calls from Syria.

For local calls you need S£1 coins to operate the telephone booths – if you can find one. If you're unfortunate enough to want to make a call elsewhere in Syria, you can try the telephone offices. Inside and out are rows of telephone booths, many disconnected. They each have a destination written up in Arabic only – so if you want to call someone in, say, Homs, you have to find a *working* booth marked Homs and wait in line. For local calls you're better off calling from your hotel.

Some of the important dialling codes in Syria are:

Damascus	11
Aleppo	21
Homs	31
Hama	331
Lattakia	41
Tartus	431
Deir ez-Zur	51

Fax, Telex & Telegram

It is possible to send telexes and telegrams from telephone offices, but they too are expensive. Although the post office in Aleppo claims to have 'electronic mail', getting hold of a fax machine is virtually impossible. The state has all but banned them as a security risk; the big hotels don't seem to have them, and some Western diplomats reckon even they have trouble getting clearance for them.

TIME

For details see the Regional Facts for the Visitor chapter.

ELECTRICITY

The current in Syria is 220 volts, 50 AC. The sockets are of the two-pronged European variety.

A lot of Syria's electricity is generated using thermal power, but the biggest source of electricity is the hydroelectric generating station at the Lake Assad dam on the Euphrates River.

The only problem seems to be that there isn't enough of it. Every town and city is without power for up to four hours a day, and not always at the same time, so it can be difficult to plan around it. The main inconvenience is that during those periods the hotels will have no fans or lights and sometimes no water.

This chronic problem seemed to have been solved in the late '80s, but in September 1991, something went wrong. Explanations abound. One official reason is that the supply is being illegally tapped, but they never say by whom. Westerners in Syria believe a generator was overloaded and went out of commission in the run-up to the 1992 elections, when the authorities 'lit Syria up'. Another possible contributing factor is, the Syrians claim, that the turbines at Lake Assad don't get enough water because the Turks hold it back for their own huge dam further upstream.

LAUNDRY
Syria's laundries are not always that easy to find, so if you want to use one ask your hotel where the nearest one is. They may organise it for you. The going price is S£15 an item, but we are not talking about one-hour laundromats. Expect a three-to-four day turnaround time! Don't be surprised to find things scribbled in wash-resistant black felt pen inside your garments too – that's just to remind them who they belong to!

WEIGHTS & MEASURES
Syria uses the metric system. For a metric conversion table see the back of the book.

BOOKS & MAPS
History
A couple of general Arab histories that are worthwhile are Philip Hitti's *History of the Arabs*, (MacMillan paperback) and Albert Hourani's more recent *A History of the Arab Peoples* (Faber, 1991). Of course neither of them are available in Syria.

Travel Guides
There is not an awful lot available on Syria, but you could try the officially sanctioned *Guide to Syria* by Afif Bahnassi (published by Avicenne). It's a saccharine but in places informative book that covers most of the sites. Another Avicenne production is E Claire Grimes' *A Guide to Damascus*.

Slightly better are Bahnassi's *Damascus* and *The Mosques of Damascus* – he may be an official mouthpiece, but he does seem to know his stuff.

Archaeological Sites
For those who read German, there is an extremely solid guide to the historical sites called *Syrien*, by Johannes Odenthal (DuMont

Kunst-Reiseführer, Cologne, 1989). It is heavy going in parts, but it *is* available in Syria.

Photography
If it's coffee-table tomes you're after, you could do worse than Michael Jenner's *Syria in View* (Longman), which contains some stunning photography and is available in Damascus. Bahnassi has also done a weighty illustrated volume called *Damascus*.

Maps
Apart from the free hand-out maps available at Syrian tourist offices, GEOprojects, based in Beirut, publishes a slightly better map of Syria. It's not great, but there's not a lot around.

MEDIA
Newspapers & Magazines
Although censorship is undeniably a feature of Syrian life, the locals do have a broad range of Arabic-language papers and magazines to choose from, not only Syrian, but from Jordan, Egypt, Lebanon and some of the Gulf states.

For everyone else, the situation is a bit more dire. The English-language daily newspaper, the *Syria Times*, is published under direct government control and is predictably big on anti-Zionist, pro-Arab rhetoric and short on news. It does have a 'What's on Today' section listing exhibitions, lectures and films as well as important telephone numbers and radio programmes.

Foreign newspapers and magazines such as the *The Middle East*, the *International Herald Tribune*, *Le Monde*, *Der Spiegel* and *Newsweek* are irregularly available in Damascus, Aleppo and Homs. Any articles on Syria or Lebanon are so lovingly torn out you'd hardly notice there was something missing.

Radio & Television
The Syrian Broadcasting Service has a foreign-language service operating on 344, 280 and 228 metres medium wave from 10 am to midnight. Programmes are in French,

English, Turkish, German and Russian. For broadcast times see the *Syria Times*.

If you have a radio the best way to keep in touch with events both inside and outside the country is through the BBC World Service, which can be picked up from about 3 am to midnight on 1323 kHz short wave or 227 mHz medium wave. They also occasionally broadcast on 720 kHz and 417 mHz.

The Syrian TV service reaches a large audience and programmes range from news and sport to American soaps. There is news in English on Syria 2 at around 10.30 pm, and a strange pop music programme in which the presenter shows some surprisingly up-to-date video clips and reads out greetings from one Syrian to another in English.

You can see Turkish TV as far south as Aleppo, and Iraqi TV in the east of the country.

FILM & PHOTOGRAPHY

Kodak, Fuji and Konica print film is readily available but a lot of it looks like it has been on the shelf for years. Slide film is only available in Damascus and Aleppo, and then with difficulty. There are places around to have your film developed, but quality is often poor.

Photography is not a problem as long as you avoid taking snaps of military sites. Be discreet if photographing women – show them the camera and make it clear that you want to take a picture of them – some may object, and if they don't, their male companions may instead. A powerful lens is helpful for good people pictures.

WOMEN TRAVELLERS

Unfortunately, many Syrian men have a slightly twisted view of Western women. Muslims are very conservative when it comes to sex and women, and men have little or no contact with either before marriage. Western movies and TV give them the impression that all Western women are promiscuous and will jump into bed at the drop of a hat.

Regardless of this, women travelling alone or in pairs should experience few problems if they follow a few tips: avoid eye contact with a man you don't know; ignore any rude remarks and act as if you didn't hear it; dress modestly at all times, but particularly in smaller towns which are likely to be more conservative than the cities.

A wedding ring will add to your respectability in Syrian eyes, but a photo of your children and even husband can clinch it – if you don't have any, borrow a picture of your nephew or niece. If you have to say anything to ward off an advance, *imshi* (clear off) should do the trick. A few women have found laughing at the importunate individual or staring at his shoes, as if to say, 'What kind of a cheap scumbag are you?', are equally effective.

In hotels, a wad of spare tissue paper or the like can come in handy for plugging up key and other holes if you're worried about peeping Toms.

DANGERS & ANNOYANCES

Despite being depicted in the Western media as a land full of terrorists and similar nasties (many Syrians are aware of and hurt by this reputation), Syria is really a safe country to travel in. You can walk around at any time of the day or night without any problem, although the area around the bars in central Aleppo and the red light zone in Damascus should be treated with a little caution.

Most Syrians are very friendly and hospitable. Don't hesitate to take up an offer if someone invites you to their village or home.

Foreigners are still enough of a novelty that they're not seen as easy targets for a rip-off. There's no such thing as one price for locals and another for foreigners and if you pay someone too much it would be rare indeed that they'd pocket the extra. I even came across one taxi driver who refused to take any money at all! On the other hand, asking a taxi to take you to one of the big hotels is sometimes seen as an invitation to ask for silly sums of money in fares.

Theft

As in Jordan, the general absence of theft has got to be one of the most refreshing things about travelling in Syria. Your bags will be quite safe left unattended virtually any-where. This is no excuse for inviting trouble through carelessness, but at least you don't have to keep a hawk-like watch over your stuff like you do in other parts of the world.

WORK

Just as Syria is not top of the pops as a tourist destination, so it is few people's dream location for work, which means teachers *do* have limited possibilities. Until the British Council re-opens (possibly 1993), the American Language Center (☎ 247236) is the only decent place to try. It is the best English-training school in Damascus and the only one that can secure residence for its employees. The school, if it needs anyone, wants people with a Bachelor's degree and some form of teaching experience. If you have a TEFL qualification, your chances improve considerably of getting work with them at US$10 or so a teaching hour.

Police

You'll see lots of uniforms and guns in Syria, partly because the military make up the police force but also because military service for men is compulsory (the only exemptions are only sons). The usual length of service is 2½ years (it used to be four). Jobs have to be found for all these men in uniform, so public buildings, ministries, embassies, banks and even bus stations are all guarded by armed soldiers. Out around the embassies and swish parts of Damascus, many of the armed men you'll see belong to virtually private armies attached to one or other bigwig or retired general – don't aggravate them, and they'll leave you alone.

Due to trouble in the past, the authorities can be touchy about what people carry on public transport. Occasionally, there may be a cursory baggage search when boarding a train or entering a bus station, although such searches and passport checks are much less frequent than they were in the mid-1980s. They're only looking for explosives and are not really interested in anything else you may be carrying.

Secret Police

Syria has several internal intelligence organisations and it's no exaggeration to say that there are secret police all over the place. If a Syrian starts talking politics to you or tries to drag you into a conversation about Assad, don't reciprocate unless it's someone you know well. The official line is that Assad is the best thing since sliced bread and to say anything to the contrary would be inadvisable. Common sense is all that's required and you shouldn't worry too much. One guy even announced to me that he was with the *mukhabarat* (intelligence service) and proceeded to expound the virtues of Assad, then asking for an opinion. 'I think he's a clever man' is a safe, fairly accurate and non-committal response to this type of question.

Just to give you an idea of the array of security forces, the following is a list of the major ones known to exist by Amnesty International, the international human rights organisation.

*   *Siraya ad-Difa' 'an ath-Thawra* – the Brigades for the Defence of the Revolution are estimated to number between 15,000 and 25,000. Their main function is to protect the President, the administration and the revolution.
*   *Al-Wahdat al-Khassa* – the Special Units comprise about 5000 to 8000 paratroopers and commandos.
*   *Al-Mukhabarat al-'Ama* – the General Intelligence responsible to the Minister of Interior.
*   *Al-Mukhabarat al-'Askariyya* – the Military Intelligence collects and acts upon intelligence affecting the armed forces. It is responsible to the Ministry of Defence.
*   *Mukhabarat al-Quwwa al-Jawiyya* – the Airforce Intelligence is the same as military intelligence, but with respect to the airforce.
*   *Al-Amn as-Siyassi* – the Political Security monitors political activity and acts upon information gathered. It is responsible to the Ministry of Interior.
*   *Al-Amn ad-Dakhili* – the Internal Security is responsible to the Ministry of Interior.
*   *Maktab al-Amn al-Qawmi* – the National Security Bureau is responsible to the Presidential Security Council. ■

The local schools, including the language faculty of the university, all tend to pay around S£100 an hour (just over US$2). Tutoring is another possibility, but that requires time to build up a clientele – tutors generally charge S£400 to S£600 an hour. For tutoring, the best thing to do first up is contact the ALC for tips and possible contacts.

Work (often unpaid) occasionally crops up on archaeological sites. It's obviously better to check this out through universities before leaving home, but your embassy might be able to help in Damascus.

ACTIVITIES
Language Courses

If you develop a more than passing interest in the Arabic language, there are several options in Damascus. The Arabic Teaching Institute for Foreigners (☎ 722328), Muhajireen, Murabet, Damascus, runs two courses: an intensive one in summer (June-September); the other in winter (October-May). Tuition is in classical Arabic (there is quite a difference between the 'standard' language and dialects) and costs about US$400. It also claims to arrange trips to archaeological sites.

Unfortunately, few students are happy with this place, but enrolment here is one of the few means of acquiring residence, saving you the hassles of continually applying for small visa extensions, which tend not to be granted beyond the second or third time anyway. Many people enrol in the course to gain residence and then go off and do something else.

The Goethe Institut and the French Cultural Centre run courses in colloquial Arabic, and there is an expensive school that is used mostly by embassies and foreign companies working in Syria, MATC (☎ 243997). Enrolment in these or any 'cowboy' school will not allow you to get residence. In fact, some schools won't take you unless you have residence. Get the picture?

HIGHLIGHTS

The two single biggest attractions lie outside the big cities. The Crac des Chevaliers is the best preserved Crusader castle in the Middle East. This largely intact medieval fortress dominates the valley between the Mediterranean port of Tartus and the city of Homs.

The ancient city of Palmyra (which under the rebellious Queen Zenobia rose and challenged Rome's authority) rises out of the glaring desert. It is, unlike many other sites of its type, visited by comparatively few tourists. Stay overnight and spend the early morning hours out among the ruins alone.

Of the main cities, Damascus, with the Omayyad Mosque and the winding alleys of the surrounding medieval city, is by far the most interesting place to spend a few days, but the citadel and souqs of its cosmopolitan northern rival, Aleppo, run a close second.

ACCOMMODATION

There are no longer any youth hostels in Syria so it's hotels or camping, although, as in Jordan, the formal possibilities for the latter are limited. You'll find every level of hotel accommodation in Syria, from the five-star, characterless, could-be-anywhere hotels down to the noisy, filthy shitboxes that you can also find in virtually any city in the world, all with prices to match.

Rooms in most of the cheap hotels are let on a share basis and will have two to four beds. If you want the room to yourself you'll often have to pay for all the beds. For solo male travellers these shared rooms are quite OK and your gear is safe when left unattended. Solo females will have to take a room.

The biggest drawback with cheap hotels is that they're often noisy, both from the street and other guests. A pair of earplugs can mean the difference between a good night's sleep and being kept awake by loud chatter, music and the TV. Rooms at the back, away from the street, are usually quieter and sometimes cheaper.

Most hotels will want to keep your passport in the 'safe' overnight, an arrangement I certainly don't like, especially when the safe is usually only a drawer at the reception desk. The purported reason for keeping it is that the police very occasionally come around checking in the middle of the night. If you tell the hotel owner that you don't mind being woken at any time he'll let you hang on to it. The common motivation is to have a security for payment of your bill.

The supply of electricity, and therefore water, is erratic all over Syria and if the hotel has no power or water when you check it out, it probably will later on. Don't take it for granted that there'll be hot water.

Note that hotels officially rated two-star and up generally require payment in US currency or equivalent and often actually want *cash*. If you feel you may not want to stay in the cheapest places and pay in local currency, it would be advisable to have a fair amount of US cash with you, however uncomfortable that may make you feel. The more expensive hotels sometimes accept credit cards and with some it is possible to change travellers' cheques for the appropriate amounts. Others again will require bank receipts with Syrian cash showing it has been changed at the official hotel rate.

ENTERTAINMENT

There is not a huge range of night-time entertainment to choose from. Most of the cinemas run heavily censored Chuck Connors to Kung Fu sort of drivel or Turkish titillation, and are only interesting for the (largely all-male) crowds that have no alter-native. The cultural centres in Damascus occasionally show more serious films.

Other than the belly-dancing and musical performances the big hotels often stage, the only other real possibility is the sleazy night clubs, of which there is no shortage in Aleppo and Damascus.

THINGS TO BUY Shopping

In the souqs of Damascus and Aleppo, you can pick up anything from silk and cotton to 100-year-old handmade carpets from Iran and antique silver jewellery, and compared with prices in Europe these are incredibly cheap.

Inlaid backgammon boards and jewellery boxes are popular buys and look great, even though the inlay work is not actually inlay but a thin veneer of ready-made wood, plastic and fake mother-of-pearl.

Other good souvenirs include brassware; narjilehs (water pipes); embroidered tablecloths; and traditional clothing, particularly the *kafiyyeh* (head cloth) and *'aghileh* (black cord) so characteristic of the region. If you buy footwear, like sandals, don't expect it to last long.

If you don't have enough Syrian pounds with you, most shopkeepers will accept hard currency, travellers' cheques and sometimes even personal cheques. Check the rate of exchange they are offering and keep the transaction quiet.

Getting There & Away

There are three ways of getting to Syria: by air, overland or sometimes by sea. Most travellers will be arriving by the overland routes from either Turkey or Jordan.

AIR

Syria has two international airports: Damascus and Aleppo. Both have regular connections to Europe, other cities in the Middle East, Africa and Asia. Most air travellers, however, will arrive in Damascus, and indeed it is not always easy to find an agent who can get you on an international flight to Aleppo.

For general hints on where to look for information and tickets in America, Europe, Asia and Australasia, as well as advice on what to watch for when buying tickets, air travellers with special needs and a glossary of air travel terminology, refer to the Jordan Getting There & Away chapter.

To/From the USA & Canada

As with Jordan, you are better off flying to London and searching around for the best deals on offer there for the onward flights.

Syrian Arab Airlines have no direct flights from North America.

To/From the UK

As it's not a popular destination you won't find much discounting on fares to Syria. Some of the eastern European airlines such as Tarom are cheaper than airlines which are members of IATA, but often require an unwanted stop.

Rumania's Tarom will do an excursion return fare (maximum stay 40 days), flying out of London, in the low season for £260, with a stop in Bucharest. For details on stopovers in Bucharest see the Jordan Getting There & Away chapter.

Yugoslav Airlines sells excursion returns for £270 or year-long flexible tickets for £300.

Among the other airlines serving Damascus KLM, Air France and EgyptAir do one-way tickets from £220 up and returns rising to as much as £495.

The cheapest way may be to take a charter plane to Adana, in southern Turkey, and a local bus from there (see the following section).

To/From Europe

From Athens and Istanbul, some agents offer one-way flights with Syrian Arab Airlines for around US$150 one way and US$300 return. Students fly for less. Shop around!

To/From Australia & New Zealand

There are no direct flights from Australia to Syria, but STA have a ticket flying Thai and Royal Jordanian from the east coast in high season for A$1094 one way and A$1947 return.

It's worth looking around for better deals on more popular destinations, like Turkey, Egypt or even Greece and going overland.

To/From Asia

Hong Kong, and to a lesser extent Bangkok and Singapore, can be good sources of discount or at least cheaper tickets, although Syria is not one of the big destinations.

Syrian Arab Airlines have flights from Delhi and Bombay in India. The quoted fare is Rs 18,702 one way or Rs 22,552 return. From Karachi, Pakistan, there is a four-month excursion return for Rs 16,100. The standard one-way fare is Rs 15,300.

To/From North Africa

Syrian Arab Airlines have regular connections to Cairo and Tunis, but unless you have to fly it is better to go overland, as ticket prices are high and in Syria they are inflated by the low aviation exchange rate. Syrian Arab Airlines and EgyptAir, for instance, will fly to Cairo for US$195 one way.

LAND

Bringing Your Own Vehicle

As with Jordan, you will need a *carnet de passage* if you bring your own car or bike. For more details see the Jordan Getting There & Away chapter.

Third-party insurance has to be bought at the border at the rate of US$36 a month. This supposedly also covers you for Lebanon, but double check. Its value is questionable, and it is worth making sure your own insurance company will cover you for Syria, especially as some Middle Eastern countries are considered 'war zones' and are not covered.

An International Driving Permit is mandatory in Syria, and you will need your vehicle's registration papers.

To/From Turkey

Bus There are at least seven border posts between Syria and Turkey. The most commonly used one links Antakya and Aleppo via the Bab al-Hawa border station. Traffic can get fairly congested here and crossing usually entails a wait of a couple of hours. Other posts may be less crowded.

You can buy tickets direct from Istanbul to Aleppo (22 hours), Damascus (30 hours) and even beyond to Amman and Medina if you wish. Usually a change of buses occurs along the way. If you buy tickets from travel agents in Istanbul, you'll pay up to TL60,000 over the odds, so it's better to head straight out to Topkapi bus station yourself and check out what the various bus companies have to offer – compare prices and bargain down where possible.

One-way to Aleppo should be TL170,000; one way to Damascus TL190,000. Buses leave every day, with at least five services a day, the last leaving in the early evening.

From Adana, in southern Turkey, buses to Aleppo and Damascus (many of them en route from Istanbul) cost TL50,000 to TL65,000 and TL70,000 to TL85,000, respectively. They cost marginally less from Antakya. Catching a bus from Istanbul to Antakya for TL100,000 and then another bus from there for TL50,000 will save you a bit. Or you can catch a *dolmus* from the last

Turkish town to the border, cross the border yourself and continue by microbus (called *meecro*) on the Syrian side. The only problem is that you may have a hard time finding a dolmus or microbus at the border when you want one. A dolmus between the border at the al-Hawa crossing and the nearest town, Reyhanli, costs TL3000.

For direct buses to Istanbul, book through the Karnak bus offices in Damascus or Aleppo, or at the Turkish bus stations in those cities. You can also find Turkish buses running from Lattakia and Homs. It's much cheaper to get local transport to Aleppo and catch a bus from there. For other destination and details of fares see the Damascus Getting There & Away chapter.

Train Every Thursday a train leaves Haydarpasha railway station on the Asian side of Istanbul at 8.20 am for the 40-hour trip to Aleppo. No advance booking is necessary. There are no sleepers, and in Istanbul you will only be sold 1st-class tickets at TL206,000. Don't believe travel agents who tell you the train only goes as far as the border, although you may have to change trains there. For details of the journey from Aleppo to Istanbul see the Getting There & Away section in the Aleppo chapter.

To/From Jordan

There's only one border crossing between Syria and Jordan and that's at Der'a/Ramtha. Consequently, it's extremely congested at times; however, it's easy to tackle on your own. You can cross by direct bus, service-taxi or by using a combination of local transport and walking. For details see the Der'a (Syria) and Irbid (Jordan) sections.

Bus There is one air-con Karnak bus and one JETT bus daily in each direction between Amman and Damascus. For details of departure times and fares see the Getting There & Away section in the Damascus chapter.

From Amman, the tickets cost JD4.500. Book two days in advance as demand for seats is high. The trip takes about seven hours, depending on the wait at the border.

Train At the time of writing, there was much talk of extending the Damascus-Der'a service along the old Hejaz railway to Amman. A weekly train leaving Damascus on Saturday and returning from Amman on Monday was envisaged at a cost of S£160 for a 1st-class ticket, with no options on 2nd class. It was alleged that this narrow-gauge excursion would take only seven hours.

Service-Taxi The service-taxis are faster than the buses but tend to get more thoroughly searched, especially at the Jordanian end of the border, and don't save you much time at all. They cost JD4 or S£300 either way. Service-taxis run between Damascus and Irbid for the same price.

To/From Lebanon

Since early 1992, when some Lebanese diplomatic missions again began issuing tourist visas, travellers have been trickling back into what was once known as the Switzerland of the Middle East.

Bus There are daily buses to Beirut and Tripoli. For details see the Getting There & Away section in the Damascus chapter.

From Aleppo you can get private buses for S£255 to Beirut. Daily Karnak buses from Lattakia cost S£125 to Tripoli and S£175 to Beirut.

Service-Taxi Service-taxis operating out of Damascus run to Tripoli for S£412 or to Beirut for anything from S£182 to S£277, depending on which part of the city you want to reach.

To/From Saudi Arabia & Kuwait

Bus It is possible to go direct from Syria to Saudi Arabia, simply passing through Jordan in transit. For details see the Getting There & Away section in the Damascus chapter.

There are also irregular services all the way across to Kuwait.

Service-Taxi For S£3000 a head, you can take a service-taxi from near the Karnak bus station in Damascus to Riyadh.

SEA

There were no passenger services operating out of Syria in mid-1992, although the weekly, 36-hour Lattakia run to Alexandria in Egypt was due to be reinstated after completion of repairs on the boat. Tickets cost US$60.

At one time or another there have also been services between Lattakia and Volos in Greece, Mersin (via Famagusta in Cyprus) in Turkey and Odessa in the Ukraine. At the time of writing, there seemed no prospect of any being restored.

TOURS

Many tourists to Syria choose to join organised tours and, as with Jordan, there are quite a few organisations to choose from. British Museum Tours (☎ (071) 323-8895), 46 Bloomsbury St, London WS1B 3QQ, offers 16 days' intensive touring accompanied by a museum lecturer for £1750 (about US$3000), for example.

Jasmin Tours (☎ (0628) 531-121), High St, Cookham, Maidenhead, Berks SL6 9SQ, does 15-day tours with half board for up to around £1900. It also runs combined tours to Syria and Jordan.

Prospect Art Tours Ltd (☎ (081) 995-2151/2163), 454-458 Chiswick High Rd, London W4 5TT, organises 13-day guided tours from £1350.

You should hunt around for the deal that suits you best, looking especially at the content and speed of the programme, amount of free time, level of accommodation, the extent to which visas, tickets and other documentation is handled by you or the operator, insurance, tour conditions and obligations.

LEAVING SYRIA

On leaving Syria, have your yellow entry card, or the equivalent you received on getting a visa extension, ready to hand in.

Departure Tax

People flying out of Syria must pay S£100 airport departure tax, but there is no tax for those leaving by land.

Getting Around

AIR

Local Air Services

Syrian Arab Airlines operates a limited internal air service that has been cut back to essential routes since big price hikes in November 1991. By Western standards, flights are cheap, but they are out of reach for most locals.

There are internal connections between Damascus and Aleppo, Damascus and Qamishle, and Qamishle and Aleppo. For details see the Damascus, Aleppo and Qamishle Getting There & Away sections.

There is talk of reopening Deir ez-Zur airport, but Lattakia appears destined to remain closed.

BUS

Syria has a well-developed road network and public transport is frequent and cheap. Private cars are relatively rare.

Distances are short so journeys are rarely more than four hours. About the longest single bus ride you can take is nine hours from Damascus to Qamishle in the north-east.

Whatever type of transport you use, make sure you are carrying your passport and it's not in your luggage or left in the hotel if you're on a day trip. You often need to show your passport to get into bus (and railway) stations, and there are sometimes checks en route.

Holidays

Note that Karnak, the Pullman companies and even the normal buses and microbuses charge up to 25% extra on official holidays (this does not apply to normal Fridays).

Caution

It is generally offensive for men to sit themselves next to women on the buses. If, when boarding, a male traveller only finds free seats next to local women, it would be prudent to remain standing. Often passengers will rearrange themselves so that women sit together, or with family members, and free the spare seats. If a male traveller does sit down next to a local woman and people get animated, the best advice is not to argue about it.

Karnak Bus

The orange-and-white air-con Karnak (government) buses connect every major town and city in Syria. They are fairly cheap, comfortable, fast and reliable and the cost is up to double what you would pay for a regular bus.

They are staffed by a crew of two – a driver, and a conductor who serves passengers with water and bonbons at regular intervals during the trip.

You need to reserve a seat at least a day in advance as they are popular among the well-to-do and the military. One big advantage Karnak buses have over regular buses and microbuses is that the office/terminal is almost always well located in the centre of town. Microbus stations tend to be further out of town, making for long walks or even obliging you to take a taxi if you're in a hurry, the price of which can exceed that of the bus trip itself.

The regular buses are a more interesting way to travel but if you just want to get from A to B with a minimum of fuss, Karnak is the way to do it.

From Damascus buses go to: Der'a, Palmyra, Deir ez-Zur, Hassake, Homs, Hama, Aleppo, Tartus and Lattakia. See the relevant sections for details of fares and travel time.

Buses also run to Baniyas, Jabla, Ras al-Ain, Albu Kamal, Suweida, Safita, Idlib and other destinations.

Pullman

Semi-private companies run Pullman buses in competition with Karnak. They are cheaper than the state-run company but, unlike the more chaotic and luridly decorated buses and microbuses that form a third, yet cheaper category, they run to a set timetable.

The Pullmans often have a separate station and you must buy tickets for pre-allocated seats at any one of the numerous competing companies' offices; it is rarely necessary to book much in advance. It can be a little confusing, especially as most of the company signs are in Arabic only. In Damascus, for example, there are companies called Yarmouk, Amin, Tawfiq, and al-Fahd.

Shop around, as the prices can vary.

Bus/Microbus

The bottom category of buses connect all major towns, and microbuses serve the smaller places. They have no schedule and leave when full, so on the less popular routes you may have to wait for an hour or so until they fill up. Sometimes you are obliged to buy tickets for pre-allocated seats – those right up the front behind the driver are not numbered but titled *khususi* (special), a spot sometimes assigned to foreigners.

If you find yourself being shunted around by passengers or the conductor, as they point to your ticket, it'll be because this time you've actually bought a seated ticket and chosen the wrong seat. On popular routes one reason for all this kerfuffle is that people holding tickets *get* a seat, while those who just pay when they jump on must stand.

From the outside the buses, most of them of ancient vintage, look fairly plain, but on the inside they are always decorated with an incredible array of gaudy ornaments – plastic fruit and plants, lights and mirrors. The driver usually has just enough uncluttered window to see some of the road ahead! Then there's the cassette player – no bus would be complete without one. The sound is invariably tinny, the tapes worn out and the volume loud. These buses are far less comfortable than the Karnak buses or Pullmans but as the distances are short it's no real hardship, and it is one of the best ways to meet the local people.

Journey times are generally longer than with the other buses, as they set people down and pick them up at any point along the route. This has earned them the nickname of 'stop-stops' among some of the locals. Conversations on buses will often lead to an invitation to someone's house or village. Try to keep your schedule flexible enough to make the most of Syrian hospitality.

Fares are cheap. See the Getting There & Away section in the Damascus chapter for destinations, fares and travel times.

TRAIN

Syria has a fleet of fairly modern trains made in East Germany. They are cheap and punctual, but the main disadvantage is that the stations are usually a few km from the town centres.

First class is air-con with aircraft-type seats; 2nd class is the same except it's not air-con. On the Qamishle-Damascus run there are 1st-class sleepers available, but unless you're a train buff who particularly wants to take the train, the bus is quicker and marginally cheaper.

The main line connects Damascus, Aleppo, Deir ez-Zur, Hassake and Qamishle. A secondary line runs along the coast from Aleppo to Lattakia, Tartus and on to Homs and Damascus. For further details see the relevant Getting There & Away sections.

In 1908, the French-built Hejaz Railway was opened to take pilgrims from Damascus to Medina (Saudi Arabia). The station is a bit of a propaganda show piece – only the daily service to Der'a and the summertime trains to the Barada Valley run along the Hejaz line. For this last trip, see the Around Damascus section.

SERVICE-TAXI

The share taxis, which also go by the name of service-taxis (servees), in Syria are usually old American Desotos and Dodges from the '50s and '60s – and some from before. One driver called his an ancient monument. There's a chronic shortage of spare parts but ingenuity and improvisation keep them running.

They only operate on the major routes and

cost up to three times the microbus fare. Unless you're in a tearing hurry, or you find yourself stuck on a highway and it's getting late, there's really no need to use them.

The advantage of the share taxis is that they are fast and, as there are only five seats in each, you never have to wait long for them to fill up.

CAR
Road Rules

Traffic runs on the right-hand side of the road in Syria and, as in Jordan, a good dose of common sense is the best advice. Remember that vehicles and people in some places often compete for space. Develop the habit of using the horn liberally.

Rental

For a long time there was only one car hire firm to choose from in Syria, Europcar, but this is slowly beginning to change. Europcar is still by far the biggest, with agents all over Syria in most of the big hotels. Their cheapest car is a Peugeot 205, which costs US$23 a day for a minimum of two days with 100 km (18c for each km above that). You can get unlimited kms with the same car for a minimum of three days for US$37 a day.

There is a Europcar agent at the airport, although the counter is often unattended.

In Damascus, two relatively new and small operations are Marmou and Palmyra. For details see the Getting There & Away section in the Damascus chapter.

Petrol

If you are driving a car in Syria you'll be better off if it runs on diesel (mazout), which seems to be the most widely available fuel, although regular (benzin) and, to a lesser extent, super (mumtaz) can also be found. All are of poor quality, and mechanics in neighbouring Jordan can always tell when a car has been running on Syrian petrol! All types generally cost about S£4 a litre – very cheap.

BICYCLE

There is no real problem with riding a bike through Syria, although the summer heat is not ideal for it, particularly in desert areas. People will think you a bit odd, as bicycles tend to be seen as a desperate means of transport and hardly appropriate for 'rich' Western tourists.

HITCHING

Hitching is even easier in Syria than in Jordan, as still fewer people have private cars, and it is an accepted means of getting around. Similar rules apply in Syria as in Jordan; some payment is often expected, as the driver will take passengers to subsidise their own trip. Unless you are skint, the best policy is to offer a small amount (try not to be insulting, though) and nine times out of 10 you'll find it being knocked back.

As always, women should think twice before hitching alone. It's been done without incident, but it is risky.

LOCAL TRANSPORT
To/From the Airport

Damascus International Airport is about 35 km south-east of the city. A local bus leaves from outside the terminal every half hour for S£5, and takes about 45 minutes to the centre. From the city, it leaves from Choukri Kouwatli Ave. The service begins at 5.30 am and ends at midnight.

Taxis are a rip-off from the airport, but if you must take one don't offer more than S£100. They will start at S£300 or more but stand your ground – or just catch a bus.

Aleppo airport is about 25 km east of the city. Buses run from the Karnak bus station for S£5 and take about half an hour.

Bus

All the major cities have a local bus system but as the city centres are compact, you can usually get around on foot. This is just as well because, with the exception of Damascus, the buses have no signs in English (and often nothing in Arabic either) to indicate where they are going. They can be useful (and cheap) for getting out to distant microbus or railway stations.

Service-Taxis & Taxis

Taxis in most cities are plentiful and cheap. In Damascus they have meters, although not all drivers use them – a trip right across town should never cost more than S£20. In Aleppo a cross-town ride should not cost more than S£10 to S£15. There is a flagfall of S£3. Where they don't use a meter, it's a matter of negotiating the fare when you get in.

It's a real surprise to find taxi drivers who aren't all sharks. In Syria, if you get into a taxi and ask how much it is to the bus station or wherever you will often be told the correct fare and bargaining will get you nowhere.

Although they are not in evidence in the capital, some other cities, notably Aleppo, are served by local service-taxis that run a set route, like a bus, picking up and dropping passengers along the way for a set price. For the outsider, there is no obvious way to distinguish between them and normal taxis – both are yellow, but the service-taxis sometimes have the name of their service-taxi company on the side in Arabic. If you end up sharing with other people and the taxi doesn't take you exactly where you want to go, you're probably in a service-taxi!

TOURS

If time is important or you're just in Damascus for a couple of days, there are tours run by Karnak Tourism & Transport, but they're not cheap. The tours use four-seater vans, and as you have to charter the whole thing, it becomes a lot cheaper per head if there are four of you.

In addition to the set tours listed, Karnak also organises a train trip to Ain al-Fijeh by steam engine, a walking tour of restaurants, cafés and bath houses of Damascus with local people, and a visit to a Bedouin family out by Palmyra. The following tours start and finish in Damascus:

Around Damascus – half-day, S£450 per person for four people, S£650 per person for two

Bosra – half-day, S£2000 per person for four, S£2900 per person for two

Maalula – half-day, S£1050 per person for four, S£1375 per person for two

Crac des Chevaliers – one day, S£2200 per person for four, S£3400 per person for two

Palmyra – one day, S£2350 per person for four, S£3750 per person for two

Shahba/Qanawat – one day, S£2000 per person for four, S£2900 per person for two

Damascus

Damascus (*ash-Sham* or *dimashq* in Arabic) is the capital of Syria and, with a population of 1.5 million, its largest city. It is a fascinating city of contrasts. Veiled women in traditional garb walk alongside women dressed in trendy Western clothes and adorned with make-up. Old men in *jalabiyyehs* and *kafiyyehs* pass young men in Michael Jackson T-shirts selling black market Johnny Walker whisky. In the old city you can hear the busy sounds of the artisans at work and the cries of the hawkers, while the new city assaults the ears with the roar of traffic and the constant wail of Arabic music from the cassette shops.

At night you will occasionally see lorries moving around with a huge spray pipe, leaving an eerie grey fog that hangs in the air. The fog is in fact an insecticide, and apparently the posher parts of town get a double serving. I don't know what it does to the bugs, but it sure doesn't do much for people in the streets!

The city owes its existence to the Barada River, which rises high in the Jebel Lubnan ash-Sharqiyah (Anti-Lebanon Mountains). The waters give life to the Ghouta Oasis, which makes settlement possible in what is an otherwise uninhabitable area.

HISTORY

Damascus claims to be the oldest continuously inhabited city in the world, although its northern rival city, Aleppo, hotly disputes this. The hieroglyphic tablets of Egypt make reference to 'Dimashqa' as being one of the cities conquered by the Egyptians in the 15th century BC, but excavations from the courtyard of the Omayyad Mosque have yielded finds dating back to the 3rd millennium BC.

It has been fought over many times and some of the earliest conquerors include King David of Israel, the Assyrians in 732 BC, Nebuchadnezzar (circa 600 BC) and then the Persians in 530 BC. In 333 BC it fell to Alexander the Great. Greek influence declined when the Nabataeans occupied Damascus in 85 BC. The Romans soon sent the Nabataeans packing in 64 BC and Syria became a Roman province. It was here that Saul of Tarsus was converted to Christianity and became St Paul the Apostle.

Damascus was an important city under the Romans and it became a military base for the armies fighting the Persians. Hadrian declared it a metropolis in the 2nd century BC and during the reign of Alexander Severus it became a Roman colony.

By the end of the 4th century AD most of the population had adopted Christianity. The Temple of Jupiter became a cathedral dedicated to St John the Baptist, whose head supposedly lies in a tomb inside the Omayyad Mosque.

With the coming of Islam, Damascus became an important centre as the seat of the Omayyad Caliphate from 661 to 750. The city expanded rapidly and the Christian cathedral was turned into a mosque. When the Abbassids took over and moved the caliphate to Baghdad, Damascus was plundered once again.

After the occupation of Damascus by the Seljuq Turks in 1076, the Crusaders tried unsuccessfully to take it in 1148 before it finally fell to Nureddin, a general of Turkish origin, in 1154. Many of the monuments in the city date to the time of his successor Saladin, when Damascus became the capital of a united Egypt and Syria.

The next to move in were the Mongols who, after only a brief occupation, were ousted by the Mamluks of Egypt in 1260. During the Mamluk period, Damascene goods became famous worldwide and attracted merchants from Europe. This led to the second Mongol invasion under Tamerlaine, when the city was flattened and the artisans and scholars were deported to the Mongol capital of Samarkand. The Mamluks returned soon after and proceeded to rebuild the city.

From the time of the Ottoman Turk occupation in 1516 the fortunes of Damascus started to decline and it was reduced to the capital of a small province in a large empire. The only interruption in 400 years of Ottoman rule was from 1831 to 1840 when it once again became the capital of Syria under the Egyptians, following the rise to power there of Mohammed Ali Pasha. Fearing the consequences of an Ottoman collapse, the West intervened to force Ibrahim Pasha, Ali's lieutenant, to withdraw from Syria.

By 1878 the city's population had grown to 150,000 and great improvements were made in sanitary conditions and a transport system was built. By 1908 Damascus had a network of tramlines and was connected by rail to Beirut and Medina.

The Turkish and German forces used Damascus as their base during WW I. When they were defeated by the Arab Legion and the Allies, the first Syrian government was set up in 1919.

The French, having been given a mandate by the League of Nations, occupied the city from 1920 to 1945. They met with a lot of resistance and at one stage in 1925 they bombarded the city to suppress rioting. French shells again rained on the city in the unrest of 1945, which eventually led to full independence.

With the evacuation of the French and British forces in April 1946, Damascus became the capital of an independent Syria.

ORIENTATION

The city centre of Damascus is fairly compact and finding your way around on foot is no problem, although the official street signs do not always correlate with their commonly known names.

The real heart of the city is the Martyrs' Square (Saahat ash-Shuhada), which most locals call 'Al-Merjeh' (a name dating to Ottoman times and meaning something along the lines of 'pasture' or 'park'). The martyrs were victims of French bombardments of the city in 1945. The rather curious bronze colonnade in the centre commemo-

rates the opening of the first telegraph link in the Middle East – the line from Damascus to Medina. Most of the cheap hotels and restaurants are around here.

The main street, Said al-Jabri Ave, begins at the Hejaz railway station and runs northeast, changing its name to Port Said Ave at the Choukri Kouwatli Ave flyover, and then again to 29 Mai Ave at the Peasant's Monument (Midan Youssef al-Azmeh), finishing at the Central Bank Building. The whole street is only about one km long and along here you'll find the post office, tourist office, various airline offices and many mid-range restaurants and hotels. Al-Jala'a Ave heads out to the Jordanian Embassy. The area around it is known to everyone as Abu Roumaneh.

The Barada River is unfortunately not much more than a smelly drain flowing from north-west to south-east through the city, although it tumbles quite strongly past the old city after some rain. Right in the centre it has been covered over. On its banks to the west of the Martyrs' Square is the Takiyyeh as-Sulaymaniyyeh Mosque and the National Museum, and close by are the university, Karnak bus station and the Immigration Office.

The old city lies to the south of the river, just east of Martyrs' Square. Apart from the old Roman road, now known as the Street Called Straight (no need to explain why) or Via Recta, it's a tangle of narrow and twisting roads with the old houses often almost touching overhead.

To get a good view of the city, take a No 1 bus to Muhajireen from the bus station opposite the Hotel Venezia. Ride the bus to the end and then climb the stairs to higher up on Jebel Qassioun. It's best to go in the late afternoon when the sun is behind you.

INFORMATION
Tourist Office

This is on 29 Mai Ave, just up from the Peasant's Monument. It's open from 9 am to 7 pm everyday except Fridays, and the friendly, English-speaking staff are very helpful. They have a good free map of Syria

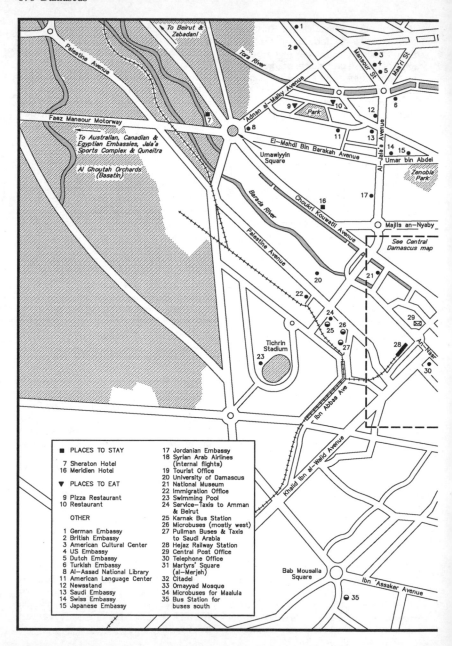

PLACES TO STAY

7 Sheraton Hotel
16 Meridien Hotel

PLACES TO EAT

9 Pizza Restaurant
10 Restaurant

OTHER

1 German Embassy
2 British Embassy
3 American Cultural Center
4 US Embassy
5 Dutch Embassy
7 Turkish Embassy
8 Al-Assad National Library
11 American Language Center
12 Newsstand
13 Saudi Embassy
14 Swiss Embassy
15 Japanese Embassy
17 Jordanian Embassy
18 Syrian Arab Airlines (internal flights)
19 Tourist Office
20 University of Damascus
21 National Museum
22 Immigration Office
23 Swimming Pool
24 Service—Taxis to Amman & Beirut
25 Karnak Bus Station
26 Microbuses (mostly west)
27 Pullman Buses & Taxis to Saudi Arabia
28 Hejaz Railway Station
29 Central Post Office
30 Telephone Office
31 Martyrs' Square (al-Merjeh)
32 Citadel
33 Omayyad Mosque
34 Microbuses for Maalula
35 Bus Station for buses south

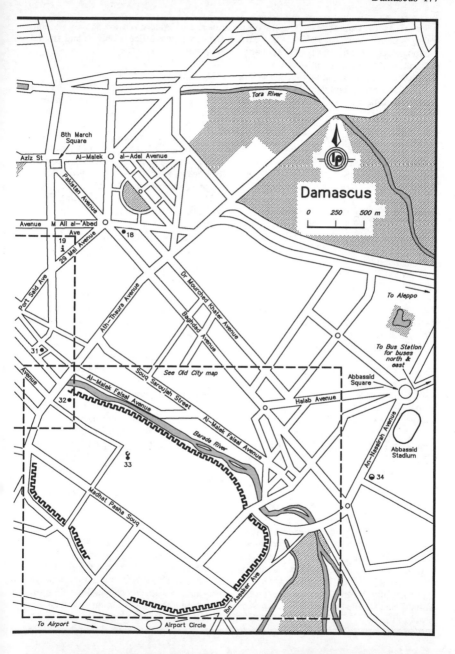

8th March Square

Aziz St — Al—Malek al—'Adel Avenue

Avenue — M Ali al—'Abed Ave

19

29 Mai Avenue

Pakistan Avenue

•18

Port Said Ave

Ath—Thaura Avenue

Dr Mourched Khater Avenue

Baghdad Avenue

31•

Avenue

Al—Malek Faisal Avenue

Souq Saroujah Street

See Old City map

32•

Al—Malek Faisal Avenue

Barada River

Halab Avenue

33

Madhat Pasha Souq

An—Nassirah Avenue

Ibn Assaker Ave

To Airport — Airport Circle

Tora River

Damascus

0   250   500 m

To Aleppo

To Bus Station
for buses
north &
east

Abbassid
Square

Abbassid
Stadium

34

with plans of Damascus, Aleppo and Palmyra on the back. They also stock a collection of maps of other parts of the country and can provide local city information.

If you go to the Ministry of Tourism by the Takiyyeh as-Sulaymaniyyeh Mosque, you can get the same maps and sometimes colour posters as well.

The information booth at the airport is irregularly staffed, not overly informative and sometimes plain misleading – don't believe them when they claim you should pay taxis into the city S£400 in hard currency.

Money

There are several branches of the Commercial Bank of Syria as well as more straight-forward exchange booths where you can change money fairly easily. The booth on Martyrs' Square is open from 9 am to 6.30 pm and 10 am to 2 pm on Fridays and will change cash and travellers' cheques. So will the booth (formerly a bank branch) opposite the Hejaz railway station, which is open from 10 am until 6 pm seven days a week.

Several bank branches take cash and cheques, but are not open as long. Branches in the Meridien and Sheraton hotels also accept cash and cheques. There is also a branch of the Commonwealth Bank of Syria at the airport, which is supposedly open seven days a week.

The American Express agent is Chami Travel (☎ 111652) in the Mouradi Building, Fardous St. The postal address is PO Box 507, Damascus.

Post

This is on Said al-Jabri Ave. You can't miss it – it's a big imposing building. It's open from 8 am to 8 pm every day, except Fridays and holidays, when it closes at 1 pm. When the power goes out, the interior is very dark and gloomy. The poste restante counter is fairly efficient – they let you look through alphabetically ordered bundles under your initials. You'll need to have your passport as proof of identity.

You can also have mail sent to you c/o American Express; see the Money section. The parcel post office is outside and around the corner.

Telephone & Telegram

The telephone office is a block south-east of the Hejaz railway station on An-Nasr Ave, and is open around the clock. Bring money, your passport and lots of patience. Go to the crowded counter on the right, fight your way to the front and tell them the country, city and number you want. They'll call for you an hour or two later.

Calls to Europe cost S£100 a minute and S£115 to North America or Australia. There is a three-minute minimum.

Telegrams are even more expensive and can only be sent during vaguely set daytime hours.

Visa Extensions

For visa extensions, the immigration office is on Palestine Ave (Shari'a Filastin), one block up from the Karnak bus station. As with all government departments, it's open from 8 am to 2 pm every day but Friday. Go to the 2nd floor to begin the process for which you need three photos, will have to fill in four forms, and buy a revenue stamp for S£2 at a stall outside the building.

A couple of photographers with ancient cameras across the road can do some awful photos for you. You can get extensions of up to one month. They cost S£25 and take a working day to process – pick them up at 1 pm.

Foreign Embassies

See the Syria Facts for the Visitor chapter for addresses of foreign embassies in Damascus.

Cultural Centres

The US Cultural Center (☎ 228527) is behind the US embassy in Mansour St and open from 9 am to 1 pm and from 2 to 5 pm Monday to Friday. It has a library, newspapers and occasionally shows films. Don't be daunted by the massive security screen.

The British Council was not expected to reopen its doors before the end of 1993.

Other cultural centres include the German, incorporating the Goethe Institut (☎ 247842), in Maysaloun St (Dar as-Salam Building); the French Cultural Centre (☎ 246181) in Youssef al-Azmeh St and its Spanish equivalent (☎ 714300) in Nazem Pasha St.

Bookshops

There's a good bookshop, the Librairie Universelle, on the short street up from the Hotel Venezia. As well as books on Syria and the Middle East, it also stocks magazines such as *Time* and *Newsweek*, and a reasonable map of Syria by GEOprojects for S£150.

The Meridien and Sheraton hotels both have fairly decent bookshops, with some foreign press and a selection of books on Syria and, in the case of the Meridien, even the odd book on surrounding countries.

The newsstand marked on the map sells a better than average range of foreign press and magazines, often stocking more than the bookshops.

A predominantly French-language bookshop that might be worth a peek is the Chachati bookshop, virtually across the flyover from the Turkish bus station.

THINGS TO SEE
Old City

Most of the sights of Damascus are in the old city, which is surrounded by what was initially a Roman wall. The wall itself has been flattened and rebuilt several times over the past 2000 years. What stands today dates from the 13th century.

The wall is pierced by a number of gates *(bab* – the Arabic plural is *abwab)*, only one of which (the restored Bab Sharqi – East Gate) dates back to Roman times. The best preserved section is between Bab as-Salama (the Gate of Safety) and Bab Touma (Thomas Gate – named after a son-in-law of the emperor Heraclius) in the north-east corner. For most of its length, the wall is obscured by new buildings constructed over and around it. Bab as-Salama is a beautiful example of Ayyubid military architecture, but unfortunately it is now draped with electric cables and telegraph wires.

Bab Kisan houses St Paul's Chapel. This is where tradition has it that the Christians lowered St Paul out of a window in a basket to escape the wrath of the Jews (Acts 9:25).

The whole area is a labyrinth of winding alleys and chaotic markets, stretching from the mainly Muslim and touristed souqs around the Omayyad Mosque to the predominantly Christian sector around the Bab Sharqi.

Citadel The citadel forms part of the western wall at the end of an-Nasr Ave. It used to be the home of the National Guard but is now closed for restoration.

You can peer through the loosely chained gateway into the courtyard, where stonemasons can be seen chipping away at the enormous blocks that will be added to the partly reconstituted walls. It is easy enough to slip in through the gate and climb up onto the ramparts for some good views of the city, but it is technically off-limits to tourists and the workers will probably gently nudge you back out.

Souq al-Hamadiyyeh Next to the citadel is the entrance to one of the main covered markets, the Souq al-Hamadiyyeh. The gloomy cobbled souq with its bustling crowds, hawkers and tenacious merchants is worlds away from the traffic jams and chaos of the streets outside. It's also the closest thing to a tourist trap in Syria.

Most of the shops sell handicrafts – inlay work, brass and copperware, jewellery, traditional costumes, silk and carpets – and the shopkeepers stand outside trying their best to entice you in. It's a good place to buy souvenirs, but if you have the time and patience, penetrate further into the city and less frequented markets for better prices. If you don't have so much time, remember the golden rule – bargain and bargain hard.

At the far end of the market the vaulted roof gives way to two enormous Corinthian columns supporting a decorated lintel – the remains of the western gate of the old Roman

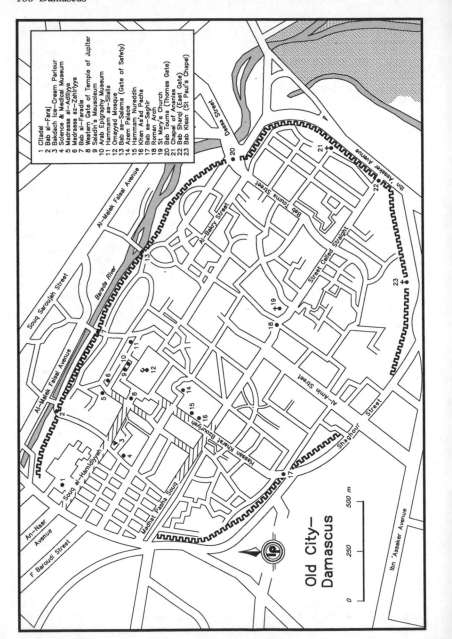

1 Citadel
2 Bab al–Faraj
3 Bakdach Ice–Cream Parlour
4 Science & Medical Museum
5 Madrassa al–Adiliyya
6 Madrassa az–Zahiriyya
7 Bab al–Faradis
8 Western Gate of Temple of Jupiter
9 Saladin's Mausoleum
10 Arab Epigraphy Museum
11 Hammam as–Silsila
12 Omayyad Mosque
13 Bab as–Salama (Gate of Safety)
14 Azem Palace
15 Hammam Nureddin
16 Khan As'ad Pacha
17 Bab as–Saghir
18 Roman Arch
19 St Mary's Church
20 Bab Touma (Thomas Gate)
21 Chapel of Ananias
22 Bab Sharqi (East Gate)
23 Bab Kisan (St Paul's Chapel)

Old City–
Damascus

0   250   500 m

Temple of Jupiter dating back to the 3rd century AD. It is draped with all manner of electric cables, telegraph wires and lights. At the foot of the columns the stalls sell, among other things, books of all descriptions and souvenirs for the religious – Korans, pictures of Mecca and wall-hangings with calligraphic messages of the 'One True God' and 'Allah is Great' variety.

Omayyad Mosque Opposite the end of the market is the entrance to the Omayyad Mosque – daunting in size and impressive in its construction. Take your time on a visit.

It's a peaceful place and a respite from the heat and hustle and bustle outside. The tourist entrance is temporarily right next to the main entrance while restoration work is carried out – usually it is 30 metres to the left. Here you pay the S£10 entry fee.

All women, and men in shorts, have to use the black robes supplied. As in all mosques, you must remove your shoes, and it's best to keep them with you. Non-Muslims are admitted on Fridays too, but not during the main midday prayer time, when the mosque is closed to tourists for a couple of hours. It's quite OK to take photos anywhere inside.

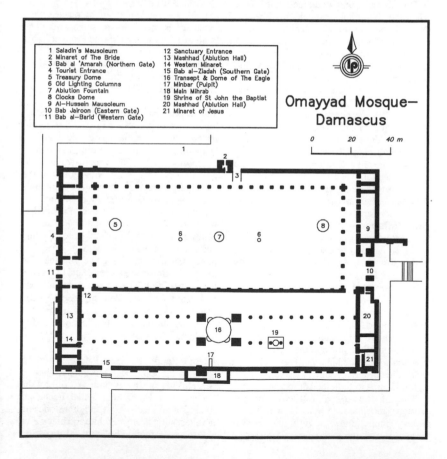

1 Saladin's Mausoleum
2 Minaret of The Bride
3 Bab al 'Amarah (Northern Gate)
4 Tourist Entrance
5 Treasury Dome
6 Old Lighting Columns
7 Ablution Fountain
8 Clocks Dome
9 Al-Hussein Mausoleum
10 Bab Jairoon (Eastern Gate)
11 Bab al-Barid (Western Gate)
12 Sanctuary Entrance
13 Mashhad (Ablution Hall)
14 Western Minaret
15 Bab al-Ziadah (Southern Gate)
16 Transept & Dome of The Eagle
17 Minbar (Pulpit)
18 Main Mihrab
19 Shrine of St John the Baptist
20 Mashhad (Ablution Hall)
21 Minaret of Jesus

Omayyad Mosque–
Damascus

0   20   40 m

The history of the site goes back almost 3000 years to the 9th century BC, when the Aramaens built a temple to their god, Hadad (mentioned in the Book of Kings in the Old Testament). The huge Temple of Jupiter, measuring 380 by 310 metres, was built on the site by the Romans in the 3rd century AD. With the rise of Christianity in the 4th century, the temple was converted into a church and named after St John the Baptist. When the Muslims entered Damascus in 636 they converted the eastern part of the temple into a mosque and allowed the Christians to continue their worship in the western part.

This arrangement continued until 705, when the sixth Omayyad caliph, Al-Walid, decided that he wanted to 'build a mosque the equal of which was never designed by anyone before me or anyone after me'. Consequently, all the old Roman and Byzantine constructions within the enclosure were flattened and for the next 10 years more than 1000 stonemasons and artisans were employed in the construction of the grand new mosque. Most of the interior was reconstructed at the end of the last century after a fire swept through the original building.

The three minarets all date from the time of the original construction but were renovated and restored at later dates by the Ayyubids, Mamluks and Ottomans. The one on the northern side is the Minaret of the Bride (Minaret al-'Arous), while the one on the south-eastern corner is the Minaret of Jesus, so named because local tradition has it that this is where Jesus will appear on Judgement Day.

The northern part of the rectangular mosque is an open courtyard with a beautiful, smooth marble floor – cool to walk over even on hot days, but mind the pigeon shit. The courtyard is flanked on three sides by a double-storeyed portico that used to be covered with veined marble. The two pillars either side of the fountain in the centre used to hold lamps to light the courtyard.

The small octagonal structure on the western side is the old treasury, which used to keep public funds safe from thieves. It is decorated with intricate mosaics.

On the southern side of the court is the prayer hall. It's a rectangular hall of three aisles divided by a transept. High above the transept is the Dome of the Eagle, so called because it represents the eagle's head while the transept represents the body and the aisles are the wings. If you stand under the dome facing the mihrab (prayer niche) to the south and look up, you'll see eight names in Arabic. From the bottom right clockwise they are Allah, Mohammed and then the first four caliphs (who had been Companions of the Prophet), Abu Bakr, Omar, Othman and Ali. The last two names are Hassan and Hussein, Ali's two sons.

Looking somewhat out of place in the sanctuary is the structure surrounding the tomb of John the Baptist (the Prophet Yahia to the Muslims). It is believed that his head was buried on this spot. The original wooden tomb was replaced by the present marble one after the fire of 1893.

Mausoleum of Saladin Saladin's mausoleum was originally built in 1193 and restored with funds made available by Kaiser Wilhelm II of Germany during his visit to Damascus in 1898. The walnut-wood cenotaph is richly decorated with motifs of the Ayyubid period and still contains Saladin's body. Next to it is the modern tomb in marble, also donated by Kaiser Wilhelm, where Saladin's body is supposed to lie.

The mausoleum is covered by a red dome and is in a pleasant garden setting outside the northern wall of the Omayyad Mosque. The caretaker almost seems reluctant to let you in, but will do his best to answer questions in broken English. You supposedly need your ticket to the mosque to get in here, but he seems oblivious to this. Doubtless a tip would be appreciated.

Azem Palace The Azem Palace, just to the south of the Omayyad Mosque, is another peaceful haven. It was built in 1749 by the Governor of Damascus, As'ad Pacha al-Azem, out of black basalt and limestone and the alternating layers of white and black give a curious effect. The cool, flourishing gardens and intricate interior decoration of some of the rooms lend the palace a restrained beauty and charm.

The rooms of the modest palace also house the exhibits of the Museum of the Arts & Popular Traditions of Syria (see under Museums).

The palace is open from 9 am to 4 pm daily, except Tuesday. On Fridays it closes for about two hours from 12.30 pm. Entry is S£10.

Al-Adlliyya & Az-Zahiriyya Madrassas

Not more than 100 metres down the market lane to the left of the Western Gate of the Temple of Jupiter, you will find two old Koranic teaching schools, erected in the 13th century during the ascendancy of the Ayyubids. The first, on the left, is the Madrassa al-Adiliyya, begun under Nureddin and continued under a brother of Saladin, Al-'Adil Saif ad-Din, whose grave it contains. Its facade is considered a classic example of Ayyubid architecture. It is now a library.

The Madrassa az-Zahiriyya opposite, begun in 1277, houses the body of Sultan Baibars, who went a long way to eliminating the Crusaders. It is now used as a school.

Hammams

Turkish baths are a great way to spend a couple of hours but unfortunately it is usually a men-only activity. There are a few of them close to the Omayyad Mosque and all seem adamant about not allowing women in. None have signs in English.

The first, called Hammam Nureddin, is in the covered street that runs between the Omayyad Mosque and the Street Called Straight. Next door to it is another legacy of the Turkish Governor al-Azem, a caravanserai known as the Khan As'ad Pacha, built in the same year as the palace. At the Hammam Nureddin the full massage, bath and sauna with towel, soap and tea will cost you S£200. Men can even have their hair cut. Open from 9 am to midnight seven days a week, it is the plushest and most expensive of the bath houses in the area.

Next door to the Madrassa az-Zahiriyya is

a hammam of the same name. The works cost you S£150, and it is open from 7 am to 10 pm seven days a week.

More or less opposite the Minaret of the Bride is the Hammam as-Silsila, also open seven days a week – from 8 am to 11 pm. Here you can get a massage, sauna and bath for S£110.

Churches

About two-thirds of the way along the Street Called Straight (Via Recta) are the remains of a Roman arch. This roughly marks the boundary of what might be called the Christian quarter.

There are a few churches in this area but the only one of any historical interest is the **Chapel of Ananias** (Kaneesat Hananya), the old cellar of the house of Ananias. Ananias, an early Christian disciple, was charged to 'go into the street which is called Straight, and enquire in the house of Judas for one called Saul of Tarsus (St Paul) (Acts 9:11) so that he might be able to touch him and restore Saul's sight'.

The entrance to the chapel is just inside the wall between Bab Sharqi and Bab Touma. From Bab Sharqi take the first lane on the right and follow it to the end. The chapel is actually in a crypt below the house where you (sometimes) pay S£5 to enter. It is open seven days a week from 9 am to 6pm. In the chapel, the story of Paul is told in a series of panels in Arabic and French.

The **St Paul's Chapel** in Bab Kisan marks the spot where the disciples lowered St Paul out of a window in a basket one night so that he could flee from the Jews, having angered them after preaching in the synagogues. You can't enter the Bab from the outside. Follow the drive up to the new convent on the left and push open the heavy wooden doors into the back of the Bab, now containing the small chapel.

Takiyyeh as-Sulaymaniyyeh Mosque

This mosque, on the banks of the Barada River just to the west of the post office, was originally built by the Turkish architect, Sinan, in 1554. It is a particularly graceful mosque built in alternating layers of black and white stone with two towering minarets. It's very peaceful to sit by the fountain and watch the world go by, away from the traffic outside. The grounds also house the Army Museum.

Next to the mosque is the Artisanat – a handicraft market in an old caravanserai built under the Ottoman Sultan Selim in 1516 to accommodate poor pilgrims. The former quarters, kitchens and offices are now workshops where you can see all sorts of crafts practised, from weaving to glass-blowing.

Museums

National Museum This is the most important of the city's four museums and it is next to the Takiyyeh as-Sulaymaniyyeh Mosque. It is well worth at least one visit and is open from 9 am to 6 pm every day except Fridays, when it opens from 9 am to 12.30 pm and 2 to 6 pm. The entry fee is S£10. All bags and cameras have to be left in the office at the entrance. Unfortunately, most of the exhibits are labelled only in French or Arabic and some have no label at all.

The large shady garden in the front of the museum has bits and pieces of statuary from sites all around the country and the small café sells tea and soft drinks. To sit under the large eucalyptus trees and sip a *shay* on a hot afternoon is a good way to recharge your system.

The facade of the museum is imposing – it is the entrance to the old Qasr al-Hayr al-Gharbi (a desert palace/military camp near Palmyra dating to the time of the Omayyad Caliph Hisham in 688). It was transported to Damascus stone by stone and reconstructed, but looks somewhat cramped by the wings of the museum.

Inside is a fantastic array of exhibits: written cylinders from Ugarit using the first known alphabet, dating from the 14th century BC; statuary from Mari, dating from the 3rd to 2nd millennium BC; two halls full

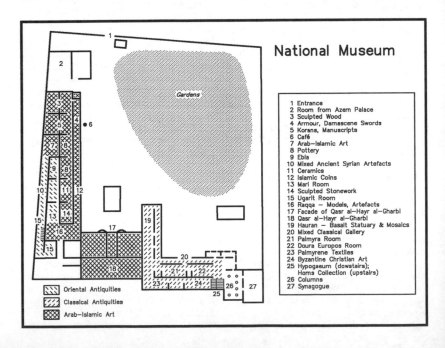

National Museum

1 Entrance
2 Room from Azem Palace
3 Sculpted Wood
4 Armour, Damascene Swords
5 Korans, Manuscripts
6 Café
7 Arab–Islamic Art
8 Pottery
9 Ebla
10 Mixed Ancient Syrian Artefacts
11 Ceramics
12 Islamic Coins
13 Mari Room
14 Sculpted Stonework
15 Ugarit Room
16 Raqqa – Models, Artefacts
17 Facade of Qasr al-Hayr al-Gharbi
18 Qasr al-Hayr al-Gharbi
19 Hauran – Basalt Statuary & Mosaics
20 Mixed Classical Gallery
21 Palmyra Room
22 Doura Europos Room
23 Palmyrene Textiles
24 Byzantine Christian Art
25 Hypogaeum (dowstairs); Homs Collection (upstairs)
26 Columns
27 Synagogue

Gardens

Oriental Antiquities
Classical Antiquities
Arab–Islamic Art

of marble and terracotta statues from Palmyra; a reconstruction of an underground burial chamber, or hypogaeum, from the Valley of the Tombs, Palmyra; frescoes from Doura Europos; sculptures of black basalt from the Hauran around Bosra; Damascene weapons; old surgical instruments from doctors' graves; Islamic glassware from the 13th century BC; a collection of Korans dating back to the 13th century; a complete room decorated in the style of the Azem Palace of the 18th century; and an extensive collection of coins and gold jewellery.

To get to the latter exhibit, known as the **Homs collection** because much of it was found in and around that city, you'll need to ask the curator's permission, but it's worth the effort. They say the room (upstairs above the Byzantine and Palmyra displays) is generally kept locked up for lack of staff. Alongside some exquisite gold jewellery, there are coins depicting Venetian Doges, the Roman emperor Phillip the Arab and Alexander the Great, among others.

The **synagogue**, removed from Doura Europos and reconstructed here, is out the back past a small colonnaded courtyard. Inside, you can see benches around the sides and niches where the five books of the Torah were kept. The frescoes around the walls depict episodes from the Old Testament, from the crowning of King Solomon through the reign of David, the story of Moses and the flight from Egypt. Don't be surprised if the old guy showing you around makes furtive enquiries about your religion and lets you know in hushed tones that he is a Christian.

Army Museum This is in the grounds next to the Takiyyeh as-Sulaymaniyyeh Mosque. It has a fine collection of weapons and armour. As is often the case in Syrian museums, the descriptions are mostly in French and Arabic. Outside are various cannons and planes, mostly relics of attacks by the French on Damascus during rebellions under the mandate, notably in 1925 and 1945, or leftovers from WW II and the Arab-Israeli war of 1967. There's also a pile of the

twisted remains of planes shot down in the war in 1973.

On the same theme, a whole room is dedicated to captured Israeli war material from the 1973 war, and one of the soldiers who act as curators of the museum is bound to want to explain to you the ins and outs of the war. It is a sobering propaganda showroom covering what was a ferocious but largely failed attempt by the Syrians to recover territory in the Golan Heights lost to Israel in 1967.

An interesting anachronism is a display on the theme of Soviet-Syrian space cooperation. Hammers and sickles and smiling portraits of Gorbachev seem to indicate the Syrians' desire to keep alive memories of the good old days.

The museum is open daily from 8 am to 2 pm, except Tuesday, and the entrance fee is S£5.

Science & Medical Museum This is in the old city, just off the Souq al-Hamadiyyeh. The museum is housed in a 12th century hospital and is open from 8 am to 2 pm daily except Tuesday. The entry fee is S£5. Descriptions are in French and Arabic.

The hospital, founded by Nureddin, was renowned throughout the world. The building itself is more interesting than the museum exhibits. The collection of old medical and surgical odds and ends from Roman to Ottoman times look more like implements of torture – there's even an old electric-shock machine. It's easy to see why many patients carried good-luck charms. There's also a display of 100 or so medicinal herbs and spices used in ancient times.

What the room full of stuffed animals and birds is doing here is anybody's guess.

Museum of the Arts & Popular Traditions of Syria This impressively titled museum is housed in the Azem Palace. Unfortunately, the displays do not make quite the same impact, but they do manage to give some idea of Syria as it was. It is not well labelled, so try to latch on to one of the attendants to show you around.

This kind of display, which features mannequins dressed in the traditional costumes of people from all walks of life, seems to be a well-worn museum genre throughout the Middle East, and you'll find no shortage of them in Syria.

Arab Epigraphy Museum

This is another case of a museum building being more engaging than its contents for most visitors. The small calligraphic exhibit will attract those with a particular interest, but it is limited. Located about 20 metres down from Saladin's Mausoleum, it was built in the 15th century as the Madrassa al-Jaqmaqiyya. It's open from 8 am to 2 pm every day but Tuesday, and entrance is S£5.

Damascus International Fair

This is a trade exhibition that takes place annually in the first two weeks of September. Although it is of little interest to the traveller, during the show there are often cultural events put on by some of the participating countries. Check the *Syria Times* for what's happening.

Saida Zeinab Mausoleum

This mausoleum to one of the granddaughters of Mohammed, in the southern outskirts of Damascus, is an object of pilgrimage for Shi'ites, many of whom come from Iran to visit the shrine. Numerous travellers have written to say that it is well worth seeing.

ACTIVITIES
Swimming

Some of the bigger hotels have swimming pools open to nonguests, but they are not terribly cheap. The Meridien, for instance, charges S£400 for the day. Otherwise, you may be able to use a public pool, open only (if at all) in the summer months. Entrance to public pools is around S£50. The easiest one to get to is at the Tichrin stadium, south of the bus and taxi stations.

Language Courses & Work

It is possible to enrol in Arabic language courses in Damascus. Most people who want to secure residence start off at the government Arabic Teaching Institute for Foreigners.

There are occasional openings for teachers of English through the American Language Center. For details of both see the Syria Facts for the Visitor chapter.

PLACES TO STAY
Places to Stay – bottom end

Damascus has a big selection of cheap hotels, most of them grouped around Martyrs' Square, but finding one with a free bed is not always easy. Many hotels in this area double as brothels, and either turn away foreigners who genuinely want just a bed or invite them in for a bed with extras. Some will give you a bed and hit you for more than it's worth the next day, since you've taken up valuable space.

Although it's not nearly as bad as it was some years ago, you will still find hotels that seem permanently reserved for Iranian pilgrims to the modern Shi'ite mausoleum built for Saida Zeinab. The accommodation shortage is particularly bad around the time of the hajj, when many Turks stop on their way to or from Mecca. Try to arrive in the morning before places fill up.

Many hotels still demand payment in US dollars, and because they calculate the price at the official rate of S£11.20 to the dollar, pretty crummy rooms can be ridiculously costly. However, there are enough cheap places, and a few of higher quality, that will accept Syrian pounds to make it generally unnecessary for the traveller on a tight budget to worry about parting with lots of dollars for little comfort.

A hotel wanting foreign currency but charging locals S£150 (about US$3.50 at the bank exchange rate) for a bed will ask the foreigner for about US$14. Some of these hotels are enforcing old and tighter restrictions on hotel billing that date back to 1987, when they are no longer compelled to make such charges. Others really still are leaned on by the mukhabarat and risk serious trouble if they accept local currency in payment from foreigners.

One of the better cheap hotels is the

Najmet al-Shark Hotel (☎ 217798), just south-west of Martyrs' Square. The location is lively and noisy, but the hotel has had favourable reports. A bed in a room costs S£100, or S£150 in a room with bath.

Quieter is the *Syria Grand Hotel*, located a block west of the Citadel. It has beds for S£100 in sometimes quite large rooms with fan, but no hot water. The proprietor is a gloomy sort of fellow, but then so is the building.

Another of the dirt (literally) cheapies is the *Hotel Qasr al-Chark*, a noisy hole that seems to distinguish itself by being surrounded by brothels without indulging in the same trade itself. You can take a room for yourself for S£300 or a bed for S£100 to S£125. Insist on the lowest possible rate, as they will try to get as much as they can out of you.

The *Abdeen Hotel* is right in the centre of things, but at S£300/500 for doubles/triples (the management doesn't seem keen on letting single beds) is not terribly enticing. The beds are rock-hard and there's not much in the line of blankets during the cooler months. Much better, and just a couple of doors away, is the slightly pricier *Hotel Said*, which has quite comfortable rooms with balcony, fan and hot water for S£200/375.

The *Rida Hotel* has some rooms the size of cupboards and others that are quite OK. At S£200 for a single it's a bit steep, but S£300 for a double or triple is not so bad and it usually seems to have room when all the others are full. The entrance is a few doors down from a cinema by the barrier across Furat Ave and the hotel is on the 4th floor.

The *Pakistan Hotel* must be a strong contender for the title of 'worst hotel in the world'. This flea-pit-cum-brothel is in a big old bluestone building and has the air of an old insane asylum. If you're really stuck late at night it's better than sleeping in the street, but not much. Beds should not cost more than S£125, but one traveller reported being stung for S£300 for company he didn't want or get.

In the street next to the Hejaz railway station, *L'Oasis Hotel*, or Al-Waha in Arabic

(☎ 227724), is quiet and secure and the guys running it are helpful. A bed in rooms with fan and bath costs S£300 for singles or doubles, but try bargaining.

A reasonable bargain by Damascus standards is the quiet and friendly *Salam Hotel* (☎ 216674) in a side street just behind the Takiyyeh as-Sulaymaniyyeh Mosque. Although the toilets sometimes leave something to be desired and there is no hot water, it's pleasantly situated halfway between Martyrs' Square and the Karnak bus station. There is a nice single room off the TV lounge and a couple of double rooms; the rest are shared rooms. Beds all cost S£100, but watch out in the doubles if you're alone, as you may find yourself paying for both beds.

Higher up the price scale, but worth every qirsh, is the *Barada Hotel* (☎ 212546) on Said al-Jabri Ave. The main stairway takes you past chandelier-lit sitting rooms to comfortable rooms costing S£300/400, and there is hot water.

Camping If you really want to pitch a tent in an approved ground, *Damascus Camping* (☎ 455870), four km out of town on the road to Homs, charges S£200 per person a day. It has a toilet, shower and cooking facilities, but is hardly worth it, particularly when you add in the cost of taxis to the middle of town and back (unless you hitch). Nevertheless, it is popular with some of the overland trucks that come through this way.

Places to Stay – middle
Going upmarket a bit generally means a fairly hefty leap in prices, and not always a commensurate increase in quality. You'll be lucky, even with bargaining, to find anything much under about US$15 for a single.

One of the better ones in this category is the *Sultan Hotel* (☎ 225768), nicely located just west of the Hejaz railway station on Moussallam Baroudy Rd. Good, clean rooms with hot water and breakfast included are US$20/30, and the staff are helpful.

The *Hotel Damas*, closer to Martyrs' Square, is cheaper but nothing special. Rooms here are US$15/22. Right behind the

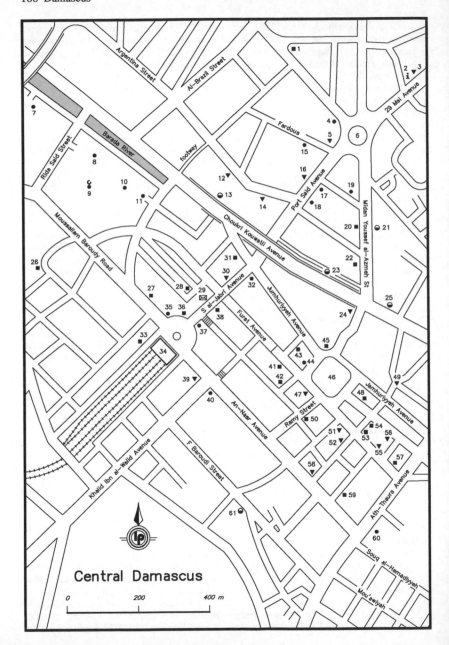

Central Damascus

0   200   400 m

post office is the *Afamia Hotel*, which has adequate rooms with ensuite bath and air-conditioning. It is sometimes necessary to book rooms, which cost US$18/22, a day or two in advance.

Slightly grander is the *Orient Palace Hotel*, across the road from the Hejaz railway station. Rooms are a little expensive at US$30/39. It has retained something of its old-world, French mandate charm, but can fill up with people from the Commonwealth of Independent States (formerly the Soviet Union) who come down on short trips to flog everything from alarm clocks to vodka.

On Martyrs' Square itself is the *Omar al-Khayyam Hotel* (☎ 211667), which is well overrated and overpriced at US$45/56. More reasonable, and also on the square, is the *Ramsis Hotel* which has singles/doubles/triples for US$15/22/25.

Other similar hotels include the *Hotel Siyaha* on Martyrs' Square and the *Hotel Semiramis*, down by the Choukri Kouwatli flyover, which might be worth avoiding given the noise of the traffic. There is a collection of hotels in this category (and some more expensive still) between the flyover and Midan Youssef al-Azmeh.

Heading up to the top end is the *Faradis Hotel*, tucked away in a side street a block west of Martyrs' Square. Good, but fairly sterile rooms go for US$62/78.

Places to Stay – top end

For those who want the best available, there's the *Sheraton, Meridien* and four hotels of the *Cham* chain, where the amount spent on a bed for the night is enough to keep most travellers going for a couple of weeks.

The *Meridien Hotel* (☎ 718730) is on the north bank of the Barada River, about 10 minutes' walk north-west of the centre.

■ PLACES TO STAY

1 Cham Palace Hotel
20 Hotel Venezia
22 Hotel International de Damas
26 Salam Hotel
27 Sultan Hotel
28 Al-Afamia Hotel
31 Hotel Semiramis
33 L'Oasis Hotel
36 Orient Palace Hotel
38 Barada Hotel
41 Rida Hotel
42 Najmet al-Shark Hotel
43 Faradis Hotel
45 Omar al-Khayyam Hotel
48 Hotel Siyaha
50 Pakistan Hotel
53 Abdeen Hotel
54 Hotel Said
57 Hotel Qasr al-Chark
59 Syria Grand Hotel

▼ PLACES TO EAT

3 Al-Kamal Restaurant
5 Ali Baba Restaurant
12 Open Terrace Restaurant
14 Café
16 Restaurant
24 Restaurant
30 Felafel Shop
39 Open Air Café
47 Shawarma Shops
49 Vegetable Market & Kebab Stalls
51 Al-Arabi Restaurant
52 Ghassan Restaurant
55 Sahloul Restaurant
56 Al-Awami Restaurant
58 Juice Stall

OTHER

2 Tourist Office
4 Commercial Bank of Syria (cash & cheques)
6 Peasant's Monument
7 National Museum
8 Army Museum
9 Takiyyeh as-Sulaymaniyyeh Mosque
10 Artisanat (Handicraft Market)
11 Ministry of Tourism
13 Turkish Bus Station
15 Chami Travel (American Express)
17 Karnak Tours
18 Commercial Bank of Syria (cash only)
19 Librairie Universelle
21 Bus to Muhajireen
23 Airport Bus
25 Buses to Jobar, Qaboun & Ticket Booth
29 Central Post Office
32 Commercial Bank of Syria (cash & cheques)
34 Hejaz Railway Station
35 Commercial Bank of Syria (cash & cheques)
37 Syrian Arab Airlines (international flights only)
40 Telephone Office
44 Exchange Booth (cash & cheques)
46 Martyrs' Square
60 Citadel
61 Local buses to South Bus Station

Rooms start at $195/215 and head upwards. The *Sheraton Hotel* (☎ 229300) has a pleasant situation by the river, a km further west along Choukri Kouwatli Ave. You can read the latest news on agency teletype printouts in the foyer. It is a little more expensive again, at $210/250 plus taxes.

The *Cham Palace* (☎ 232300), complete with revolving restaurant, is one of the more conveniently located of the biggies. It's just one block west of the Peasant's Monument and is one of a rapidly expanding chain. It has singles/doubles starting at US$135/140, plus 10% taxes. Two smaller versions, the *Jala'a* and *Techrine* hotels, further away from the centre, have singles/doubles for US$80/90.

Out on the airport road, the *Ebla Cham* has singles starting at US$180 and reaching US$3500 for a presidential room!

PLACES TO EAT
Cheap Eats
Martyrs' Square is the focus for cheap restaurants. There are small stalls and restaurants dotted around selling the usual kebabs, chicken, shawarma and felafels.

A good sign is a full restaurant, and one of the best eateries in the cheaper bracket is the *Al-Arabi*, just a little way off the square towards the Citadel. It offers an unusually wide range of meat and vegetable dishes (including that old favourite, lamb's testicles). A hearty meal won't cost much more than S£150, and the filling vegetable dishes are cheaper still. There are menus in English and you can take away.

For a cheap meal, a beer and a view over the square, you will find it hard to beat the *Al-Karnak* restaurant above the Siyaha Hotel. It is not marked in English; just head up the stairs in the street entrance off the square. This is one of the few cheap places that seems to have a late licence, as it only really begins to get crowded after 11 pm. A meal of kebabs, salad and hummus costs S£90.

The *Ghassan Restaurant* has excellent chicken, and a filling meal with typical side orders like hummus, salad, bread and a coke will cost you about S£100.

Next door to the Najmet al-Shark Hotel is a small restaurant serving rice and a mixed meat and vegetable stew for S£60.

For a good felafel (if you can face another one) try the small shop about 10 metres past the post office towards the Choukri Kouwatli flyover.

There are also excellent juice stalls all over the city. You can't miss them as they have string bags of fruit hanging outside. Apple, orange, banana and pomegranate are favourites and cost from S£20 to S£25. The tiny stall close to the An-Nasr Ave does good, cheap juices and also has cheese and jam sandwiches.

The vegetable market on the edge of Martyrs' Square becomes the nighttime kebab stalls. It's interesting in the evening when it throngs with kebab and fruit stalls. Black marketeers sell Amstel beer from Lebanon (S£40 a can) as well as whisky and araq (the local firewater), and you can hear the cigarette sellers cry, 'Marl-poro, Marl-poro!'.

On An-Nasr Ave, between the Hejaz railway station and the telephone office, there is a couple of shawarma stalls and an enormous café with tea, coffee and narjileh.

For one of the best ice creams you are likely to taste, head for *Bakdach* in the Souq al-Hamadiyyeh. There is at least one 'imitation' place before your get to it (they are both on the right heading towards the Omayyad Mosque), but wait for the best.

A bowl of ice-cream, covered with pistachio nuts, or sahlab (a kind of smooth, sweet milk pudding) covered with same, costs S£10 and is worth every one of them. That's all they serve, but they do it well.

Mid-Range
There is any number of restaurants in Damascus, and throughout Syria for that matter, where a good meal will cost around S£200 plus. There is a string of them along 29 Mai Ave, and the *Al-Kamal Restaurant* next to the tourist office is typical. Most of the more expensive places also serve beer, something that cannot always be taken for granted.

The glitzy 'three-star' *Sahloul Restaurant*, just off Martyrs' Square, has all the standard fare as well as a variety of meat and vegetable stews, rice and macaroni, but is considerably more expensive. A big meal of chicken shish tawooq (marinated and barbecued pieces of chicken) and side orders costs S£230. There's a similar place, the *Al-Awami* (with no name in English), a few doors further along – the entrance is also a hotel entrance.

There is a good open-terrace restaurant up in the street behind the Turkish bus station. It's a pleasant location and S£200 will get you a decent meal of kebabs with the usual side dishes. If it's just a beer you want, a half litre of Barada costs S£28.

You can dine al fresco at the *Al-Khater Restaurant*, on the 3rd floor in the Hotel Venezia, but the food is overpriced and overdone.

The *pizza restaurant* in the park is nothing outstanding and not overly cheap, but makes a change from the usual fare. Just up from the Meridien, on the other side of the road, is a kind of Italian takeaway self-service, where you can get bitesize snacks without laying out too much.

GETTING THERE & AWAY

Air

International Almost all the airline offices and travel agencies for international travel are located in or around Fardous, a small side street left of Port Said Ave, just before the Peasant's Monument. Be warned that buying an international air ticket entails changing money at the artificially low 'aviation rate'.

For details on international flights to Damascus, see the Syria Getting There & Away chapter.

Some travellers have reported being subjected to repeated searches by unpleasant plain clothes officials prior to boarding planes at Damascus Airport.

Domestic For information and ticketing on internal flights, go to the Syrian Arab Airlines office up by the Central Bank Building, at the end of 29 Mai Ave. The square is known as Saahat as-Sabe. The other Syrian Arab Airlines offices you'll see scattered about deal mainly in international flights and can give you no details on internal timetables.

Syrian Arab Airlines fly once or twice daily to Aleppo for S£600. It flies three times a week (Saturdays, Mondays and Thursdays) to Qamishle for S£900.

Bus

Karnak Bus The Karnak bus station is about a 15-minute walk to the west of Martyrs' Square. You may need to show your passport here, although such checks have become far less common than they were in the mid-1980s. It's a big, bustling place that even has a reasonable restaurant.

Buses go from Damascus to all major towns in Syria. Buses (not all of them Karnak) also leave here for destinations in Turkey, Lebanon, Jordan and the Gulf. It is essential to book at least one day in advance.

There is a daily departure for Istanbul (30 hours, S£1500) that also stops at Antakya (S£550), Iskenderun (S£650), Adana (S£750) and Ankara (S£1200). It leaves at 10 pm. It is *much* cheaper to get local transport to Aleppo or the Turkish border and get Turkish buses from there.

Twice daily, buses leave for Amman in Jordan and cost US$5 or JD4. You can't pay in Syrian pounds. The first departure is at 7 am; the second (actually the Jordanian JETT bus making the return trip) at 3 pm. The journey takes six or seven hours, depending on hold-ups at the border.

Karnak buses leave at the same times for Beirut in Lebanon. The trip takes about three hours and costs S£125. There is also a daily service to Tripoli leaving at 8 am for S£175.

A Saudi bus company, Aman, has a daily service to Riyadh (24 hours, S£2000), which also goes to Jeddah. There are occasionally departures for Kuwait, too. You will be asked to present your Saudi visa, and it may pay to get a transit visa for Jordan in advance.

There are departures at least once daily to many destinations within Syria, including the following:

destination	travel time	fare
Aleppo	five hours	S£88
Deir ez-Zur	six hours	S£111
Der'a	1½ hours	S£24
Hama	2½ hours	S£52
Hassake	seven hours	S£153
Homs	two hours	S£39
Lattakia	five hours	S£82
Palmyra	three hours	S£82
Tartus	3½ hours	S£64

Pullman The pullman bus station is next door to the Karnak bus station and competing companies run most of the main routes inside Syria at slightly lower rates than Karnak. Sample Pullman bus fares from Damascus are: Aleppo, S£78; Lattakia, S£75; Deir ez-Zur, S£96; Raqqa, S£116. See the Syria Getting Around chapter for more details.

Bus/Microbus There are two main bus stations (known as 'garages') in Damascus for regular buses and microbuses. There is also a couple of minor bus stations. Buses run to no set schedule and just leave when full.

For buses north, east and to the coast, the station is about three km east of the centre past the traffic circle contrarily called Abbassid Square (or Abbassayeen). To get there catch a local bus going to Qaboun (the destination is sometimes written in English on the side). Get off at the first roundabout after the big football stadium on the right. You have to be careful to get the *right* Qaboun bus, as there are several and not all go via Abbassid Square. All you can do is ask.

This is the cheapest category of buses. Estimated journey times should be taken with a grain of salt. Some fares include:

destination	travel time	fare
Aleppo	five-six hours	S£50
Deir ez-Zur	seven hours	S£100
Homs	2½ hours	S£25
Qamishle	nine hours	S£135
Tartus	four hours	S£46

The station for buses south is just south of the Bab Moussala Square roundabout, about two km from the centre. Take a No 13 Sinaa bus from F Baroudi St and get off at the first stop after the roundabout. Microbuses leave for Der'a (1½ hours, S£20), Suweida (1¾ hours, S£20) and Shahba (1¼ hours, S£15).

In addition, there are two smaller bus stations for buses doing short runs north (such as Maalula) and west (like Bloudan and Zabadani). See the appropriate Getting There & Away sections for these two destinations.

Turkish Buses There is a bus station for Turkish buses just where the Choukri Kouwatli flyover begins. Buses leave for Istanbul and other destinations from here at 7 am and 10 pm and tickets can be bought at the bus station or from travel agents dotted around the city. They cost exactly what a ticket from the Karnak office would, and the same advice applies on making your way at least to Aleppo by internal transport before picking up a Turkish bus. It may be necessary to book in advance.

You can supposedly buy tickets for destinations as far flung as Cairo, Moscow and Western Europe at the same bus station, but caution is advisable.

Train
The Hejaz railway station is right in the centre of town. It's an impressive old building and the ceiling inside is intricately decorated. But before you get too excited, most trains actually leave from the Khaddam railway station, about five km away and most easily reached by taxi. Trains are infrequent and slower than the buses and run daily to Homs, Hama, Aleppo, Raqqa, Deir ez-Zur, Hassake, Qamishle, Tartus and Lattakia. The trip to Qamishle can take 16 hours or more.

The only trains leaving from the Hejaz railway station are the daily run south to Der'a (three hours, S£24) and the summertime daytrippers' train to the mountain 'beauty spot', Zabadani (the train is known to some expat wits as the 'Zabadani Flyer').

The big disadvantage with the trains is that the railway station is usually right on the outskirts of the towns and it can be a hassle to get to the centre. Some fares include:

Top Left: Citadel, Damascus (DS)
Top Right: Treasury, Omayyed Mosque, Damascus (DS)
Bottom Left: Convent of St Thecla, Maalula (DS)
Bottom Right: House in Maalula (HF)

Top Left: The Roman theatre at Bosra (HF)
Top Right: Workmen at Bosra (HF)
Bottom: Saladin from the north-west (DS)

destination	sleeper	1st class	2nd class
Homs		S£44	S£29
Hama		S£54	S£37
Aleppo	S£320	S£81	S£55
Deir ez-Zur		S£150	S£101
Qamishle		S£195	S£130
Lattakia		S£86	S£58

Service-Taxi There is a service-taxi station next to the Karnak bus station. Taxis leave throughout the day and night for Amman (five hours, S£300 or JD4) and Beirut (three hours, S£182 or S£277 depending on where in Beirut).

There is another service-taxi station behind the Pullman bus station. Service-taxis to Riyadh cost S£3000 a head.

Car Rental
Europcar has agents in most of the big hotels. For details of the limited options on renting a car, see the Syria Getting Around chapter.

Two relatively new and small operations are Marmou (☎ 335959), opposite the American School, and Palmyra (☎ 243854), opposite the Cham Jala'a Hotel. Their rates are not much different to Europcar's, so the effects of competition have yet to be felt.

GETTING AROUND
To/From the Airport
Damascus International Airport is 35 km south-east of Damascus. Local buses leave every half hour from next to the Choukri Kouwatli Ave flyover from 5.30 am to midnight. The trip costs S£5 and takes 45 minutes.

Bus
Damascus is well served with a local bus network, but as the centre is so compact you'll rarely have to use them. Tickets have to be bought before you get on and there are small booths for this – there's one on Choukri Kouwatli Ave where the bus to Qaboun leaves from.

A book of 10 tickets costs S£10 and each ticket is good for one journey. You are supposed to punch both ends of it in a machine on the bus. Although a lot of people seem not to bother with buying tickets, there is a S£25 fine for travelling without one.

Taxi
All the taxis are yellow, and there are hundreds of them. They are cheap, but make sure the driver uses the meter. A cross-town ride should never cost more than S£20.

Around Damascus

MAALULA
Set in a narrow valley in the foothills of the Anti-Lebanon range, Maalula is an interesting little village where the houses cling to the cliff face. They are often plastered in yellow, blue or mauve, which makes the village far more attractive than most Syrian villages with their generally drab, grey, concrete buildings.

Although there are some Muslims, most of the residents are Greek Catholics. The village's real claim to fame, however, is that a dialect of Aramaic is still spoken here. Dating from the 1st millennium BC, Aramaic was the language that Jesus spoke. The Lord's Prayer and the Old Testament book of Daniel were first written in Aramaic. Two nearby settlements, Jaba'deen and Bakh'a, are also Aramaic-speaking.

At the main intersection in the village, the road forks. The right fork leads to the Convent of St Thecla, tucked snugly against the cliff. The convent itself is of no particular interest, but carry on past it along a narrow cleft cut through the rock by the waters draining the plateau above the village. Turn back to the left where the cleft opens out and walk along the cliff edge for some spectacular views of the town and valley. The atmosphere is unfortunately spoiled by the presence of the sprawling Safir Hotel.

Past the hotel is another convent, dedicated to St Sergius (Mar Sarkis). The low doorway leads into the monastery where there is a small Byzantine church. Take the road leading down from the monastery and it brings you out at the fork in the village.

Places to Stay & Eat

Maalula is an easy day trip from Damascus, and it is hard to believe that many people would want to spend the money availing themselves of the services of an expensive hotel there. However, the *Safir Hotel* (☎ 27250) offers four-star accommodation at $66/83 for singles/doubles, along with a bar, pool and restaurant.

In the centre of town and by the Convent of St Thecla there are a few small snack places and shops. You may be able to stay overnight at the convent.

Getting There & Away

Microbuses run to Maalula every hour or so from a separate station in Damascus. To get to it from the centre take a Jobar bus from Choukri Kouwatli Ave, which drops you right by the small station south of Abbassid Square. The microbuses are more frequent in the morning, although even then can take a while to fill up. The trip costs S£9 and takes about an hour.

ZABADANI, BLOUDAN & 'AIN AL-FIJEH

These three small towns are in the valley of the Barada River as it makes its way down from the Anti-Lebanon range to the Ghouta Oasis and Damascus.

The countryside is very pleasant but the main attraction is the narrow-gauge train trip up the valley, which you can take any day of the week in summer. Damascenes flock there on Fridays to escape the city and picnic by the river. The train is loaded with a real variety of people – from elderly veiled women with children and grandchildren in tow, to teenage boys sporting their latest Western clothes and ghetto-blasters.

The train crawls as far as Zabadani, taking about three hours to cover the 50 km from Damascus. It then stops for about three hours before making the return trip. If that's too long for you, catch a microbus down to 'Ain al-Fijeh to have a look around before picking the train (or another microbus) up on the downward journey, or simply ride all the way back to Damascus.

Bloudan is seven km further on again from Zabadani and cannot be reached by train. It is another in a line of favourite weekend getaway spots for stressed out Damascenes. Although pleasant enough, it really doesn't have much to offer the traveller.

Getting There & Away

Trains (the 'Zabadani Flyer') only run during the summer, leaving from the Hejaz railway station. Fares hover around the S£10 mark.

Microbuses leave from the station next to the Karnak bus station. They take about an hour and cost S£10 to Zabadani and S£12 to Bloudan.

South of Damascus

The area from Damascus south to the Jordanian border, about 100 km away, is fertile agricultural land and intensively farmed, particularly with watermelons. In the late summer you'll probably see more melons for sale by the side of the road than you've ever seen in your life. Often, however, it looks as though the farmers are trying to grow polythene bags – the fields are littered with them.

The Golan Heights in the south-west were originally Syrian territory but have been largely in Israeli hands since the Arab-Israeli war of 1967. For the Syrians, Golan remains the most pressing issue in any peace process, ahead of resolution of the Palestinian dilemma. The Syrian response to developments on the latter front are guided by how their interest in retrieving the Golan can best be served.

The area known as the Hauran is a black

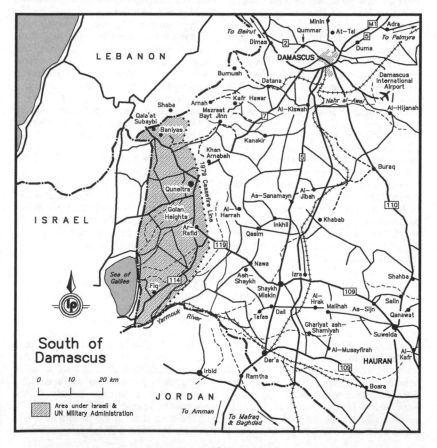

South of
Damascus

0   10   20 km

Area under Israeli &
UN Military Administration

basalt plain that straddles the Jordan-Syria border and also goes by the names of Jebel Druze and Jebel al-Arab. The black rocks used for construction give the villages and towns of the area a strange brooding quality.

GOLAN HEIGHTS

The Golan is a name that most people would have heard in news reports on the Middle East, but probably have only a vague idea where it is or what its significance is.

It is the only area where Israel and Syria have a common border and so it has been the scene of bitter conflict over the years. The 1967 war saw the Israelis clear the Golan of Syrian troops and Damascus itself was threatened.

During the war of 1973, a delicate truce was negotiated between Israel and Syria by the US Secretary of State, Henry Kissinger, who spent almost a month shuttling back and forth between Damascus and Israel. The truce saw Syria regain some 450 sq km of territory lost to the Israelis during the war as well as some small, symbolically important pieces lost in the 1967 war. A complicated demilitarised buffer zone supervised by UN forces was also established. It varies in width from a few hundred metres to a couple of km.

In 1981 the Israeli government formally annexed part of the Golan and settlers moved in. In Israeli eyes the area serves as an indispensable buffer against potential Syrian attack. The Syrians, quite naturally, see things differently, but have so far refrained from taking military action.

In September 1992 Israel declared it would be prepared to hand back at least part of the Golan Heights in exchange for a lasting peace agreement with the Syrians.

Before the Israelis withdrew from the biggest town in the Golan, Quneitra, they evacuated the 37,000 Arab population and set about systematically destroying the town, removing anything that could be unscrewed, unbolted or wrenched from its position. Everything from windows to light fittings were sold to Israeli contractors. Once the buildings had been stripped, they were pulled apart with tractors and bulldozers. It is reported that some graves were even broken open and ransacked.

All this makes Quneitra look more like a bombed-out city than anything else. It has become something of a national propaganda showpiece demonstrating the hard-nosed approach of the Israelis and it is an eerie place to visit. As the demilitarised zone is only a few hundred metres wide at this point, the Israeli flag can be seen flying not far away.

Since Quneitra has passed from the direct control of the UN and is now under UN-supervised Syrian administration, it has become virtually impossible to get in. You used to be able to get a permit from the UN with no trouble. This is no longer the case, so don't waste your time trying any of the various UN offices scattered around the capital. The permit now has to come from the Ministry of the Interior, but to get it, you supposedly have to get your embassy to make a request via the Foreign Ministry. If your embassy can be bothered, and the Syrians actually agree, you might have the permit after a matter of weeks.

Getting There & Away

Microbuses from the station next to Karnak bus station take one hour and cost S£10. You could always try just hopping on and seeing what happens. You won't be stopped by any UN checkpoints, but almost definitely by the Syrians. The bus driver probably won't even let you on without the permit.

SHAHBA

The modern town of Shahba is about 90 km south of Damascus. The town entered into its own when it was refounded by its son, emperor Phillip, in 244 AD, the year of his accession to the ultimate position of authority in the Roman Empire. The only Arab to rule the empire, his reign lasted only five years, but Phillipopolis continued to thrive long after he had gone, as the magnificent 4th-century mosaics now held in the museum of Suweida testify.

The main street of the modern town was the cardo. This was intersected by the decumanus at the town centre. Head right along the partly intact paved **Roman road**, past four columns on the right, and you'll see a number of buildings on the left.

The best preserved of them appears to have been a family **shrine**, dedicated to a god Martinus, probably Phillip's father. Just behind it lies a fairly modest **theatre**. Back on the main road, head a little way south and on the left you can see the jumbled remains of the town **nymphaeum**, or public baths. Further down the street is part of the original southern **gate** of the city.

Getting There & Away

Microbuses run from the south bus station (or 'garage') in Damascus. The trip takes about an hour and 20 minutes and costs S£15. You can also pick up microbuses coming up the other way from Suweida.

SUWEIDA

Anything that might once have been of interest in this provincial capital, 15 km south of Shahba, has long been swept away by modern expansion. However, there is a brand new **museum**, built and organised with the aid of the French and opened in November 1991, which holds an impressive collection covering periods in Hauran history from the Stone Age to Rome. You can see prehistoric pottery, an extensive array of mostly basalt statuary, as well as a popular tradition section (the usual wax dummies in traditional garb and various other bits and bobs).

The main attraction, however, are the mosaics from Shahba, which alone make a visit worthwhile. The best preserved and most remarkable (you can't miss it) is entitled 'Artemis Surprised While Bathing'. Unfortunately, all the labelling is in Arabic and French.

The museum is open from 9 am to 6 pm every day but Tuesdays, and costs S£5 to get in. To get to the museum walk one km directly east of the microbus station at the northern entry into the town. It's hard to mistake – it is the only huge, modern, shiny building in the area.

Getting There & Away

A microbus from Damascus (again the south bus station) takes 1¾ hours and costs S£20. For the trip back be prepared for a long wait if you leave it later than about 3.30 pm, as the number of buses running after then is minimal.

QANAWAT

A 15-minute bus ride east of Suweida lies the town of Qanawat, once a member of the Roman-inspired Decapolis that included such cities as Jerash, Philadelphia (Amman) and Gadara (Umm Qais) in Jordan. The bus drops you at the most interesting monument, known as the **Seraglio**. Historians believe it was a combination of temples, the most intact building dating from the second half of the 2nd century AD. It was later converted into a basilica and the whole area given over to Christian worship.

If you head north from here (head left from the main facade), you will come towards a river bed, where you can see remains of a **theatre**, a **nymphaeum** and a few other scattered relics.

Getting There & Away

To use public transport, you need to head about one km towards the centre of Suweida from the northern microbus station. The Qanawat shuttle leaves fairly regularly from a side street off the main road, and about the only way you'll find it is by asking at regular intervals along the way for the Qanawat bus. The quick trip costs S£3.

BOSRA

The town of Bosra lies between two wadis, both of which run into the Yarmouk River. It is 40 km east of Der'a across fertile plains littered with black basalt rocks. Once important for its location at the crossroads of major trade and, under the Muslims, pilgrimage routes, it is now little more than a backwater.

It is a weird and wonderful place. Apart from having possibly the best preserved Roman theatre in existence, the rest of the town is built in, around and over old sections of Roman buildings, almost entirely out of black basalt blocks. Those in the new houses have mostly been filched from ancient Roman buildings.

Altogether it's a strange mixture of architectural styles and, as the *Cook's Travellers' Handbook* of 1934 says, 'a zealous antiquary might find weeks of profitable enjoyment among the ruins'. That is probably quite true, but for most people one day is enough to see everything at a leisurely pace. It is possible to visit Bosra in a day-trip from Damascus using public transport, but it's less hectic if you use Der'a as a base.

History

Bosra is mentioned in Egyptian records as early as 1300 BC and during the 1st century AD it became the northern capital of the Nabataean kingdom; Petra was the capital in the south.

In 106 AD the area was annexed by the Romans and Bosra became the capital of the Province of Arabia and was named Nova Trajana Bostra. This was the seat of a praetorian legate who was administrator of the region and in command of the 3rd Legion which was garrisoned mainly at Bosra. It was this and the fact that Bosra was still on the caravan routes that allowed it to prosper. When Phillip became emperor of Rome, he raised the town to the status of metropolis and coins were minted here.

During the Christian era it was also important as the seat of a primate with 33 priests subject to him. Prior to its fall to the Muslims in 634, tradition has it that Mohammed encountered the Nestorian monk Boheira here. Although some say the monk did little more than introduce Mohammed to the basic tenets of Christianity, others claim he told him of his future vocation as a Prophet.

The Crusaders twice tried unsuccessfully to take the fortress in the 12th century and the Mongols seriously damaged it during their invasion in 1261.

The city still managed to prosper as it was on the pilgrimage route to Mecca, and because of the tradition of Mohammed and the monk, pilgrims would often stop here for up to a week. When this route became unsafe about the end of the 17th century, the pilgrims started using a route further to the west – Bosra was on the way down.

Citadel & Theatre

The citadel is a curious construction as it is largely a fortified Roman theatre. The two structures are in fact one – the fort was built around the theatre to make it an impregnable stronghold. The first walls were built during the Omayyad and Abbassid periods, with further additions being made in the 11th century by the Fatimids.

After the Crusader attacks of 1140 and 1183, it was realised that there was not enough room to house all the Ayyubid troops stationed there, so during the period 1202 to 1251 nine towers were constructed. These towers were encircled by a deep moat and a five-span bridge was erected.

The big surprise on entering the citadel is to find the magnificent 15,000-seat theatre. The theatre was almost completely obscured by later buildings and only this century have these been cleared away to reveal its fine lines. It is a rarity among theatres of the time in that it is completely freestanding rather than built into the side of a hill.

The stage is backed by rows of Corinthian columns and the whole facade was originally faced with white marble. The stage had a wooden roof and the rest of the theatre was covered by silk awnings to give protection from the elements. As if this wasn't refine-

ment enough, perfumed water was also sprayed in the air and the fine mist fell on the heads of the spectators.

There are two small museums in two of the towers, but they are often as not closed. One, in a tower in the south-east of the citadel, houses a small and not terribly inter-esting archaeological display. The other is one of the ubiquitous museums of popular culture and tradition, with scenes of Arab life depicted using mannequins and various exhibits of clothing and utensils. This south-western tower appears to have once served some official function as a residence or

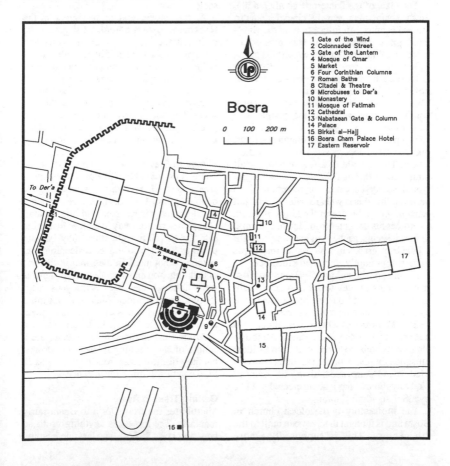

Bosra

1 Gate of the Wind
2 Colonnaded Street
3 Gate of the Lantern
4 Mosque of Omar
5 Market
6 Four Corinthian Columns
7 Roman Baths
8 Citadel & Theatre
9 Microbuses to Der'a
10 Monastery
11 Mosque of Fatimah
12 Cathedral
13 Nabataean Gate & Column
14 Palace
15 Birkat al-Hajj
16 Bosra Cham Palace Hotel
17 Eastern Reservoir

0   100   200 m

To Der'a

reception quarters. If they are closed, ask one of the people in the café to open them up for you.

The citadel is open daily from 8 am to 6 pm and entrance is S£10; in the rest of the town you can wander around at any time.

Other Things to See

North of the citadel is the **main street** of the old city running roughly east-west. At the western end is the large Gate of the Wind (Bab al-Hawa). Along the cobbled main street are the remains of columns found on the site during excavations.

The Gate of the Lantern (Bab al-Qandil), on the main street near the citadel, dates to the 3rd century. An inscription on the right-hand pillar states that it was erected in memory of the 3rd Legion, which was garrisoned here.

Next up are the four enormous Corinthian **columns**, looking somewhat out of place. This is what is left of the **nymphaeum**, which supplied water to the people and gardens.

Just past these is another column and lintel that has been incorporated into a modern house. The thought of a few tons of basalt plummeting through the ceiling one night would surely be cause for insomnia. It is believed that this is what remains of a pagan sanctuary built by one of the kings of Bosra to protect his daughter from death. A dismal failure it seems, as the daughter was brought a bunch of grapes in which a scorpion was hiding. It promptly stung and killed her.

Right opposite this are the **Roman baths**. It was a complicated series of rooms where the bather moved from one pool-room to the next, finally arriving at the steam bath.

The **Mosque of Omar** lies about 200 metres north of the main street. Although claimed by some to be one of the three oldest mosques in the world (the others are in Medina and Cairo) and built in 720, the more likely hypothesis has it being erected in 1112 by a Seljuq administrator.

The **monastery** is the oldest church in Bosra and is thought to have been built in the 4th century. This is supposedly where Mohammed met the monk Boheira. The facade has been totally rebuilt but the side walls and apse are original.

Between the monastery and the main street lies the **cathedral** in a sorry state of decay. It was the first building to have a circular dome above a square base, but it was poorly constructed in the first place (circa 512 AD), and had been rebuilt a number of times before its final demise. The emperor Justinian used the church as the model for cathedrals he built at Constantinople and Ravenna. His architects managed to do a better job of it and those two cathedrals still stand.

At the eastern end of the street is the **Nabataean gate & column**. The gate is the main entrance to the palace in which the Nabataean king Rabbel II lived. The column is the only one of its kind in Syria and bears the typical simple Nabataean capital.

Further out of town are two **cisterns** or reservoirs that used to supply the town with water. The one to the east of the Nabataean gate is a popular swimming location with the local kids, although not overly inviting.

Places to Stay & Eat

There is only one hotel in Bosra, the expensive *Bosra Cham Palace*, where singles/doubles go for US$100/120. It is located a few hundred metres south of the theatre. Otherwise, you can stay in a room inside the café for S£100 a night (they may bargain down to S£50). You'll need a sleeping bag, as there is not much in the room in the line of bedding. You may be able to cook there as well, although the cafés employees seem reticent about that idea. Make up your mind before 6 pm, as you get locked inside then. Damascus or Der'a offer better alternatives.

Around the entrance to the citadel are a couple of shops selling felafels and drinks, but they like to charge over the odds – S£25 for a can of soft drink for instance.

Getting There & Away

Microbuses run from Der'a to Bosra fairly regularly. The trip takes anything up to an hour and costs S£7.50. The last one heading back to Der'a leaves about 4.30 pm. There is no direct service from Suweida, but you may be able to make it with a combination of microbuses and hitching. Don't leave this too late, as the microbuses in this part of the country slow to a trickle from around 4 pm.

DER'A

There's not a lot of interest in this southern town, 100 km from Damascus, although it can make a good base for visiting the ruins at Bosra, and you'll probably end up staying here if you want to tackle the Jordanian border by public transport. There are a couple of sights worth a quick look if you are stuck here with time to kill.

There's a tourist office on the Damascus road, just north of the railway line, and further up the same road is a post office.

Things to See

About two km south of the centre of town is the **Omari Mosque**, loosely based on the Omayyad Mosque in Damascus, although far less grand. It was built in the 13th century under the Ayyubids.

To get to it, head out along the Jordan road, then veer off it to the left before crossing the stinking dribble that passes for a river. Follow the road up around the left side of the knoll and beyond; the mosque will appear on the left.

As you leave the mosque, take the side street almost directly opposite and on your right you'll see the remains of a Roman **theatre** that are still being investigated.

Places to Stay & Eat

There is a couple of nondescript hotels in the centre of town. The *Hotel as-Salam*, in a side street south off the main road (which itself runs parallel to the railway line) is not too bad and charges S£50 a bed in a double room (with bargaining). On the main road itself is the *Hotel al-Ahram*, where S£100 will get you a quite disgusting cupboard and they'll try to charge you extra for a cold shower. They have the gall to ask

US$20 for a quite pleasant (but hardly enchanting) double on the other side of the hotel. Stay clear of this place.

The best deal by far is in a hotel on the Damascus road, north of the post office. It has no name in English, but is a big place. The staff are friendly, it has hot water and good clean doubles/triples for S£300.

There are a few small felafel, chicken and shawarma places in the main street.

Getting There & Away

Bus The Karnak bus station and microbus stations are grouped together about three km east of the centre of town – a real pain. Microbuses and bigger buses to and from Damascus (south bus station) cost S£20 and take about 1½ hours. Microbuses to Bosra take up to an hour and cost S£7.50. Competition for the Damascus buses can be pretty tough in the afternoons.

There are two Karnak services between Der'a and Damascus. Tickets cost S£24 and the trip takes about an hour. You can't pick up the Damascus-Amman bus here.

Train There is a daily departure for Damascus along the Hejaz Railway. The train leaves at 6 am, the trip takes three hours and costs S£24. The same train leaves Damascus for the return trip at 2.40 pm.

To/From Jordan This border is straightforward enough, although it can involve a bit of hiking. Service-taxis shuttle between the bus stations in Der'a and Ramtha (on the Jordanian side), and cost S£125 or JD2 a head.

Otherwise you will need to hitch or walk. To save yourself some of the effort, try to get a local bus from the bus station into the centre; that will save you the first three km. From there head south out on the Jordan road (it's signposted) and hitch or walk the four km to the Syrian checkpoint. Once through formalities here, it's another three or four km to the Jordanian checkpoint. The soldiers here may not allow you to walk the last km or so to the immigration post, but are friendly and will flag down a car or bus for you. From the Jordanian side, at Ramtha, minibuses go on to Mafraq, Irbid and Zarqa, from where you can proceed to Amman.

The number of trucks lining the road on this border is staggering – at times they are queued up for kms waiting to cross. The drivers are well prepared. Each truck has a well-stocked food-box on the side complete with teapot and gas stove, and you'll see the drivers sitting next to their trucks making a brew and having a chat while they sit it out.

Getting Around
There's little need for an extensive local transport system. However, it is worth noting that if you arrive at the bus station and want to get back into the centre, there are fairly regular local buses between the two for S£1.

Mediterranean Coast

The 183-km-long Syrian coastline is dominated by the rugged mountain range which runs along its entire length. The coastal strip is narrow in the north, and widens towards the south and it is extremely fertile and heavily cultivated.

The port city of Lattakia (Al-Lathqiyya) with its beach resorts, and the ruined ancient city of Ugarit, lie in the north. From here roads head north to Turkey, east across the mountains to Aleppo, and south to Tartus, Syria's secondary port.

The mountains behind Lattakia contain Syria's only forests and these are easy on the eyes after the often monotonous country in the interior. Excessive clearing of the forests for timber have led to large areas being reduced to scrub, although the government has laid aside some areas for preservation.

The beaches along the coast are certainly

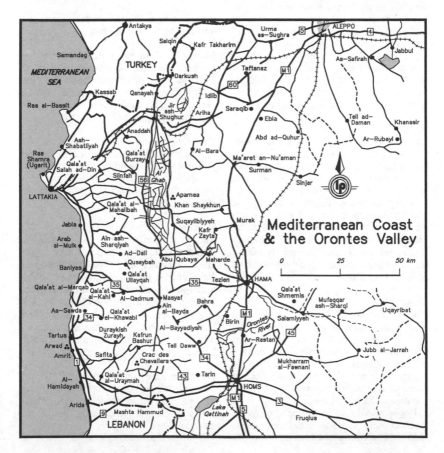

Mediterranean Coast & the Orontes Valley

nothing to rave about as the water is murky and the sand is littered with garbage, but they are popular with Syrians on holiday.

LATTAKIA

This busy port city is dominated by the harbour facilities and the freighters anchored just offshore. Most of Syria's imports and exports come through here and car ferries connect it to Cyprus and Turkey.

It's certainly not a typical Syrian town. It has almost a European feel with its wide tree-lined streets and the occasional café with chairs and tables on the footpath. It's also one of the least conservative cities in Syria. The people are very snappy dressers and, apart from the odd *hijab* (woman's head scarf), you'll see little traditional dress.

The city itself has no real attractions but it makes a good base for visits to the ruins of the ancient city of Ugarit, Jabla, Qala'at Salah ad-Din (Saladin) and, at a pinch, the northernmost beach of Ras al-Bassit.

History

Lattakia became a city of importance under the Seleucids in the 2nd century BC and was named Laodicea by Seleucus I. It came under Roman control in the 1st century AD and Mark Antony made it a free town.

Many serious earthquakes during the Middle Ages took their toll and with the rebellions of the Alawites against the ruling Muslims in the 1800s, it had little chance of regaining its former prosperity. Only recently has it boomed with the development of the port facilities.

Orientation

The lower end of 14 Ramadan St, the main road running from the north-east into town and culminating at the central mosque, is where most of the cheap hotels, cafés and the like are gathered, spilling into the streets immediately around it. The buses (except Karnak) and service-taxis all leave from somewhere along this road.

Baghdad Ave, the north-south boulevard that becomes 8 Azar St by the main local bus station, is the chic axis of Lattakia. There are charming (and pricier) European-style cafés on the footpaths. Although of no great interest, it is not an unpleasant place to wander around a bit.

Information

Tourist Office The Tourist Centre is in the impressive new building at the fork in the main road, beyond the second microbus station. It is open from 9 am to 2 pm every day except Fridays, and the friendly staff will bend over backwards to help, even if they really don't have that much to offer in terms of literature or concrete advice.

Post The post office is south of the centre towards the harbour entrance.

Money The Commercial Bank of Syria is on Baghdad Ave and is open from 8.30 am to 1.30 pm. There are three entrances. Take the middle one, which leads into a kind of exchange booth that is surprisingly efficient. You can change cash and cheques.

Visa Extensions For visa extensions, the immigration office is on the 3rd floor of the police building. The office is open every day, except Fridays, from 8 am to 2 pm, and supposedly from 8 to 9 pm. Extensions are issued on the spot.

Museum

There's a small museum down near the waterfront housed in what was once an old khan, or caravanserai. The 2nd floor was built during the French mandate. Most descriptions are in Arabic, but the caretaker is quite helpful if you don't speak Arabic. There's some pottery and written tablets from Ugarit, chain-mail suits and a section of contemporary art. It's open from 8 am to 2 pm daily except Tuesdays. Entry is S£5.

Places to Stay – bottom end

For some reason, Lattakia seems to play host to some of the cheapest hotels in Syria. These cheap hotels are concentrated around the mosque.

The *Hotel Kawkab ash-Sharq* ('Hotel' in

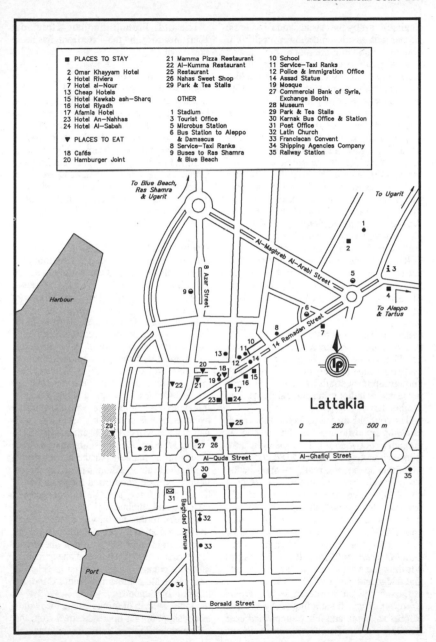

PLACES TO STAY
2 Omar Khayyam Hotel
4 Hotel Riviera
7 Hotel al-Nour
13 Cheap Hotels
15 Hotel Kawkab ash-Sharq
16 Hotel Riyadh
17 Afamia Hotel
23 Hotel An-Nahhas
24 Hotel Al-Sabah

▼ PLACES TO EAT

18 Cafés
20 Hamburger Joint

21 Mamma Pizza Restaurant
22 Al-Kumma Restaurant
25 Restaurant
26 Nahas Sweet Shop
29 Park & Tea Stalls

OTHER

1 Stadium
3 Tourist Office
5 Microbus Station
6 Bus Station to Aleppo
  & Damascus
8 Service-Taxi Ranks
9 Buses to Ras Shamra
  & Blue Beach

10 School
11 Service-Taxi Ranks
12 Police & Immigration Office
14 Assad Statue
19 Mosque
27 Commercial Bank of Syria,
   Exchange Booth
28 Museum
29 Park & Tea Stalls
30 Karnak Bus Office & Station
31 Post Office
32 Latin Church
33 Franciscan Convent
34 Shipping Agencies Company
35 Railway Station

To Blue Beach,
Ras Shamra
& Ugarit

To Ugarit

Al-Maghreb Al-Arabi Street

8 Azar Street

Harbour

14 Ramadan Street

To Aleppo
& Tartus

Lattakia

0   250   500 m

Al-Quds Street

Al-Ghafiqi Street

Baghdad Avenue

Port

Borsaid Street

English), just by the Assad statue, has basic singles with ensuite cold shower for S£50. If you wait until mid-afternoon, the shower, with a bit of solar aid, will probably be pleasantly tepid anyway. It also has doubles with a balcony that go from S£100 to S£150, depending on your bargaining efforts.

Closer to the mosque is the *Afamia Hotel*, where beds come for as low as S£45/75 for singles/doubles. A hot shower costs S£25 extra. Turn down the street to the left and you'll come across the *Hotel an-Nahhas* (☎ 38030), where the friendly Algerian manager has rooms for S£75/125, but only cold water. He sells coffee, tea and juices on the premises and speaks English and French. Across the road, the *Hotel al-Sabah* has clean rooms with balconies. Singles/doubles cost S£50/75 but, again, there is no hot water.

Right by the mosque are a few more cheapies, but they're so close by that you may as well have a loudspeaker hooked up in each room for the early morning call to prayer.

Places to Stay – middle
A couple of doors down from the Kawkab ash-Sharq is the *Hotel Riyadh*, a comfortable place boasting relatively modern rooms high enough up to neutralise much of the street noise and with hot water and balconies. The snag is they cost $18/23.

The sour old chap at the desk of the *Hotel al-Nour*, opposite the first bus station, is enough to put you off before you even start. Singles/doubles/triples cost $18/22/25.

Further up the same road, just opposite the Tourist Centre, is the *Hotel Riviera* (☎ 21803) where the reception is markedly friendlier and rooms (with hot water, TV and fridge) are more expensive. Singles/doubles cost $50/55.

Another roundabout further on is the *Hotel Haroun* (☎ 27140). It's a bit sombre, but the rooms also come with hot bath, TV and fridge and cost $25/30.

Down by the stadium is the *Omar Khayyam Hotel*. It's nothing really special. Rooms are clean and fairly simple and cost $20/25.

The old, French-mandate Hotel du Tourisme, down by the waterfront, has been shut down.

Places to Stay – top end
About six km north of town on Blue Beach is the four-star *Hotel Meridien* (☎ 29000). Rooms here cost $85/$108 plus 10% taxes, but in the off-season it's pretty easy to get a 25% discount. They only charge for use of their reasonably clean beach in high season.

To get to the Meridien you actually pass Lattakia's premier establishment, the *Côte d'Azur* (☎ 26329), where prices for singles/doubles range from $111/263 to $198/367. They charge nonresidents S£150 to use the beach.

Places to Eat
As with hotels, the cheap restaurants and street stalls are around the mosque area. A quick hunt around will turn up the old faithfuls – felafel, chicken, kebabs and shawarma.

For the same food in better surroundings there's a partly open-air restaurant upstairs on the first corner south of the mosque. A decent meal will cost you about S£150.

Along similar lines is the *Al-Kumma* restaurant, a block closer to the waterfront, up on the 2nd floor. Try to get a window seat in this quite cosy little place. Prices are fairly average for this kind of restaurant. A good half chicken will cost S£90 and a beer S£25.

The *Mamma Pizza* restaurant, for those who want a change from the usual fare, is pretty good value. Although there isn't much variety, they do good pizza for about S£60. They also have spaghetti bolognese, escalope and hamburgers!

A block further north, you can get a reasonable imitation takeaway burger and chips from a bright, new little spot in a side street.

All over Lattakia shops sell cheap locally made ice cream which is similar to gelati. If you can handle the lurid colours, the ice cream is quite good.

On the subject of things sweet, the *Nahas* sweet shop, not far up a side street from the Commercial Bank of Syria, has an amazing range of local and imported chocolates and sweets. If you've been on the road for a while and have forgotten what, say, Maltesers taste like, this is about the only place in Syria you're likely to be able to remind yourself.

Getting There & Away
Air Lattakia airport has been closed since November 1991.

Bus The Karnak bus station and office is in the southern end of the town centre, just off Baghdad Ave. Book one day in advance for buses running daily to Aleppo (S£44), Damascus (S£82, stops in Tartus and Homs) and Beirut (S£175, with a stop in Tripoli).

There are two other bus stations on 14 Ramadan St. The first, a few hundred metres up from the Assad statue, is for buses to Aleppo and Damascus only. The trip to Aleppo takes 3½ to four hours and costs S£26. The other bus station, a further 100 metres along, is the microbus station for buses to all other destinations. The trip to Tartus takes 1½ hours and costs S£17.

Train The railway station is about a km east of Baghdad Ave. There are two daily departures for Aleppo (S£51, 1st class; S£24, 2nd class).

Service-Taxi There are taxi ranks on both sides of the school and others gather at other points on and near 14 Ramadan St. Bargain hard for whatever destination you want.

Ferry At the time of writing there were no passenger ferries operating out of Lattakia. The ferry used on the weekly, 36-hour run to Alexandria, in Egypt, was undergoing repairs, and there was some hope that it would eventually re-enter service. The Shipping Agencies Company assumed a ticket would cost around US$60 per person.

At one time or another, there have been other ferries to Cyprus, Volos in Greece and Odessa in Ukraine, but there were no immediate plans to reinstate them. The best bet is to go down to the Shipping Agencies Company in person and find out what, if anything, is going on. The Tourist Centre *may* have some other ideas, but don't bet on it.

Getting Around
Bus The city's local bus station is at the point where Baghdad Ave becomes 8 Azar St, widening out to allow for a narrow garden through the middle of the road. On the west side is the ticket booth and this is also where buses for Ras Shamra (Ugarit) and Blue Beach leave from. The first of these passes fairly close by Blue Beach, turning off at the Côte d'Azur Hotel. A ticket, which is good for four rides (or four people), costs S£10. For each ride you clip a corner of the ticket on the machine you'll see on the bus.

To/From Turkey To get to Antakya take a microbus to Kassab (1½ hours, S£15) and from there a dolmus (if you can find one) to Antakya. You may have to walk or hitch from the town to the border crossing itself.

Alternatively, there are Turkish bus companies in Lattakia itself, but they are not so easy to find. The Tourist Centre can actually come in handy here. One company, Al-Nouras (☎ 24955), has two daily departures to Antakya for S£300 – a little expensive.

AROUND LATTAKIA
Ras Shamra
Although there's not much to see today, Ras Shamra (Ugarit) was once the most important city on the Mediterranean coast. It first came to prominence in the 3rd millennium BC, when it traded with Cyprus and Mesopotamia. Its golden age, however, was from about the 16th to the 13th century BC when it was a centre for trade with Egypt, the Aegean Sea, Cyprus, Mesopotamia and the rest of Syria. Offerings were sent by the kings of Egypt to the famous Temple of Baal and Ugarit became a centre of learning. The city was destroyed by the Philistines when they invaded in about 1190 BC.

In the 13th century BC, the royal palace at Ugarit was one of the most imposing and famous buildings in western Asia. It started out as a modest structure but in time was enlarged to cover more than one hectare and featured courtyards, piped water, drainage and burial chambers. Similar features were also found in the houses of the well-to-do. At its peak, Ugarit was a very wealthy city.

The city had a library and it is here that written clay tablets were found. The writing on the tablets is widely accepted as being the earliest known alphabet. It was adapted by the Greeks, then the Romans, and it is from this script that all alphabets today are derived. The texts found here are the most important source of information on early religion and life in Syria. They contain various texts and myths of religious significance as well as lists of gods and dictionaries. The tablets are on display in the museums in Lattakia, Aleppo and Damascus, as well as the Louvre in Paris.

Things to See On the right of the track up to the ruins is the original entrance to the city, although now it looks more like a large drainage outlet. From the top of the small hill the site is laid out before you – a massive jumble of blocks with poorly defined streets and buildings. In the ruins there are vaulted tombs, wells and water channels. Water played an important part in the funerary rites. The dead had to have water near them, hence the elaborate wells and channels.

Two temples once stood on the highest point of the site. One was dedicated to the storm god, Baal, the supreme god for the Canaanites, Phoenicians and Aramaens. The father of all gods (except Baal) is El, the creator of man. The second temple was dedicated to Dagon, the father of Baal and the god associated with the fertility of crops.

The Mediterranean is just visible through the trees to the west. It has receded 100 metres or so since Ugarit's heyday. Don't try to walk directly through to the water as it's a military area and you're likely to get a less than friendly reception. However, if you follow the road back a way, you'll find some quiet stretches of water and bits of beach, usually too liberally strewn with garbage to be greatly tempting. There are a few little shops where you can get something to drink.

Getting There & Away Local town buses make the 16-km trip to Ras Shamra every hour or so from Lattakia (see Getting Around above). Ask the driver where to get off for the *athar* (ruins). It's easy to hitch back to Lattakia or flag down a microbus or service-taxi.

The road goes through some extremely fertile country full of orchards surrounded by high cypress hedges. Fruit stalls along the road sell apples and oranges in season.

Blue Beach
The road to Ras Shamra also passes Blue Beach, the major coastal resort in Syria. It's between the sports complex (built for the 1987 Mediterranean Games) and the Meridien Hotel. There are expensive bungalows set up along the beach and some effort is made to keep it cleared of garbage. The murky brown water, however, is none too inviting.

Ivory head from Ugarit

Out on a point, the multistorey Meridien Hotel sticks out like a sore thumb. Here the beach is a little better, but in high season you have to pay to use it. They also have pedal boats and sailboards for hire.

There's a squalid little camping area next to the Meridien but it has absolutely nothing to recommend it.

Getting There & Away Catch the Ras Shamra bus and get off in front of the Côte d'Azur Hotel, or catch a Blue Beach bus, which goes out to the Meridien Hotel.

Ras al-Bassit

The black-sand beaches just south of the Turkish frontier are probably the best of a pretty bad lot along the Syrian coast. Jebel Aqra forms a dramatic back-drop, and if you're coming down the awful road from the town of Kassab the views are spectacular.

If you get here outside the summer holiday period, it can be quite pleasant. There are not too many people around, the water is clean and so too, unusually enough, are the beaches. When the holiday crowds hit, get out.

Kassab itself is a popular mountain escape with Syrians, and is pleasant enough on the eye, without being anything remarkable. It is possibly the most inviting route into and out of Syria. There are a few hotels and snack places.

Places to Stay & Eat There are quite a few beach bungalows, cabins and 'chalets' dotted along the length of the beaches, but most are closed out of season. There are also the usual snack places. You may want to stay in one of the hotels up in Kassab, but the only way to get down will be to negotiate with taxi drivers.

Getting There & Away There are one or two microbuses from Lattakia, but the service is unreliable, especially for the return trip. There is no microbus back after about 4 pm. Otherwise, you can catch an irregular microbus up through the mountains to Kassab (1½ hours, S£15) and negotiate your way down to the beaches by taxi.

Qala'at Salah ad-Din

Perched on a heavily wooded ridge, and made almost impregnable by the surrounding ravines, 'Saladin's Citadel' (also known in Arabic as 'Qala'at Sahyun') is so called in memory of the Muslim leader's taking of the Crusader-held citadel in 1188 after the fall of Lattakia. It ranks behind the Crac des Chevaliers and Qala'at Marqab to the south, and is well worth a visit. Originally in Byzantine hands, it was taken by the Franks and expanded in the first half of the 12th century. Sultan Baibars brought it under Mamluk control in 1272.

Things to See The Crusaders' single most astounding feat of engineering was to clear an artificial **gorge** on its east side, through which the modern road now passes but which, at the time, served to cut the castle off from assault. The pillar of stone in the middle of the road helped prop up a draw bridge.

Today, the entrance is behind the high tower on the south-eastern side. Once inside you can see the remains of a pillared room that served as **stables**, and next to it a two-storey **dungeon**, the main defensive structure. To the left of the entrance are the remains of baths and a mosque installed by the Muslims, and further down again what's left of a Byzantine fort and chapel. A ditch separates the main part of the castle from its lower, western half. The castle is closed on Tuesdays and costs S£5 to enter, if the caretaker is around.

Getting There & Away Take a microbus from Lattakia to Al-Haffeh (40 minutes, S£5). From there, it is about a seven-km walk or hitch to the castle. Keep heading east along the main road out of town and follow the signs. Alternatively, haggle with a taxi or with one of the *trezeenas*, the odd-looking, locally assembled three-wheeled 'vans'. They occasionally do a run to villages beyond the castle but are irregular and sharks. Pay no more than S£15 per person. This is still outrageous but apparently what they hit the locals for, too.

Jabla

Only about half an hour south of Lattakia, the Phoenician settlement of 'Gabala' was founded by the island state of Arwad. It is worth a quick look for its **Roman theatre**, which is just a couple of hundred metres south of the microbus station, and perhaps more so for a stroll along the coast road.

There is a wonderful café perched over the rocks just past the two little fishing boat harbours as you head south. It is a perfect spot to have a coffee, smoke a narjileh and watch the sun go down over the Mediterranean. Up on the promenade you may see a rare sight indeed – women in traditional dress also sitting around enjoying a narjileh!

There is a couple of cheap hotels by the theatre, but transport to Lattakia is so regular that it is hardly worth it. The microbus costs S£5.

BANIYAS

Baniyas is south of Lattakia, halfway to Tartus. It is a busy port town with a large oil refinery. The only reason to stop here is to visit the old Crusader fort of Qala'at Marqab, six km south of the town.

Getting There & Away

Microbuses to and from Lattakia cost S£10 and take about an hour. Competition for a place on them is fierce, especially in the mornings, and you have to pay for an assigned seat at a booth just to get on. The microbuses to Tartus take only half an hour but cost the same.

QALA'AT AL-MARQAB

This citadel was originally a Muslim stronghold, possibly founded in 1062, and has extensive views of the Mediterranean to the west and surrounding valleys falling away to the east and south. After falling into Crusader hands in the early 12th century, the fortifications were expanded. The main defensive building, the dungeon, is on the southern side, as the gentler slopes made that point the castle's most vulnerable. After several attempts, Saladin gave up trying to take Marqab, which only fell to the Mamluks from Egypt in 1285.

The walls and towers are the most impressive element of what is left over today, and the interior of the citadel is rapidly being overrun with vegetation. The entrance now is through the **gate tower** in the west wall. After getting through the main gate (just push it open if 'nobody's home'), turn off to your right and, across what was the central courtyard, you will see the **chapel** which has two fine doorways and frescoes. Keep heading south past the chapel to the cylindrical **dungeon** and, next door, a great **hall**. To the north and east (stretching off to the chapel's left) are the barely distinguishable remains of **storerooms** and possibly dining and living quarters.

Entrance is S£5 (if the caretaker is actually around). Although technically closed on Tuesdays, the main gate may be left unlocked.

Getting There & Away

Take a microbus (S£10) from Baniyas – it goes right past. You may have to wait a while for the microbus, and hitching is your best bet on the way back.

TARTUS

Tartus, Syria's second port, is an easy-going – some might say dead, at least in the cooler months – town with what could be a reasonable beach if it weren't so utterly covered in garbage. The compact remnants of the old city (known to the Crusaders as Tortosa) are a fascinating warren of old and new, as is the once fortified island offshore, Arwad. Stench and rubbish seem to be a big theme here though, spoiling Arwad as well as the beach. Anyone game to pick through the junk strewn over the sand to go for a dip should note the occasional dribble of sewage into the sea.

Women should wear at least a modest one-piece bathing suit – a bikini would be inappropriate, especially when the Muslim women hop into the water fully clothed.

Just south of Tartus is the virtually untouched Phoenician site of Amrit, and not far inland the soaring, white Crusader dungeon of Safita. Tartus is also a good base from which to visit the beautifully preserved Crusader castle, the Crac des Chevaliers. It is also possible to see the Crac en route from Tartus to Homs or vice versa, as long as you don't mind carting your gear around with you all day.

History

Tartus seems to have been first established as a service town for the island of Arados (later called Ruad, now called Arwad) and given the name Antarados. It was taken over by Alexander the Great and then rebuilt by Constantine in 346 AD and renamed Constantina.

A chapel devoted to the Virgin Mary was built and the town became a popular pilgrimage site during the Crusader period. It was then that it acquired the new name of Tortosa. The town first came into Crusader hands in 1102. Later that century, it became the seat of a bishop and the cathedral was constructed on the site of the ancient chapel.

In 1188, Saladin conquered all but the dungeon, the town's last redoubt. He eventually withdrew and the Knights Templar set about building the town and its defences up again. Only in 1291 did the Mamluks force the Crusaders to flee to Cyprus. Another garrison managed to hang on to Arwad for a further 11 years.

Information

Tourist Office The tourist office is located north of the cathedral and is open from 8 am to 2 pm, except on Fridays when it is closed. The staff have a few of the usual brochures, but are happy to help in whatever limited way they can.

Money The Commercial Bank of Syria has two branches: the main one, on a corner just up the road from the tourist office, is open from 8 am to 12.30 pm and takes cash or travellers' cheques. The other, down the street towards the port from the clock tower, supposedly opens from noon to 6 pm, but take this with a pinch of salt. It only takes cash.

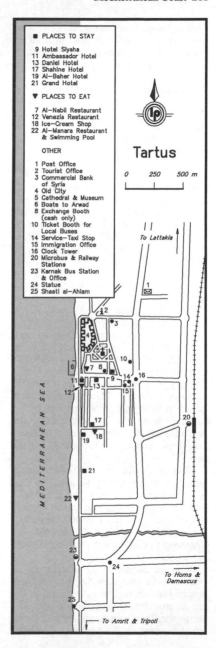

Tartus

■ PLACES TO STAY
9 Hotel Slyaha
11 Ambassador Hotel
13 Daniel Hotel
17 Shahine Hotel
19 Al–Baher Hotel
21 Grand Hotel

▼ PLACES TO EAT
7 Al–Nabil Restaurant
12 Venezia Restaurant
18 Ice–Cream Shop
22 Al–Manara Restaurant & Swimming Pool

OTHER
1 Post Office
2 Tourist Office
3 Commercial Bank of Syria
4 Old City
5 Cathedral & Museum
6 Boats to Arwad
8 Exchange Booth (cash only)
10 Ticket Booth for Local Buses
14 Service–Taxi Stop
15 Immigration Office
16 Clock Tower
20 Microbus & Railway Stations
23 Karnak Bus Station & Office
24 Statue
25 Shaati al–Ahlam

Post & Telephone The post office is open
only from 8 am to 2 pm, and not at all on
Fridays. The telephone office, in the same
building, is open until 10 pm.

Visa Extensions The immigration office for
visa extensions is in a small street just behind
the clock tower, and is open from 8 am to 2
pm. It is upstairs and the street entrance is
just a doorway with a black and white sign
and a Syrian flag overhead.

Cathedral & Museum

Don't be put off by the rather austere exterior
of the 12th century cathedral, the interior is
all graceful curves and arches and houses a
good little museum. On this site, more or
less, a chapel dedicated to the Virgin Mary is
thought to have been destroyed as early as
367 AD. It is from that chapel that an altar
and icon that became the object of pilgrimage supposedly survived to be incorporated
into the cathedral.

From the outside it looks more like a
fortress, and that is no coincidence, as its
construction was conceived with its own
defence in mind. The only decoration is the
five-arched windows (which were only finished shortly before the Mamluks took over
the city in 1291) and the reconstructed
doorway. The interior consists of a nave with
aisles on either side. Fragments of earlier
buildings have been incorporated into the
construction; most obvious are the Corin-
thian-style capitals used in two pillars in the
nave.

The second pillar on the left of the nave is
built on top of a rectangular structure containing an arched passage. This is believed
to have been the entrance to the original
chapel where pilgrims made their devotions
to the icon of the Virgin Mary, which the
Crusaders took with them when they finally
abandoned the city.

Items on display in the museum come
from various sites including Ras Shamra,
Arwad and Amrit. The sarcophagus in the
central apse dates from the 2nd century AD,
during the Roman era, as do the four to the
left of the entrance. The headless statue in the
nave is of Bacchus, the god of revelry. Left
of the sarcophagus, in the apse, is a mural
taken from the Crac des Chevaliers depicting
Christ, Mary and St Simon.

The cathedral is supposedly open from 8
am to 2 pm daily except Tuesday, but these
hours seem flexible. Entry is S£5.

Old City

If you head down to the waterfront, pretty
well directly in front of the cathedral, you
will see remains of the medieval town walls
and ramparts. The area of the old city is small
and still buzzing with the activity of its
crowded inhabitants. New structures have
been added to or blended in with the old, and
the whole area is honeycombed with low
archways, stairways seemingly leading
nowhere, narrow lanes and tumbledown
houses. It is, unlike so many medieval city
centres in Europe cleaned up by modernity,
to all intents and purposes the direct heir of
its Crusader past, a living microcosm of a
world long gone, unpolished for any passing
visitors, although some limited excavation
and restoration is being done. It's to be hoped
they can strike the right balance between
living town and museum.

Arwad

This small island, a few km south-west of
Tartus, is a real gem. If only it were not so
filthy! There are no cars or wide streets, only
a maze of narrow lanes that twist and turn
between the tightly packed buildings and,
with each turn, reveal something new.

In Phoenician times the island was a prosperous and powerful maritime state, with
colonies on the mainland at Amrit, Banias
and Jabla (Gabala). It gradually declined in
the 1st millennium BC and was of little
importance by the time it became part of the
Roman Empire. During the Crusades it
assumed strategic importance and was the
last 'Frankish' outpost to fall to the Muslims,
in 1302.

Today the island is an interesting, somewhat claustrophobic place to wander around.
Right next door to the modern cafés you can
see fisherfolk mending their nets and build-

ing boats with a mixture of traditional methods and modern tools.

Little is left of the island's defensive walls, but two forts remain; the one on the highest point houses a small museum. Nothing is labelled but the attendants are eager to show off their English and guide you around. It's closed on Tuesdays and entry is S£5.

The stalls down by the boat harbour sell the most amazing array of tacky souvenirs, from shell-encrusted ashtrays to plastic toys. You can get an expensive cup of tea at the waterfront café, but if you want a more reasonably priced snack, wait until you stumble across one of the several small shops in the tangle of lanes. It won't take too long, the whole island only measures 800 by 500 metres.

Small boats head out to the island every 15 minutes or so from the small fishing harbour. The two-way trip costs S£15, which you pay on the island, and takes about 20 minutes each way. The last boat leaves the island around sunset – don't get stranded as there is no accommodation.

Shaati al-Ahlam

This beach, the Dream Beach, where no attempt is made to keep it clean, is anything but a dream. In fact, there seems to be more rubbish on it than on the beaches closer to town! It is a little more relaxed than Tartus and women should have no problems swimming in bikinis. You may have to pay a fee to use the beach, and the money hopefully goes to a bit of muck-raking!

There are bungalows, called chalets, for rent at S£430 per day. They have three beds, bath and cooking facilities. The fancy *Shaati al-Ahlam Restaurant* is very up-market and has live music in the evenings.

Places to Stay – bottom end

One of the best deals in Syria is the *Daniel Hotel* (☎ 20581). The elderly owner is a great old character, but you'll hardly ever see him. Unfortunately, the relatives and employees seem to have coasted a bit on the place's reputation. The rooms are still very good – spotlessly clean and spacious with

their own bath. Don't count on hot water though, even if they tell you they have it.

Bargain on the prices too, which seem to change every time you ask. Singles/doubles/triples cost about S£150/200/225 but bargain them down. They can get a bit grouchy if you come in much after 10 pm. They will sometimes do breakfast for a little extra.

Across the road and a little way up towards the clock tower is the *Hotel Siyaha* (which means 'Tourism'). It has pokey singles for S£60 and reasonable doubles with balcony for S£100. A hot shower costs S£25 extra.

Up closer to the clock tower there are a few others, like the *Arab Unity Hotel*, which charge in the vicinity of S£60/80 for singles/doubles and occasionally simply direct Westerners down to the Daniel!

Places to Stay – middle

The only other places start at about US$15 a single. The *Ambassador Hotel* (☎ 20183) down on the waterfront (the entrance is in the back street) is enormous and has rooms with balconies overlooking the water for $15/20/24. Rooms in the back can be had for less. Next door, the *Blue Beach* hotel's proprietor speaks Spanish and offers similar rooms with shower for $15/22. Both have hot water, but apart from that and the views, offer little that the Daniel doesn't.

Further down the beach and with much better rooms is the *Al-Baher Hotel* (☎ 21687). Singles/doubles cost $18/22.

Then comes the *Grand Hotel* (☎ 25475), where rooms cost $33/38 and the only significant improvement is a TV and fridge in the rooms. The new *Shahine Hotel*, back a bit from the beach, has doubles for $44 – solo visitors pay the same.

Places to Eat

The cheap restaurants and snack places are clustered around the clock tower and the road leading south from it.

The small restaurant just behind the boat harbour, *Al-Nabil*, sells baked fish that is heavily spiced and salted. The fish is really quite good, but a meal with extras and a beer or two will set you back S£300. They also do more regular dishes (like kebabs), which cost about half.

Along the waterfront are a few outdoor restaurants. The *Al-Manara Restaurant* at the southern end of the corniche (the coastal road) is right on the beach, but seems only to open during the summer months.

Next to the Ambassador Hotel is the *Venezia Restaurant* which supposedly serves pizza, but there are no guarantees of this. They *do* (surprise, surprise) serve things like kebabs, hummus and salad without fail. At about S£200 a full meal with a drink or two, it's nothing great.

Opposite the Shahine Hotel is a new and quite reasonable ice-cream shop.

Getting There & Away

Bus The Karnak bus station and office are a couple of km south of the town centre along the coastal road, just after the sludgy stream that poses as a river. As usual it's necessary to book in advance. There is a daily departure at 7 am for Tripoli (S£100) and Beirut (S£150), three buses for Damascus via Homs (S£64) and one at 2 pm for Aleppo for the same price.

The chaotic microbus station is also quite a walk; a taxi from the clock tower will probably cost you more than your bus fare. Buses leave regularly when full.

The trip to Lattakia takes 1½ to two hours and costs S£17; Baniyas is 30 minutes and S£10 away. There are also plenty of buses heading for Homs (1½ hours, S£20) and Damascus (four hours, S£35). You can get a microbus to Safita (45 minutes, S£8) from here.

Train The railway station is right behind the microbus station. The attendant insists the only train for Damascus leaves at 1.23 am and costs S£64 (1st class) or S£43 (2nd class). Presumably it stops in Homs as well.

Service-Taxis Service-taxis congregate around the clock tower. Demand is not high so you may have to wait quite a while for one to fill up. They charge way over the bus prices. Destinations include Damascus, Homs and Lattakia.

Getting Around

Although you're not likely to need to use them much, the local buses can make life a little easier. A ticket booth is located about 200 metres north of the clock tower. A pink ticket valid for four rides (punch a corner at a time) will cost S£4. From the stop just south of the clock tower buses head south to the Karnak bus station and, in summer, to Shaati al-Ahlam.

AROUND TARTUS
Amrit

Two quite odd-looking monuments, presumed to be tombs, lie about eight km south of Tartus, and mark part of the site of Amrit, or the ancient Marathos. Little is known about the thriving Phoenician settlement, taken over by Alexander the Great in 333 BC and later by the Romans. Virtually no excavation work has been done in the area.

Getting There & Away Hitching is probably the simplest option; just head on south from the corniche. Otherwise, a city bus supposedly goes that way. Ask at the ticket booth for the Hamadiyeh bus and get the driver to let you off at Amrit.

Safita

This restful mountain town is dominated by the white tower, the Castel Blanc of Crusader times, that locals simply know as the burj (tower). It was built and rebuilt several times by the Knights Templar as the result of earthquake damage, and fell shortly before the Crac des Chevaliers to Sultan Baibars in 1271.

Two steep, cobbled lanes lead up to the donjon, and you enter from the western side. On this level there is a church that is still in use. Stairs in the south-west corner lead up to spacious living quarters. Another flight takes you to the roof, from where the tower was defended. To the south-east you can see the Crac (the two were thus linked in the Crusaders' chain of communications), and directly to the south the snow-capped peaks of northern Lebanon.

It's supposedly open from 8 am to 1 pm and 3 to 6 pm, but this is not to be taken too literally. Entrance is free, but the poor old guardian deserves a small tip for his troubles.

Places to Stay & Eat Where the town's two main streets meet in the centre, not far from where the microbuses terminate, there is a small hotel above a shop, the *Hotel Siyaha*. They charge S£100 for a bed in a basic room.

The only other options are beyond the budget traveller. A few km south-east of the central square, where the buses terminate and the taxis hang about, is the *Hotel Burj Safita*, which offers decent singles/doubles/triples for $18/22/25.

Even further out of the range of most mortals is the *Safita Cham Palace*, unfortunately the most prominent building in the town next to the tower itself. Rooms cost US$105/130.

Quite a few travellers swear that you can organise to stay in a private home.

There are a few snack places in the middle of town, including one just by the Castel.

Getting There & Away The microbus from Tartus costs S£8 and takes about 45 minutes to wind its way up to Safita. There appears to be no direct microbus service to Homs.

There is a daily Karnak connection to Damascus via Homs.

CRAC DES CHEVALIERS

The Crac des Chevaliers (Castle of the Knights, or Qala'at al-Hosn) is one of Syria's prime attractions and should not be missed. It is very well preserved and can't have looked much different 800 years ago. It's open from 9 am to 5 pm seven days a week (except public holidays) and the entry fee is S£10. A flashlight would be handy to explore some of the darker passages.

The fort is sited in the only significant break in the mountain range between Antakya (Turkey) and Beirut (Lebanon), a distance of some 250 km. Anyone who held this gap was virtually assured of authority over inland Syria by controlling the flow of goods and people from the ports to the interior.

Even today, this gap is important and carries the major road link from Homs to Tartus, as well as the oil pipeline from the fields in the far east of the country to the terminal at Tartus.

The Crusaders built and expanded the fort over a period of about 100 years from around 1150; when completed, it could house a garrison of 4000. Local basalt was used in early stages of construction; later, limestone was also employed. After holding off a number of concerted attempts to take the fort, in 1271 they were finally forced to surrender to Sultan Baibars. He allowed them to march out of the castle on condition that they left the country, although it seems that they only went as far as Tartus and Tripoli. Additional towers were built by Baibars and the different Frankish and Arabic styles can be clearly seen.

Things to See

The stronghold has two distinct parts: the outside wall with its 13 towers and main entrance; and the inside wall and central construction, which are built on a rocky platform. A moat dug out of the rock separates the two walls.

The main entrance (No 1 on the plan) leads

to a gently sloping ramp with steps wide enough to allow the garrison's horses to ride up. The first tower on the left (2) was a guard room and, next to it, the long hall served as stables (3). The ramp (4) continues up to a point where it turns sharply to the right and leads to the inner fortress. The tower (5) at this point is massive, with a doorway leading out to the moat through a five-metre-thick wall. On the outer wall above the doorway are the figures of two lions facing each other, supposedly symbols of the English Crusader king, Richard the Lionheart.

The moat here is usually full of stagnant water. When the castle was occupied, this water was used to fill the baths (6) and water the horses. Near the baths is the easily missed and largely overgrown entrance to what was a secret passage into the Crac.

The cavernous room (7) on the south of the moat (8) measures 60 by nine metres and the roof is totally unsupported. The square tower (9) bore the brunt of the attack in 1271 and was rebuilt by Sultan Baibars. The long room leads to the tower (10) in the south-west corner. The central pillar which supports the upper level of the tower bears an inscription in Arabic recording Sultan

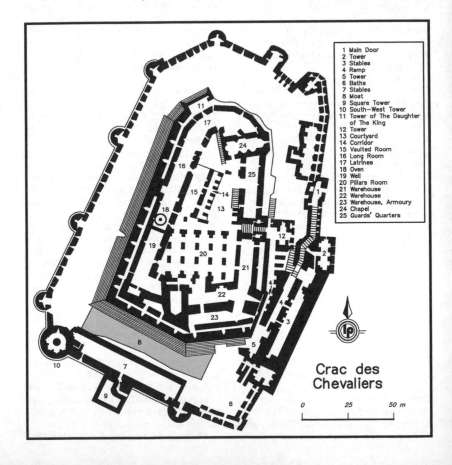

1 Main Door
2 Tower
3 Stables
4 Ramp
5 Tower
6 Baths
7 Stables
8 Moat
9 Square Tower
10 South—West Tower
11 Tower of The Daughter
   of The King
12 Tower
13 Courtyard
14 Corridor
15 Vaulted Room
16 Long Room
17 Latrines
18 Oven
19 Well
20 Pillars Room
21 Warehouse
22 Warehouse
23 Warehouse, Armoury
24 Chapel
25 Guards' Quarters

Crac des Chevaliers

0   25   50 m

Baibars' name in full: 'Al-Malek az-Zaher Rukh ad-Dunya wad-Din Abu al-Fath Baibars'!

Walking around between the two walls from the south-west tower, you reach the Tower of the Daughter of the King (11). You'll know you're inside the right place by the flies and stench of rotting rubbish piled up at the bottom. This tower is unusual in that it is wider than it is deep. On the facade are three rows of triple-pointed arches. A large projecting gallery, where rocks were hurled at assailants, is concealed in the face. The only danger visitors face today is the kitchen garbage nonchalantly hurled off the top of the tower from the café. The eastern face of this tower has a rear gate opening on to the moat.

Continue around and enter the inner fortress through the tower (12) at the top of the access ramp into an open courtyard (13). The corridor (14) on the western side of the yard is the most impressive structure in the Crac. Of the seven trusses facing the yard two are open doorways, while the other five each hold a pillar with delicate carvings.

The doors through the corridor lead to a large vaulted room (15), which was probably a reception room. On the far side of this is a 120-metre-long room (16) which runs the whole length of the western wall. A few old latrines (17) are still visible at the northern end. In the middle of the room are the remains of an old oven (18) measuring more than five metres in diameter. The room has been bricked up just behind it, but you can walk into the other half from the pillars room and see a well (19) and, right at the end, another oven in the wall.

The pillars room (20) has five rows of heavy squat pillars and it is vaulted with fist-sized stones. It has been suggested that it was used as a refectory. Rooms 21, 22 and 23 were used as warehouses. In room 22 are the remains of massive pottery oil jars and in 23 there's an old oil-mill, more oil jars and a well.

Back in the courtyard, the chapel (24) has a nave of three bays of vaults. It was converted to a mosque after the Muslim

conquest and the *minbar* (pulpit) still remains. The staircase which obstructs the main door is a later addition and leads to the upper floors of the fortress.

The upper floor of the Tower of the Daughter of the King (11) has been converted into a café selling tea, beer and snacks. From various vantage points on this level there are some magnificent views if the haze clears: the snow-capped peak of Kornet as-Saouda (3088 metres) in the Anti-Lebanon Range to the south and the valley of the Nahr al-Kabir (Big River) to the east.

For the best view of the Crac itself, walk along the road around to the right of the entrance and up to the small hill behind the south-west corner.

Places to Stay & Eat

The restaurant inside the castle is called the *Knights of the Round Table* and is a little expensive. Outside, to the left of the entrance and up the road a little way is another more modest restaurant, where you also might be able to get a bed for S£100. Otherwise, there is quite an expensive hotel a few km down the road that winds around and up behind the Crac.

The Crac is an easy day trip from Tartus, Homs or even Hama, which all offer better accommodation possibilities.

Getting There & Away

The Crac lies some 10 km north of the Homs-Tartus motorway. It is roughly halfway between the two towns and can be visited in a day trip from either or en route from one to the other.

From Homs there are two or three buses to the village of Hosn before noon. They will drop you right at the Crac, take about 1½ hours and cost S£16. Otherwise, there are a few others that will take you to within a few km, leaving you to hitch the rest or catch a local microbus (S£13). In fact, you are quite likely to end up on one of these even if you ask for the direct bus to Qala'at al-Hosn at the Homs bus station.

The other alternative, and the only choice from Tartus, is to catch one of the buses shuttling between the two cities and alight at the turn-off. Tell them where you want to go and they'll charge you S£10, not the full fare. From there, again, you have to hitch or pick up a passing local microbus.

To return, hitch or take a local microbus back to the highway and from there flag down another one back to Homs or Tartus. A microbus supposedly leaves Hosn for Homs at about 1.30 pm.

Orontes Valley

The Orontes River (Nahr al-Assi in Arabic – the 'rebel river') has its headwaters in the mountains of Lebanon near Baalbek. It enters Syria near Tell Nabi Mend, the Kadesh of ancient times where, in around 1300 BC, the Egyptians were beaten back by the Hittites in a bloody confrontation.

Just south of the city of Homs is a dam dating back to the 2nd millennium BC. With some modern additions, it is known today as Lake Qattine and supplies Homs with drinking water and irrigates some 200 sq km.

The river flows through the industrial city of Homs before reaching Hama, where the only obstruction to the flow is the ancient *norias* or water wheels. The Orontes used to flow north-west from Hama and drain away in the swamps of the plain of Ghab. Now the swamps have been drained to form one of the most fertile plains in Syria and the river flows north through Antakya in Turkey before finally reaching the Mediterranean.

HOMS

There's little of interest to see in Homs but it's a busy city with a lively air. It is also one of those crossroads that most travellers have to pass through at some stage. Roads head north to Hama, east to Palmyra and the Euphrates, south to Damascus and west to Tartus and the coast.

Homs, Syria's third largest city, is an industrial centre where half the country's total oil refining capacity is based. Superphosphates are produced here, there is a sugar refinery and also some light manufacturing.

Despite its long history, almost nothing is left as a witness to its past. The few remaining items of interest only really justify a stop for travellers with time to kill.

History

In ancient times, the city was known as Emesa and its people are mentioned among those who opposed the Roman conquest. In 194 AD, emperor Septimius Severus married Julia Domna who came from an Emesa family of priests.

His successor, Elagabalus, was proclaimed emperor in 218 AD and made a sun god cult from Emesa the main official religion of Rome. The central object of this cult, a large, black conical stone, was sent to Rome. By 222 AD the slightly eccentric Elagabalus had gone mad. He was assassinated by Praetorian guards and the stone was promptly returned to Emesa.

Aurelian defeated the troops of Zenobia, the ambitious queen of Palmyra, in Emesa 50 years later, and thus destroyed her burgeoning empire.

Information

Tourist Office There is a small information booth by the footpath in Kouwatli St. There is no printed information in any language here and the woman running it, who seems to know very little, locks up shop and disappears all the time. Officially, it's open from 8 am to 2 pm and pm to 9 pm daily except Fridays.

Money A few blocks north of Kouwatli St is the main branch of the Commercial Bank of Syria, where you can change cash or cheques from 8 am to 12.30 pm every day except Fridays. Otherwise, there is an exchange booth close to the souqs that also takes cash and cheques and is open from 8 am to 8 pm. The guy here shuts for an hour or two in the early afternoon for lunch.

Post The post and telephone office is near the clock tower roundabout at the western end of Kouwatli St, and is open Saturday to Thursday from 8 am to 4.30 pm. The telephone service may be open later.

Visa Extensions For visa renewals, go to the 3rd floor of a multistorey administration building (marked Immigration Office on the map) at the end of a tiny side lane north of Kouwatli St. This place houses everything from the passport office to the traffic place and is chaotic to say the least.

At street level there are passport photo places and a booth (on the left) where you will inevitably have to buy revenue stamps for your visa extension forms. It's open 8.30 am to 2 pm Saturday to Thursday.

Things to See

The only building of great note is the **Khalid Ibn al-Walid Mosque** on the Hama road about a km north of the town centre. It holds the tomb of the commander of the Muslim armies who brought Islam to Syria in 636 AD, and is something of an object of pilgrimage. The present building was begun in 1908 and is topped by nine cupolas.

East of central Homs is the Syrian Orthodox **Church of the Girdle of Our Lady**, or 'Kaneesat Um Zumaar' in Arabic. In 1953, the patriarch of Antioch, Ignatius Aphraim,

declared a delicate strip of woven wool and silk found in the church six months earlier to be a girdle worn by the Virgin Mary. The story is that it had survived intact since the Ascension of Mary into Heaven, preserved in one container or another in a church on this spot. You can ask a caretaker to see the girdle, but don't expect much. It is a fairly flimsy piece of cloth.

To get there, follow the extension of Kouwatli St east through the souqs. Turn right at the second street after a building marked 'Archevêché syrien catholique' (Syrian Catholic Archbishopric) and you'll see the church at the end of the street.

Heading back to the main street, there is a small Ottoman building in a lane off to the right called Beit Zahrani. A small Museum of Popular Traditions & Culture – you know, the type with the wax dummies – was due to open there by the end of 1992.

The city's main **museum** is purportedly housed in the Department of Antiquities

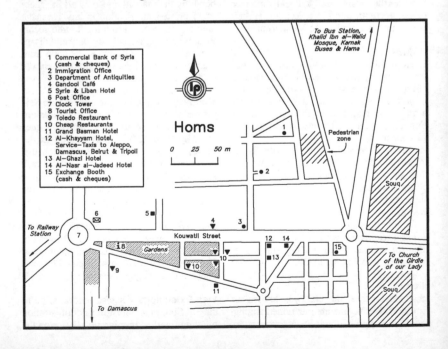

Building on Kouwatli St, but it seems to be permanently closed.

The souq is unusually large and busy but, as it's all modern, it's no great shakes.

The **citadel**, in the south of the city, is a military zone and off limits. It is little more than an outsize mound anyway.

Places to Stay

The cheap hotels are on or around Kouwatli St between the tourist office and the souq. The best is the *Al-Nasr al-Jadeed Hotel*. Its owner is a polite old guy who speaks English well and with whom you can have a long chat in the big lounge room. The entrance is in a side street off Kouwatli and clean singles/doubles cost S£100/200. A hot shower is S£30 extra.

Next door on Kouwatli is the *Al-Khayyam Hotel*. It has singles/doubles for S£150/200, as does the *Al-Ghazi Hotel* next to it. Neither have hot water or anything much else to recommend them.

If it's dirt cheap you want, the *Syrie & Liban Hotel* in the block behind the post office and opposite a medical lab is the place to go. It's basic, but you can get a bed in a shared room for S£65 or a double for S£125, including warm shower.

Across the road from the Khalid Ibn al-Walid Mosque is the *Az-Za'afran Hotel* (just 'Hotel' in English). With no hot water and at S£150 for one person, it has little to recommend it above the others.

For something a bit more up-market, the *Grand Basman Hotel* has rooms with bath and fan for US$15/20. The entrance is in the middle of a small shopping arcade. It's not bad, but as so often with the hotels charging dollars at the lower end of the scale, it's well overpriced.

Places to Eat

The *Toledo Restaurant*, set back a little from the gardens around the tourist information booth, serves a reasonable variety of stews, soups and rice dishes and a filling meal can easily be had for under S£100.

Other cheap restaurants are all in a group one block south of Kouwatli St and have the same old stuff – kebabs, chicken, felafel, hummus and salad.

On Kouwatli St there is a big shady café, the *Gandool*, where you can sit down for a drink and narjileh, but they don't do any food.

Getting There & Away

Bus Homs is a busy transport hub serviced by Karnak, pullman and microbuses.

Karnak Bus The Karnak bus station is about two km north of the city centre. There are six daily buses to Damascus, the first at 6.30 am and the last at 6.30 pm. The trip costs S£40. Two buses run to Aleppo (calling at Hama), at 10 am and 6 pm, for S£52. There is a daily departure for Palmyra for S£45.

The staff insist there is no bus to Lattakia or Tartus, which seems a bit odd considering Karnak buses *from* those cities pass through Homs on the way to Damascus. Book a day in advance for the buses that *do* run.

Bus/Microbus The regular bus station is next to the Karnak bus station, and because Homs is a transport hub, it's pretty busy. Microbuses do the half-hour hop to Hama frequently (S£10). There are at least two direct buses to Qala'at Hosn (for the Crac des Chevaliers) before noon (1½ hours, S£16).

Other destinations include: Damascus (1½ hours, S£25); Aleppo (three hours, S£26); Tartus (1½ hours, S£20) and Palmyra (two hours, S£25).

There are a few Pullmans leaving from out the back – the main destination seems to be Deir ez-Zur via Palmyra. Establish the price first, as rip-offs definitely occur on these buses.

Train The railway station is about 20 minutes' walk from the centre. Take the street heading south-west of the clock tower until you hit the main road (Tarablos St). Turn right there and walk for about a km to the big intersection with lights at the corniche – the railway station is just off to the left.

There are four departures a day south to

Damascus (S£44, 1st class; S£29, 2nd class) and north to Aleppo (S£42, 1st class; S£29, 2nd class). Two of the latter go on to Qamishle and all stops in between.

Service-Taxi All the service-taxis gather around the corner of the Al-Khayyam Hotel on Kouwatli St and run to Damascus, Aleppo, Beirut and Tripoli (Lebanon).

HAMA

This is one of the most attractive towns in Syria with the Orontes River flowing through the centre, its banks lined with trees and gardens and the ancient, groaning norias. There's not an awful lot to see, but the town's peaceful atmosphere makes it a pleasant place to spend a few relaxing days. It is also a good base for excursions to the ruins of Apamea and Qala'at Sheisar. You can even get to the Crac des Chevaliers via Homs and back in a day.

The people here are some of the most conservative in Syria and it is common to see smartly dressed women with their faces completely veiled in black. In contrast to this are the many women in local costume of full-length black dresses boldly embroidered in bright reds and yellows, their unveiled faces often tattooed with traditional markings.

Hama is also an important industrial city, and the bulk of Syria's iron and steel industry is centred here.

History

Although its history is not well known, Hama has been an important place for centuries. Excavations have revealed settlement as long ago as the New Stone Age.

During the reigns of David and Solomon (1000 to 922 BC), the Aramaean Kingdom of Hamah (or Hamath) traded with Israel. In 853 BC, in concert with Damascus, it revolted against Assyrian occupiers and defeated the troops of Samalnasar. Under Sargon II, the Assyrians got their revenge in 720 BC and deported all its citizens. In the time of the Seleucids it was known as Epiphania after Epiphanes (Antiochus IV), and was called Emath in the early Christian era.

During the early years of the Crusades, Damascus, Aleppo (then divided) and the Franks all competed to win influence over Hama. Finally, under the tutelage of the Mamluks, the Arab poet Abu al-Fida was made sultan of Hama.

In recent times Hama has become famous, or infamous, as the place where the true, repressive nature of Assad's regime was brutally demonstrated in 1982. The details of what happened in that bloody February are hazy at best, but it appears that about 8000 troops moved in to quash a rebellion by armed members of the then outlawed Muslim Brotherhood.

Townspeople willing to talk describe bombing attacks by the air force, tank assaults and fierce fighting. In all, up to 25,000 people may have died in fighting and as a result of mass executions and atrocities. As the city was sealed off for that month, water and electricity supplies were cut and food became scarce. One man said he was only alive because he slept over at work one night. When he got home the next day, he found his father and all his brothers had been rounded up and shot the night before.

Even today, it is possible to see evidence of the damage. The old city area around the museum and An-Nouri Mosque is still a mess, although as new buildings (a big modern school for example) are slowly built, it becomes harder to distinguish war damage from the usual chaos of construction sites. One area the authorities were quick to cover up was on the other side of the river. The Apamee Cham Palace Hotel is, as a few locals point out, built on the 'houses and bodies of thousands'.

Obviously this event is something that the government would rather like to pretend never happened, so it's prudent not to discuss the subject, even if someone wants to raise it with you.

Information
Tourist Office This is in a small building in the gardens in the centre of town. Apart from the usual free hand-out map, the staff here don't have an awful lot to tell you.

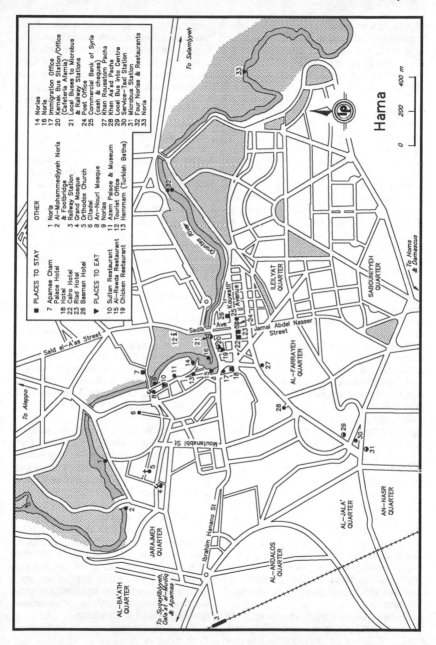

Hama

0   200   400 m

To Salamiyeh

To Homs
& Damascus

To Aleppo

To Suqayibiyyeh,
Qala'at al-Mudiq
& Apamea

PLACES TO STAY
7   Apamee Cham
    Palace Hotel
18 Hotel
22 Cairo Hotel
23 Riad Hotel
26 Basman Hotel

▼ PLACES TO EAT
10 Sultan Restaurant
15 Al-Rawda Restaurant
19 Chicken Restaurant

OTHER
1   Noria
2   Al-Mohammediyeh Noria
    & Footbridge
3   Railway Station
4   Grand Mosque
5   Orthodox Church
6   Citadel
8   An-Nouri Mosque
9   Noria
11 Azem Palace & Museum
12 Tourist Office
13 Hammam (Turkish Baths)

14 Norias
16 Noria
17 Immigration Office
20 Kernak Bus Station/Office
    (Cafeteria Afamia)
21 Local Buses to Microbus
    & Railway Stations
24 Post Office
25 Commercial Bank of Syria
    (cash & cheques)
27 Khan Rousstom Pacha
28 Khan Assad Pacha
29 Local Bus Info Centre
30 Service-Taxi Station
31 Microbus Station
32 Four Norias & Restaurants
33 Noria

JARAJMEH
QUARTER

AL-BA'ATH
QUARTER

Said al-A'as Street

Sadik

Kouwatli
Ave

Jamal Abdel Nasser
Street

Moutanabbi St.

Ibrahim Hanano St

AL-FARRAYEH
QUARTER

LEILYAT
QUARTER

SABOUNIYYEH
QUARTER

AL-JALA'
QUARTER

AL-ANDALOS
QUARTER

AN-NASR
QUARTER

Money The brand new offices of the Commercial Bank of Syria on Kouwatli Ave, next door to the post office, are open longer than most – from 8 am to 8 pm, with a three-hour break from 2 pm. They accept cash and cheques.

Post The main post office, open from 8 am to 4.30 pm, is on the corner of Kouwatli Ave and the old Damascus-Aleppo highway (Sadik Ave). The posting box is an anonymous wooden box inside on the left.

Visa Extensions To have your visa extended, the immigration office is hidden away up three flights of stairs in a building just opposite the footbridge in the centre of town. There is a small sign saying 'passports' in English next to a pharmacy near the traffic island. The office is open every day, except Friday, from 8 am to 1 pm.

Citadel

For a good view over the city walk up to the park on top of the citadel. Apart from a few unrecognisable fragments, nothing remains of the old fortress as all the stone has been carted off for use in other buildings. Danish archaeologists did extensive work on this tell and found evidence of continuous settlement since Neolithic times, particularly during the Iron Age.

The area has been landscaped and developed into a picnic and recreation area. There is a café for those who don't bring their own.

Norias

Hama's main attraction is the norias – wooden water wheels up to 20 metres in diameter – built centuries ago to provide water for the town and for irrigation. They still turn today, although the water is not used. Of the more than 30 norias that characterised medieval Hama only about a dozen remain. Because both the wheels and the blocks on which they are mounted are wooden, the friction produces a mournful groaning.

The norias right in the centre of town make for a pleasant spot. In the surrounding park

people come to rest and children swim in the waters by the wheels, which are also lit up at night. The most impressive wheels, however, are about one km upstream from the centre at a place known as The Four Norias of Bichriyat. As the name suggests, there are four norias here – two pairs on a weir which spans the whole river. It's unfortunate that this weir also collects all the rubbish and debris that happen to be drifting down the river – everything from plastic bottles to dead sheep. On the downstream side on the left bank are two flash restaurants with terraces looking across to the wheels.

About one km from the centre in the other direction is the largest of the norias known as the Al-Mohammediyyeh. It dates from the 14th century and used to supply the Grand Mosque with water. At this point there is a small stone footbridge across the river which leads to an uninteresting area of parkland.

Grand Mosque

The Grand Mosque, about 150 metres south of the Al-Mohammediyyeh Noria, is gradually being restored after its complete destruction during the 1982 uprising. Once the most striking of Hama's monuments, it was built by the Omayyads along the lines of their great mosque in Damascus. It had a similar history, too, having been converted from a church that itself had stood on the site of a pagan temple.

Although the mosque is not on the city's free hand-out map, the tourist office staff are less coy about its existence than they used to be. This should not be interpreted as a cue for launching into a discussion of *why* it is in its present state.

Azem Palace & Museum

The museum is housed in the old Azem Palace, the residence of the governor, As'ad Pacha al-Azem, who ruled the town from 1700 to 1742. The palace reminds its visitors of the more grandiose building of the same name in Damascus, which is hardly surprising, as the latter was built by the same man upon his transfer to Damascus.

The shady courtyard has various bits of

Top Left: Qala'at al-Marqab (DS)
Top Right: Beating the heat in Tartus (HF)
Bottom Left: Taxi in Tartus (HF)
Bottom Right: Mending fishing nets, Arwad (HF)

Top: Crac des Chevaliers (DS)
Left: Ibn al-Walid Mosque, Homs (DS)
Right: Noria, Hama (HF)

ancient sculpture lying around, some bearing Arabic and Christian inscriptions. When the palace was extended in the late 18th century, this area became known as the Haramlik, reserved for family and women. Stairs from here lead up to what is known as the Royal Hall, where it is supposed As'ad Pacha had his sleeping quarters. It is being repaired – presumably still suffering from the pounding the building took during the uprising. Opposite are three small rooms with some mannequins depicting scenes from local life.

Back on the ground floor, another door leads into a small museum containing artefacts discovered in the citadel. The most interesting of the exhibits is a 3rd century mosaic found near Hama. Historians have found its depiction of musicians a rich source of information on ancient instruments.

The Haramlik was connected to the Salamlik by the baths. The Salamlik was reserved for men and guests and today offers little for the visitor. The top floor is closed.

The museum is open from 8 am to 2 pm daily except Tuesday. Entry is S£5.

An-Nouri Mosque
Just north of the palace is the An-Nouri Mosque, built by the Muslim commander Nureddin in the 12th century. The building is more interesting on the outside than the inside. The three norias here all have names: from east to west they are the Al-Kilaniyyeh, As-Sahuniyyeh and Al-Ja'abariyyeh.

Hammam
The hammam (Turkish baths) marked on the map is supposedly open every day from 8 am to noon and 7 pm to midnight for men, and from noon until 5 pm for women. Judging by the often firmly shut doors, this timetable is to be interpreted flexibly.

Caravanserais
The two caravanserais (khans) are notable only for their stone entrances built in alternating colours. The Khan Rousstom Pacha was at one time an orphanage but is being converted into a school, although the tourist map claims it is being converted into a handi-

crafts market. At any rate, you are not allowed in. The big door has a feature known as an 'eyelet', which only allows one person through at a time. The Khan As'ad Pacha, built in 1751, is now a technical school.

Places to Stay
Two of the best value-for-money places in Syria are right next to one another in Kouwatli Ave in Hama. The *Cairo Hotel* (☎ 22280) is spotlessly clean, has a great shower and the friendly owner, Bader, speaks English and German. A bed in a shared room is S£125 and doubles S£250. If you don't mind having no shade to retreat to in the heat of summer, a bed on the roof will cost you less.

The *Riad Hotel* is in direct and not necessarily friendly competition with the Cairo and you can get a cheaper deal here. A bed in a shared room will cost S£100. Singles/doubles with TV, fridge and ensuite bath cost S£200/300. It's pretty much a toss-up between the two – both even ply you with complimentary tea on arrival.

There's a couple of cheap flophouses where S£40 gets you a bed in a basic, noisy but otherwise satisfactory hotel. The one at the end of Kouwatli Ave is upstairs and just has a green, black and red sign in Arabic above the door.

Hama's only mid-range hotel is the *Basman Hotel*, also on Kouwatli Ave. Here you'll be paying US$25/30 for singles/doubles with fan, bath, TV and balcony. It's a reasonable place but, given the price, offers little more than the Cairo or Riad.

At the top of the range is the *Apamee Cham Palace Hotel* (☎ 27712) where singles/doubles cost US$100/120. It's across the river from the An-Nouri Mosque.

Places to Eat
In the couple of blocks along Kouwatli Ave west of the Cairo Hotel are all the usual cheap kebab and chicken restaurants. There's about half a dozen of them here so if one doesn't have what you want, just try next door.

On the small street running from Kouwatli

Ave to the river are a couple of chicken restaurants – the one nearer the river is good and has fans. The standard half-chicken, salad and hummus is S£70.

If you want to dine in style, the *Al-Rawda Restaurant* on the banks of the river has a fine setting overlooking the norias. The food is only average, the prices are not, and don't be surprised if the waiter deducts a tip for himself before giving you the change, not that there'll be much change from S£200 for a meal of kebabs, chips, salad and hummus. Occasionally, there is a band and dance performances.

For similar food at similar prices, but in a different setting by the river, head for the *Sultan Restaurant*, which you can reach by the low vaulted tunnel under the An-Nouri Mosque.

As mentioned above, there are two very pleasant but fairly upmarket restaurants out by the Four Norias, which is in fact the name of one of them.

For just a tea or coffee, and maybe a narjileh and a game of backgammon, you can't beat the outdoor café next to the Al-Rawda. It's set in a garden of shady eucalyptus trees and has views of the river and norias. It is a great place to escape the heat. Every so often a waiter will come around with a shiny silver coffee pot and very small cups; this is very strong Arabic coffee and is strongly flavoured with cardamom. It is drunk in tiny doses which you just knock back in one hit – a real heart-starter. When you've had enough, hand the cup back with a quick jiggle of the wrist.

Although you can find it outside Hama, the *halawat al-jibn* is a not-to-sweet dessert speciality of the city. It is a cheese-based soft doughy delicacy drenched in honey or syrup and often topped with ice-cream. A lot of places around Kouwatli Ave sell it; some sell nothing else.

Getting There & Away

Bus If you're coming or going by Karnak bus, the bus station/office (open from 7 am to 7 pm) is right in the centre of town, tucked away on the 1st floor inside the Cafeteria Afamia. There are buses to Damascus (7.30 am, 2.30 pm, S£52), Homs (8.10 am, S£16) and Aleppo (5.30 pm, S£40).

The microbus station is on the southern outskirts of town, about two km from the centre and half an hour's walk. You can catch a local bus from Kouwatli Ave for S£1. Regular microbuses go to Homs (half an hour, S£10), Aleppo, Suqaylibiyyeh (Apamea) and surrounding towns.

Train The railway station is way out of town to the south-west. A local bus from Kouwatli Ave is S£1, and a taxi about S£20. The new railway station is still being completed, so the area is a bit of a mess.

There are four daily trains to Damascus (S£54, 1st class; S£37, 2nd class) which take about four hours. To Aleppo there are also four services, taking about 2½ hours (S£31, 1st class; S£21, 2nd class). Two of these trains go all the way to Qamishle.

Service-Taxi The service-taxi station is right across the road from the microbus station.

Getting Around

The local buses may come in handy for getting to and from the bus and railway stations, both of which are uncomfortably far from the town centre. Buses leave from the corner of Kouwatli and Sadik Aves. Ask at the booth for the bus station or train *(qitaar)*. You pay the S£1 fare on the bus.

To get into town from the bus station, the stop is about 200 metres to the north. It's not marked, but the people milling around will be a clue.

QALA'AT AL-MUDIQ

From Hama the Orontes River flows north-west and into the vast Ghab depression, some 50 km away. Once a stagnant swamp, this low-lying area of some 40 sq km has, with World Bank help, been drained and irrigation ditches dug, turning it into one of the most fertile areas in Syria. Major crops are wheat, barley, sugar beet and a range of fruit trees.

In olden times it is said that the Pharaoh Thutmose III came here to hunt elephants. A thousand years later Hannibal was here teaching the Syrians how to make use of elephants in war. On the eastern edge of this valley lie the ruins of the ancient city of Apamea ('Afamia' in Arabic), now known as Qala'at al-Mudiq.

Founded by Seleucus I in the 2nd century BC and named after his wife, the city became an important trading post and crossroads for the East. It was connected by road to Lattakia (Laodiceia), which served it as a port. In its heyday, Apamea boasted a population of about 500,000 (120,000 free people) and was visited by many dignitaries including Mark Antony, accompanied by Cleopatra, on his

return from staging a campaign against the Armenians on the Euphrates.

The city declined after the Roman era but again assumed importance during the Crusades when the Norman commander, Tancred, took possession of the city. The occupation was short-lived, however, and Nureddin won the city back 43 years later, in 1149.

The fortifications around the hill-top that dominates the valley are still standing after being restored following the earthquakes of 1157 and 1170.

Museum

In the small village at the foot of the hill is a restored Ottoman caravanserai dating from the 18th century, which has been converted into a museum. The floors of the vaulted rooms surrounding the massive courtyard have been covered with the brilliant mosaics found in Apamea during excavations.

The most impressive, located in a room in the south-west corner of the khan, are two large mosaics found in church ruins at the eastern end of the main east-west boulevard. A third one is being restored in Damascus and will also be transferred to the museum when work is complete.

Unfortunately, what labelling there is is in Arabic. It's a real crime that there's nothing to stop visitors from just walking all over these priceless pieces. The museum is open from 8 am to 2.30 pm daily except Tuesdays; entry is S£5.

Fortifications

The fortifications on the hill are, typically, more impressive from the outside. They date from the 13th century and occupy what had been the acropolis of the ancient city. Inside is the village of Qala'at al-Mudiq, where local hustlers will try to sell you glass and coins from the ruins. A few of the pieces are obviously old and most are just as obviously made in the local workshop, so if you're interested, it's a case of buyer beware.

Ruins

The main area of ruins is about 500 metres

east of the village where the re-erected columns of the two-km-long cardo look quite incongruous standing in the middle of wheat fields and thistles. The northern end was bounded by the Antioch Gate and the southern end the Emesa (Homs) Gate. The columns themselves, originally erected in the 2nd century AD, are unusually carved with straight or twisted fluting.

Along the length of the cardo and the decumanus (which now serves as the modern access road to the site), the ground is littered with great chunks of rock that were once part of structures such as a temple, theatre, churches and shops. Many of these pieces are sculpted or have Greek inscriptions. The whole site covers a large area, and even in the small area where the reconstruction has taken place, excavation has been far from exhaustive. Glass fragments are everywhere and there must still be some fine pieces waiting to be unearthed.

As you approach the site from the village, the first significant ruins to appear belong to the **theatre**, largely destroyed by earthquake and pilfering. It has a diameter of 135 metres, making it the largest of its kind in Syria. Just south of the intersection of the decumanus and cardo stand a largely destroyed circular building (erected in the 6th century under Justinian) on the right and, across the cardo, a church.

The remains at the end of the decumanus include a Roman **villa** on the left and a **cathedral** from about the 5th century on the right. Underneath it were discovered the two outstanding mosaics now on display in the museum.

Back at the intersection and facing north up the cardo, there are remains of the city **nymphaeum** on the right and, a bit further on, the **agora**, or market, on the left. Behind this was a **temple** to Zeus.

If you didn't go to the 'antiquities' hustlers in the citadel, don't worry, they'll come to you on motorbikes. They are insistent and a real pain. The best remedy seems to be to ignore them studiously. When the occasional tour bus arrives, they swarm in.

Places to Stay & Eat

There's nowhere to stay in Qala'at al-Mudiq and, apart from a couple of small general stores where you can get a drink and some biscuits, there's nowhere to buy something to eat. Fortunately, it's an easy day trip from Hama (Fridays can be a bit exasperating) but bring some food, a water bottle and hat – it can be really scorching.

Getting There & Away

Microbuses (S£10) and service-taxis run regularly from Hama to Suqaylibiyyeh (Apamea), 45 km from Hama, and from there microbuses go on to Qala'at al-Mudiq (S£2.50). The whole trip takes about an hour, except on a Friday, when you can wait for ages for a connection.

There will be little point in asking people where 'Apamea' is. Use the Arabic 'Afamia' (with the stress on the second syllable) and you'll be understood.

QALA'AT SHEISAR

About halfway between Hama and Suqaylibiyyeh, in the Christian town of Maharde, the ruins of Qala'at Sheisar rise above the escarpment on the right and a small ruined noria groans away slowly by the river on the left. You can hop off the Hama-Suqaylibiyyeh bus here to have a look at the castle, an Arab fortification dominating the right bank of the Orontes.

The castle was the base for opposition to the Crusaders during their occupation of Apamea and resisted all attempts to take it. Only the northern gate complex and the main defensive tower, or dungeon, are still reasonably well preserved.

It is also believed to be the site of the ancient town of Caesarea, although nothing is left of it now.

Aleppo

Called Halab by the locals, Aleppo (population about one million), is Syria's second largest city. Since Roman times it has been an important trading centre between the countries of Asia and the Mediterranean, and the long presence of a strong corps of merchants from Europe goes some way to accounting for the vaguely European feel of its tree-lined streets, parks and up-market restaurants. Trading routes led to Aleppo from Istanbul, Mosul (in Iraq), Lattakia and Damascus. After WW I, it came under the French mandate and consequently lost a lot of its importance as a commercial centre, as it no longer served as a trading outlet for the south of Turkey.

There is a large Christian population comprised mainly of Armenian refugees from Turkey, and if you walk around certain quarters of the city, you'll see as many signs in the condensed-looking script of Armenian as you'll see in the familiar 'shorthand' with which many people equate Arabic.

With its fascinating covered souqs, the citadel, museum and caravanserais, it is a great place to spend a few days. There are also interesting places in the vicinity such as the Church of St Simeon (Qala'at Samaan), which was the largest Christian building in the Middle East when it was built in the 4th century, and the ancient city of Ebla.

HISTORY

Texts from the ancient kingdom of Mari on the Euphrates show that Aleppo was already the centre of a powerful state as long ago as the 18th century BC. Its pre-eminent role in Syria came to an end with the Hittite invasions of the 17th and 16th centuries BC, and the city appears to have fallen into obscurity thereafter.

During the reign of the Seleucids it was given the name Beroea, and with the fall of Palmyra at the hands of the Romans, it became the major commercial link between the Mediterranean to the west and the countries of Asia to the east. The town was completely destroyed by the Persians in 611 AD and was taken by the Muslims during their invasion in 637. The Byzantines overwhelmed the town in 961 and again in 968, although they couldn't take the citadel. In 1124, the Crusaders under Baldwin laid siege to the town.

After three disastrous earthquakes in the 10th century, both the town and fortress were rebuilt by Nureddin. After raids by the Mongols in 1260 and 1401, in which Aleppo was practically emptied of its population, the city finally fell to the Ottoman Turks in 1517. It prospered greatly until another earthquake struck in 1822, killing over 60% of the inhabitants and wrecking many buildings, including the citadel. During the decade of Egyptian rule from 1831 to 1840, the city once again prospered, although its importance as a trading centre declined with the discovery of the Cape route to India.

European merchants – particularly French, English and Venetian – established themselves here and set up factories, although the flood of cheap goods from Europe killed off a lot of local manufacturing. Today the major local industries are silk-weaving and cotton-printing. Products from the surrounding area include wool, hides, dried fruits and, particularly, the pistachio nuts for which Aleppo is famous.

ORIENTATION

The centre of town and the area where the cheap hotels are clustered is a compact zone centred on Kouwatli and Baron Sts. A lot of the restaurants, the main museum and places to change money are all located here. About one km to the south-east is the citadel, and to the left of it, the souqs. North-east of the centre are the main Christian quarters, the majority of their inhabitants Armenians. Directly to the north, beyond the chic area around the main park (parched in summer but quite pleasant otherwise), is the poorest

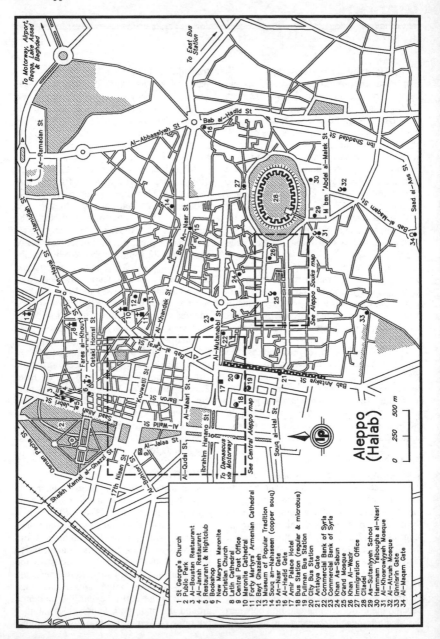

Aleppo
(Halab)

0   250   500 m

1 St George's Church
2 Public Park
3 Al–Boustin Restaurant
4 Al–Barah Restaurant
5 Restaurant & Nightclub
6 Bookshop
7 New Maryam Maronite
     Christian Church
8 Latin Cathedral
9 Central Post Office
10 Maronite Cathedral
11 Forty Martyrs' Armenian Cathedral
12 Bayt Ghazaleh
13 Museum of Popular Tradition
14 Souq an–Nahaseen (copper souq)
15 An–Nasr Gate
16 Al–Hadid Gate
17 Amir Palace Hotel
18 Bus Station (regular & microbus)
19 Pullman Bus Station
20 City Bus Station
21 Antakya Gate
22 Commercial Bank of Syria
23 Commercial Bank of Syria
24 Khan As–Sabun
25 Grand Mosque
26 Khan Al–Wazir
27 Immigration Office
28 Citadel
29 As–Sultaniyyeh School
30 Hammam Yalbougha al–Nasri
31 Al–Khosrowiiyeh Mosque
32 Al–Atrush Mosque
33 Qinnirin Gate
34 Al–Maqam Gate

part of the city, and it shows. To the west are the newer suburbs and university district.

INFORMATION
Tourist Office
The tourist office, in the gardens opposite the museum, is next to useless, and doesn't seem to be staffed half the time. It is theoretically open from 9 am to 2 pm every day but Friday. They have a reasonable free map and little else. The tourist police are based here, too.

Money
You may find yourself getting the run-around if you want to change travellers' cheques, but the only place to do it is 'Branch No 2' of the Commercial Bank of Syria, on Baron St north of Kouwatli St. There is a big sign in English, but the entrance is hidden away at the back of an arcade and the office up on the 1st floor. It's open from 8 am to 12.30 pm, and changes cash as well.

There is another branch close by where you can only change cash. Down on the corner of Kouwatli and Bab al-Faraj Sts is an exchange booth open from 9 am to 7 pm. You can only change cash here, but most currencies are accepted. There are a couple of other branches of the bank south of the town centre.

Post & Telephone
The main post office is the enormous building on the far side of the square opposite Kouwatli St. It's open every day from 8 am to 8 pm (and until 9 pm for telephones; the counter is off to the left).

There is a sign claiming you can send 'electronic mail'. Since fax machines are all but illegal, what they mean by this is anybody's guess. If you've forgotten anything from postcards to envelopes, there are plenty of guys set up on the steps of the post office selling them.

The parcels office is around the corner to the left of the main entrance.

Visa Extensions
The immigration office for visa extensions is on the 2nd floor of a building just north of the citadel. Here they want *five* passport photos,

but are prepared to give an extension of up to two months. It takes them a day to process. The office is open from 8 am to 1.30 pm.

Newspapers & Magazines
The odd copy of *Time* and similar magazines may turn up in the big hotel bookshops, but generally foreign newspapers are hard to come by. You don't even see the *Syria Times* all that often.

A couple of blocks east of Saad Allah al-Jabri St and just north of Al-Abbarah St you'll find the Reed stationery shop. It sells a small range of foreign magazines and newspapers, which are often quite a bit out of date, but better than nothing at all.

Bookshops
There is a small bookshop, on the corner of Al-Azmeh and Fares al-Khoury Sts, that sells a few second-hand novels and the like. It stocks more French books than English.

THINGS TO SEE
Souqs
The fabulous covered souqs are the main attraction of the city. This labyrinth extends over a couple of hectares and once under the vaulted stone ceiling, you're swallowed up into another world. All under one roof are the smells of cardamom and cloves from the spice stalls, the cries of the hawkers and barrow pushers, the rows of carcasses hanging from the doorways in the meat souq, and the myriad of stalls selling everything from rope to prayer mats.

A walk through the souqs could take all day, particularly if you accept some of the many invitations by the merchants to stop and drink tea. There's no obligation or pressure to buy – this is just Syrian hospitality.

While wandering around you may well find yourself latched onto by a young Syrian who wants to be your 'guide' and take you to the shop of his 'cousin'. They may be helpful for finding what you want, if you don't mind paying extra for their commission.

A couple of blocks north of the citadel is the Copper Souq, not far from the An-Nasr Gate. The souqs are dead on Fridays.

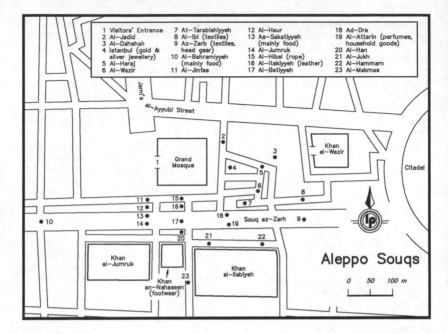

1 Visitors' Entrance
2 Al—Jadid
3 Al—Dahshah
4 Istanbul (gold & silver jewellery)
5 Al—Haraj
6 Al—Wazir
7 At—Tarabishiyyeh
8 Al—Ibi (textiles)
9 Az—Zarb (textiles, head gear)
10 Al—Bahramiyyeh (mainly food)
11 Al—Jinfas
12 Al—Haur
13 As—Sakatiyyeh (mainly food)
14 Al—Jumruk
15 Al—Hibal (rope)
16 Al—Itaklyyeh (leather)
17 Al—Batiyyeh
18 Ad—Dra
19 Al—Attarin (perfumes, household goods)
20 Al—Han
21 Al—Jukh
22 Al—Hammarn
23 Al—Makmas

Jami'a al—Ayyubi Street

Grand Mosque 1

Khan al—Wazir

Citadel

Souq az—Zarh

Khan al—Jumruk

Khan al—Ilablyeh

Khan an—Nahaseen (footwear) 23

Aleppo Souqs

0   50   100 m

Citadel

The citadel dominates the city and is at the eastern end of the souqs. It is surrounded by a moat, 20 metres deep and 30 metres wide, which was dug in the 12th century. The site had already been in use since at least the 10th century BC, when it hosted a temple.

To enter, you cross the bridge on the southern side and pass through a 12th century gate, behind which is the massive fortified main entrance. Although finely decorated on the outside, the inside is a succession of five right-angle turns, where three sets of solid steel-plated doors made a formidable barrier to any would-be occupiers. Some of the doors still remain and one of the lintels of the doorways has carvings of entwined dragons; another has a pair of lions. The main entrance area was actually finished in the 16th century under the Mamluks, after Aleppo was freed from Mongol hands.

Just before you pass the last door into the interior of the citadel, a door to the right leads

to the **armoury**. If you follow the path, which doglegs to the right and left, you'll see an entrance to your right leading to what is now called the **Byzantine Hall**. Double back and head up the stairs. Here you enter the **Royal Palace** built in 1230 by King Al-Aziz Mohammed and largely destroyed 30 years later by the Mongols. You pass through what originally was the servants' quarters and an antechamber before entering the lavishly restored **throne room**, whose dominating feature is the intricately decorated wooden ceiling.

Two buildings inside the citadel survived pillage and an earthquake in 1822. Halfway up the main path on the left is the entrance to a small 12th century **mosque** attributed to Nureddin, although it retains little of its original charm. At the northern end of the path, opposite what is now a café, is the 13th century **big mosque**. The café is housed in what was the *thukna* (barracks) of an Ottoman commander, Ibrahim Pasha.

The views from the walls are terrific and you get a good idea of just how big this city is. The citadel is open from 9 am to 5 pm daily except Tuesday. Entry is S£10.

Caravanserais

The caravanserais, or khans, are found in among the souqs. It was in the caravanserais that the bulk of the European commercial representatives were to be found, the first of whom to set up a trade bureau were the Venetians in 1548. Unfortunately, most are of limited interest because they are almost totally obscured by modern additions.

The Khan al-Wazir (Minister's Khan), built in 1682, has an interesting doorway and inside is at least one low-key souvenir and carpet shop. The Khan al-Jumruk (Customs Khan) is the old headquarters of the French, Dutch and English merchants of the 16th and 17th centuries.

Grand Mosque

On the northern edge of the souqs is the Grand Mosque (Jami'a Zakariyyeh) with its freestanding minaret dating back to 1090. The mosque itself dates back to early Islamic times but most of what remains today is from the Mamluk period. Inside the mosque is a fine, carved wooden pulpit (minbar) and behind the railing to the left of it is supposed to be the head of Zacharias, the father of John the Baptist, after whom the mosque is named.

This is one of the few mosques where non-Muslims are admitted on Fridays, and you may even be permitted to participate in the main midday prayers.

Museums

Archaeological Museum Aleppo's main museum, right in the middle of town, has a fine collection of artefacts from Mari (Tell Hariri), Ebla (Tell Mardikh – a centre of great political power in northern Syria, Anatolia and part of Mesopotamia around 1800 BC) and Ugarit (Ras Shamra). There are sculptures from Hama, and the black basalt statues at the entrance are from the temple-palace at Tell Halaf (a 9th century BC settlement in the

north-east of Syria, near present-day Ras al-'Ain). Upstairs, the collections are mainly from the Classical period and include Greek and Roman pottery, a lot of material from Palmyra and Byzantine coins.

It is a fine museum and, as usual, you'll be virtually the only one there. On sale at the entrance is a guidebook to the museum for S£200. It is open from 9 am to 2 pm and 4 to 6 pm daily except Tuesday. Entry is S£10, although the attendants don't seem to take too much notice of people who just wander in.

Statues from Tell Halaf, now guarding the entrance to the Archaeological Museum

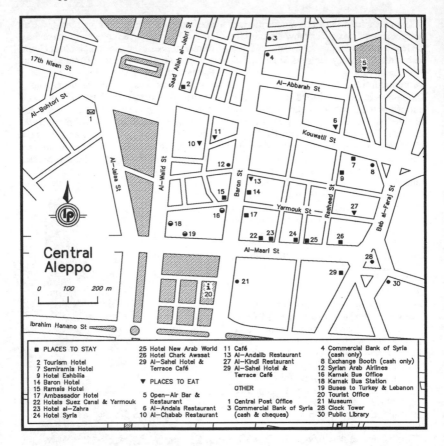

Central
Aleppo

0   100   200 m

Ibrahim Hanano St

■ PLACES TO STAY	25 Hotel New Arab World	11 Café	4 Commercial Bank of Syria
	26 Hotel Chark Awssat	13 Al–Andalib Restaurant	(cash only)
2 Tourism Hotel	29 Al–Sahel Hotel &	27 Al–Kindi Restaurant	8 Exchange Booth (cash only)
7 Semiramis Hotel	Terrace Café	29 Al–Sahel Hotel &	12 Syrian Arab Airlines
9 Hotel Eshbilia		Terrace Café	16 Karnak Bus Office
14 Baron Hotel	▼ PLACES TO EAT		18 Karnak Bus Station
15 Ramsis Hotel		OTHER	19 Buses to Turkey & Lebanon
17 Ambassador Hotel	5 Open–Air Bar &		20 Tourist Office
22 Hotels Suez Canal & Yarmouk	Restaurant	1 Central Post Office	21 Museum
23 Hotel al–Zahra	6 Al–Andals Restaurant	3 Commercial Bank of Syria	28 Clock Tower
24 Hotel Syria	10 Al–Chabab Restaurant	(cash & cheques)	30 Public Library

Museum of Popular Tradition Tucked away in the former residence of an Ottoman official in the narrow Souq as-Souf (wool market), the museum contains the by now all-too-familiar scenes of local life in bygone centuries and displays of clothing, tools, weapons, furniture and the like. The house has stood for 250 years, and from the top you can see across to the citadel to the south-east. Entrance is S£5 and it's open daily from 8 am to 2 pm except Tuesdays.

To find the museum, turn left from Al-Khandak St into the narrow lane that veers right and serves as a souq. The museum is on the left a few metres before the lane opens out onto a little square.

Christian Quarter The area immediately surrounding the Museum of Popular Tradition is a Christian, mainly Armenian, quarter called Al-Jadayda, and there are a number of stately old homes dating back to the 17th and 18th centuries that can be visited. Various people have the keys to these places. One is the museum attendant, another is the owner of a big souvenir shop on another small square about 200 metres north of the opening to the Souq as-Souf by the museum. Otherwise, just ask around. You actually pass one of the houses, Bayt Ghazaleh, on the left as you walk up towards the shop. To get a price per person comparable to museum entrance, you'll need a group of four or five and some determined bargaining.

The whole area is fascinating to wander around on a Sunday, when it's busy with the faithful of five Christian faiths thronging together. Along the Souq as-Souf is the entrance to the Forty Martyrs' Armenian cathedral. A little way to the north is the Maronite cathedral, and squeezed between them are Latin (Roman Catholic), Greek Catholic and Syrian Orthodox churches.

ACTIVITIES
Hammam
Just to the south-east of the bridge to the citadel is the Hammam Yalbougha al-Nasri (☎ 333155). Originally constructed in 1491, it had been destroyed and rebuilt several times before the latest restoration, completed in 1985. The corridor leading in acts as a mini-museum. Noteworthy is the sun clock inside the dome above the reception area – three intricate designs mark out four o'clock, eight o'clock and 12 o'clock.

It will cost S£240 for as long as you want inside, full massage, sauna and baths, along with soap, towels and complimentary tea. Women only get to go on Thursdays and Saturdays from 9 am to 5 pm (which is better than nothing, and recommended). It's open to men from 5 pm until midnight Thursdays and Saturdays, and from 9 am to midnight every other day.

Swimming
People wanting to cool off with a simple swim will have a harder time. The Cham Chahba Hotel charges S£3000 for a monthly membership of their pool and gym.

The local hand-out map indicates two pools in the north of the town. One doesn't exist and the other seems closed all the time. The hassle involved in trying to find the pool makes a stint under a cool shower in your hotel an easier alternative.

Public Library
Just behind the clock tower is the public library, where there are occasional art and photographic exhibitions.

PLACES TO STAY
Places to Stay – bottom end
There is a stack of cheap hotels on Al-Maari St. The *Hotel Yarmouk* (☎ 217510) shares its entrance with the *Hotel Suez Canal* (☎ 217564). Both are quite reasonable cheapies that have been recently renovated and cleaned up. The Yarmouk is the better of the two, and a good clean single with hot shower is S£150. There is a TV lounge on each floor. Also, most of the rooms are up on the high floors, well above the street noise. The price per person is the same next door, but they'll make you pay for both beds in a double if you are alone.

Further down towards the clock tower is the *Hotel Syria* (☎ 219760). You pay S£125 (you can sometimes get them down to S£100) a person. It's OK but there have been some bad reports about the place being virtually turned into an all-night market place by bus loads of Armenians and others from the former Soviet Union who descend on Syria on trading sprees.

This is something you see a lot of in Aleppo and, to a lesser extent, in Damascus. The black marketeers bus overland from all over the former Eastern Bloc bringing whatever they think they can flog. They then try to buy up goods unavailable to them for resale back home. The nearby *Hotel Asia* is quieter and charges the same.

Others in a similar bracket on Al-Maari St include the *Al-Zahra, New Arab World* and the *Chark Awssat*. The *Hotel Eshbilia* (☎ 221830) on Rasheed St is the favoured accommodation choice of a bunch of girls who perform in the nightclub next door, and is rumoured to be a brothel. A bed in a shared double is S£125, but they may want you to pay for the whole double if you are alone. Hot showers are extra at S£25 a go. It's all right and there's no hassle, but the nightclub is loud and late.

Failing all these, there is a plethora of pits

around and behind the clock tower; few have signs in English, but a bed usually won't cost you more than S£100.

Places to stay – middle

There's really only one place to stay – the *Baron Hotel* (☎ 210880). If you're going to splurge once in Syria, this is the place to do it. When it was built in 1909, the hotel was on the outskirts of town 'in gardens considered dangerous to venture into after dark'. The hotel was opened by two Armenian brothers and called the Baron because residents of Aleppo addressed the brothers as 'baron' (although some say the title meant little more than 'mister' in Armenian at the time).

The Baron quickly became famous for being one of the premier hotels of the Middle East, helped by the fact that Aleppo was then an important trading centre and staging post for travellers. The Orient Express used to terminate in Aleppo and the rich and famous travelling on it would often stay at the Baron.

A look through the old leather-bound visitors book (kept securely stashed in the safe) turns up names such as T E Lawrence (Lawrence of Arabia); Agatha Christie; aviators Charles Lindbergh, Amy Johnston and Charles Kingsford-Smith; Theodore Roosevelt and Lady Louis Mountbatten. You can see a copy of Lawrence's bill in the lounge.

Today, the Baron is run by the grandsons of the original 'baron' brothers. It's still a handsome building but if it's luxury you're after, forget it! Nothing much has changed since 1909 – the beds are old and squeaky, the walls need painting and the plumbing is antediluvian. For all that the place has heaps of character and if you don't want to stay, at least stop by and have a drink in the bar. If you are staying, single/double rooms with breakfast cost US$23/31. A lot of package tourists in more comfortable and expensive places seem to end up in the bar half wishing they were staying here, at least for a night or two.

The *Ramsis Hotel* (☎ 216700), opposite the Baron, is more modern and squeaky clean, and air-con rooms with hot bath cost

US$22/28. On the same side of Baron St as the Baron is the *Ambassador Hotel* (☎ 211833), a dingy and unfriendly place that doesn't seem to encourage guests. Singles (if you can get one) are US$15 and doubles US$22.

Just by the exchange booth is the *Semiramis Hotel* (☎ 219990), with rooms little better than those in some of the better basic hotels. Prices are the same as at the Ambassador, but the manager seems to enjoy wheeling and dealing.

Heading up the scale is the three-star *Tourism Hotel* (☎ 210156) on the corner of Kouwatli and Saad Allah al-Jabri Sts. Quite reasonable rooms with TV, hot bath and air-conditioning cost US$38/48/57.

Places to Stay – top end

Just near the microbus and Pullman stations is the *Amir Palace* (☎ 214800). Pretty much a standard four-star hotel, its principal advantage is its relative proximity to the places of interest compared with the other biggies. Singles/doubles/triples go for $US52/88/101, plus 10% taxes.

Out near the university is the *Pullman Shahba Hotel*, opened in 1989. There is a local bus to and from the centre, not that you'll be likely to use it if you can afford to stay here in the first place. Rooms are US$90/100 plus taxes.

At the top of the scale and also well out in the west of the city is the five-star *Chahba Cham* (☎ 249801), which has everything, right down to CNN plugged into each room. You pay US$135/165 plus taxes, and that does not include breakfast.

PLACES TO EAT

In the block bounded by Al-Maari, Bab al-Faraj, Kouwatli and Baron Sts are the cheapies offering the usual stuff – the price is more variable than the food so check before you sit down.

Al-Chabab is a good alfresco restaurant with a fountain in a side street off Baron St, just up from the Syrian Arab Airlines office. It's a pleasant and inexpensive place to sit in the evenings. Along similar lines, but brighter, noisier and more expensive, is the big café/restaurant on Al-Abbarah St.

The *Al-Kindi Restaurant* on Yarmouk St offers quite filling meals of kebabs and the usual side orders for about S£100. There is quite a wide menu written in English. A bottle of Al-Chark beer costs S£28.

Quite a decent upstairs place with tables for two on separate little balconies is the *Al-Andals* on Kouwatli St. They serve a reasonable dish of meat, salad, hummus and something to drink for around S£150. It's a pleasant vantage point from which to contemplate the lunacy below and sip a slow beer.

For about the same price you can eat in the *Al-Andalib*, a few doors up from the Baron Hotel. It's a good place in the summer, but the food is less than special.

A respectable meal in the Tourism Hotel's restaurant will set you back about S£250, and although there is nothing wrong with the food, you're really just paying to be posh. (Speaking of posh, there's an Italian restaurant in the Pullman Shahba Hotel.)

If it's just a drink you're after, the outside terrace at the *Baron Hotel* takes a lot of beating, but it's only open in summer and the beer will cost you S£40.

There are a few cafés worth trying. Opposite the entrance to the citadel there are two with some shady trees where you can linger over a shay and watch the world go by. Back in the downtown area there's an upstairs café right by the clock tower. It has a view of the hectic intersection and the antics of the drivers and pedestrians are good entertainment. The entrance is in the side street, through the Al-Sahel Hotel.

ENTERTAINMENT
Cinema
There is no shortage of cinemas, all of them showing rubbish so heavily censored that it is impossible to know what is going on. In fact, most of the slightly risqué stills used to entice the almost exclusively male customers belong to scenes removed from the film!

Nightclubs
There is no shortage of nightclubs in the centre of town. The number of drunk Syrian men spilling out of these sleazy joints late at night create one of the few areas and moments it might be wiser to avoid.

GETTING THERE & AWAY
Air
Aleppo has an international airport with some connections to Turkey, Europe and other cities in the Middle East, although it is not easy to find a travel agent who will organise international flights to Aleppo. Syrian Arab Airlines has flights to Istanbul for US$393 and to Cairo for US$195 – hardly great bargains.

Internally, there is a flight at 10 am on Mondays to Qamishle in the north-east for S£600, and at least one flight daily to Damascus for the same price.

If you want to book international flights with other airlines, most foreign airline offices are on Baron St.

Bus
Karnak Bus The Karnak bus office is on Baron St diagonally opposite the Baron Hotel. The buses leave from around the back, almost opposite the tourist office.

There are daily connections to Lattakia (S£44), Deir ez-Zur (4½ hours, S£82), as well as Hama (S£40), Homs (S£52) and Damascus (five hours, S£88). Book at least one day in advance.

Pullman Bus The Pullman bus station is directly behind the local city bus station, itself behind the Amir Palace. Different bays are allotted to various competing companies.

Buses go to most long-distance destinations and you buy tickets before boarding.

Pullman buses are cheaper than Karnak (the trip to Deir ez-Zur, for instance, costs S£58) and more comfortable than the regular buses and microbuses.

Bus/Microbus The station for regular buses and microbuses to the north, west and south is across the road from the city bus station. For many destinations you actually have to buy tickets from a window. This supposedly ensures you a seat. Alternatively, you can hop on at the last moment and join the standing-room only squash.

Buses to Damascus take six hours (S£50), to Homs about three hours (S£26), and to Lattakia three to four hours (S£40). Microbuses to Azaz (for Turkey) also leave regularly from here.

For destinations east of Aleppo it is easier to catch a Pullman. However, if you want to save every possible pound, you'll have to make your way to the East bus station for services to the east and south-east, which, appropriately enough, is on the eastern side of town. As it's about three km from the centre, the only sensible way to get there with luggage is by taxi, thus killing any saving you'd make over the Pullman.

Note also that, if you arrive in Aleppo by microbus from the east, you'll also end up in the East bus station, and have the long trek (or taxi ride) into the centre ahead.

Turkish Buses Buses leave from next to the Karnak bus station for Istanbul (24 hours, S£950) and other destinations in Turkey. Book in one of the booths at the bus station or enquire at one of the nearby travel agencies.

There are other private long-haul buses to Beirut (S£255) and supposedly Amman, in Jordan (S£400). For this you're better off getting down to Damascus and organising something from there.

Train
The railway station is just to the north of the big public park, about 15 minutes' walk from the downtown hotel area. Local trains run daily to Damascus, Lattakia, Deir ez-Zur and Qamishle in the north-east.

Once a week there's a train from Aleppo to Istanbul. It takes forever (anything up to 48 hours) and costs S£460 in 1st class or S£219 in 2nd class. There is no sleeper. It leaves Aleppo at 11 am on Saturdays. For details on the trip from Istanbul to Aleppo see the Syria Getting There & Away chapter.

Service-Taxi
There are service-taxi ranks in Al-Maari St and dotted around the city, but the main station is just behind the pullman bus station.

Car Rental
Europcar is about the only place you'll be able to find a hire car in. Try their (frequently vacant) desk at the Amir Palace. For other details, see the Syria Getting Around chapter.

GETTING AROUND
All the sights of interest are in a compact area so getting around on foot poses no problems.

Bus
You'll hardly need the local buses, and if you go to the bus station behind the Amir Palace it's all but impossible to get any sensible information. A ticket good for four rides (punch a corner each time) costs S£5 and can be bought on the bus.

Taxi
Car buffs may like to ride in a regular taxi just for the hell of it. They are mostly enormous, lumbering old American limousines from the 1940s and '50s and have the usual assortment of lights and decorations inside – some light up like Christmas trees at night. The vintage is beginning to change with the relaxation of car import laws. An average cross-town ride should not cost more than about S£15.

There are some service-taxis running set routes and picking up passengers for standard rates along the way, but it's difficult to tell them apart from the regular taxis which multiple hire, until you're in one and find you can't go to exactly your chosen destination.

Around Aleppo

The ruins and historical sites to the north, west and south of Aleppo have come to be known collectively as the Dead Cities. The area is crowded with the remnants of towns and monuments, many dating from early Byzantine Christianity. The majority are in such an advanced state of decay that they possess only limited interest for the passing traveller and many are hard to reach. For the expert or amateur historian, they represent a still largely unexplored archive in stone.

QALA'AT SAMAAN

This is the Basilica of St Simeon, also known as St Simon of Stylites, who was one of Syria's most unusual early Christians. In the 5th century this shepherd from northern Syria had a revelation in a dream and joined a monastery. Finding monastic life not sufficiently ascetic, he retreated to the barren hills.

In 423, he sat on top of a three-metre pillar and went on to spend the next 36 years atop this and other taller pillars! For his last 30 years, the pillar was some 15 metres high. There was a railing around the top and an iron collar around his neck was chained to the pillar to stop him toppling off in the middle of the night. Rations were carried up a ladder by fellow monks and twice a week he celebrated mass on top.

Pilgrims started coming from as far away as Britain, hoping to see a miracle. St Simeon would preach to them daily from his perch, and shout back answers to their shouted questions. He refused to talk to women, however, and even his mother was not allowed near the column.

After his death in 459, an enormous church was built around the famous pillar. It was unique in design in that it was four basilicas arranged in the shape of a cross, each opening onto a central octagonal yard covered by a dome. In the centre stood the sacred pillar. One basilica was used for

Basilica of St Simeon

worship; the other three housed the many pilgrims. It was finished in 490 and at the time was the largest church in the world. A monastery was built at the foot of the hill to house the clergy and a town with inns soon sprang up.

The church today is remarkably well preserved, with the arches of the octagonal yard still complete, along with much of the four basilicas. The pillar is in a sad state and is nothing more than a boulder on top of a platform. After St Simeon's death, pilgrims chipped away at it and took small fragments home as souvenirs of the holy place.

The views of the barren hills to the west are stunning and the ruins of the monastery can be seen down to the left at the foot of the hill in the village of Deir Samaan. A family has actually taken up residence in the ruins but they don't mind if you wander around.

The site is open daily and entry is S£10. The ruins can be quite a popular spot with Syrians and Lebanese up from Tripoli for a visit.

Getting There & Away

Microbuses from Aleppo leave every hour or so from the main microbus station for the one-hour trip to the village of Daret 'Azze for S£5. About two-thirds of the way there you'll notice the 5th century Mushabbak basilica, isolated in an empty field to the left.

It is about 15 km from Daret 'Azze to Qala'at Samaan and it's a matter of negotiating with a local for transport. Hitching is a reasonable possibility on weekends, when a lot of locals head out. Sometimes the microbus from Aleppo will take you the whole way – after all, they've got no timetable to stick to – but only for a substantial amount of money.

The last microbus from Daret 'Azze to Aleppo leaves at about 8 pm.

QATURA

About five km before Deir Samaan are the old Roman tombs at Qatura. They are about one km off the road to the west. The tombs are cut into the rock and it's easy to scramble

up to them. The Greek inscriptions are still clearly visible.

Right below the tombs is a natural well where young village girls bring their goats. They collect water using buckets made from old truck tyres.

'AIN DARA

A thousand years before Christ, a Hittite temple dedicated to the mountain god and the goddess Ishtar stood on an acropolis off the modern road that led north from Qala'at Samaan to the mainly Kurdish town of 'Afreen. The temple was destroyed in the 8th century BC, rebuilt and then gradually gave way to other constructions.

Excavations since the mid-50s have revealed the layout of the site and, most interestingly, some extraordinary basalt statues and reliefs, which litter the site. The single most impressive statue is a huge lion tipped over on its side.

As you climb the path up the side of the hill, a local chap (who is caretaker while archaeologists are absent) will probably greet you and do his best to show you around. He will also demand a tip.

Getting There & Away

You can continue hitching from Deir Samaan towards 'Afreen (you may be able to pick a local microbus), or catch a microbus from Aleppo direct to 'Afreen (S£10) and from there one of the irregular pickups to 'Ain Dara (S£5). It will drop you at the turn-off just before the village; you can see the acropolis in the distance. Follow the road around (about two km), or cut across the path and onion fields directly to the site.

CYRRHUS

Overlooking the Turkish border and deep in Kurdish territory is the 3rd century provincial town of Cyrrhus (Nabi Houri, or Prophet Cyrrhus, to the locals). Little is left of the town today, which once held a strategic position for troops of the Roman Empire. From the dusty town of Azaz (a windy, putrid little dump) the road takes you through cheerful countryside, dotted by wheat fields and olive groves, across two 3rd century Roman **bridges** on the Sabun River and past a Roman era **mausoleum**. This pyramid-capped monument has survived well, partly because it was preserved by local Muslims as a holy site. Here you branch right off the road to the ruins.

The easiest to distinguish is the **amphitheatre**. Of the town walls, colonnaded street and basilica in the north of the town, not a lot remains, but it is quite fun to scramble up through the ruins past the theatre to the Arab **citadel** at the top, from where you have sweeping views. You can be virtually guaranteed of having this place to yourself.

Getting There & Away

Microbuses run from Aleppo to Azaz, from where you have no real choice but to bargain with one of the taxis. Do not be surprised to be hit for as much as S£400 for the ride there and back. You can try to hitch, but there is precious little traffic on this road. The same taxis also run people to the Turkish border for S£50 (for the car, not per person).

EBLA

About 60 km south of Aleppo on the highway to Hama lay the ancient city of Ebla (Tell Mardikh), where more than 15,000 clay tablets in a Sumerian dialect have been unearthed, providing a wealth of information on everything from economics to local administration and dictionaries of other tongues. The Italian teams that have been excavating the site since 1964 have discovered that it was one of the most powerful city-states in Syria in the late 3rd millennium BC. By 1600 BC, it had been largely destroyed by Hittite invaders and never again rose to any importance. Troops of the First Crusade passed by thousands of years later, when it was known as Mardic hamlet.

The modern road takes the visitor to what was the ancient northwest gate. You won't be overwhelmed by towering remains; in fact the bulk of the site is rather flat. The most interesting ruins for the casual visitor are probably those of what has been labelled 'Palace G', which lies east of the acropolis and displays remains of a royal staircase, walls and columned halls.

The site is scattered with evidence of other palaces and temples.

Getting There & Away

Take any Hama-bound microbus, or to be sure of not paying the full fare for Hama, one of the less frequent ones to Ma'aret an-Nu'aman, and get off at the turn-off. You shouldn't have to pay more than S£10. From there it is a 40-minute walk to the site.

MA'ARET AN-NU'AMAN

This lively little market town is nothing special in itself, but if you want to get some idea of how many of the buildings of the Dead Cities were decorated, the **mosaic collection** housed in an Ottoman Khan is well worth a visit. Most of the mosaics covered the floors of the more important or luxurious buildings and private houses of the 5th and 6th century Byzantine towns. Not quite as old is the lovingly executed mosaic of Assad, which takes pride of place facing the entrance. The museum is about 50 metres to the north of the bus station, on the right side of a large square. Entry is S£5.

Further north and off to the right is the 12th century **Grand Mosque**. From the mosque, head away to the right of the square and north for a few hundred metres – where the street opens out you'll see the sad remains of a medieval **citadel**, which now serve as cheap accommodation for a few families. All up, it's about one km from the mosque.

Getting There & Away

Every hour or so a microbus leaves Aleppo (one hour, S£10), passing the Ebla turn-off on the way.

AL-BARA (AL-KAFR)

About 20 km west of Ma'aret an-Nu'aman is just one of many sets of ruins belonging to the Dead Cities. In the late 5th century it was one of the most important centres of wine production in the region, and today boasts remains of at least five **churches** among ruins that cover a two by three km square. Small plots are still intensively worked in among the ancient buildings. The land is good and olives, grapes and apricots thrive here.

The most striking structures are the **pyramid tombs**, of which there are two. Just ask the locals in the modern town which path to take to the brooding grey basalt ruins (you can see them from the town) and head out. Take plenty of water and food as there's not

much to be had in the town, although you will stand out so much that an invitation to tea is more than likely.

Getting There & Away
The road from Ma'aret an-Nu'aman is bad and you'll have to negotiate with a trezeena driver to get a lift to the modern village. It's easier to get a microbus from Aleppo to Ariha and hitch, or try to track down local transport from there as the roads are better and carry more traffic.

The Desert

The Damascus-Aleppo highway marks roughly the division between the cultivable land to the west and the barren desert which runs east all the way to the Euphrates.

The wide fringe of the desert gets sufficient rain to support enough vegetation to graze sheep and goats. The desert fringe-dwellers build beehive-shaped houses as protection against the extreme heat. You can see these houses on the road from Homs to Palmyra, in the area south of Lake Assad and around Aleppo.

The desert proper extends south-east from Palmyra into Jordan and Iraq. Its Arabic name is Badiet es Sham and it is also known as the Syrian Desert. It is not a sand desert but consists of stony treeless plains stretching to the horizon. Rainfall is extremely irregular here and it's not uncommon for two or three years to pass between falls.

Dotting this desert are the oases – the main one is Palmyra – which used to serve as way-stations for the caravans on their way between the Mediterranean and Mesopotamia.

PALMYRA

Known to the locals as Tadmor (its ancient Semitic name), Palmyra is Syria's prime attraction and is one of the world's great historical sites. If you're only going to see one thing in Syria, make it Palmyra. Even if you have seen enough ruins to last you a lifetime and the thought of one more is enough to make you groan, make the effort to see this one as it really is something special.

Although mass tourism is beginning to make itself tentatively felt and the place's popularity is growing, you'll more often than not find you virtually have the site to yourself – a rare pleasure. Apart from a few locals, some of them looking for a chance to practise their English or change a bit of money, and the occasional traveller or tourist, the ruins of Palmyra are deserted.

The oasis is really in the middle of nowhere – 150 km from the Orontes River to the west and 200 km from the Euphrates to the east. This is the very end of the Anti-Lebanon Mountains, and the final fold of the range forms a basin. At the edge of the basin there is a spring, known as Efca ('source' in Aramaic). It is slightly sulphurous and is said to have medicinal qualities.

The ruins of the 2nd century AD city have been extensively excavated and restored and cover some 50 hectares. The new town is rapidly growing around it, spreading out with especial speed towards the west, and now counts 40,000 inhabitants. Nearby is an air force base, and the sight of fighters screaming over the ancient ruins (thankfully, they don't come in too low) in training runs is curious to say the least.

Tucked well out of sight to the west of the old and new cities is a high-security prison with a reasonably grim reputation.

History

Tadmor is mentioned in tablets as early as the 19th century BC. It became an important staging post for caravans travelling from the Mediterranean to the countries of the Gulf. It was also an important link on the old Silk Route from China and India to Europe and the city prospered greatly by levying heavy tolls on the caravans.

As the Romans pushed the frontier of their empire further east during the 1st and early 2nd centuries AD, Palmyra's importance as a buffer between the Persians and the Romans grew. The Romans dubbed the city Palmyra (the City of Palms), but the locals retained the old name of Tadmor (the City of Dates). It appears that, in spite of Rome's growing influence, the city retained considerable independence, profiting also from the defeat of the Petra-based Nabataean Empire by Rome.

The emperor Hadrian visited the city in 130 AD and declared it a 'free city'. In 217

AD, under the emperor Caracalla, the city became a Roman colony. This gave its citizens equal rights with Rome and freed them from paying Roman taxes. During this period the great colonnaded street was enlarged, temples were built and the citizens grew extremely wealthy on the caravan trade – some even owned ships sailing in the Arabian Gulf.

In 137 AD an enormous stone tablet bore the inscription of the 'Tariff of Palmyra' (now in a museum in St Petersburg). It set out the taxes payable on each commodity that passed through the city, as well as the charges for the supply of water.

The colony gradually evolved into a kingdom ruled by Odenathus, a brilliant military leader who had earned the gratitude of Rome by freeing the emperor Valerian from capture by the Persians. For this Valerian bestowed upon him the title of 'Corrector of the East' and put all Roman forces in the East under his command.

The city's downfall began when Odenathus was assassinated in 266 in suspicious circumstances. His second wife, the famous half-Greek/half-Arab Zenobia, took

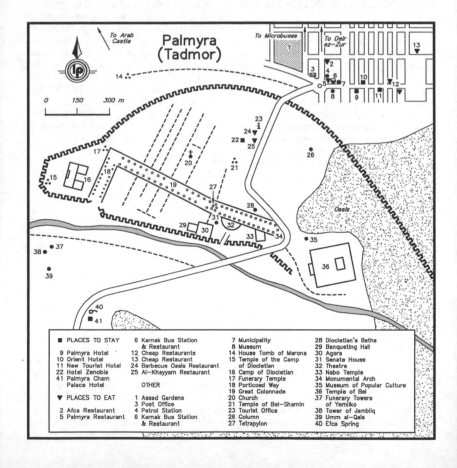

Palmyra (Tadmor)

To Arab Castle
To Microbuses
To Deir ez-Zur

0   150   300 m

Oasis

■ PLACES TO STAY	6 Karnak Bus Station & Restaurant	7 Municipality	28 Diocletian's Baths
		8 Museum	29 Banqueting Hall
9 Palmyra Hotel	12 Cheap Restaurants	14 House Tomb of Marona	30 Agora
10 Orient Hotel	13 Cheap Restaurant	15 Temple of the Camp	31 Senate House
11 New Tourist Hotel	24 Barbecue Oasis Restaurant	of Diocletian	32 Theatre
22 Hotel Zenobia	25 Al-Khayyam Restaurant	16 Camp of Diocletian	33 Nabo Temple
41 Palmyra Cham		17 Funerary Temple	34 Monumental Arch
Palace Hotel	OTHER	18 Porticoed Way	35 Museum of Popular Culture
		19 Great Colonnade	36 Temple of Bel
▼ PLACES TO EAT	1 Assad Gardens	20 Church	37 Funerary Towers
	3 Post Office	21 Temple of Bel–Shamin	of Yemliko
2 Afca Restaurant	4 Petrol Station	23 Tourist Office	38 Tower of Jambliq
5 Palmyra Restaurant	6 Karnak Bus Station & Restaurant	26 Column	39 Umm al-Qais
		27 Tetrapylon	40 Efca Spring

over in the name of their son, who was still a minor. He claimed the titles of his father, but Rome was not keen to recognise them. Zenobia was suspected of involvement in her husband's death, but it was never proved.

Claiming to be descended from Cleopatra, Zenobia was a woman of exceptional ability and ambition. Fluent in Greek, Latin, Aramaic and Egyptian, she effectively turned Palmyra into an independent empire, wresting control of Egypt from Rome and marching deep into Asia Minor. The 18th century traveller, Edward Gibbon, in his book titled *The Decline & Fall of the Roman Empire* said of her:

She equalled in beauty her ancestor Cleopatra and far surpassed that princess in chastity and valour. Zenobia was esteemed the most lovely as well as the most heroic of her sex. She was of dark complexion. Her teeth were of a pearly whiteness and her large black eyes sparkled with an uncommon fire, tempered by the most attractive sweetness. Her voice was strong and harmonious. Her manly understanding was strengthened and adorned by study.

She was also a ruler with a sense of humour. A merchant was to be punished for overcharging and was summoned to the theatre to appear in front of the queen and the public audience. The merchant stood alone in the arena and shook with fear, thinking that a wild beast was to be set upon him. When the beast was released the crowd roared with laughter – the merchant turned around to be confronted by a chicken.

With her sights set on Rome, Zenobia declared complete independence and had coins minted in Alexandria bearing her image and that of her son, who assumed the title of Augustus. The emperor Aurelian, who had been prepared to negotiate, couldn't stomach such a show of open defiance and after defeating her forces at Antioch and Emesa (Homs) in 271, he besieged Palmyra itself. Zenobia was defiant to the last and instead of accepting the generous surrender terms offered by Aurelian, made a dash on a camel through the encircling Roman forces. She headed for Persia to appeal for military aid, only to be captured by the Roman cavalry at the Euphrates. The city then surrendered but escaped with only a fine for its insurrection.

Zenobia was carted off to Rome as Aurelian's trophy and was paraded in the streets, bound in gold chains. She spent the rest of her days in Rome, some say in a villa provided by the emperor, others say she chose to fast to death rather than remain captive.

Whatever became of her, it was the end of Palmyra's prosperity and its most colourful figure. The emperor Aurelian wrote of Zenobia:

Those who say I have only conquered a woman do not know what that woman was, nor how lightning were her decisions, how persevering she was in her plans, how resolute with her soldiers.

Zenobia's coin

The city itself was destroyed by Aurelian in 273 following another rebellion, when the inhabitants massacred the 600 archers stationed there. Aurelian's troops were particularly brutal. The residents were slaughtered and the city was set to the torch.

Palmyra was never able to recover its former glory and became a Roman outpost. The emperor Diocletian fortified it as one in the line of fortresses that marked the boundary of the Roman Empire. Justinian rebuilt the city's defences in the 6th century but by this stage it had lost all its wealth and declined steadily with the drop in caravan traffic.

The city fell to the Muslims in 634 and was finally and completely destroyed by a devastating earthquake in 1089. It seems that a Jewish colony existed there in the 12th century but the city had passed into legend by then.

In 1678 it was rediscovered by two English merchants living in Aleppo and the tales of Odenathus and Zenobia fascinated Europe, mainly because nobody had any idea that this once-important city had even existed.

Excavations started in 1924. Until then, the Arab villagers had lived in the courtyard of the Temple of Bel (or Baal), before being moved to the new town. Restoration has seen the number of standing columns go from 150 in the 1950s to over 300 now. Some of the earlier restoration work, particularly noticeable on the tetrapylon (four groups of four pillars), was crudely executed.

Today, it's easy to spend a couple of days wandering around the site, the funerary towers, and the 17th century Arab castle on the hill.

Information

Tourist Office Open from 8 am to 2 pm and 5 to 7 pm, the tourist office is about halfway between the town and the site proper.

Money There is no bank or exchange office in Palmyra, so you'll need to bring all you need or look around, discreetly, for someone willing to change money on the black market.

Post The post office is a very laid-back place with flexible opening hours – don't count on it being open much after 2 pm.

The Ruins

Tempting though it may be to think of Palmyra as simply another Roman city, it is in fact anything but. Its layout does not follow classical Roman town planning at all, although Roman and Greek influences are obvious. Despite the power of its neighbours

(whether Roman, Persian or Parthian) Palmyra retained a distinct culture and expression in its own language, a dialect of Aramaic.

Temple of Bel The best place to start is the Temple of Bel at the eastern edge of the site. The temple itself is in a massive courtyard some 200 metres square. Originally this courtyard was surrounded by a 15-metre-high wall but only the northern side is original, the rest is of Arab construction. The western wall, which contains the entrance and a small souvenir shop, was built out of fragments of the temple when it was fortified. A double colonnade used to run around three sides of the interior while the fourth side (the western side) had a single row of columns much taller than the others. Some of these can be seen to the right and left of the entrance.

Just to the left of the entrance inside the courtyard is a passage that enters the temple from outside the wall and gradually slopes up to the level of the courtyard. This is where sacrificial animals were brought into the precincts. In front of the shrine are the ruins of a banquet hall. The podium of the sacrificial altar is on the left, and the remains of another platform on the right, which was possibly used for religious purification ceremonies.

The shrine itself is unusual in design in that the entrance is in one of the sides rather than the ends, and is offset from the centre. Inside, the shrine has porticoes at either end, with ceilings cut from single blocks of stone. The northern one is highly decorated and the ceiling has a rosette. The centre is a cupola featuring a bust of Jupiter and signs of the zodiac. The stepped ramp leading to the southern portico suggests that it may have contained a portable idol used in processions.

Around the back of the shrine is a pile of old railway tracks that were used to remove trolleys of rubble during the original excavations. The temple enclosure is open daily from 8 am to 1 pm and 4 to 6 pm. Entry is S£10.

There is a selection of books available

here on Syria and Palmyra, and this is one of the rare locations where you can buy slide film.

The Great Colonnade This column-lined street formed the main artery of the town and ran from the main temple entrance to the monumental arch, and then on for 700 metres or so, ending at the funerary temple. The section between the Bel Temple and the arch no longer exists and the main road from Palmyra to Damascus now winds through here. Overloaded trucks come thundering through within a couple of metres of the arch and this traffic can't be good for the ruins. In fact it looks as though the keystone of the arch is ready to fall out at any moment.

The street itself was never paved, to allow camels to use it, but the porticoes on either side were. The section up to the tetrapylon is the best restored and is impressive in its scale. Each column has a small jutting platform about two-thirds of the way up, designed to hold the statue of some rich or famous Palmyrene who had helped to pay for the construction of the street. One of these statues has been replaced on its pedestal, virtually in front of the Museum of Popular Culture.

The street itself is evidence of the city's unique development. At the arch and again at the tetrapylon it takes a slight turn, quite unimaginable in any standard Roman city.

Nabo Temple The first ruin on the left as you pass the arch is a small trapeze-shaped temple built in the 1st century BC to the god Nabo. It seems the temple underwent a few changes, as some of the construction stretched into the 3rd century AD.

Diocletian's Baths Next up on the right, but pretty much indistinguishable, is the site of baths built by Diocletian.

Theatre The theatre is on the south side of the street between two arches in the colonnade. Beneath the platforms on many of the columns are inscriptions with names for the statues that once stood there. It seems the statues were of prominent people such as emperors, princes of Palmyra, magistrates and officials, high-ranking priests and caravan chiefs. The theatre has been the subject of extensive restoration work, and for better or worse, large sections of it now look just a bit too shiny and new.

The freestanding facade of the theatre is designed along the lines of a palace entrance, complete with royal door and smaller doors on either side. From the rear of the theatre a pillared way led south past the senate house and agora to one of the gates in the wall built by Justinian.

Agora The agora was the equivalent of a Roman forum and was used for public discussion, and as a market. Four porticoes surrounded a courtyard measuring 84 by 71 metres. The dedications of the statues that once stood on the pillars and walls provide important clues for historians. The portico on the north had statues of Palmyrene and Roman officials, the eastern one had senators, the western was for military officers while on the south side, merchants and caravan leaders were honoured. Today there is nothing left of the statues and most of the pillars are only a metre or so high.

Adjoining the agora is the **banqueting hall** used by the rulers of Palmyra.

Tetrapylon About a third of the way along the street is the reconstructed tetrapylon. Only one of these pillars is of the original granite (probably brought from Aswan in Egypt). The rest are just coloured concrete and look pretty terrible – a result of some rather hasty and amateurish reconstruction.

Each of the four groups of pillars supports 150,000 kg of solid cornice. A statue used to stand between the pillars on each of the four pedestals, one of them of Zenobia herself. Unfortunately, no vestiges of the latter have ever been found.

This monument marks a major intersection of the city. From here the main street continues north-west, and another smaller pillared street leads south-west to the agora.

Funerary Temple The main street continues for another 500 metres and ends in the impressive, reconstructed portico of the funerary temple, dating back to the 3rd century. This was the main residential section of town and streets can be seen leading off to both sides.

Camp of Diocletian This lies to the south of the funerary temple along the porticoed way. The area here is littered with fallen stones and the intricacy of the carvings can be seen at close quarters.

It is believed that Diocletian built this camp on the original site of the Palace of Zenobia, but excavation so far has not been able to prove this. The camp, erected after the destruction of the city by Aurelian, lay near what was the Damascus Gate, which gave on to a 2nd century colonnaded street linking Emesa (Homs) to the Euphrates.

Temple of Bel-Shamin This small shrine is near the Zenobia Hotel and is dedicated to the god of storms and fertilising rains. Bel-Shamin was a Phoenician god, not unlike Bel a master of sun and moon, but only really gained popularity in Palmyra when Roman influence was at its height.

Although it is permanently closed, the six columns of the vestibule have platforms for statues and bear inscriptions. The one on the far left has an inscription in Greek and Palmyrene praising the secretary of the city for his generosity during the visit of 'the divine Hadrian' and for footing the bill for the construction of the temple. The text is dated at 131 AD.

A branch road led to the temple from the tetrapylon.

Funerary Towers of Yemliko & Jambliq These lie to the south of the city wall at the foot of the hill of Umm al-Qais. The square towers were built as tombs and contained coffins in niches on up to five levels. The interior was often decorated with cornices and friezes.

The towers are worth visiting, and the views from the top in late afternoon are great.

Those closest to the town are not kept locked and can be easily explored; however, the best towers are locked. The only way to see them is to hire a trezeena and get the museum attendant to bring the keys along. Although it's within walking distance they don't allow you to take the keys, and the attendant is not prepared to walk.

You'll have to bargain hard to budge them from their starting price of S£100 a person. The exorbitant price can only be put down to the preparedness of some better-off tourists to part with this kind of money at the drop of a hat.

Qala'at Ibn Maan

To the west the dominant feature is the Arab castle, Qala'at Ibn Maan, built in the 17th century by Fakr ad-Din the Maanite. You can't miss it, just jump the wall and head uphill. It is surrounded by a moat and a footbridge across it still stands. The castle is not open, although one traveller reported being able to scramble inside.

The views of Palmyra and the surrounding desert make the 45-minute scramble up the rubble slope well worthwhile. It's best to go up in the late afternoon when the sun is behind you and the shadows are long.

Museum

The museum is on the edge of the new town and open daily, except Tuesday, from 8 am (9 am in summer) to 1 pm and 2 to 4 pm. The entrance fee is S£10.

The museum has an excellent array of statuary from Palmyra, most in surprisingly good condition considering they have been buried in the sand for a thousand years. A couple of dead Palmyrenes are on display, looking a little worse for wear. The descriptions of the displays are in English, which is unusual for Syrian museums.

You will also find fairly detailed explanations of the Palmyrene language, which had 22 letters and remained the main tongue of the region until the arrival of Islam, when it was gradually usurped by Arabic. The upstairs part of the museum has been closed since its exhibits were transferred to the Museum of Popular Culture.

Museum of Popular Culture

The whitewashed building with the air of a Beau Geste fort, just by the Temple of Bel, houses the Museum of Popular Culture. It contains the by now overly familiar scenes from Arab life, recreated using mannequins, but is better than most. The guardian may even play you a tune on the traditional Bedouin single-string rababa.

There is a lot of interesting information on the Bedouin tribal system – the catch is it's all in French. The museum is open from 8 am to 1 pm and 2 to 4 pm, but they may open up if they see you hanging around outside these hours. Entry is S£10.

Efca Spring

Just past the Palmyra Cham Palace, on the way in to the town, is the Efca Spring. Here you can visit a grotto said to date back to Roman times and have a swim in the slightly sulphurous water for S£50 (includes shower afterwards, towel and soap). For an extra S£50 you can get a mud massage, but watch out for the groping hands.

The chaps running it are relaxed and friendly, will probably drown you in tea and suggest, without much insistence, that you might like to buy one of the souvenirs they have for sale.

Places to Stay

The cheapest hotel in town is the *New Tourist Hotel*, where a bed in a shared room goes for S£100, a small single room for S£125 and a double for S£200. There is a hot communal shower and some rooms have their own (cold) bath. It's basic but OK. The mosque is nearby, so you will be subjected to the early morning call to prayer.

A good place, a little closer to the ruins, is the *Orient Hotel* ('ash-Sharq' in Arabic). This hotel is clean and quiet, and most rooms come with their own hot shower (the Algerian owner has to heat them up in the evening). Singles/doubles go for S£175/250, but you may be able to bargain down a little.

The owner runs a little restaurant downstairs, although it seems more often than not to be closed.

Close by, in the main street, is the relatively new *Palmyra Hotel*. It's pleasant enough, with a nice lounge on the 1st floor, but is not really worth the asking price – US$14/20.

Since late 1991, the *Hotel Zenobia* out by the ruins has been in the hands of new owners, the Damascus-based tourism company Orient Tours. At the time of writing, refurbishing was still being done, although some rooms were available. It originally dates back to the French mandate, and although the present work will leave it with very comfortable and even attractive rooms, don't expect to find much of the old elegance.

Improvement has also pushed prices up to US$35/45. For S£150 a day they'll let you camp out the back and use the showers – hardly worth the hassle really, especially as you can get a hotel room a few hundred metres into town for the same amount.

By the Efca Spring, some three km from town on the road to Damascus, is the *Palmyra Cham Palace Hotel* (☎ 37000) with five-star facilities (although it has been heftily criticised by a couple of tourists) and prices. Singles/doubles cost US$135/165.

Places to Eat

The range of choice in Palmyra is slowly increasing. Out by the Zenobia Hotel on the road to the ruins are two outdoor restaurants next to the tourist office. The *Barbecue Oasis* and the *Al-Khayyam Restaurant* next door are much of a muchness, and a fly-blown meal of kebabs, hummus, salad and a coke will set you back about S£100.

The garden restaurant by the Karnak bus station/office is quite shady and not a bad place to wait for a bus. However, a cup (admittedly quite big) of tea will cost a staggering S£15.

Four or five 'breakfast' places have sprung up along the main town road between the museum and the New Tourist Hotel, and there are a few cheap restaurants also as far down as the town square. A half chicken and the usual trimmings should not cost more than about S£80.

Short of eating out at the Palmyra Cham Palace, the *Palmyra Restaurant* is probably the poshest place you can eat in. The food's not bad and a satisfying meal will not cost more than about S£150 (they'll want a tip). A block back is the *Afca Restaurant*, which is nothing special.

Next door to the mosque is the local tea shop where you can sit and watch the world go by. The much trumpeted Assad Gardens supposedly sport a café, but there's precious little evidence of it.

Getting There & Away

Bus A variety of bus services operate out of Palmyra. You can choose between Karnak, Pullman or microbus.

Karnak Bus The Karnak bus station/office is just at the entrance to the new town. There are seven daily buses to Damascus, but as some of them are in transit from Deir ez-Zur or even Hassake, seats are not guaranteed. Some of the buses go direct to the capital (three hours), others via Homs (about four hours) and cost S£82. The ride to Homs costs S£44. Four buses go to Deir ez-Zur (two hours, S£52), and two of them on to Hassake (five hours, S£96). Most of these are in transit from Damascus, so seats are limited. Book at least one day in advance.

Pullman/Microbus The local microbuses leave for Homs three times a day for S£25. The bus station is about 500 metres north of the post office. Otherwise, you can try to flag down a microbus or Pullman passing through in front of the Karnak office to Damascus, Homs or Deir ez-Zur.

Service-Taxi A few service-taxis and their drivers hang around the café by the mosque and New Tourist Hotel. They don't seem too keen on going anywhere much, and as a result tend not to be a good deal. Stick with the buses.

QASR AL-HAYR ASH-SHARQI

With some spare cash, a worthwhile excursion will take you 120 km east of Palmyra into the desert to see one of the most isolated and startling monuments to Omayyad Muslim rule in the 8th century. The Qasr al-Hayr ash-Sharqi falls into the category of 'desert castles', such as those that can be fairly easily visited in Jordan (see the East of Amman chapter), but is much larger.

The palace held a strategic position, commanding desert routes into Mesopotamia. As support from the nomadic Arab tribes (of which they themselves were a part) was one of the main Omayyad strengths, it is no coincidence that they made their presence felt in the desert steppes.

The palace complex and rich gardens, once supplied by an underground spring about 30 km away, covered a rough square with 16-km sides. Built by Hisham around 730, the palace long outlived its Omayyad creators. Harun ar-Rashid, perhaps the best known of the Abbassid rulers, made it one of his residences, and evidence suggests it was only finally abandoned in the 14th century.

The partly restored walls of one of the main enclosures, with their mighty defensive towers, are the most impressive remaining sign of what was once a sumptuous anomaly in the harsh desert. The ruins to the west belong to what may well have been a khan. In the south-east corner are remnants of a mosque – the column with stairs inside between the two areas was a minaret. The remains of baths are to be found just to the north of the main walls. Remnants of the old perimeter wall can just be made out to the south, and in fact border the best track.

This castle has a counterpart west of Palmyra, Qasr al-Hayr al-Gharbi, but little of interest remains on the site (most of it, including its impressive facade, is in the National Museum in Damascus).

Getting There & Away

The only way to get out here is by private transport or taxi. A planned asphalted road will considerably facilitate the trip, but until then a 4WD is, although not essential, probably the best idea for the last part of the ride (about 35 km from the town of Sukhna, which is just off the Palmyra-Deir ez-Zur highway). A local driver or guide, at least from Sukhna, is indispensable. In the unlikely event that it has rained in the previous days (it does happen), it is best not to attempt it – getting bogged in the desert is few people's idea of fun.

You can get a taxi to go from Palmyra, but it is an unusual request. Expect to pay a lot, as they simply won't go otherwise. They'll start at S£2000 for the car and you'll be doing well (or they badly) to get them below S£1500. Take plenty of water and some food with you. Unless you end up in one of the few Bedouin houses scattered around the desert (none of them very close to the site) for a cup of tea, it can be a thirsty way to spend the day, especially if your driver or guide gets lost in the labyrinth of tracks left in the desert by Bedouin pick-ups!

The Euphrates River

The Euphrates River ('Al-Furat' in Arabic) starts out high in the mountains of eastern Anatolia in Turkey and winds through the north-east of Syria into Iraq, finally emptying into the Shatt al-Arab waterway and the Persian Gulf – a total distance of over 2400 km. The Euphrates is a cool green and it makes a change to see some water and fertile land after all the steppes and desert of the interior.

One of the few tributaries of the Euphrates, the Kabur, flows down through north-eastern Syria to join it below Deir ez-Zur. These two rivers make it possible to irrigate and work the land, and in recent years the cotton produced in this area has become an important source of income for the country.

The Jezira (literally 'island'), bounded very loosely by the Kabur and, further east, the Tigris (which just touches Syria on its way from Turkey into Iraq), now constitutes some of the richest land in the country.

Locals say the best land is to be found in the strip just south of the Turkish border, mostly in Kurdish territory. Cotton and wheat are the two big crops.

A local sign of prosperity is the new high-powered pick-up trucks imported from Japan or the USA that seem to be multiplying in the region. People will tell you that 'nowhere else in Syria will you find these', and they're right.

Oilfields at Qaratchok in the far north-eastern corner of the country have been producing oil for two decades, but only low-grade stuff that had to be mixed with better imported oil for refining. Big high-grade oil finds around Deir ez-Zur in the '80s have changed all that. Production from the area, which stood at zero in the early '80s, was expected to reach 400,000 barrels a day by the end of 1992. National and foreign companies are still searching for yet more reserves.

Beehive village near Lake Assad

LAKE ASSAD

By the time the Euphrates enters Syria at Jarablos (once the capital of the Hittite Empire) it is already a mighty river. A dam was constructed to harness the Euphrates for irrigation water and hydroelectricity production.

Work on the dam began at Tabaqah in 1963 and the reservoir started to fill in 1973. Now that it's full, it stretches for some 60 km. The dam is Syria's pride and joy and the electricity produced was supposed to make the country self-sufficient. Recently, however, the flow of the Euphrates has been reduced by the construction of another large dam in Turkey, and Syria and Iraq are concerned that the Turks may at any time decide to regulate the flow for political reasons. The two Arab countries in fact claim there have been examples of this, but the Turks deny everything, attributing any slowing in the flow to natural causes.

The lack of water in the river has been a disappointment, but by the late 1980s the regular power cuts across the country had all but been eliminated. Now, however, for whatever reason, the cuts are back, and most parts of the country are without electricity for anything up to four or five hours a day.

The dormitory town of Ath-Thaura (the Revolution) was built at Tabaqah to accommodate dam workers and peasants who had to be relocated because of the rising water levels. Not only were villages inundated, but also some sites of historical and archaeological importance. With aid from UNESCO and other foreign missions, these were investigated, documented and, where possible, moved to higher ground. The 27-metre-high minaret of the Maskana Mosque and the 18-metre-high minaret from Abu Harayra were both segmented and transported, the latter to the centre of Ath-Thaura.

QALA'AT NAJM

The northernmost citadel and castle of its kind along the Euphrates in Syria, Qala'at Najm, which is partly restored, has commanding views of the river. Built around the time of Saladin, it's not in bad condition at all.

Watch out for the warden – he or his son will soon get wind of your presence and invite you in for a friendly cup of tea in their house at the foot of the castle. The hand will then be out for a friendly piece of baksheesh.

Getting There & Away

Take a bus for 'Ain al-Arab from the East bus station in Aleppo (two hours, S£25) and get off at the village of Haya Kabir (tell people on board where you want to go). From there it is 15 km to the castle, and hitching is the only way.

The earlier you get going the better, as there is not a lot of traffic on this dead-end trail. The road passes through rolling wheat fields that form a cool green carpet in spring.

QALA'AT JA'ABAR & ATH-THAURA

An impressive sight from a distance, this citadel does not add up to all that much once you're inside. It is situated on a spit of land connected to the bank of Lake Assad, about 30 km north of Ath-Thaura. Before the lake was built, the original castle had rested on a rocky perch since before the arrival of Islam, and had then been rebuilt by Nureddin and altered by the Mamluks. The castle makes a great backdrop for a day by the lake, and on Fridays this is an extremely popular spot with Syrians. It's a great place for a swim and picnic.

You will have to pass through Ath-Thaura to get to the citadel, and it may be worth a quick visit anyway to have a look at the dam. The town itself, however, has nothing at all to recommend it and is a confusing place to get around when searching for the right road to the citadel or anywhere else. Even the buses don't seem to terminate in the same place. Ask and you shall, eventually, work it out.

Getting There & Away

Without your own car, it can be a pain to get to. You'll have to go via Ath-Thaura, either coming from Raqqa or Aleppo (S£40 by Pullman). Raqqa is the much closer base; from Aleppo it can be a long and hassle-filled day. From the centre of Ath-Thaura, you have to head out towards the north of town and try to hitch across the dam (as-sidd). The turn-off for the citadel is a few km further on to the left. From here it is 10 km.

Friday is a good day to hitch across the dam, as the place is crawling with day trippers. If you want peace and quiet on the other days, be prepared for longer waits.

Note that there are few, if any, buses or microbuses from Ath-Thaura anywhere after about 4 pm.

RAQQA

From 796 to 808 AD, the city of Raqqa (then Ar-Rafika) reached its apex as the Abbassid caliph, Harun ar-Rashid, made it his capital. The area around the city had been the site of numerous cities that had come and gone in the preceding millennium, including that founded by the Seleucids, Nikephorion. After the Mongol invasion in 1260, Ar-Rafika virtually ceased to exist. It is only since the end of WW II that it has again come to life and become an important Euphrates basin commercial centre.

Things to See

Practically nothing of the city's old glory has been preserved, but there are a couple of exceptions. The partly restored **Baghdad Gate** lies about a 10-minute walk to the east of the clock tower, a central landmark when you arrive in the city. The old Abbassid city **wall**, restored at some points to a height of five metres, runs north from the gate past the **Qasr al-Binaat** (Daughters' Palace), which served as a residence under the Ayyubids.

To the north-west are the remains of the old **grand mosque**, now being replaced by an Iranian-financed monstrosity behind the Baghdad Gate. A small **museum**, located roughly halfway between the Baghdad Gate and the clock tower, has some interesting artefacts from excavation sites in the area. The museum is open from 8 am to 2 pm daily except Tuesdays, and entry costs S£5.

Places to Stay

There are a few hotels around the clock tower, all of them amazingly expensive. The

Hotel Tourism, along the street running east-west between the clock tower and the Baghdad Gate, charges S£250 per person for uninspiring rooms and the owner seems in no mood to negotiate.

West of the clock tower is the very basic *Andalus*, where they ask S£150 a head – and they have no bath at all! The best of a bad lot is the *Ammar Hotel* (☎ 22612), which charges S£200/300 for singles/doubles. It is clean, has hot showers and is perfectly all right. Don't accept the kind offers of coffee or tea – they'll only add them to the bill at double the normal price.

Getting There & Away

Bus There are the usual options when choosing which type of bus to travel on.

Karnak Bus The Karnak bus station/office are about 100 metres north of the clock tower. There are daily departures for Damascus (7½ hours, S£133) and Deir ez-Zur (1¾ hours, S£40) and two buses a day to Aleppo (2½ hours, S£52).

Pullman The various Pullman offices are virtually across the road from Karnak. They have similar departure times at slightly lower prices, and you don't need to book in advance.

Microbus From the bus station, about 200 metres south of the clock tower (on the road leading out of town), there are regular microbuses west to Ath-Thaura and Aleppo (three hours, S£25), and east along the Euphrates to Deir ez-Zur (2½ hours, S£20).

Train The railway station lies about two km north of the clock tower – just follow the road up past the Pullman buses. There are three trains a day to Aleppo (1st class, S£52; 2nd class, S£35) and Deir ez-Zur (1st class, S£35; 2nd class, S£25).

Two trains a day go to Damascus, calling at Aleppo, Hama and Homs on the way. The trip takes the best part of nine hours and costs S£125 in 1st class and S£85 in 2nd class.

RASAFEH

This old walled city is in the middle of nowhere, and seems to rise up out of the featureless desert as you approach it. The walls, enclosing a quadrangle measuring 500 by 300 metres, are virtually all complete. Rasafeh is a bit of a hassle to get to, but it can be done in a day trip from Raqqa and is worth the effort.

Inside the walls are the remains of a Byzantine basilica built to honour Saint Sergius. The city was taken over by the Omayyad caliph, Hisham, who built a palatial summer residence here. This was completely destroyed by the Abbassids in 743 and the city fell into ruin.

There is nobody at the site selling water, or anything else for that matter, so bring food and water with you – it gets stinking hot in summer.

Getting There & Away

It requires a little patience to get to Rasafeh as transport is infrequent. Catch a bus from Raqqa for Ath-Thaura or Aleppo and get off at Al-Mansura (20 minutes, S£5) – that's the easy bit. Now it's just a matter of waiting at the signposted turn-off for a pick-up to take you the 35 km to the ruins for about S£20.

Wait a while – one will turn up eventually. If you're impatient, you can ask one of the pick-up drivers lounging around here to take you there and back for some extraordinary sums – S£200 would not be unusual. The difference seems to be an I'm-going-out-of-my-way-for-you fee.

HALABIYYEH & ZALABIYYEH

Halabiyyeh was founded by Zenobia, the rebellious Palmyrene leader, in the years immediately preceding her fall in 273. It was later re-fortified under emperor Justinian, and it is mainly the result of his work that survives today.

The fortress town was part of the Roman Empire's eastern defensive line against the Persians, who took it in 610 AD. The walls are largely intact, and there are remnants of the citadel, basilicas, baths, a forum and the north and south gates. The present road follows the course of the old colonnaded street.

Across the river and further south is the much less intact forward stronghold of the main fort, Zalabiyyeh. In summer, the Euphrates is sometimes passable between the town and the fort, which is what made Zalabiyyeh necessary.

Getting There & Away

Neither Halabiyyeh or Zalabiyyeh is easy to get to. Halabiyyeh is the more interesting of the two, and at least the first stage of this hike is straightforward enough. Get a Raqqa bus from Deir ez-Zur and get out at the Halabiyyeh turn-off a few km after the town of Tibni (one hour, S£5). From here you'll have to hitch or, if you feel up to it, do the three-hour walk. Alternatively, get off at Tibni and negotiate with a local to take you out there.

For Zalabiyyeh, the hardest bit is getting back. Ask for Zalabiyyeh at the Deir ez-Zur microbus station. The trip takes 1½ hours to the turn-off and costs S£10. From there it's a half-hour walk west. There aren't many buses plying the right bank of the Euphrates, and that's what makes the return trip a pain. If you're here in the afternoon, you'll just have to sit it out and hope for a passing truck.

The railway line passes by Zalabiyyeh, and you could follow it north a couple of km to a small railway station and wait for a train – locals swear they actually stop here.

DEIR EZ-ZUR

This is a pleasant town on the Euphrates and a crossroads for travellers visiting the northeast of Syria. Roads fan out north-east to Qamishle and Turkey; south-east to Mari, Abu Kamal (or Albu Kamal) and Iraq; south-west to Damascus via Palmyra; and north-west to Raqqa and Aleppo.

Deir ez-Zur ('Deir' to the locals) seems destined to grow in importance. Oil discoveries throughout the surrounding area have provided a huge fillip to the economy and locals will probably assume you are an oil company employee. There were about 20 fields being worked by mid-1992, and plans to bring another 80 on line.

There's not much to see in the town, but a stroll along the river bank, particularly at sunset, is a popular activity. This has been temporarily spoiled by the new road and bridge construction works taking place along the narrow stretch of river in the town. To get to the main body of the river, you need to cross the tributary at the point where bridge works are being done and head north straight on to the suspension bridge, which is only for pedestrians and bicycles. On the other side of the bridge is a small recreation ground where you can swim with the locals.

The main north-south axis running from the river through the square and on up past the new post office to the microbus station is called Hassan Taha St. The main east-west axis runs through the square and is called Shari'a 'Am (Main St).

Information

Tourist Office This is in a side street right off Shari'a 'Am, about 10 minutes east of the square. It's not much use, but the staff are friendly. It's open from 9 am to 2 pm daily except Fridays.

Money The Commercial Bank of Syria is about 15 minutes' walk west of the square on Shari'a 'Am. It's open from 9 am to 12.30 pm, and they take ages to do anything.

Post At the time of writing the big new post office, halfway between the square and the microbus station on Hassan Taha St, was still not open. The other post office is west along Shari'a 'Am, a few hundred metres short of the bank and open from 8 am to 8 pm.

Visa Extensions Another 500 metres on from the bank, turn left at the roundabout and left again. The big immigration and passports building is just on the corner. It is open from 8 am to 1.30 pm. They issue extensions on the same day, but it seems to take *all* day. One guy seems to take special pleasure in making you wait. A lot of patience is required to maintain a sense of humour.

Museum

Closed at the time of writing, the museum is on Hassan Taha St, about 20 metres in from the river. It contains artefacts from the Euphrates area. Entrance is S£5.

Places to Stay – bottom end

The best place in this price range is probably the *Hotel Damas* (☎ 21481). It's on the corner of Hassan Taha St, by the river. A bed in a shared room costs S£45, including hot shower.

The *Hotel Amal*, in among the noisy souqs on the square, is a dump where rooms cost S£100/150. East of the square, along Shari'a 'Am, are several pretty crummy places, including the *Ghassan*, *Semiramis* and the *Hotel al-Arabi al-Kabir*. The latter has dingy singles for S£100 and equally dingy doubles that the cagey old man behind the counter will let a lone traveller have for S£150.

The *Oasis Hotel*, out by the railway station, is popular with some travellers.

Places to Stay – top end

Just around the corner from the Damas is the *Hotel Raghdan* (☎ 22053), which has quite acceptable rooms for US$21/31/37. It's really not bad, if you have the money.

For those who have loads of money, you can rub shoulders with foreign oil-company employees at the *Furat Cham* (☎ 25418), five km out of town along the river. Singles/doubles go for US$135/155. You can use the pool for S£100 a day.

Places to Eat

Around the hotels on the main street you'll find the same roast chickens, kebabs, hummus and salad that you get everywhere.

For the same food in different surroundings, the *Restaurant Cairo*, also on the main street, is a big cavernous place. The part at the back is really just a drinking area, although it's perfectly OK to have a drink with your meal. A meal of very salty fish, chips, salad and hummus will cost about S£120. A 750 ml bottle of Al-Chark beer comes for S£25. Araq and other spirits are also available.

Top Left: Citadel, Aleppo (HF)
Top Right: Souq stall, Aleppo (HF)
Bottom Left: Goat herders & Roman tombs, Qatura (HF)
Bottom Right: Cyrrhus (Nabi Houri) (DS)

Top Left: Palmyra (HF)
Top Right: Arab castle, Palmyra (DS)
Bottom Left: Inside the Basilica, Rasafeh (DS)
Bottom Right: The Euphrates River from Doura Europas (DS)

Down at the river by the footbridge are a couple of outdoor restaurants right on the river banks. They are great places to sit in the evening and sip a beer. Food here costs about the same as in the Cairo.

Getting There & Away
Air The airport is about seven km east of town and, at the time of writing, was closed. There is talk of reopening it for three flights a week to Damascus. The flight between Deir ez-Zur and Damascus would cost S£602.

A shuttle bus was planned from the Syrian Arab Airlines office, a block north of the bank.

Bus Karnak, Pullman and microbuses all service Deir ez-Zur.

Karnak Bus The Karnak bus station is right in the thick of things in the centre of town. It's part of a new shopping complex one block back from the river tributary, but has no identifying signs. It's open from 7 am to 8.30 pm.

There are departures for Damascus at 7.30 am and 4 pm (5½ hours, S£111) and one for Aleppo at 2 pm (4½ hours, S£82). The bus to Aleppo passes through Raqqa (two hours, S£36), while the Damascus bus calls at Palmyra (2½ hours, S£52). A bus also passes through Deir ez-Zur, shuttling between Abu Kamal and the capital, but getting a seat is generally not easy.

Bus/Microbus The local bus station is a couple of km south of town, towards the end of Hassan Taha St. There's a local shuttle-bus service from a stop about five minutes' walk south of the square, on the right hand side, for S£1.

Buses and microbuses head south as far as Abu Kamal, north-west towards Raqqa and north-east to Hassake.

Train The railway station is across the river to the north of town, about three km from the centre. If you feel like a half-hour walk to get there, cross the footbridge, continue to the T-junction and turn right. The alternative is to catch one of the yellow shuttle buses which run from the railway booking office (next to the Karnak office) to the railway station for S£5. These only run when a train is due to leave. The booking office itself is open from 9 am to 1 pm and 4 to 8 pm.

Trains to Aleppo leave at 10 am and 1 am (1st class, S£85; 2nd class, S£56). The 9.30 pm train to Damascus (1st class, S£150; 2nd class, S£101) also stops in Aleppo. There are at least five trains to Hassake and on to Qamishle (1st class, S£55; 2nd class, S£37), but the bus trip is much more interesting as it follows the heavily cultivated region alongside the Kabur River, passing through many small mud-brick villages.

SOUTH OF DEIR EZ-ZUR
The route south-east of Deir ez-Zur follows the Euphrates down to the closed Iraqi border. It is dotted with sites of archaeological and historical interest. The impatient traveller with a car could visit the lot and be back in Deir ez-Zur for dinner in the same day. With a very early start, it might just be possible to do the same with a combination of microbuses and hitching.

Qala'at ar-Rahba
The 13th century defensive citadel, which was finally abandoned after the battles between Mongols and Mamluks, is a few km south of the town of Mayadin. You can see it in the distance (it's about four km west of the main road) shortly after leaving Mayadin.

Like many castles it is more impressive from the outside than in, but the views of the desert to the west, and the Euphrates and occasional oil field to the east are breathtaking. Ask on the bus where to get off, and hitch or walk out (about an hour).

Tell Ashara
Just 17 km south of Mayadin is the sleepy village of Ashara. Three sites that date back to the early centuries AD are being excavated by Italian teams, but there is little of real interest here. An old mud-brick mosque, with only a fragile eight-storey minaret sur-

viving, is the main item of note. Most of the area under excavation overlooks or is near the Euphrates.

Doura Europos

For the uninitiated, the extensive, largely Hellenistic/Roman fortress city of Doura Europos is by far the most intriguing site to visit on the road from Deir ez-Zur to Abu Kamal. Based on earlier settlements, the Seleucids founded the city of Europos here in around 280 BC. It also retained the ancient Syrian name of Doura (wall), and is now known to locals as Tell Salhiye.

The riverside walls overlook the left bank of the Euphrates, 90 metres below. In 128 BC the city fell to the Parthians. It remained in their hands, although under the growing influence of Palmyra, until the Romans succeeded in integrating it into their defensive system in 165 AD. As the threat from Persia to Roman pre-eminence grew, so did the importance of Doura Europos. It is reputed for its apparent religious tolerance, seemingly confirmed by the presence of a church, synagogue and other Greek, Roman and Mesopotamian temples side by side.

The Sassanids seized control of the site in 256 AD, and from then on its fortunes declined. A French team has been working on the site since 1985.

Ruins The western wall stands out in the stony desert two km east of the main road, its most imposing element the **Palmyra Gate**. Just inside the wall was a church to the right and a synagogue to the left. The road leading towards the river from the gate passed first Roman **baths** on the right, a **khan** on the left and then the site of the Greek **agora**.

Opposite this are the sites (little remains) of three temples – Artemis, Atargatis and the Two Gads. In the north-eastern corner were further palaces and other buildings, mainly from the Roman period. Overlooking the river is the **citadel**.

Getting There & Away Any microbus between Abu Kamal and Deir ez-Zur will drop you on the highway. Just walk straight out, you can't possibly miss it.

Mari

The ruins of Mari (Tell Hariri), an important Mesopotamian city dating back some 5000 years, are about 10 km north of Abu Kamal. Although fascinating for its age, the mud-brick ruins do not grab the imagination as much as you might hope.

The most famous of Mari's ancient Syrian leaders was Zimrilim, who reigned in the 19th century BC and controlled the most important trade routes across Syria into Mesopotamia, making his city-state the object of several attacks. The Royal Palace of Zimrilim was enormous, measuring 200 by 120 metres with over 300 rooms. The palace is the main point of interest; it is now covered by a modern protective roof to shelter it from the elements. It was finally destroyed in 1758 BC by the Babylonians under Hammurabi.

There are quite large chunks of pottery lying around all over the place. Most of the good stuff found here is on display in the museums in Aleppo and Damascus. Excavations begun in 1933 revealed two palaces (including Zimrilim's), five temples and the remains of a ziggurat, a kind of pyramidal tower peculiar to Mesopotamia and usually surmounted by a temple.

A statue of the god Itur-Shamagan, from Mari

Getting There & Away There is a microbus from Abu Kamal that goes right by Mari. It leaves from a side street east of the square and takes about half an hour by a circuitous route (S£5).

ABU KAMAL

Abu Kamal (also known as Albu Kamal) is a frontier town 140 km south-east of Deir ez-Zur, close to the Iraqi border. This border has been closed for some years because of Syria's support for Iran in the first Gulf war, and its subsequent participation in the anti-Iraq coalition after Baghdad's invasion of Kuwait in 1990. The frontier is actually about 10 km out of town.

Places to Stay & Eat

There only appears to be one cheap hotel in the centre – the *Jumhuriyyeh* (there is no sign in English), in a side street three blocks south of the square. Ask around. It has pretty awful doubles for S£100. There are a few cafés and cheap eateries around the square.

Getting There & Away

Karnak buses run daily from Abu Kamal to Damascus at 8 am (seven hours, S£141). The office is on the main square in the centre of the town. Local microbuses run alongside the river to Deir ez-Zur (three hours, S£25). The bus station is about a km north of the centre. You can catch a trezeena (or 'motor') between the two, but don't pay more than S£5.

The microbus for Mari leaves from a side street east of the square (30 minutes, S£5).

The North-East

Bordered by Turkey and Iraq, there are no major monuments or sites in the north-eastern corner of the country, but this does not mean it is empty of attractions. Perhaps the greatest is the chance to meet the Kurds, a people without a country, who have yet to give up their struggle. Only about one million of a total of maybe 20 million Kurds

live in Syria. The rest are spread across south-eastern Turkey, northern Iraq and north-western Iran.

The area between the Kabur and Tigris rivers is also known as the Jezira and is an increasingly rich agricultural zone, helped along by the irrigation schemes born of the Lake Assad project on the Euphrates to the west. The numerous tells (artificial hills) dotted around the place are a sign that it has long been inhabited, its mainstay the wheat and cotton crops that still predominate.

The heavy crude oil fields right up in the north-east corner have paled into insignificance beside the recently opened fields around Deir ez-Zur.

HASSAKE

The capital of the muhafaza of the same name, Hassake doesn't offer the visitor an awful lot to do, but it's not a bad base from which to explore the area, unless you're planning on entering Turkey here, in which case you may as well push on to Qamishle. The main drag, where the Karnak and Pullman buses arrive, is Fares al-Khouri St. The central square and clock tower are off to the left of the statue of Assad.

There is a tourist office hidden in a building complex on Fares al-Khouri St with no sign in English. Don't worry, they have no hand-outs, no information and no English. There is a Commercial Bank of Syria on the road left from the Assad statue.

Places to Stay & Eat

There are two basic hotels near the clock tower, although one, the *Heliopolis* seems to be a phantom. The *Hotel Ramsis* has basic rooms for S£125/175. Near the sports ground in the east of the town is the *Boustan*. It claims to be a two-star joint and charges US$20/25/30 for singles/doubles/triples, plus taxes. On top of this, they have the nerve to ask US$4 for breakfast. It's not even much good, so unless you have money to burn, forget it.

There are a few of the usual places to eat around the centre, mostly run by Iraqi Christians from the nearby refugee camp at Al-Hol.

Getting There & Away
Bus Hassake is serviced by Karnak, Pullman and microbuses.

Karnak There are two departures for Damascus, at 9.15 am and 11 am, via Deir ez-Zur. Buses leave from the little ticket booth in Fares al-Khouri St. Tickets cost S£153. As usual, you'll have to book a day or two in advance.

Pullman The Pullman buses leave from much the same area as the Karnak buses. There is no ticket office, and no rhyme or reason to their departures times (at least none that is obvious). The trip to Aleppo takes five hours and costs S£70. The main rule is to get there in the morning and ask.

Microbus The bus station for destinations like Qamishle, Deir ez-Zur and Ras al-'Ain is about two km south of the clock tower. Follow the road across the bridge over the Kabur. You can catch a shuttle there from a side street just east of the clock tower for S£1.

Train To get to the railway station, walk about 50 metres north along Fares al-Khouri St and turn left. The railway station is at the end of the street, about 10 minutes' walk. There are at least two departures a day for Qamishle (S£21, 1st class; S£15, 2nd class), Deir ez-Zur, Aleppo, Damascus (S£180, 1st class; S£111, 2nd class) and all stops in between.

Service-Taxi The service-taxi station is just south of the bridge on the left-hand side.

RAS AL-'AIN
This largely Kurdish town on the Turkish border (you cannot cross here) has little to offer, although the chances are high you'll be invited to eat and stay with the locals. Don't be surprised if the subject of conversation turns to politics. The Kurds are not much more pleased with their position in Syria than elsewhere, and discretion may be the better part of valour when chatting. In summer, the attraction is the restaurant in the main park (near the road to Hassake), where they set the tables in the shin-deep water from nearby sulphur springs. You cool your heels as you eat!

Three km away is Tell Halaf, the site of an ancient northern Mesopotamian settlement. Although plenty more artefacts are said by locals to be buried here, the visitor will see nothing other than a bald artificial hill. The bulk of what has been found can be seen in the museum in Aleppo.

Getting There & Away
Microbus The microbus from Hassake takes about 1½ hours and costs S£15. There seems to be no public transport going back in the afternoon, especially on Fridays and holidays.

QAMISHLE
Situated right at a crossing point on the Turkish border in the north-east, the place is full of Kurds and Turks and the cheaper hotels will sometimes quote prices in Turkish lire rather than Syrian pounds.

There is nothing to see in Qamishle, but the mix of people makes the place interesting. Because of its proximity to the border, you can expect passport checks at the hotels (even during the night), and when getting on or off buses or trains.

Places to Stay & Eat
About 100 metres south of the microbus station is the town's top establishment, the two-star *Hotel Semiramis*, which charges foreigners US$15/22/24 for clean rooms with fan. Expatriate workers in the oilfields often stay here.

Just around the corner is the *Chahba Hotel*, which is nothing to write home about and asks S£100 a bed (women must take a double). The upstairs terrace is OK.

The *Mamar*, a block south, is better value, although a tad more expensive. Singles/doubles cost S£150/200. The rooms with balconies are quite good and they have hot water.

The cheapest is the *Omayad Hotel*, in a

side street across from the Semiramis. A bed here costs S£50.

Across from the Chahba is quite a pleasant restaurant with an outdoor section. A good meal of kebabs and the usual side orders will cost about S£175 for two.

Getting There & Away
To/From Turkey The Turkish border is only about one km from the centre of Qamishle – a 15-minute walk.

Air The airport is about two km south of town. Take a taxi or any Hassake-bound bus. The Syrian Arab Airlines office is just off the main street, two blocks south of the Semiramis. There are several flights a week to Damascus (S£900) and one flight a week to Aleppo (S£600).

Bus/Microbus For some reason, Karnak does not operate buses this far, but the Pullman bus station is about 200 metres down the road from the Chahba Hotel. The trip to Damascus takes up to 10 hours and costs S£160. For Aleppo, reckon with at least five hours and S£100.

The microbus station is on the main street, 100 metres north of the Semiramis. There are departures for Hassake, Ras al-'Ain and Al-Malkyer in the east.

Train The railway station is, typically, a long way from the centre, and you'll have to catch a taxi there.

There is, however, a booking office in the centre, virtually opposite the Chahba Hotel. It's open until about 7 pm, but closes for a long stretch in the middle of the day. The friendly official speaks English and is helpful, and not just with train info.

There are four trains that go as far as Aleppo, and two of them go all the way to Damascus (S£735, sleeper; S£195, 1st class; S£130, 2nd class). The Damascus trains leave at 2.30 and 6 pm and call at all stops on the line – snaking down to Deir ez-Zur, up to Aleppo and back down to Damascus. The trip take from 16 to 19 hours.

'AIN DIWAR
In the extreme north-east corner of the country is an impressive medieval bridge over the Tigris. Unfortunately, relations between Turkey and Syria are not brilliant, and a Syrian border garrison may stop you from getting out to it – they say because the Turkish border troops tend to shoot first and ask questions later. You may have guessed that there is no crossing here.

There are great views from the plateau overlooking the Tigris (which may be as far as you can safely get) of the snow-capped mountains of southern Turkey to the north-east and Jebel Zakho in Iraq (some locals call it Jebel Barzani, after one of the rebel Kurdish leaders there) to the east . On a clear day, you might just make out mountains in Iran through the gap between Jebel Zakho and the Turkish ranges.

Getting There & Away
If you want to try your luck, take a microbus from Qamishle to Al-Malkyer (about two hours, S£15). From there, negotiate with one of the kids to take you out on a motorbike, or just hitch. Bear in mind that there is not much traffic on this last stretch of road.

Glossary

This glossary is a list of Arabic (a) and French (f) words commonly used in Jordan and Syria.

Abassids – Baghdad-based successor dynasty to Omayyads, which lasted from 750 until the sack of Baghdad by the Mongols in 1258. By that time, the Abassid caliphs had lost much of their power, although in the first three centuries of their rule, Arab and Islamic culture flourished. The Abbassid caliphate was maintained in Cairo until 1517 after the sack of Baghdad, but had no power.
Ayyubids – the dynasty founded by Salah ad-Din (Saladin) in Egypt in 1169. He was largely responsible for uniting the fractious Muslims in the fight against the Crusaders, retaking Jerusalem and most of the Crusaders' other possessions.

bab (abwab) (a) – gate.
bayt ash-sha'ar (a) – goat-hair tent.
bayt (a) – house.
benzin (a) – regular petrol.
burj (a) – tower.

caliph – 'successor'. The Muslim rulers who succeeded Mohammed were religious and secular rulers at once, whose power reached its apogee under the early Abbassids. As the power of this dynasty declined, numerous others sprang up in the disintegrating Muslim world, and the caliphate lost importance. It remained the highest authority in the Muslim world, but increasingly in name only.
caravanserai – large inn enclosing a courtyard, providing accommodation and a marketplace for caravans.

deir (a) – monastery.
donjon (f) – dungeon.
doura (a) – wall.
duwaar (a) – circle.

garage – commonly used term for bus and service-taxi stations in Syria (from French).

Hajj (a) – the pilgrimage to Mecca.
hammam – Turkish-style bathhouse with sauna and massage.
hijab (a) – woman's head scarf.

iwan – vaulted hall, opening onto a central court, usually in the madrassa of a mosque.

jalabiyyeh (a) – full-length robe worn by men.
jazira (a) – island
jebel (a) – hill or mountain.

khan (a) – see caravanserai.
khususi (a) – special.

madrassa – theological college that is part of a non-congregational mosque, also school.
Mamluks – 'slaves'. This Turkish slave and soldier class rose to power in Egypt and ruled it and later Syria from 1250 to the coming of the Ottoman Turks in 1517. Their reign was characterised by seemingly unending bloodletting and intrigue for the succession.
mashad (a) – ablution hall.
al-Medina al-riyadiyya (a) – sports city
mazout (a) – diesel.
meecro – microbus (local dialect from French; used in Syria only).
medina (a) – city
midan (a) – town or city square.
mihrab (a) – niche in the wall of a mosque that indicates the direction of Mecca.
minbar (a) – pulpit in a mosque.
muezzin (a) – mosque official who calls the faithful to prayer five times a day from minaret.
muhafaza (t) (a) – governorate(s).
mukhabarat (a) – secret police.
mumtaz (a) – super petrol.

narjileh (a) – water pipes used to smoke tobacco.

noria – wooden water wheels, built centuries ago.

Omayyads – first great dynasty of Arab Muslim rulers, based in Damascus, and which lasted from 661 to 750 AD.

qasr (a) – castle or palace. Used generically in reference to a series of buildings that were erected, mostly in the 8th century, across the desert in southern Syria and Jordan by Omayyad rulers.

rababah (a) – traditional single-string Bedouin instrument.

ras (a) – headland, also head.

servees – service-taxi (local dialect from French).

sharq al-awsat (a) – Middle East.

sidd (a) – dam.

siq (a) – gorge.

souq (a) – market.

tell (a) – hill.

tetrapylon – four groups of four pillars.

thukna (a) – barracks.

trezeena (a) – three-wheeled motorised cart (local dialect).

wadi (a) – valley formed by watercourse, that is often dry except in time of heavy rainfall.

Index

TEXT

Guides to the Middle East

Arab Gulf States
The Arab Gulf States are surprisingly accessible and affordable with an astounding range of things to see and do – camel markets, desert safaris, ancient forts and modern cities to list just a few. Includes concise history and language section for each country.

Egypt & the Sudan - a travel survival kit
This guide takes you into and beyond the spectacular pyramids, temples, tombs, monasteries and mosques, and the bustling main streets of these fascinating countries to discover their incredible beauty, unusual sights and friendly people.

Iran - a travel survival kit
The first English-language guide to this enigmatic and surprisingly hospitable country written since the Islamic Revolution. As well as practical travel details the author provides background information that will fascinate adventurers and armchair travellers alike.

Turkey - a travel survival kit
This acclaimed guide takes you from Istanbul bazaars to Mediterranean beaches, from historic battlegrounds to the stamping grounds of St Paul, Alexander the Great, the Emperor Constantine, King Croesus and Omar Khayyam.

Trekking in Turkey
Explore beyond Turkey's coastline and you will be surprised to discover that Turkey has mountains with walks to rival those found in Nepal.

Yemen - a travel survival kit
The Yemen is one of the oldest inhabited regions in the world. This practical guide gives full details on a genuinely different travel experience.

West Asia on a shoestring
Want to cruise to Asia for 15 cents? Drink a great cup of tea while you view Mt Everest? Find the Garden of Eden? This guide has the complete story on the Asian overland trail from Bangladesh to Turkey, including Bhutan, India, Iran, the Maldives, Nepal, Pakistan, Sri Lanka and the Middle East.

Also available:
Arabic (Egyptian) phrasebook, **Arabic (Moroccan)** phrasebook and **Turkish** phrasebook.

Keep in touch!

We love hearing from you and think you'd like to hear from us.

The Lonely Planet Newsletter covers the when, where, how and what of travel. (AND it's free!)

When...is the right time to see reindeer in Finland?
Where...can you hear the best palm-wine music in Ghana?
How...do you get from Asunción to Areguá by steam train?
What...should you leave behind to avoid hassles with customs in Iran?

To join our mailing list just contact us at any of our offices. (details below)

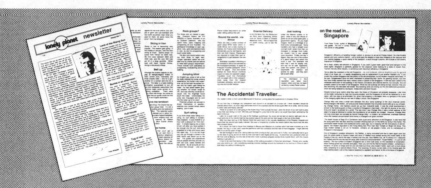

Every issue includes:

- *a letter from Lonely Planet founders Tony and Maureen Wheeler*
- *travel diary from a Lonely Planet author - find out what it's really like out on the road*
- *feature article on an important and topical travel issue*
- *a selection of recent letters from our readers*
- *the latest travel news from all over the world*
- *details on Lonely Planet's new and forthcoming releases*

Also available Lonely Planet T-shirts. 100% heavy weight cotton (S, M, L, XL)

LONELY PLANET PUBLICATIONS
Australia: PO Box 617, Hawthorn, 3122, Victoria (tel: 03-819 1877)
USA: Embarcadero West, 155 Filbert Street, Suite 251, Oakland, CA 94607 (tel: 510-893 8555)
UK: Devonshire House, 12 Barley Mow Passage, Chiswick, London W4 4PH (tel: 081-742 3161)

Lonely Planet Guidebooks

Lonely Planet guidebooks cover every accessible part of Asia as well as Australia, the Pacific, South America, Africa, the Middle East, Europe and parts of North America. There are five series: *travel survival kits*, covering a country for a range of budgets; *shoestring guides* with compact information for low-budget travel in a major region; *walking guides*; *city guides* and *phrasebooks*.

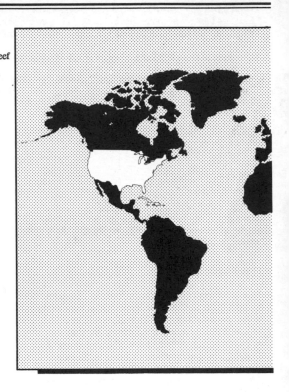

Australia & the Pacific
Australia
Bushwalking in Australia
Islands of Australia's Great Barrier Reef
Fiji
Melbourne city guide
Micronesia
New Caledonia
New Zealand
Tramping in New Zealand
Papua New Guinea
Papua New Guinea phrasebook
Rarotonga & the Cook Islands
Samoa
Solomon Islands
Sydney city guide
Tahiti & French Polynesia
Tonga
Vanuatu

South-East Asia
Bali & Lombok
Bangkok city guide
Myanmar (Burma)
Burmese phrasebook
Cambodia
Indonesia
Indonesia phrasebook
Malaysia, Singapore & Brunei
Philippines
Pilipino phrasebook
Singapore city guide
South-East Asia on a shoestring
Thailand
Thai phrasebook
Vietnam, Laos & Cambodia
Vietnamese phrasebook

North-East Asia
China
Mandarin Chinese phrasebook
Hong Kong, Macau & Canton
Japan
Japanese phrasebook
Korea
Korean phrasebook
Mongolia
North-East Asia on a shoestring
Taiwan
Tibet
Tibet phrasebook
Tokyo city guide

West Asia
Trekking in Turkey
Turkey
Turkish phrasebook
West Asia on a shoestring

Middle East
Arab Gulf States
Egypt & the Sudan
Egyptian Arabic phrasebook
Iran
Israel
Jordan & Syria
Yemen

Indian Ocean
Madagascar & Comoros
Maldives & Islands of the East Indian Ocean
Mauritius, Réunion & Seychelles

Mail Order

Lonely Planet guidebooks are distributed worldwide. They are also available by mail order from Lonely Planet, so if you have difficulty finding a title please write to us. US and Canadian residents should write to Embarcadero West, 155 Filbert St, Suite 251, Oakland CA 94607, USA; European residents should write to Devonshire House, 12 Barley Mow Passage, Chiswick, London W4 4PH; and residents of other countries to PO Box 617, Hawthorn, Victoria 3122, Australia.

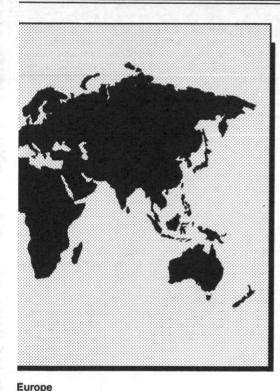

Indian Subcontinent
Bangladesh
India
Hindi/Urdu phrasebook
Trekking in the Indian Himalaya
Karakoram Highway
Kashmir, Ladakh & Zanskar
Nepal
Trekking in the Nepal Himalaya
Nepal phrasebook
Pakistan
Sri Lanka
Sri Lanka phrasebook

Africa
Africa on a shoestring
Central Africa
East Africa
Kenya
Swahili phrasebook
Morocco, Algeria & Tunisia
Moroccan Arabic phrasebook
South Africa, Lesotho & Swaziland
Zimbabwe, Botswana & Namibia
West Africa
Mexico
Baja California
Mexico

Central America
Central America on a shoestring
Costa Rica
La Ruta Maya

North America
Alaska
Canada
Hawaii

Europe
Eastern Europe on a shoestring
Eastern Europe phrasebook
Finland
Iceland, Greenland & the Faroe Islands
Mediterranean Europe on a shoestring
Mediterranean Europe phrasebook
Poland
Scandinavian & Baltic Europe on a shoestring
Scandinavian Europe phrasebook
Trekking in Spain
Trekking in Greece
USSR
Russian phrasebook
Western Europe on a shoestring
Western Europe phrasebook

South America
Argentina, Uruguay & Paraguay
Bolivia
Brazil
Brazilian phrasebook
Chile & Easter Island
Colombia
Ecuador & the Galápagos Islands
Latin American Spanish phrasebook
Peru
Quechua phrasebook
South America on a shoestring
Trekking in the Patagonian Andes

The Lonely Planet Story

Lonely Planet published its first book in 1973 in response to the numerous 'How did you do it?' questions Maureen and Tony Wheeler were asked after driving, bussing, hitching, sailing and railing their way from England to Australia.

Written at a kitchen table and hand collated, trimmed and stapled, *Across Asia on the Cheap* became an instant local bestseller, inspiring thoughts of another book.

Eighteen months in South-East Asia resulted in their second guide, *South-East Asia on a shoestring*, which they put together in a backstreet Chinese hotel in Singapore in 1975. The 'yellow bible' as it quickly became known to backpackers around the world, soon became *the* guide to the region. It has sold well over half a million copies and is now in its 7th edition, still retaining its familiar yellow cover.

Today there are over 100 Lonely Planet titles – books that have that same adventurous approach to travel as those early guides; books that 'assume you know how to get your luggage off the carousel' as one reviewer put it.

Although Lonely Planet initially specialised in guides to Asia, they now cover most regions of the world, including the Pacific, South America, Africa, the Middle East and Europe. The list of *walking guides* and *phrasebooks* (for 'unusual' languages such as Quechua, Swahili, Nepalese and Egyptian Arabic) is also growing rapidly.

The emphasis continues to be on travel for independent travellers. Tony and Maureen still travel for several months of each year and play an active part in the writing, updating and quality control of Lonely Planet's guides.

They have been joined by over 50 authors, 48 staff – mainly editors, cartographers, & designers – at our office in Melbourne, Australia and another 10 at our US office in Oakland, California. In 1991 Lonely Planet opened a London office to handle sales for Britain, Europe and Africa. Travellers themselves also make a valuable contribution to the guides through the feedback we receive in thousands of letters each year.

The people at Lonely Planet strongly believe that travellers can make a positive contribution to the countries they visit, both through their appreciation of the countries' culture, wildlife and natural features, and through the money they spend. In addition, the company makes a direct contribution to the countries and regions it covers. Since 1986 a percentage of the income from each book has been donated to ventures such as famine relief in Africa; aid projects in India; agricultural projects in Central America; Greenpeace's efforts to halt French nuclear testing in the Pacific and Amnesty International. In 1992 $45,000 was donated to these causes.

Lonely Planet's basic travel philosophy is summed up in Tony Wheeler's comment, 'Don't worry about whether your trip will work out. Just go!'